# Global Pharmaceuticals

# Global Pharmaceuticals

## Ethics, Markets, Practices

*Edited by Adriana Petryna, Andrew Lakoff, and Arthur Kleinman*

Duke University Press
Durham and London 2006

2nd printing, 2007

© 2006 Duke University Press

All rights reserved

Printed in the United States of America on acid-free paper ∞

Designed by Heather Hensley

Typeset in Minion by Tseng Information Systems, Inc.

Library of Congress Cataloging-in-Publication Data

appear on the last printed page of this book.

# CONTENTS

vii    Acknowledgments

1    The Pharmaceutical Nexus
ADRIANA PETRYNA AND ARTHUR KLEINMAN

33    Globalizing Human Subjects Research
ADRIANA PETRYNA

61    The New Medical Oikumene
DAVID HEALY

85    Educating for Global Mental Health: The Adoption of SSRIs in Japan
KALMAN APPLBAUM

111    High Contact: Gifts and Surveillance in Argentina
ANDREW LAKOFF

136    Addiction Markets: The Case of High-Dose Buprenorphine in France
ANNE M. LOVELL

171    Pharmaceuticals in Urban Ecologies: The Register of the Local
VEENA DAS AND RANENDRA K. DAS

206    Pharmaceutical Governance
JOÃO BIEHL

240    Treating AIDS: Dilemmas of Unequal Access in Uganda
SUSAN REYNOLDS WHYTE, MICHAEL A. WHYTE,
LOTTE MEINERT, AND BETTY KYADDONDO

263    References

289    Contributors

291    Index

# Acknowledgments

The Michael Crichton Fund, Department of Social Medicine, Harvard Medical School, and the Asia Center of Harvard University generously supported the conference upon which this volume is based and preparation of the volume. The essays collected in this volume grew out of the Third Annual W. H. R. Rivers Workshop held at Harvard University in May 2002. The coeditors thank the participants, presenters, and discussants of this forum, for their insightful contributions: Kalman Applbaum, João Biehl, Jean Comaroff, Ranendra Das, Veena Das, Joseph Dumit, Michael M. J. Fischer, Byron Good, Mary-Jo Del-Vecchio Good, David Healy, Jim Yong Kim, Joan Kleinman, Margaret Lock, Anne Lovell, Ilana Lowy, Harry Marks, Paul Rabinow, and Susan Reynolds Whyte; as well as members of Harvard's Department of Anthropology and Department of Social Medicine, and the Program in Science, Technology, and Society of the Massachusetts Institute of Technology. We also thank the two anonymous reviewers for Duke University Press for their constructive comments, and Ken Wissoker for his enthusiasm and support of this project.

# The Pharmaceutical Nexus

ADRIANA PETRYNA AND ARTHUR KLEINMAN

Worldwide, images of well-being and health are increasingly associated with access to pharmaceuticals. Media advertisements invite arthritis sufferers to celebrate with co-sufferers who have become pain free after consuming the latest blockbuster anti-inflammatory drug.[1] A playful bouncing ball asks us if we suffer from malaise and hopelessness as it transforms into a lock-and-key chemical-based model of depression. Given the magic of such self-transforming images, it is not surprising that marketing and advertising had their beginnings in the pharmaceutical industry. Images of magical make-over represent a multi-billion-dollar-a-year commerce that promises innovative drugs to wipe out disease and alleviate suffering in the world. In their attempt to achieve universal reach, however, these marketing efforts and images traverse vastly different worlds with vastly uneven social and economic conditions.

Juxtapose these images with other images, such as those of the massive crisis of global AIDS and multi-drug-resistant tuberculosis — crises that threaten national securities and require complex forms of intervention. Over 60 million people have been infected with HIV, and more than 25 million have died since the beginning of the epidemic.[2] In some African countries, one in four adults is HIV-positive and five million people are newly infected each year. Diminishing access to public health services and treatment, and political instability around the globe have increased the flow of pathogens and the likelihood of resistance, and have made infection hypermutable. While infectious diseases that primarily affect poor societies remain undertreated, global markets for antidepressant and antipsychotic treatments have grown. Numbers tell a story. In 2002, global sales of antidepressants grew by 5 percent and sales of antipsychotics rose by an astonishing 19 percent. Among the leading therapy classes in global pharmaceutical sales, antidepressants rank fourth and antipsychotics rank fifth.[3]

The modern pharmaceutical industry got its start in the nineteenth century when several potent compounds — including alkaloids such as morphine, strychnine, quinine, nicotine, and cocaine — were isolated and mass produced. Major pharmaceutical breakthroughs occurred during and after World War II, including the discovery of penicillin (and methods to mass produce it), streptomycin to treat tuberculosis, and the first broad-spectrum antibiotic, chloramphenicol. Corticosteroids, tetracyclines, oral contraceptives, antihistamines, tranquilizers, amphetamines, diuretics, and hundreds of other medicinal compounds were patented in the late 1940s and early 1950s.[4] Even before World War II, the pharmaceutical companies operated internationally by relying on licensing and marketing agreements, subsidiaries, and joint ventures.[5] After the war, the industry used sophisticated marketing methods to transform from a commodity chemicals business (with individual pharmacists compounding the dose) to one heavily concentrated in several large firms and dependent on large investments in research and marketing.[6] Global pharmaceutical spending reached almost $500 billion in 2003; approximately half of that was attributed to the United States and Canada. In 2003, the top ten drug companies enjoyed a profit of 14.3 percent of their annual sales (compared with a 4.6 percent median for other industries; see Angell 2004:11).

Behind these figures lies a morass of economic and moral paradoxes. Some therapeutic markets are launched (for example, antidepressant sales have risen sharply among low-income groups) while other no less urgently needed markets are ignored.[7] The alarmingly slow development of the anti-HIV drug market in Africa has been attributed to the allegedly unreliable medical and economic behaviors of that continent's desperately poor HIV sufferers.[8] These characteristics are said to heighten investment risk, which traditionally justified the industry's failure to make low-cost drugs accessible to those who need them. Inertia also exacts a high cost: misguided policy and insufficient private incentives often keep in place the wrong types of intervention. For example, the ongoing use of ineffective treatments for malaria is causing a dramatic rise in malaria-related deaths.[9] Tropical diseases in poor countries do not present the same kind of economic incentives that drive the proliferation of chronic disease treatments in rich countries. Witness the relative abundance of lifestyle treatments versus the scarcity of treatments for disorders uncommon in the West. Industry discourse reinforces this gap in value as it sponsors cures for diseases that have a proven consumer base, or extends the limits of treatable illness to enlarge markets for new products (Lexchin 2001; Moynihan, Heath, Henry 2002).[10] Thus, at least two distinct pharmaceutical markets have evolved based on group behavior, culture, or economic characteristics and their potential to enhance industry profits.

Advertisements present us with distinctive, and highly disputable, imagery that supports this consumption-oriented logic. Well-being is recast as a commodity and as a distinct personal achievement. Side by side with depictions of individualized health are images of more collective forms of suffering that are portrayed as inchoate or hopelessly untreatable. These images convey distinct moralities, suggesting that illnesses can be valued and treated differently (Kleinman and Kleinman 1996). As moral economy becomes based on political economy, possibilities are foreclosed and violence is perpetrated when populations and communities are treated in drastically unequal ways. Life*style* is fostered pharmaceutically for some while benign neglect is the order of the day for others. New major initiatives such as the Global Fund, private foundations, and public-private partnerships for drug research and development have evolved to promote investment in health research and technology transfer for diseases and countries that are deemed unprofitable investments for research and development.[11] The continued existence of separate spheres of risk raises questions about the anthropological dimensions of new pharmaceuticals and about the innovative empirical work that is required to convey the moral and ethical realities of emergent global drug markets.

The coexistence of effective life-extending technologies and lost life chances in local places where essential medications remain unavailable presents contemporary ethnography with an urgent challenge to make sense of this paradox — to plumb its technical, political, and social depths. Anthropological studies have significantly advanced our understanding of the relationship between income inequalities and health (Chen et al. 1994; Desjarlais et al. 1995; Kim et al. 2000; Farmer 2003), showing how health inequities build on socioeconomic and political divisions within and between countries and among racial and ethnic minority groups. They have shown, for example, how differences in the structure and organization of institutions authorized to deal with health problems (state bureaucracies, welfare agencies, insurance companies, medical facilities, and religious/humanitarian organizations) result in distinct programs and policies that not only differ greatly in form and content but also can create different courses of health and disease and influence their outcomes of both. Other authors have removed the air of obviousness with which the concept of culture is deployed to explain local health practices. In refuting the notion that the poor are somehow less responsible regarding treatment regimes, they have exposed how cultural assumptions in health planning can further entrench inequality, justifying some interventions while disallowing others (Farmer 1999).

This body of anthropological work has shown how the local trajectories of pandemics are influenced by international policy and choices (Das 1999). There is little doubt that a failure to respond adequately to the AIDS pandemic has contributed to an exponential growth of infection in South Africa — from 0.7 to 20.1 percent in the adult population between 1990 and 2001.[12] Other patterns of delay have been found in regions in political transition. In Eastern Europe in the early 1990s, for example, rapidly opening markets combined with economic shock therapy threatened the lives of vast numbers of people as social services were being reduced.[13] The reality of these threats was counterbalanced by the euphoria accompanying the advent of social and political freedoms and the promises of democratic governance. The World Bank and the

International Monetary Fund (the two international agencies most influential in advising developing countries) focused resources on institutional reforms rather than on health. Pharmaceuticals needed to fight AIDS and tuberculosis were distributed too late, and the delay produced a new set of local health concerns. Anthropologists have pointed to the inadequacies of ethical discourse for assessing health equity and health rights in politically and economically devastated communities because it does not have a way to account for local moral worlds as social processes (Kleinman 1998). They have argued for a lifting of the ban on moral engagement with worlds that are unjust, chaotic, and riddled with violence and premature death (Scheper-Hughes 1992; Bourgois 1995; Das et al. 2000; Biehl 2005).

This volume's ethnographies complement these studies and bring new perspectives — anthropological and cross-cultural — to bear on the issues posed by the growth of the international pharmaceutical trade.[14] The essays gathered here grew out of the Third Annual W. H. R. Rivers Workshop held at Harvard University in May 2002. The workshop assembled leading anthropologists working in the field of science and medicine and historians of medicine — scholars who in their own areas of research are concerned with the human consequences of pharmaceutical use and their market expansions in cross-cultural and everyday contexts. The combined viewpoints of the authors acts as a prism, breaking these issues into their component parts and providing a multilayered look at the interests and stakes involved in the production of pharmaceuticals and their consumption in particular times and places. They undertake at least two levels of analysis. On the one hand, the authors examine the cultural, scientific, and economic practices that contribute to the growth of the drug industry; and on the other hand, they investigate how this expansion, as well as the proliferation of treatments, affects various forms of inequality and health practice. Many extend the anthropological technique of the close analysis of such practice to broader structuring agencies — governmental, nongovernmental, corporate, professional — whose decisions affect the well-being of populations. The essays in this volume examine the proliferating global institutional ecology of pharmaceuticals created by intense competition for regional markets and a tug-of-war between pharmaceutical

importation in poorer countries and the evolution of drug production capa-
bilities in medium-poor countries like China, India, and Brazil. Elements in
this new ecology include the World Bank, the World Trade Organization, and
TRIPS, and a host of emerging international and national regulation and law,
which set the terms for pharmaceuticals' worldwide and regional circulation.
This institutional ecology moves within and across more traditional, territori-
ally bounded apparatuses of governance. Analyses of medical professions, advertising agencies, audit companies, and contract research organizations also
highlight the recurrent theme of territoriality in these essays: how social and
institutional geographies of healthcare are remapped and how physician practices and patient agency are remade.

These fine-grained studies of the global movements of pharmaceuticals also
reveal an emerging "values gap." Its symptoms include the growing division
between populations that have access to life-saving drugs and the ability to pay
for them, and populations that have neither and must rely on some other form
of distribution. The gap is intensified by the choices made by industry: afflic-
tions whose treatments are relatively easily produced and have ready markets
are deemed more worthy of research and development. It is also reinforced
by the subtle and not so subtle ways by which the significance of others' well-
being is judged. Human experiences of suffering and its costs can have little
bearing on economic measures of costs of "morbidity" and other indicators
configuring social need (Kleinman and Kleinman 1996). In other instances it
is economic worth — specifically, market readiness (or lack of it) — that can determine the fate of whole populations. Arguably, this is a most critically important issue presented by the flow of pharmaceuticals: Whose illness is worth
treating? Whose life is worth saving? Jim Kim, an anthropologist and physician who is the former director of the World Health Organization's HIV/AIDS
Department, questions why, given empirical data showing that it is possible to
save the lives of the desperately poor, these men, women, and children are routinely cut off from needed medical treatments. A key source of this paradox, he
claims, is a pervasive "public health machismo," the idea that "someone has to
make the decision as to who lives and who dies" at the highest levels of international health planning.[15] What is new about the globalization of pharma-

ceuticals is the dramatic degree to which action, resources, and coordination are required and can be mobilized to counteract the extreme and debilitating effects of pharmaceutical triage. Debates over access to new medical technologies must consider complex care delivery systems for the poor; and the role of state and non-state actors in securing "health" as a fundamental good and right of citizenship has never been more profound.

The question of the social good and to whom it applies filters through every phase of pharmaceutical production, from preclinical research to human testing, marketing, distribution, prescription, and consumption. Each step is marked by a "particular context, actors, and transactions and is characterized by different sets of values and ideas" (Van der Geest et al. 1996:153). Each phase entails specific ethical concerns and problems. Decisions about what therapeutic entity to develop are connected to institutional priorities that may have little to do with the realities of disease and treatment demand. A telling example is provided by Anne Lovell's discussion of heroin addiction in France and the current lack of antiaddiction pharmaceuticals. The market potentiality of drug compounds is more typically defined by country than by need. And as Adriana Petryna notes in her essay, the settings in which new drugs are clinically tested may be entirely different from the settings in which they are sold. Which populations should researchers include in their research cohorts? Sometimes public pressure and interest group activists can accelerate the development of innovative drugs, as in the case of antiretrovirals (Epstein 1996) and cancer therapeutics (Lowy 2000). This form of research activism is taken as standard policy today, as access to experimental therapies is being broadened and drug trials are increasingly viewed as therapeutic rather than experimental commodities (especially for populations historically underrepresented in clinical research, such as women, children, the elderly, and members of racial and ethnic minorities).

How are pharmaceutical markets launched? What are the ethical challenges to the imposition of a market-based approach to drugs that in one context may be affordable but in another are not? As drug costs escalate and access becomes hyperindividualized, pharmaceuticals markets generate new social distinctions based on the individual's ability to pay. How do pharmaceuticals enter communities, and how do the most essential drugs circulate? How does the "social liveliness" of the drug displace other meaningful interpretations of suffering and disease (Whyte et al. 2002)? We take as a starting point of an ethnographically engaged analysis that the alleviation of suffering and death that pharmaceuticals promise can hardly be dissociated from larger social and political determinations. Unquestionably, pharmaceuticals affect the human body as a site of control and creative experience (Scheper-Hughes and Lock 1991). But drugs and treatment strategies also go beyond the body, affecting and potentially reshaping interpersonal, family, and community domains.[16]

## Standards, Secrecy, and Trust: The Science of Pharmaceuticals

"By definition medicines are substances that have the capacity to change the condition of the living organism—for better or for worse. The secret of their attributed power lies primarily in their concreteness or their ability to transform a problem at hand into 'thinginess.' . . . By applying a 'thing,' we transform the state of dysphoria into something concrete, into some thing to which the patient and others can address their efforts" (Van der Geest et al. 1996:154). Claude Lévi-Strauss's classic essay "The Sorcerer and His Magic" provides insights into the effectiveness of drugs and why they become potent commodities. Lévi-Strauss tells the story of a sorcerer's apprentice who was initially a skeptic of his enterprise of healing but learned to believe in its potency once he saw that it was his skill in manipulating social expectations that endowed him with magical gifts. His expertise rested on his secret ability to focus community attention on an object, believed to be the object of affliction, and to remove it in a dramatic fashion (Lévi-Strauss 1967; see also Hahn and Kleinman 1983 and Harrington 1997). Healing involves actions that hold the promise of some physical curing effect. The practices of the Ndembu doctor described by Victor Turner (1967) instruct that before any physical treatments can be effective, a first order of healing must take place. This first order involves a complicated divination of problems happening at the sociostructural level and a subsequent diminishing of the negative force of such problems. Treatment in this conception is viewed "not only in a private or idiographic but also in a public and social structural framework" (1967:361). Put forth as a classic medical anthropological vantage, this social principle of healing is based on a consideration of healing as an interactive, social and cultural process that is especially attentive to the symbolic and narrative aspects of health and illness.

Today, however, treatment methods bypass this classic conception — overfetishization of pharmaceuticals aimed at repairing the body can miss the social principle of healing altogether. Such overfetishization remains standard in the minds of most American consumers (Elliott 2003). The body in American society and elsewhere is isolated — broken up conceptually into technologized imagery (on magnetic resonance imaging, see Dumit 2000; on chromosomal risk, see Rapp 1999) — as other ways of dealing with social problems are replaced by the workings of the pharmaceutical magic bullet (Brandt 1985). There is much magic in the way pharmaceutical companies target individuals and their bodies, influence the course of therapeutic events, and manipulate collective needs and wants, particularly in the area of antidepressants, as David Healy discusses in his essay. Under the aegis of an epidemic of attention deficit disorders, for example, the promotion, demand, and abuse of Ritalin and Adderal in American secondary schools have become widespread. Overreliance on pharmaceuticals allows us to avoid dealing with problems of family, the lack of public financing for schools, school discipline, and child rearing. The pharmaceuticalization of certain disorders is sometimes more a product of popular culture (in part, resulting from the 1997 FDA decision to relax strictures on direct-to-consumer advertising) than of professional interests. Notably, more parents than pediatricians or psychiatrists are seeking diagnoses for their children (Lakoff 2000).

The pharmaceutical industry applies a large proportion of its resources to marketing and advertising operations. Such attention to nonmedical forms of influence seems to run counter to the trajectory of modern biomedicine. Materia medica became modern when medical reformers began to ground its practices in scientific methods in the early part of the twentieth century (Marks 1997). The history of modern medicine highlights the importance of government regulation in the form of the institutionalized standard in bolstering medical expertise. Testing results in a laboratory, peer review, and, later, the establishment of randomized clinical trials were intended as protective barriers against the encroachment of false beliefs and business interests into medicine. The increased standardization of the therapeutic process was believed to promote scientific progress in medicine while protecting the public against inflated claims about the effects and uses of substances claimed as remedies to restore health. One unintended effect of such regulation has been that it works as a barrier to market entry for prescription drugs — thus ensuring profits for those who are allowed to enter.

Standards are important cultural and social markers of modernity. Standardization organizes vast bureaucratic arenas and divisions of labor involving networks of specialists, researchers, information, and institutional spaces worldwide. As Anthony Giddens notes (1991), universal standards have a validity that is not derived from local settings. Their objectivity is unquestioned at the same time that they are a "disembedding" force. The category of depression, for instance, is said to be a universal condition with consistent cross-cultural prevalence; its treatments are said to be applicable everywhere. Such supposed universality implies vast amounts of trust backed by vast amounts of coordinated expert know-how whose end product becomes a set of primary documents: surveillance guidelines that narrow core symptomatology to fairly fixed interpretations.

The trust vested in the experts can be volatile, however (Starr 1982; Abbott 1988). The wave of accounting scandals, scientific mismanagement in environmental policy, and influence peddling in politics represents only a few of the institutional domains which have undergone a crisis of public trust. Transparency is crucial for any industry, yet there is a special onus on the pharmaceutical industry to maintain scientific integrity and tell consumers the truth about the economic and therapeutic value of its products.[17] Most of us use drugs, some on a daily basis. We ingest them, inhale them, or insert them with the idea that these actions will produce some desired physical effect (Van der Geest et al. 1996:154). Insurance companies, health maintenance organizations, and state governments, also relying on scientific assessment, influence how we use drugs by deciding which drugs are worth paying for and which drugs physicians should prescribe. Yet when data about efficacy are tampered with we lose trust; and we worry that industry-sponsored research can produce biased results. There is much controversy over whether the data that the industry provides — to think tanks, for example — are reliable (Relman and Angell 2002). The drug industry claims it spends over $897 million — a highly contested figure — on the development of each new drug and uses this number to validate its claim against individual U.S. states that are attempting to control prices and lower drug costs. These same numbers are an index of how much we value drugs — how much we are willing to pay for them — and they have become the centerpieces of controversy over who will bear the burden of paying for the more expensive drugs.

Scandals in the pharmaceutical industry — be they related to questionable marketing practices or the withholding of information about dangerous drug side effects — are often traced back to the same root cause: a conflict of interest. It is now required among researchers and even medical ethicists to declare any financial conflicts of interest at the end of their lectures or journal articles. Yet such ritualized acts of transparency often hide more than reveal the scope of private activity involved. (The drug industry funds universities, academic departments, and continuing medical education programs, for example. It pays a "user-fee" to American regulators for every new drug that is reviewed).[18] Conflicting interests are now at the heart of the pharmaceutical industry's growing ability to transform the sociocultural landscape: institutionally and "biopolitically," everyone in rich countries is now seen as a lifelong "market share." The essays in this volume deal explicitly with these lines of conflict — or rather, fit — between privatizing interests and professional obligations in pharmaceutical science: from its influence on clinical trial design and overemphasis on positive research findings to what some see as the abandonment of the scientific method to characterize harm to the more profitable task of characterizing benefit.[19] To what extent have financial or other personal conflicts always plagued the pharmaceutical research process, and how are they new? Medical school and hospital faculties are so enmeshed in the life sciences industry, especially pharmaceutical companies, that the question of what constitutes conflict of interest is undergoing fundamental reassessment. It is difficult to assemble an institutional review committee for psychopharmacology studies without including members with commercial and industry ties. How are we thus to control potential bias, and is there any sense in trying to hold back the tide? This is a research issue that transfers quickly into a clinical doctor-patient concern in terms of how information derived from industry-mediated networks is judged clinically and used in patient settings. Other clinical issues include the pharmaceutical industry's financial support of global research on mental health problems that are also targets for new drugs. The last issue suggests that the globalization of pharmaceuticals is too extensive and complex to be dealt with by all-or-none regulation.[20]

The global market in pharmaceuticals is structured by regulation—incomplete, underdeveloped, or imperfect though it may be. The role of trustworthy standards is particularly crucial today as every aspect of drug production, including human testing, moves to ever distant shores. Transnational regulatory bodies have become central in promoting standardization of pharmaceutical activities and in regulating the ways in which state health institutions and market actors engage each other. Other realms of standardization involve patent rules and rules over intellectual property rights, which have led to bias in negotiations over fair drug pricing and access. Most recently, institutions such as the International Conference on Harmonisation of Technical Requirements for Registration of Pharmaceuticals for Human Use encourage national regulatory authorities to standardize procedures for drug testing and registration, speeding the entry of drugs into new markets.

Global standards are difficult to enforce, however. Moreover, they are much more than cross-cultural quality assurance mechanisms; they are also "mediators of action" that can promote desired outcomes by the holders and purveyors of those standards (Bowker and Star 2000:17). As standards travel, their social and economic embeddedness is revealed. Several essays in this volume take Bowker's and Star's call to take standards and classifications out of their supposed neutrality and "reclassify" them as central sites of power—organizing and channeling flows of knowledge, capital, and resources in specific directions, and blocking others. How are standard biological models of human behavior linked to the development of international markets for behavioral medications? How do global practices of vaccination for infectious diseases reveal inadequately formulated ethical obligations of international organizations and state bureaucracies in disclosing the realities and local contexts of disease? Issues extend beyond those considered in this book to include the regulation of bioprospecting for herbal compounds among indigenous people and deciding who benefits and who loses with respect to the capital flow of pharmaceuticals (Eisenberg 2001; Hayden 2003; Coombe 2003; Juma 1989; Etkin 2001).

Standards also encompass monopolies over strategic knowledge (Bourdieu 1999). The high degree of uncertainty regarding domains of drug production and consumption tends to limit the sharing of information. On the production side, researchers can never be certain that they have the solution to a problem before they test it with a compound representing the potential drug. This technical uncertainty spills over to the economic domain. Information about the efficacy of new drugs is intensely guarded because news of the success or failure of drugs in clinical trials can drastically affect the price of stock market shares. Once drugs are produced, their sales and marketing involve more proprietary knowledge. Audits of physician prescription practices inform behind-the-scenes promoting, which in turn helps to solidify markets and demand. Advertising influences drug research and medical education about new treatments, and negative information may be selectively withheld to increase the desirability of a given drug. Market forecasting is increasingly dependent on privately generated epidemiological data that aid in the prediction of future disease trends and new drug markets. Andrew Lakoff's essay reveals that industry think tanks, audit firms, advertising agencies, and health-marketing companies are all involved in the formulation of "interested knowledge."

One particularly vexing issue for anthropologists who study pharmaceuticals is the industry's apparent level of secrecy. How much does the pharmaceutical industry know about the prescription practices of doctors and patient consumption patterns? How much is too much? What are the side effects of new pharmaceuticals? Do we know too little about them? Do we tend to overvalue them? These concerns in turn raise a more fundamental question regarding our own cultural positioning vis-à-vis pharmaceutical knowledge and practices. One very damaging thing that can be said to a person suffering from a mental disorder, for example, is that his or her disease is a social construct (Luhrmann 2000). While unveiling of this sort is not the point, the level of pharmaceutical advertisement and the fashioning of categories seem to substantiate the argument that people are in part "made up" through a process Ian Hacking calls "dynamic nominalism" (1999:170). Categories and the categorized emerge hand in hand. In his example of a "transient" mental illness (the nineteenth-century French fugue epidemic), Hacking shows that diagnoses change as social and historical conditions change. New "vectors" and "ecological niches" for the spread of disease are actively produced. An epidemic of poor, urban, young men traveling impulsively in confused and amnesiac states took place in France, but not, surprisingly, in England or America (Hacking 1998). Was the loss of interest in this hysteria and its subsequent disappearance related to the failure to construct a pharmaceutical market for it? Do historical transformations in pharmaceuticals make up persons as much as do historical transformations in disease? Penicillin and the antibiotics era changed how we assess vulnerability in children and the risk of traveling, for example. Clearly, the era of analgesics has contributed to a transformation in perceptions of how pain and suffering relate to a modern subjective experience of aging. Treating bereavement with antidepressants may herald yet another transformation of subjectivity.

When we analyze the global production and distribution of pharmaceuticals from an ethnographic standpoint, we find areas of practice that *defy* standardization. A variety of distinct niches — regulatory, medical, ethical, legal, scientific, and economic — related to the anthropological study of pharmaceuticals take specific forms in local contexts and affect individual and collective experience. Enormous differences in drug pricing, for example, stand out as the most politically charged issue of the world's prescription drug market. In the United States, cross-border drug sales have soared as the elderly (who generally pay high drug prices) travel to Canada or Mexico to obtain cheaper drugs. This underground importation of prescription drugs is estimated to cost the pharmaceutical industry millions of dollars. The industry is threatening to hold back new treatments from the market unless Canadian health regulators close these discount stores (some of which continue to operate without regulatory control or licensed pharmacists).[21] The astonishing social logic that results in drugs produced by American pharmaceutical firms costing less outside the United States is hardly challenged by economists and policy analysts since it is rational in the global system of trade, but it needs to be understood anthropologically as a telling critique of what has become cultural commonsense about global trade.

Prescription drug promotion practices that involve giving financial grants and valuable items to doctors are common as well. In some countries these practices are nonexistent or illegal. In others such as the United States they remain routine. This inconsistency of practice — let alone the definition of what constitutes illegality in the realm of pharmaceuticals marketing — speaks to the absence of oversight but also to the kinds of powers and influence the pharmaceutical industry can bring to bear in various countries. Such powers are dependent on countries' abilities to codify and enforce standards and to create hospitable or inhospitable business climates, and the ability of pharma to operate predictably and at times to purchase influence.

Practices of mass advertising also represent a nonstandardized field. Pharmaceutical companies today market directly to a huge body of laypersons in the developed world through magazine advertisements, newspaper articles, television, and radio talk shows. In the developing world, they may indirectly promote their products in markets or via pharmacies, where pharmacists actively recommend particular medicines. On the streets of many African towns, drugs are sold by street vendors. Susan Reynolds Whyte has noted that pharmaceuticals destined for NGOs are sold in local Ugandan markets. Sale by local itinerant peddlers may be insufficient and scientifically irrational, but it is the way most poor peasants get their medications. In Shanghai, employees of large pharmaceutical firms give samples of medicines away free on the streets in front of pharmacies and department stores. In the United States, direct-to-consumer advertisements tell us to ask our physicians about particular drugs. Their flows of supply and demand are unevenly regimented. And the Internet has made their flow even more complex and difficult to control. Messages about drugs have become part of who we are and how we live in the global market, with its enormous hold on the transnational and domestic cultural space created by television and other advertising media.

## States, Markets, Regulation

The question of the state's role looms large when pharmaceuticals are the issue. Regulatory bodies set standards for the review of new drug applications, labeling, advertising, manufacturing, and clinical trials, among other things. But inconsistent regulation across the globe generates unexpected economic and political returns that move well beyond questions of standardization and what it can control and into the realm of governmentality (Foucault 1991). China offers a disturbing example. At the red-hot edge of the Chinese economy, which is rapidly becoming the world's production center, indigenous pharmaceutical companies that manufacture biomedical and also traditional Chinese medicinal products carry out business in a setting with limited regulations and unscrupulous practices aimed at beating competition. And indeed, this nonstandardization of traditional medicines—whereby the state is just not there to enforce global standards—is precisely the means by which their economies flourish. Capsules that contain literally nothing are manufactured and marketed. What is on the label may not be in the pill. What is in the pill may not be labeled. Out-of-date medicines may be sold as if they were still active. From Westerners' vantage point, global pharmaceuticals may represent an impressive degree of standardization in drug safety.[22] But traditional Chinese medicinal products are in fact global; they are exported to Southeast Asia, Europe, Japan, Australia, and the United States, and few attempts have been made to regulate them in developed countries. Traditional medications are treated almost as if they are outside the international standards. They represent an issue to be addressed by local and international regulation, and China itself is only now starting to deal with the problem after scandals have forced a direct confrontation. American federal regulations have yet to come to terms with the globalization of traditional pharmaceuticals, though attention to health supplements is now increasing and speaks to a new development.[23]

Some countries are more active in controlling their pharmaceutical markets than others, and this difference in itself points to the benefits of ethnographic specificity. In his *Seeing Like a State*, James Scott argues that the failure of large-scale state projects can be attributed to their inattention to detail. We can question, based on the above examples, the extent to which such inattention is a deliberate choice. Scott also argues that the totalizing political schemes of the twentieth century maintained a structural, ghostlike state "through a narrowing of vision" (11), while a much messier, unstable, material, and lived reality that defied schematic means of control and manipulation existed simultaneously. The theme of informal schemes evolving around formal ones, and vice versa, is central to this volume's essays. For example, the United States and China not only seem unable to control transitional flows of illegal drugs, but are also desultory in dealing with legal drug flows. Indeed, different state agencies responsible for medical licensing, the regulation of commercial enterprises, import-export trade, and so on, have yet to organize a unified bureaucratic policy. If one asks a Ministry of Health or a Food and Drug Administration to define the arenas of healthcare where drugs are bought and sold, the blueprint often is restricted to the official pharmacies, clinics, hospitals, and public health institutes of biomedicine. But this is an inadequate mapping of the cultural positioning of pharmaceuticals, which are also found in alternative and complementary medicine settings and in the homes and workplaces of patients, family members, and members of the wider social network (for the Indian case, see Das and Das in this volume). Almost every family keeps medicines from previous episodes of illness; stocks health foods, vitamins, and tonics; borrows drugs from friends and neighbors; hears about new treatments in the media; and participates in an informal economy of exchange and use of medicaments.

Some informal drug use takes place, indeed proliferates, because of formal state schemes that may or may not have an interest in containing such use and can even encourage it. FDA approval requires that new drugs in the United States be proven effective against a placebo, and not against drugs already on the market. This standard of evaluation invites manufacturers to produce me-too drugs (drugs that are structurally similar to existing drugs); and their purpose is often to exploit established and lucrative markets, not to create new ones. Such development strategies, some claim, increase drug costs. A number of state-level efforts to reduce these costs and provide a basis for informed choices are under way. There is the Maine initiative to rationalize drug purchasing, for example, and an Oregon law which would provide doctors with unbiased information about the efficacy of new prescription drugs; all are intended to counteract the ill effects of formal regulatory, and by extension drug-marketing, practices.

Administrative practices within the United States and China provide a comparative analysis of contemporary state forms and reveal how differently each form organizes and controls pharmaceutical flows. These issues link to a wider debate over whether or not states have lost the unquestioned sovereignty they once had over their populations and citizens, a particularly salient point as public health functions formerly ordered by the state are increasingly being assigned to nonstate actors. Governments' failure to ensure citizens' basic health has in some instances made room for market responses and the privatization of healthcare services and insurance. Privatization of services has introduced new experiments with decentralized healthcare delivery systems and new criteria for resource allocation. The pharmaceutical industry has filled in the services gap in some low-income contexts and has acquired preferential treatment and influence on the kinds of drugs to be included in national formularies and essential drug lists, on the regulatory systems of drug evaluation and approvals, on prescription costs, and on the prescribing patterns of physicians.

As governmental capacities are "de-statized," social and regulatory operations once performed by states are taken over by "quasi-autonomous non-governmental organizations" (Rose 1996:56 cited in Ferguson and Gupta 2002:989). NGOs and transstate actors such as the World Bank and IMF are more powerful than some nations. Thus, for some it would appear that the state as a sovereign entity is disappearing entirely (Abrams 1988) and that we have entered a postnational era (Appadurai 1996). Indeed, many scholars no longer view states as primary units of analysis (Sassen 1996). In a globalizing age, states either do not have the capacity to deal with transnational economic processes, are too indebted, or are simply irrelevant in the control of flows of global finance. Those who favor liberalization of economic trade argue that industries should operate on a principle of convergence and integration (of standards or common interest such as profit) and relegate the idea of the state to a primitive economic backwater inasmuch as it places barriers in the way of such processes (Boyer et al. 1996).

Such interpretations of the state, however, obscure the national and political specificities of global pharma and more generally, ignore how states can exercise new powers to define national and local affairs — where national regulators harmonize and where they claim spaces of independence for themselves. Brazil inaugurated a new model of state activism when it threatened to violate international drug patent laws in its fight against AIDS, as João Biehl's essay shows. We would argue that under the rubric of global pharma, states have acquired opportunities to configure their political and institutional assets, or what Pierre Bourdieu calls "species of capital" that are economic, cultural/informational, material, and symbolic in form (1999). These types of capital are manipulated within worlds with particular economic rules and exclusions, and they have a certain limited practical reach. In the domain of economic capital, for example, states continue to exercise power by influencing the size of pharmaceutical markets. They can undercut industry attempts to establish market strength by imposing strict regulations and procedures for product approval and advertisement, as Kalman Applbaum's essay suggests. They can set public health priorities and research agendas that may conflict with private interests, or they may grant these interests substantial influence. Cultural capital can be leveraged in the form of local knowledge and therapeutic practices that may resist universalized standards, as in the case of traditional Chinese medicines. States via health ministries can also use their informational and symbolic capital by sponsoring prevention campaigns and educational programs that counteract the stigma associated with sexually transmitted diseases; or, in claiming health rights as a powerful enough human rights issue, they can dramatically reshape the landscape of everyday survival. Through the pharmaceutical lens one can observe the types of power and control that are assumed (or given up) by states in the health care of their citizens, how industry practices can be restructured at national and subnational levels, and the largely uncharted interconnections between scientific knowledge, modes of profit-making, and the meanings and experiences of health and disease. It reveals what Saskia Sassen refers to as the overlapping rather than exclusive functions of the global and the national. She suggests examining their "combined thickness and specificity," as well as the discrepant spatialities and temporalities of the national that are "among the most vital effects" of accelerated economic globalization (2000: 215).[24]

The theoretical issues prove to be far more subtle than the making of global markets or the unmaking of sovereign states. The local acquires renewed epistemological and ethical urgency in globalizing regimes of commerce, as some locales are slated for concern and others are left out. What are the forces that make some locales exemplary centers of heated debates over ethics? What makes some locales peripheral to policy? Local beliefs and cultural practices: are they a hindrance to prevention strategies or to compliant drug use? Local infrastructures: can they deliver life-saving medications? Selective visibility has decisive effects in terms of whether equitable forms of distribution continue or are discontinued, whether healing capacities of local communities are enhanced or denied. "Psychotropic nihilism"—a bleak sense that all plans have failed us and that the availability of psychotropic drugs is an improvement over nothing—must also be addressed in communities that are left on their own to handle unmet responses to human need.[25] Anthropological analysis of pharmaceuticals brings to view a local world that is more than a reservoir of detail from which to critique large-scale plans. It is a "practiced site" (Rabinow 1999)—unfinished, complicated, often misinterpreted—in which socially invisible destinies can be accounted for, remade, toward viable and valued forms of individual and collective life.

### The Pharmaceutical Nexus

The globalization of pharmaceuticals illustrates the sheer scale and complexity of our interconnected world and its uncertain social and biological outcomes in local and national settings. It is a multiscaled movement with political, economic, and ethical dimensions. Together these dimensions constitute a "pharmaceutical nexus." But because it is constantly evolving, the globalization of pharmaceuticals evokes far more and perhaps means much more than what separate scholarly divisions — medical anthropology, the anthropology of markets, the anthropology of states, the sociology of professions, international trade relations and their history — can capture. The idea of a nexus is meant to capture a broad set of political and social transitions that fall under and to some extent happen through the globalization of pharmaceuticals. We propose three ways of understanding the nexus: as an empirical object, as a problem, and as a method of inquiry. As an empirical object, the pharmaceutical nexus has what seems like an obvious focal point: the pharmaceutical industry. Yet the logics that make pharmaceuticals circulate can recast the meaning and function of other public institutions such as states via standards, regulations, and forms of distribution. The uneven availability of life-saving drugs and heightened global sensibility about such patterns raise urgent challenges of remediation and access. As pharmaceuticals transform moral and political aspects of experience, our initial, obvious object has grown to encompass a number of other core elements: states and populations, governmental and non-governmental actors, medical professions and patient groups, persons and subjectivity. As the "3 × 5 Initiative" to treat millions of people living in developing countries with antiretroviral treatments shows, the possibilities of transformation and improvement in the human condition lie in the combined effort, knowledge, and will of all of these actors.

This leads us into the second aspect of the pharmaceutical nexus: the problem of relating core elements and critically analyzing changing configurations of commercial, state/regulatory, and public interests. The nexus may appear different, and pose different kinds of problems, for different kinds of people or interests. For drug developers, the nexus may pose obstacles or opportunity structures — a set of regulatory channels through which testing and market launching are deemed possible (see the essays by Applbaum and Petryna). For policymakers and legislators of different countries, it may pose a problem of balancing different national constituencies, of weighing the challenges in international negotiations over fair pricing. For patient groups or would-be patients, access to the resources this nexus generates may be a crucial life-saving tactic (Biehl), or it may generate new sorts of competition among different patient communities in the bid for public and private support. Different ways of looking at the nexus reveal different stakes for different interests, and suddenly it matters how we look at it.

Viewed ethnographically, the pharmaceutical nexus becomes more than a symbol of imperial design on domestic political institutions, practices, or bodies. It is also a method of critical analysis: how local worlds whose intensity of experience and "experiments with life and death" ground social processes (Das and Das); how professional practice, ethical conduct, and personal agency are shaped; and how sickness is mitigated against and a chance of healing is actually produced. Big pharma and its "inner" workings are exposable and observable at many levels; smaller details become part of a larger complex. How are disease and need, misery and marginality governed? What new political capacities and drives are instantiated with globalizing pharmaceuticals? How do local medical practices, affiliations, and regimes of labor affect or betray such drives? The essays in this volume rethink the big object—big pharma—in terms of located political and ethical problems whose solutions are not predetermined, or whose solutions could be different or better. They specify modes of entry and methods of approach, and provide situated anthropological microanalyses that help us to reflect on how we think about distinctions between the experimental and the routine, excess and scarcity, inclusion and exclusion, citizenship and marginality. An ethnographic analysis of this sort opens perspectives on the bureaucratic and technological determinants of disease and health, and of the concrete institutional ethics and medical and political practices that are determining life and its managements in the pharmaceutical nexus.

### Essays in Brief

The scope of pharmaceutical experimentation and the expense of clinical development have globalized human subjects research. Adriana Petryna investigates how the rapid growth of pharmaceutical markets has led to increased demands for human subjects for drug research, particularly in low-income countries. For regulatory, economic, and even biological reasons, new populations are being pursued as human subjects for pharmaceutical trials. Her essay considers the evolution of commercialized clinical trials and ethical and regulatory environments as they contribute to a dramatic growth of human subjects' involvement in research. She focuses on the operations of U.S.-based contract research organizations, a specialized global industry focusing on human subjects recruitment and research, and on the ways in which they expedite drug testing to low-income contexts. Specifically, she analyzes how these trans-state actors interact with regulatory authorities in the United States and how they recast international ethical guidelines as they organize trials for research subjects abroad. Through case-based analyses she elaborates an "ethical variability" at work as international ethical guidelines are being recast when trials for global research are organized. In an industrial pharmaceutical context, ethical variability evolves as a tactic informing the regulation and organization of commercial clinical trials. It takes the specificities of local context and lived experience as a given and as a basis on which to consolidate a cost-effective variability in ethical standards in human research.

Psychiatric medications are a specific example of the way drug production—its regulatory, technical, and economic underpinnings—is redefining the ethics of research. As David Healy tells us, the age of therapeutic reform marked by concern for scientific accuracy and standards is now past. Healy traces the rise of a new therapeutic paradigm in which psychopharmacology—particularly psychotropic drug testing and promotion—is entirely imbricated in the marketplace. As clinical trials themselves become a form of marketing, a host of unregulated practices, including the misrepresentation of clinical data, leveraging, and ghostwriting, have become standard procedures among corporate research sponsors. The experts who publish the results of their "objective" scientific investigations often themselves have a financial stake in the research without publicly disclosing that point. He illustrates how scientifically flawed the psycho-pharmaceutical research paradigm has become, citing evidence of an excess of suicides being withheld from official data on clinical trials of some antidepressants. Pharmaceutical companies may fail to publish trials with negative outcomes, but they must make this data available to the FDA. Here they are allowed by regulators to subvert the scientific process, which misleads clinicians. Antidepressants are repackaged and marketed as antianxiety drugs with little concern for classification, diagnosis, or science, because the market for such products is much bigger. The conflict of interest between science and business is changing the moral economy of professional classification and diagnosis. In this new medical *oikumene*, the goal of knowledge improvement—and by extension, health improvement—is subverted at multiple scientific, regulatory, and clinical levels.

Precisely who is on the right side of the conflict of interest may vary depending on who wants to control the market. Kalman Applbaum provides a vivid example of how controlling processes work through the invocation of standards, focusing on the market-making activities of American pharmaceutical marketing representatives. Interviews with personnel working in Japan document attempts to regulate the entrance of ssris (selective serotonin reuptake inhibitors) into the Japanese market. Applbaum examines the "theories of practice" American marketers employ to break open markets in national contexts known for their impenetrability. They start by selling the idea of innovation as a global professional standard and moralizing strategy, creating consensus among Japanese regulators of the "backwardness" of their approach and convincing them of the need to revamp their entire testing, distribution, and pricing infrastructure. This is nothing less than an attempt to reconstruct entire local and national conditions in order to enable multinational pharmaceutical companies to operate. Applbaum engages in a kind of ethnographic "reverse engineering" (Bowker and Star 2000), revealing "the multitude of local political and social struggles and compromises" that go into the constitution of a transnational market.

Andrew Lakoff looks beyond the conflict of interests in the marketing of antidepressants and into the ways global pharmaceutical companies create and regulate demand for antidepressants, specifically in Argentina. These efforts are aimed at getting general practitioners to switch from anxiolytics to their ssris, which became indicated for anxiety disorders as well as depression. The phenomenological condition of patients is pliable since most depressive episodes are accompanied by anxiety symptoms, and it is difficult to tell which came first or is most important. As in the Japanese case, consumer interests or needs are not the starting point for the creation of markets and regulation of demand. Rather, it is digitalization and the "avalanche of printed numbers" that take center stage here: the surveillance and auditing of physician prescription practices, which themselves reflect a conditioned set of relationships. Lakoff focuses on transformations behind the numerical avalanche: gift giving in the form of sponsored trips and conferences and the forging of local relationships in the quest to build brand loyalty. These dynamics take place in a context marked by economic scarcity and an overabundance of high-priced psychotropic treatments. Argentina is one of five countries that have domestic producers with a higher market share than foreign ones, but the specific dynamic of the Argentine drug market hinges on the trajectory of intellectual property there: "institutionalized piracy." The uses of numbers and expertise suggest how neoliberal topologies of knowledge about health and disease are crafted and imply distinctive (pharmaceutical) modes of response. It is the dynamic of sales in a specific drug rep's territory rather than an epidemiology of health and disease that decides whether prescriptions are increased and how antidepressants fall into users' hands.

We witness in its full market force how the intentionality of medical perception is informed by the purpose of treatment rather than the causes or phenomenology of symptoms. The very act of prescribing, which normally involves professional medical counseling and a diagnosis of symptoms which results in an appropriate medication, is reconceived. A top-down numbers game combined with physicians' relative vulnerability and eagerness to receive gifts shapes prescription practices. Behind-the-scenes marketing activities not only promote drugs but redefine human needs and the way they are responded to or elided. The elision of such needs makes one wonder who is left out of the picture. How do communities that have been overlooked as consumers manage misfortune and disease?

Anne Lovell examines an affliction for which there is no lucrative treatment market—heroin addiction. Markets remain small, in part, because the distribution and selling of such treatments is highly stigmatized. Although they have a strong potential to reach and help large populations, addiction pharmaceuticals and their production are generally discouraged. Against this background Lovell explores the intervening forces that contribute to a novel addiction pharmaceutical market in France in the mid-1990s: how buprenorphine (a synthetic opiate introduced in the late 1980s as a postoperative analgesic) came to be routinely prescribed in general medical practice for heroine addiction. France's buprenorphine market had its beginnings in a state-run addiction management model. This model was limited in several ways: treatment, clinical surveillance, and care were highly regimented and difficult to access. The program relied on short courses of methadone to assist in behavioral screening (for apathy, for example) and subjected patients to psychological interventions. Because it was labor-intensive, the model's reach was limited, and the urban poor and immigrants had no access to it. Lovell tracks the networks of addiction and treatment that developed on the periphery of the model in an informal pharmaceutical sector. By 1996, knowledge of buprenorphine's effectiveness had reached the medical hierarchy, and the opiate was marketed and routinely prescribed as an addiction pharmaceutical. The essay highlights how formal-regulated and informal-unregulated spheres interact. It is in the latter sphere that experiments take place and constitute a frame for future operation. Lovell's analysis describes the informal economy of illicit pharmaceuticals as more than a sinister shadow of the licit market. These markets are directly and indirectly connected. Her account also suggests the extent to which a global pharmaceutical industry relies on off-label experiments and unregulated local practices of self-medication to constitute pilot projects for new markets.

Veena Das and Ranendra Das examine the worlds of the urban poor, a group both patterned and disordered by state public health managers and international health planners, but typically seen as marginal and outside the logic of market and state regulatory regimes. These worlds are different from those assumed by multinational drug marketers, who promote ways of recognizing problems that are solved by the commodity they want to sell (Whyte et al. 2002). Here, common and uncommon health problems are unevenly treated, and local possibilities of medical consumption are structured in particular ways that defy standardized conceptions. Das and Das center their concerns on the notion of self-medication, a term that is often indiscriminately used to describe the poor as irrational in their pharmaceutical consumption. The sense of self-sustenance and autonomy embedded in the idea of self-medication all too readily makes the poor blameworthy when in their efforts to heal they apparently defeat themselves. Moreover, the authors suggest that such a term misinterprets demand and obscures the nature of therapeutic choice in poor urban settings. They document how the poor choose between public (free government dispensary) and private care and ration medications according to their resources. The structure of prescription practices is often unrelated to the specifics of a person's disease and reflects the limited availability of necessary drugs. Das and Das construct a spatiotemporal map of experience, a "local ecologies of care," that is far from inchoate and is deeply entangled in the worlds of health planning and decision making. They reveal intricate networks that are established between practitioners, patients, and households that shape the course of illness and the chances of healing: how care is rationed according to cash flow, how individual therapeutic actions and practices of users and providers in poor Delhi neighborhoods take shape, and the sheer amount of time and seriously limited financial resources that are devoted to solving illness.

In the pharmaceutical intentionality mapped by Das and Das, the causes and phenomenology of symptoms are embedded in a complex local world in which meanings of suffering and disease intersect with local providers, labor regimes, and families. Constrained agency, the traffic in illness categories, and actual medication practices have very little to do with culture as it is embedded in the notion of self-medication. The problem of recognition of distress and the action to take is made much more difficult. The importance of detailed surveys of these local ecologies of care cannot be overlooked, particularly in the wake of success stories of disease control. Das and Das bring this hidden locality into view and give it geographical and spatial credence. Most important, they offer a set of new methodological tools for examining local worlds that do not reify them culturally but that allow ethical reflection on the discourses and calculations at the national and international level that affect healing possibilities locally and the countervailing human efforts to survive.

States have begun to experiment with their own responses to the healthcare crisis. The Brazilian AIDS model of state dispensation of combined antiretroviral treatments has been hailed as an example of how to intervene successfully in a low-income context. The model, as João Biehl shows, combined the interests of the Brazilian state, international agencies, multinational and national pharmaceutical enterprises, and social activism to guarantee universalized access for the poorest of the poor to complex therapies; it has averted significant numbers of hospitalizations and deaths among registered AIDS patients. We can all celebrate the success of this model, which also effectively opened new pharmaceutical markets within Brazil that in turn allowed the country to pay for the life-saving intervention. It is a primary example of how markets can be innovated for human needs. The model also became a moral leveraging tool in the negotiation over drug patent rules and the stemming of macroeconomic imperatives. In short, Biehl suggests that the experiment has succeeded on many fronts. Yet, looked at ethnographically, there is room for critical attention to the realities that the model obscures. Promising universal access at a time when state healthcare enterprises are decentralizing and privatizing, the problem of access to specialized services is addressed through a form of state triage. Biehl highlights aspects within the model that "make people invisible" and urges global health policy experts to look more carefully at local developments of inequity before the model is transposed to other low-income contexts. He shows how the innovative Brazilian AIDS response is as much a product of public health response and corporate strategy as it is of strong social activist pressure; all three came together to provide medication. With innovation at the level of cooperation and access, AIDS in Brazil is becoming a chronic disease one can live with rather than a disease one dies from.

The creation of an infrastructure, either combined with existing public health delivery or a supplement to it, is also essential in making AIDS survivable. In many countries where the AIDS crisis continues unabated, the advent of cheaper generics has brought down the price for ARVs and to some extent has alleviated need. In Uganda, on the other hand, only 10,000 of the estimated 157,000 who need them use antiretroviral drugs. Access has come to express acute differences in power and position, as Susan Reynolds Whyte and her collaborators note in their case study. And the 10,000 for whom the $28 per month required for treatment is a realistic or "almost a realistic option" face stark dilemmas. Drawing on research among middle-class families and health workers, the authors reveal the social negotiations and moral decision making among families and individuals as they prioritize their cash expenditures and decide whether or not to buy antiretrovirals. The economic question of who lives and who dies, and at what cost, becomes all too real as families (predominantly middle class) are brought into the painful and difficult dynamic of triaging care among their own children and kin. The use and the cost of these drugs are weighed against other socially valued priorities such as sending a sister or a daughter to school. Patterns of moral and economic deliberation over whether to start or to continue treatment for oneself or for a family member influence patterns of adherence. The cost of long-term treatment becomes unsustainable in many cases, and people continue to die. "AIDS is socially and pharmacologically active," the authors note, inasmuch as access to its treatment reveals new social distinctions. In this sense AIDS has opened a space of moral critique about the unevenness of access and the need for flexible systems of delivery and care, as in the Brazilian instance.

We live in an era when not only industry but institutions of science and government must be made to respond to the unprecedented scope of unmet need. The essays in this volume offer no comprehensive, definitive canvassing of the new world order of pharmaceuticals and their entanglements. But they do make palpable the images, dilemmas, moralities, and calculations that have become so consequential for individual and collective lives. And these angles of sight show that it is not just institutions that are involved; a wide-ranging set of biosocial relations (Rabinow 1996) ultimately links societies with bodies, subjectivities, and the always shifting borders between normal experience and pathology.

This is a key moment: the sensibilities of ethics, professional standards, regulatory practices, and consumer and patient protections for this millennium are being defined. The subject of global pharmaceuticals both sets a new field for anthropological research and reframes the questions central to anthropology today. In thinking through existing realities, gaps, and moral paradoxes in the pharmaceutical nexus, we come closer to a language that addresses these complex issues as a whole. In thinking ethnographically and comparatively, we also hope to achieve a form of intelligibility that equips us—citizens, patients, advocates, research participants, scientists, and consumers — to identify the collective risks and benefits of an expanding pharmaceutical regime. We might then as a collective rethink our choices regarding what we consider to be of technological and therapeutic significance, and in the process readjust our senses of value in a direction that ensures equal access and the best therapeutic practices for all.

## Notes

The authors thank Daniel Carpenter, Rosemary Coombe, Andrew Lakoff, and Nicole Luce-Rizzo for their comments and suggestions on this essay.

1. These advertisements have recently been withdrawn because the use of cox 2 inhibitors (in relatively high doses) has been associated with an increased risk of heart attacks.

2. Malaria, AIDS, and tuberculosis are primary causes of adult and/or child morbidity and mortality in some regions.

3. In 2002, global sales of antidepressants totaled $17.1 billion; global sales of antipsychotics, $9.5 billion. In 2005, global sales of antidepressants totaled $20.3 billion; global sales of antiphsychotics, $14.1 billion (figures taken from http://news.bbc.co.uk and http://www.imshealth.com).

4. The 1960s and 1970s were marked by the arrival of anticancer drugs and a growing auto-immune therapy market.

5. U.S. drug makers set up affiliates as a means of entering foreign markets; they exported active ingredients and then transformed them into finished products according to the laws of the new country (Encyclopedia of Global Industries 2005). As of 2004, a number of new books critical of the pharmaceutical industry have appeared. Among them are Marcia Angell's *The Truth about the Drug Companies*; Jerry Avorn's *Powerful Medicines*; Merrill Goozner's *The $800 Million Pill*; and John Abramson's *Overdosed America*. These publications parallel current heated debates over the cost of healthcare and prescription drugs in the United States, as well as controversies, lawsuits, and federal hearings over the regulation and safety of some prescription drugs. For a recent overview of drug regulation in the United States, see Hilts 2003.

6. The pharmaceutical industry comprises multi-national and national enterprises. The largest companies are based in the United States, Britain, France, Sweden, Germany, and Switzerland. Pharmaceutical industries such as those in Brazil, Argentina, and Japan for example, are also influential. National and international regulations shape the way their drugs are tested, approved, manufactured, and sold. The United States Food and Drug Administration and the U.S. Congress have contributed to the present profitable form of the pharmaceutical industry by allowing technology-transfers from the academic to industry sector and by supporting monopolies on patent rights, among other things (see Angell 2004).

7. Owing in no small part to the increased significance of mental health disorders world-wide. Globally, mental health disorders represent five of the ten leading causes of disability in persons aged fifteen through forty-four.

8. Persistent and resistant infection among poor people is often cited as the main cause of

lagging development and poor adherence. Recent studies on compliancy have shown just the opposite.

9. East Africa is an epicenter of drug resistance to antimalarials such as chloroquine and sulfadoxine-pyrimethamine (SP). There is an acute shortage of effective artemisinin-based combination therapy (ACT).

10. See also Lexchin 2001.

11. Full name is the Global Fund to Fight AIDS, Tuberculosis and Malaria. Other such programs include the Bill and Melinda Gates Foundation and the Geneva-based Global Forum for Health Research. Also see Kremer and Glennerster 2004.

12. It is estimated that average life expectancy in South Africa has diminished by between eighteen and twenty-five years since the AIDS outbreak.

13. In other world regions, the World Bank's structural adjustment policies (SAPs) in the 1980s can credibly be held responsible for the shrinkage of public health sector investments, especially in health, in poor countries. By the 1990s the World Bank was "Investing in Health" and had become the largest such investor worldwide. See Kim et al. 2001.

14. Examples of earlier studies that provide agendas for the anthropological study of pharmaceuticals include Vuckovic and Nichter 1994, 1997, which examine the effects of social and political-economic factors on pharmaceutical practices in the United States and elsewhere. The authors looked at shifts in demand for pharmaceuticals in relation to product proliferation, and evaluated how such shifts reflect cultural ideals. Van der Geest, Whyte, and Hardon have suggested a focus on the life cycle of pharmaceuticals in which every phase is analyzed in terms of its specific actors, contexts, values, and ideas. Such an approach offers clues to answers for larger anthropological questions concerning commodification, the body, and processes of globalization and localization.

15. Public lecture, Harvard University, May 14, 2002. Substantial progress is being made in the push to expand HIV treatment access. More people in developing countries are receiving combination antiretroviral therapy for HIV/AIDS (from 400,000 in December 2003 to approximately 1 million in June 2005). A target has been set by WHO and UNAIDS of treating 3 million people by the end of 2005 (http://www.who.int/3by5/progressreportJune2005/en/print.html).

16. A number of anthropological works provide critical empirical and theoretical insights into how these experiential domains are affected and interpreted via biomedicine. Among them are João Biehl's *Vita*; Myra Bluebond-Langner's *In the Shadow of Illness*; Charles Briggs's (with Clara Mantini-Briggs) *Stories in the Time of Cholera*; Paul Brodwin's *Medicine and Morality in Haiti*; Lawrence Cohen's *No Aging in India*; Robert Desjarlais's *Shelter Blues*; Sue Estroff's *Making It Crazy*; Byron Good's *Medicine, Rationality, and Experience*; Mary-Jo DelVecchio Good and Byron Good's "Clinical Narratives and the Study of Contemporary Doctor-Patient Relationships"; Marcia Inhorn's *Infertility and Patriarchy*; Sharon Kaufman's *And a Time to Die*; Arthur Kleinman's *The Illness Narratives*; Margaret Lock's *Encounters with Aging*; Shirley Lindenbaum and Margaret Lock's *Knowledge, Power, and Practice*; Theresa O'Nell's *Disciplined Hearts*; Lorna Rhodes's *Emptying Beds*; and Allan Young's *The Harmony of Illusions*.

17. See Fleising 2002.

18. For an analysis of the complexities of FDA drug review and the trade-offs and consequences of delay and rejection of new drug applications, see Daniel P. Carpenter, The politi-

cal economy of FDA drug review: Processing, politics, and lessons for policy. *Health Affairs* 23 (1) 2004: 52–63.

19. On the pharmaceutical industry's sponsorship of research and the outcome and its quality, see Lexchin et al. 2003.

20. As the relationship between academic medicine and the pharmaceutical industry becomes increasingly close, the lack of fit between publicly professed ethics values and private behavior only becomes more disturbing (Bosk 2000).

21. Recently, Illinois and Wisconsin announced their intention to add New Zealand and Australia as sources of low cost medications. The pharmaceutical industry has successfully pressured Canadian lawmakers and health ministry officials to limit bulk prescription drug exports.

22. As Philip Hilts notes in his book *Protecting America's Health*, the U.S. Food and Drug Administration standardized drug safety requirements only gradually, particularly after drug-related deaths and tragedies had occurred and forced it to do so.

23. The National Center for Complementary and Alternative Medicine at the National Institutes of Health, established by Congress in 1998, sponsors studies of efficacy and safety but is also policy oriented.

24. Where Sassen sees discrepant spatialities and temporalities as among the most vital effects of accelerated economic globalization (2000:215), one sees a growing disjuncture in ethics and its strategical uses (Petryna, this volume).

25. This term was proposed by Byron Good in a roundtable discussion.

# Globalizing Human Subjects Research

ADRIANA PETRYNA

The number of people participating in and required for pharmaceutical clinical trials has grown enormously since the early 1990s. The number of clinical
trial investigators conducting multinational drug research in low-income settings increased sixteenfold, and the average annual growth rate of privately
funded U.S. clinical trials recruiting subjects is projected to double by 2007.[1]
This essay considers the evolution of commercialized clinical trials and ethical and regulatory environments as they contribute to a dramatic growth
of human subjects' involvement in research. It focuses on the operations of
U.S.-based contract research organizations and on the ways in which drug
trials are being outsourced and expedited. Many of these new trials are being
performed in areas of political and economic instability and unprecedented
healthcare crises. Drug companies' accessibility to such areas raises questions
about the unequal social contexts in which research is being performed and
about how conditions of inequality remake a global geography of human
experimentation.[2]

Pragmatic issues have overwhelmed ethics in terms of who controls international guidelines for ethical research and their capacity to protect the rights,
interests, and well-being of human subjects globally.[3] Social scientists have
critiqued bioethicists for focusing discussions about new global experimental

orders almost exclusively on procedural questions of informed consent and clinical conduct, narrowing the view of the complexity of emergent ethical dilemmas in the arena of global human subjects research. Such a focus has led to a disconnect between bioethics—an abstract philosophical discourse grounding a set of codified norms for medical practice and research—and empirical reality.[4] Arthur Kleinman (1999), for example, points to a "dangerous break" between bioethics and the realities of local moral worlds that poses a danger to persons and their bodily integrity. Veena Das (1999) links international immunization programs and the manner of their implementation with the reemergence of local epidemics in India. Her work raises questions about the relation between bioethics and accountability in democratic societies and about the forms such ethics take and to whom it is accountable.

Other anthropological work on the ethics of biotechnology and new medical technologies has shifted attention away from issues of individual autonomy and has deepened the analysis of new biomedical technologies as they affect new patterns of civic, medical, and commercial organization.[5] This work examines an important dimension of ethics beyond its universal and regulatory (or normative) frameworks. New technologies raise new contexts of decision making over doing what is right; thus, beyond defining instances of moral certainty, ethics also involves a set of tactics that can generate new human conditions and events (Rabinow 1996, 2003; Fischer 2001, 2003).

In my ethnographic work with various professionals within the contract research organization (CRO) community (including company founders, CEOs, clinical trial managers, and health economists), the nurses and physicians with whom CROs contract, and pharmaceutical consultants and regulators in various countries, I came to see that the global dynamics of drug production plays an important role in shaping contexts in which ethical norms and delineations of human subjects are changing. As violations of individual bodily integrity in human research continue to be exposed in the media, social scientists are also challenged to chart and consider how whole populations are brought into experimental orders and why the available discourses and protective mechanisms are unable to intervene to assist these groups.

I also discovered an ethical variability at work in the globalization of trials, one of several modes helping pharmaceutical sponsors to mobilize much larger populations of human subjects much more quickly. Ethical variability refers to how international ethical guidelines (informed by principles and guidelines for research involving human subjects) are being recast as trials for global research subjects are organized.[6] The international standardized ethics has starkly failed to account for local contexts and lived experience (Cohen 1999; Das 1999; Kleinman 1999). In an industrial pharmaceutical context, ethical variability evolves as a tactic informing the regulation and organization of commercial clinical trials. It takes the specificities of local context and lived experience as a given and as a basis on which to consolidate a cost-effective variability in ethical standards in human research.

Variability, however, is not meant to evoke the notion of "cultural relativism," although it has been interpreted in such terms (Christakis 1992). Reliance on culture to explain differences in global health practices has been central to the field of medical anthropology for decades. Knowledge of such cultural differences, as translated into the healthcare arena, tends to focus on "unbridgeable" moral divides between Western and non-Western groups. In the ethical imperialism versus relativism debate (Macklin 1999), anthropologists working in healthcare arenas and elsewhere have been faulted for blindly defending local cultural tradition, making them susceptible, as Clifford Geertz says, to the "moral and intellectual consequences that are commonly supposed to flow from relativism — subjectivism, nihilism, incoherence, Machiavellianism, ethical idiocy, esthetic blindness, and so on" (Geertz 2000:42).

Medical anthropologists, by contrast, have recently contended that a focus on cultural and moral difference in healthcare has become dangerous to the very people and practices anthropologists have sought to understand, particularly in the contexts of massive epidemics and debates over treatment access. As Paul Farmer (1999), Jim Yong Kim et al. (2003), and others point out, culture understood as difference has been used to explain "why" the poor are somehow less responsible regarding treatment regimes. The absence of an anti-HIV drug market in Africa, for example, has been blamed on the allegedly undependable medical and economic behaviors of that continent's desperately poor HIV sufferers. Farmer and Kim et al. have addressed the way moral assumptions in international health can further entrench inequality, warranting some interventions while preventing others.

Other anthropologists have moved beyond emphasis on difference and have shown, via careful ethnography, how courses of local epidemics are influenced by international policy and its technical forms (Cohen 1999; Das 1999; Biehl 2001). Differences in how institutions assigned to administer health problems (state governments, welfare agencies, insurance companies, medical bureaucracies, and religious and humanitarian groups) are arranged produce programs and actions that can shape different courses of health and sickness and affect the outcomes of both.

These works point to the kind of empirical precision that is required to address the moral, ethical, and cultural realities of emergent global drug markets. In this essay, I explore how ethical variability works, particularly in the conjuncture of accelerated drug development and the realities of global public health crises. I specify the effects of this variability on how research that uses human subjects is governed across various political and economic spheres, particularly in the absence of clear legislation in the United States and of transnational regulatory policy.[7] Ethical variability has become central to the development and global testing of pharmaceutical drugs, and it provides the means through which pharmaceutical sponsors and their third-party CROs achieve recruitment successes.

**More Human Subjects**

What drives the demand for larger pools of human subjects? First, it is the sheer number of trials being run. One market research company estimates that as of 2000, about 7,500 new clinical projects were being designed for research and development worldwide. By 2001 that number had purportedly grown to 10,000 (Brescia 2002).[8] Second, to satisfy U.S. regulatory demands, increasingly large numbers of patients must be included in clinical trials to prove products' long-term safety, especially for drugs intended to be widely prescribed. Third, some therapeutic categories — such as hypertension — are being overwhelmed by new drugs. Competition to get these drugs approved and to bring them to market intensifies the search for subjects. Fourth, there is a "drug pipeline explosion": patent applications are flooding the U.S. Patent Office for new compounds that have yet to be clinically tested.

Shifts in the very science of drug development also influence the decision to increase subject recruitment. As a vast amount of potential molecular therapeutics is generated, making right decisions regarding which molecules to test becomes more difficult. Consider antisense, a technology made up of genetic snippets that pass through cells and prevent the expression of certain harmful proteins. Wall Street investors learned that when the technology showed signs of failure in a late-phase clinical trial for patients with skin cancer, researchers recruited more research subjects in an attempt to find a statistically significant positive result.

Finally, the available pool of human subjects in the United States is shrinking. The relatively affluent U.S. population is using too many drugs (Gorman 2004). "Treatment saturation" is making Americans increasingly unusable from a drug-testing standpoint, as our pharmaceuticalized bodies produce too many drug-drug interactions providing less and less capacity to show drug effectiveness and making test results less statistically valid.

Indeed, whatever an American is ready to provide as a human subject, owing to a belief in scientific progress, altruism, or therapeutic need, will never be enough to satisfy the current level of demand for human subjects in commercial science. And that fact is pushing the human subjects research imperative to other shores. In this section, I examine historical aspects and operations of North American CROs, members of a specialized industry that began listing and selling securities on public exchanges in the early 1990s and that focuses on efficient and cost-effective human subjects research and recruitment.

The demand for human subjects in developing countries is directly related to the dynamics of industry-sponsored pharmaceutical drug testing in the United States. The roots of the expanding drug-testing regime are traceable to the post–World War II pharmaceutical boom in the United States, when a fee-for-service industry evolved in response to a demand for more safety testing in animals. Another point of origin for the expansion of human subject recruitment efforts dates back to the early 1970s, when the use of prisoner subjects in the United States was exposed and severely limited. According to one prominent executive, widely regarded as the founder of the CRO industry, pharmaceutical companies in the United States began internationalizing their human subject recruitment efforts as a response to regulatory limitations on prison research. (He directed the internationalization effort for one company in the mid-1970s.)[9] The scale of U.S. prison research was impressive: An estimated 90 percent of the drugs licensed prior to the 1970s were first tested on prison populations (Harkness 1996). When use of prisoners was banned (for particular phases of testing), pharmaceutical companies lost almost an entire base of human volunteers. In response, they shifted a good deal of their research elsewhere, primarily to Europe (and countries with regulatory-friendly environments), but also to other areas with large subject pools whose access could be guaranteed because of centralized health systems and the closed nature of referral systems.

By the early to mid-1980s, pharmaceutical companies were routinely outsourcing laboratory and clinical services—including preclinical bioassays, in which the activity of a chemical is assessed (mainly in animal models)—and the monitoring of investigational sites and clinical data. By the early 1990s, drug development had become a globalized endeavor, in part under the aegis of the International Conference on Harmonisation, or ICH (in which the U.S. FDA played a key developmental role).[10] The ICH created international standards for ensuring and assessing the safety and quality of testing procedures for experimental compounds, including the Good Clinical Practice guidelines for investigators and the implementation of institutional review boards (IRBs). Most important, it eased the acceptability and transference of clinical data from foreign investigational sites to the FDA for regulatory approval of new drugs.[11]

Today, CROs are highly competitive transnational businesses that run clinical trials for pharmaceutical, biotechnology, and medical device industries. They offer expertise in submission of clinical trial data to regulatory bodies and in conducting market analyses of existing and prospective drugs. Their main source of revenue comes from conducting clinical trials in an efficient and cost-effective manner, particularly the second and third phases of clinical trials, and they are paid to know the constraints and opportunities afforded by country and regional regulations related to drug testing.[12] CROs are rapidly expanding into the Third World and the former Second World of Eastern Europe, statistically and innovatively carving out new populations for larger and more complicated trials to assess the drug safety and efficacy demanded by U.S. regulators and consumers.

CROS claim to recruit patients quickly and more cheaply than academic medical centers. Most firms are involved in locating research sites, recruiting patients, and in some cases drawing up the study design and performing analyses. Elements considered in situating a cost-effective trial include local levels of unemployment, population disease profiles, morbidity and mortality rates, per-patient trial costs, and potential for future marketing of the approved drug. CROS investigate the host country's regulatory environment. They ask whether universal access to health is in place. They assess regulatory priorities and capacities of host countries (e.g., efficacy of local ethical review boards outlooks and regulations on placebo use).

In managing clinical trial sites CROS sometimes work with site management organizations, which may include primary healthcare facilities, general practitioner networks, hospitals, or consortia of specialists focusing on a particular therapeutic area. U.S.-based CROS have alliances with site management organizations in countries in Eastern Europe, Latin America, the Middle East, and Africa. Some even have their own centralized IRBS for single-investigator trials or for multicenter trials that can involve studies of up to ten thousand people in ten to twenty countries.[13] IRBS are, ideally, independent boards composed of scientific and nonscientific members whose duty is to ensure the safety of patients in a trial. Their purpose is to review and approve the trial protocol and methods to be used in obtaining and documenting the informed consent of trial subjects. The ethics committee model for monitoring the conduct of research, as sociologists and anthropologists of bioethics have noted, turns the ethical universe in which researchers operate into an essentially procedural one (Guillemin 1998; Bosk 1999, 2002, 2005; Bosk and de Vries 2004; de Vries 2004) and deflects attention from structural circumstances that can contribute to increased risk and injustice (Chambliss 1996; Marshall and Koenig 2004). Do clinical researchers have the patient's informed consent? Does the local investigator agree to accept all responsibility in case of an adverse reaction or death? In the international context of drug development, the IRB model avoids the challenge of variability across distinct political and economic contexts. At stake is the construction of an airtight documentary environment ensuring the portability of clinical data from anywhere in the world to U.S. regulatory settings, even if those data were derived in the middle of an epidemic or in a war zone.[14]

## Treatment Naiveté

This work evolved out of my research and writing on the Chernobyl nuclear disaster in the former Soviet Union (Petryna 2002). Working in government-operated research clinics and hospitals in the mid to late 1990s, I observed a rapid growth of pharmaceutical and clinical trial markets in Ukraine and its neighboring countries. Physicians who tended to Chernobyl sufferers routinely expressed eagerness to learn how to conduct clinical trials and to attract clinical trial contracts from multinational pharmaceutical sponsors because of the abundance of various untreated diseases.[15] They were also eager because the scientific infrastructures on which they were dependent were quickly deteriorating in the absence of state funding. The combination of local public health crises and commercial and scientific interest led to the sudden revaluing of patients who themselves had lost state protection in the form of guaranteed healthcare. It was not quite the dream "of Neel, Chagnon, and their gold-rush, tourist-hunting allies 'to turn the Yanomami's homeland into the world's largest private reserve,' a six-thousand-square-mile research station and 'biosphere' administered by themselves," described by Geertz (2001:21).[16] But scientists' rush to reconceptualize their object of study "not as a people but as a population" to be brokered as valued research subjects on the pharmaceutical world scene was certainly there.

Currently a turf war is raging among pharmaceutical sponsors for human subjects. The competition is not only about the number of subjects a given company can recruit, it is also about recruiting subjects quickly. As one veteran recruiter told me, "It's really a problem. I don't know anybody who has really cracked the code. Sometimes you get lucky and you fill the study quickly, but for the most part, patients are really difficult to find, and they are difficult to find because everybody is looking for them." CROs see Eastern Europe as a particularly good recruitment site due to the collapse of basic healthcare there. Postsocialist healthcare systems are conducive to running efficient trials because they remain centralized. High literacy rates in this region mean that subjects offer more "meaningful" informed consent, thus smoothing potential regulatory problems in the future. Large Latin American cities such as Lima and São Paulo are also considered premium because, as one CRO-based recruiter told me, "Populations are massive. It's a question of how many patients I can get within a limited area, which reduces travel cost." CROs, he said, battle over "who gets those patients, who I can sign up to be in my alliance so that when I do attract a sponsor, I can say 'I can line up 500 cancer patients for you tomorrow morning.' You are seeing that happening a lot because recruitment is one of the most time-consuming and expensive portions of the plan." Eastern Europe and Latin America are particularly attractive because of the extent of so-called treatment naiveté, the widespread absence of treatment for common and uncommon diseases. Treatment-naive populations are considered "incredibly valuable" because they do not have any background medication (medications present in the patient's body at the time of the trial), or any medication, for that matter, that might confuse the results of the trial. CROs make themselves competitive by locating the treatment-naive. One researcher told me that these populations "offer a more likely prospect of minimizing the number of variables affecting results and a better chance of showing drug effectiveness."[17]

On the one hand, pharmaceutical markets are growing. On the other hand, drug developers are now focusing on the biology of populations experiencing acute healthcare crises—populations whose life expectancies increased and whose incidence of infectious disease and mortality rates decreased under the demographic health transition, but whose lives are now shorter, more chronically diseased, and less socially protected.[18] The public health practice of demarcating disease to prevent disease (involving epidemiology, prevention, and medical access) is now used to carve out new catchment areas of human subjects who are targeted precisely because of their treatment naiveté. This move may appear exploitative, but the pharmaceutical industry argues that it is positive because in these regions clinical trials have become social goods in themselves.[19] And they may well be: they provide healthcare where there is none (see the chapter by Whyte et al.) and medical relief for participants' specific ailments for the duration of the trial.

Although industry and U.S. regulators would not dare codify such justifications for promoting clinical trials in poor areas, in many ways such justifications have already become an industry norm. Yet the question of precisely what made the move of the human subjects research enterprise to resource-poor settings both ethical and opportune remains unaddressed. In the next section I consider some key moments in the recent ethical and regulatory discussion of globalizing research in contexts of crisis, which have implications for how experimental groups are being defined and pursued globally today.

## Ethical Variability: Constructing Global Subjects

The controversy over placebo use in Africa in 1994 during trials of short-course AZT treatment to halt perinatal transmission of HIV was a watershed in the debate over ethical standards in global clinical research (Angell 1988, 1997, 2000; Bayer 1998; Crouch and Arras 1998; Lurie and Wolfe 1998, 2000; Botbol-Baum 2000; de Zulueta 2001). Here I consider it as a watershed of another kind: for understanding how a cost-effective consolidation of variability in ethical standards overtook efforts to make a universal ethics (as codified in key ethical guidelines for human subjects research) applicable and enforceable worldwide. Underpinning this process is a more general anthropological problem of how new subject populations are forged at the intersection of regulatory deliberation, corporate interests, and crises (upon crises) of health. My specific inquiry here centers on how the ability of the pharmaceutical industry to recruit treatment-naive subjects was solidified.

In this well-known case, some American researchers argued that giving less than standard care to those on the placebo arm of the study was ethically responsible, even if in the United States the standard of care medication was already known (a placebo is an inactive treatment made to appear like real treatment; it amounts to no treatment).[20] Critics viewed the use of a placebo arm in this case as highly unethical. They charged that research carried out in developing countries was being held to a standard different from those in effect in developed countries. Marcia Angell (2000), for example, noted patterns of conduct reminiscent of the Tuskegee experiment; that is, low-income communities were providing standing reserves of exploitable research subjects. Harold Varmus of the National Institutes of Health and David Satcher of the Centers for Disease Control, among the U.S. government institutions that authorized and funded the trial, claimed the trial was ethically sound (Varmus and Satcher 1996). They cited local cultural variables and deteriorated health infrastructures as making the delivery of the best standard of care infeasible. It would be a paternalistic imposition, they argued, for critics in the United States to determine the appropriate design of medical research in a region undergoing a massive health crisis when deciding the appropriate conduct of research and treatment distribution was within the jurisdiction of local and national authorities.

Ethical imperialism or ethical relativism? The debate, as it stands, is unresolved. Yet these catchphrases represent current responses to the ethics of the trial. The first position builds on well-known cases of marginalized communities acting as human subjects, and those cases, as medical historian Harry Marks (2002) suggests, may obscure more than they reveal about the contexts of experimental communities today. The second position relativizes ethical decision making as a matter of sound science, but it fails to consider the uptake of this relativizing move in corporate research contexts. The African AZT trial — and the ethical debates that followed it — highlight the role of crisis in the consideration of differences in ethical standards in the area of human research; indeed, that crisis conditions legitimate variability in ethical standards. Historically, some crises have led perhaps inescapably to experimentation (Smith 1990; Petryna 2002). But one can also ask, are crises exceptions or are they the norm? To what extent does the language of crisis become instrumental, granting legitimacy to experimentation that otherwise might not have any?

The debate over the ethics of the AZT trial prompted the sixth revision of the Helsinki Declaration, first issued in 1964. The declaration deals with all dimensions of human biomedical research, furnishing guidelines for investigator conduct in research involving human subjects.[21] The 2000 revision reiterated a position against placebo use when standards of treatment are known: "The benefits, risks, burdens, and effectiveness of a new method should be tested against those of the best current prophylactic, diagnostic, and therapeutic methods. This does not exclude the use of placebo, or no treatment, in studies where no proven prophylactic, diagnostic, or therapeutic method exists" (World Medical Association 2000:3044).[22] Although the ethics was unambiguous, the regulatory weight of the declaration was not. In this latter domain the winners and losers of the placebo debate would be named.[23] Pharmaceutical companies, already eagerly expanding operations abroad and calculating the economic advantages of placebo use (placebos lower costs, and, many argue, placebo trials produce unambiguous evidence of efficacy), were scrambling to learn from regulators about the legal enforceability of the declaration and were finding ways to continue using the placebo arm.

Haziness brought clarification of the rules of the game. Dr. Robert Temple, associate director of medical policy of the Center for Drug Evaluation of the FDA, undercut the regulatory significance of the declaration and threw his support behind placebo advocates, stating, "We'll have to see if the Declaration of Helsinki remains the ethical standard for the world" (Vastag 2000: 2983). He cited the International Conference on Harmonisation (ICH-E10 2001) as the more authoritative guideline on the ethics of placebo use. This guideline states, "Whether a particular placebo controlled trial of a new agent will be acceptable to subjects and investigators when there is a known effective therapy is a matter of patient, investigator, and IRB judgement, and acceptability may differ among ICH regions. Acceptability could depend on the specific trial design and *population chosen*" (Temple 2002:213, emphasis added). In other words, the ethical standard for the world was claimed to be variability.

Temple's support for the placebo trial was ostensibly guided by his desire for high-quality scientific data. His reaction is also indicative of how regulatory regimes can influence the definition of experimental groups. Let me briefly trace the logic of this relation. The alternative to the placebo control is the active control trial. Its purpose is to compare a new drug with a standard one, to show superiority of the new drug to the active control or to at least show a difference. (Many patients and clinicians consider the comparative effectiveness of a new drug in relation to a standard therapy to be the most relevant information.) But showing difference or superiority is not enough because "many kinds of study defects decrease the likelihood of showing a difference between treatments" (Temple 2002:222) and make data on difference less reliable. Study defects arise from external factors like poor patient compliance, poor diagnostic criteria, and the use of concomitant medication that can obscure the effect. Other defects can include inconsistencies in how the disease is defined, the use of insensitive or inappropriate measures of drug effectiveness, and the chance of spontaneous recovery in a study population. These factors can be "fatal to a trial designed to show a difference," Temple claimed (2002:222; also see Pocock 2002:244–245). They can decrease difference or increase the chances of finding no difference, such that, in the end, in Temple's words, "you don't know if either of them worked" (Vastag 2000:2984). By contrast, a placebo control trial is capable of showing difference, and, much more important, makes it possible to distinguish between effective and ineffective treatments. That ability is considered a key marker of reliable evidence of the effectiveness of a new drug. Active control trials fail to make such a distinction and are therefore not preferable from a regulatory standpoint.

A certain kind of global human subject is at stake in Temple's description of the failure of active control trials. Most people in low-income countries, where many clinical trials are being or will be performed, are subject to the external factors that are said to lead to the study defects cited above. They may have medical histories that are patchy at best, thus making cross-cultural interpretation of the meaning of drug effectiveness less reliable. Their diagnoses can be inconsistent, also confusing evidence on drug effectiveness. Not only is quality of data in doubt with active control trials, so is the "quality" of the research subjects. Researchers must standardize medical histories if they are to ensure their comparability, and this is a time-consuming, costly, and all but impossible task.

Temple's invalidation of the active control trial is anthropologically and economically significant — the treatment-naive become preferable from a regulatory standpoint that emphasizes the importance of an efficient (and foolproof) global research subject. Precisely because they are often poor and lack a treatment history and treatment itself, the treatment-naive are the more foolproof and valuable research subjects!

## Ethics as a Workable Document

In responding to the Helsinki Declaration revision, American regulators conveyed the value of research efficiency to industrial clinical researchers. And the murky ethics of the placebo could be bypassed by providing for what is known as equivalent medication — not necessarily the best or standard treatment, but whatever is available as the best local equivalent. "Do I give them a sugar pill or vitamin C?" one researcher cynically asked me. In the meantime, the study will be ethical, the data will have integrity, and, sadly, the patients will remain treatment-naive.

Another researcher echoed this shift from concerns about redistribution to efficiency-based standards in global research when he told me that ethics has come to be seen as a "workable document." "Equivalent medication in Eastern Europe is not the same as equivalent medication in Western Europe, so you could work the Helsinki Declaration," he said. In the name of efficiency, pharmaceutical companies and CROs intensified their search for treatment-naive populations worldwide.

In tracing the relation between regulation and the making of ethics in human research, Marks notes, "it is as if ethical discourse and the regulations governing research exist in two parallel universes which share some common elements but do not connect" (2000:14). But I would argue that the aftermath of the 1994 AZT trials shows how linked those universes are. Regulatory response in the context of debates over the Helsinki Declaration's revision (itself a response to controversial uses of human subjects) is now instantiating new populations of human subjects — the treatment-naive.

The story told here is about how regulatory decision making at the transnational level encourages the evolution of "local" experimental terrains whose ethics are workable and whose subjects can be (justifiably) variably protected under current international ethical codes such as the Helsinki Declaration. I say variably because some national governments faced with a sudden growth of human subjects research have minimal bureaucracies to cope with structures of liability in cases of adverse or catastrophic events.[24] Nor do all have the bargaining power or the desire to press for fairer procedures and access to drugs during and after the trial. Thus, a distinction is to be made between ethical codes (in which the definition of what constitutes biomedical harm is fairly unambiguous) and ethical regulation (in which deliberation of those definitions is balanced against economic, scientific, and regulatory constraints and demands). Ethical regulation entails minimally enforceable procedures governing human research as inscribed in public policy and law. It is also a realm of contingent practice where the allocation of protection for human subjects research is far from settled.

The ethical arrangements that have grown up around populations and their diseases can be elucidated by examining the spatial and temporal complexities associated with global pharmaceutical development and by analyzing the practices of the CROs that fill this demand.

Starting in the early 1990s, just four years before the controversial AZT trials, the FDA began to actively promote the globalization of clinical trials, declaring "the search for sites and sources of data" to be "part of its mandate to determine the safety and efficacy" (Office of the Inspector General, Department of Health and Human Services 2001:42) through the establishment of the ICH. Participation in American-sponsored research began to swell among clinical investigators in countries that had voluntarily agreed to harmonizing standards in the field of commercial drug testing: Argentina, Brazil, Hungary, Mexico, Poland, Russia, and Thailand, among others. As a result, the number of international human subjects involved in clinical trials grew dramatically between 1995 and 1999 (in 1995, 4,000; in 1999, 400,000; these are only partial estimates; see Office of the Inspector General, Department of Health and Human Services 2001).[25]

This global growth of research brought with it a new set of unknowns related to the circumstances of research as well as concerns about possible exploitation of foreign subjects. Currently, no U.S. legislation or international regulatory policy is aimed at controlling or monitoring the conduct of these globalizing clinical trials, although many proposals have been made for improving the monitoring system. In 1999, the Office of the Inspector General (OIG), a body that carries out periodic reviews of the FDA, told that agency after careful review that "in spite of its active promotion of the search for sites and subjects elsewhere," the FDA is not able to protect human subjects in research elsewhere.[26] The OIG recommended that the FDA support and in some cases help to construct local ethical review boards.

The regulatory preference for the expansion of the IRB model is reflected in a recent National Bioethics Advisory Commission (2000) report recommending that studies submitted to the FDA receive ethical committee review both in the United States and in the country in which the research is being carried out (as opposed to the present situation, in which only foreign ethical review and approval are mandated). The report supported the idea of dual review but stated that if host countries have working ethical review committees, then only their approval is required.

These approaches involve monitoring, data collection, and more local ethics committees and lean heavily toward what Iris Young (2004) calls the "liability model" of accountability: Let regulators name the responsible local parties (in some cases, set them up first), and surely those parties can gather information and make the right decisions; surely they can stop inappropriate research from taking place. Much is also assumed about who is and is not the agent of abuse, typically defined as the individual investigator.

What about instances in which risks arise in the structure of the research itself? These instances tend not to find proper nouns in ethical discussions, beyond designation as "interesting" or "scandalous" cases. The fact is that certain conditions have to be met for liability to work: States themselves need to act as protectors and not abusers; transnational corporations need to respect the rights and dignity of all research subjects and recognize that different situations elicit different kinds of coercion; and international ethics codes must be enforceable in cases of clear violation.

None of this occurred, unfortunately, in Nigeria in 1996 during industry-sponsored research involving Trovan, a drug manufactured by Pfizer, Inc. Trovan was once one of the most widely prescribed antibiotics in the United States, but it was taken off the market because it was found to produce liver-damaging side effects. In an effort to gain FDA approval for a new use of Trovan to treat bacterial meningitis a team of Pfizer researchers traveled to the city of Kano during a bacterial meningitis outbreak (which they found out about on the Internet). They were in search of pediatric victims of this disease who were most likely treatment naive. Doctors Without Borders was already distributing a cheaper antibiotic, proven effective for treating bacterial meningitis, at a main local hospital.

The trial protocol for testing a new use of Trovan was not approved by an American ethics committee and received a grossly inadequate, perhaps nonexistent, review in the host country, which was suffering civil unrest under the Abacha military dictatorship. Legal documents show that the informed consent forms used in Pfizer's defense are backdated.[27] The Pfizer team went to the hospital where the cheaper drug was being distributed and selected one hundred children who were waiting in line to receive treatment. Researchers are alleged not to have explained the experimental nature of Trovan to the subjects; parents believed their children were receiving a proven treatment.[28] Some of these children were given Trovan in a form never before tested on humans; others were given a lower dose of the standard of care for meningitis (ceftriaxone) that, according to the complaint filed by the New York law firm representing the parents, allowed Pfizer researchers to show that Trovan was more efficacious (Lewin 2001). This low dosing, the parents claim, resulted in the deaths of eleven children.

This is the first case brought by foreign citizens against a U.S.-based multinational pharmaceutical company. The plaintiffs' lawyers suggested that a chain of complicity in making the children available for research included Nigeria's military rulers and state officials, Ministry of Health officials, and local hospital administrators; U.S. FDA regulators who authorized an unapproved drug's export to Nigeria for "humanitarian" purposes; and the Pfizer researchers who selected subjects for an industry-sponsored clinical trial. All were involved, lawyers claimed, in violating principles of the Nuremberg Code and other codes of human subjects protection, referred to in plaintiffs' court documents as "customary laws" that are "made up of fundamental principles of a civil society that are so widely held that they constitute binding norms on the community of nations" (*Rabi Abdullahi et al. v. Pfizer Inc.*, 01 Civ. 8118 (WHP) [2000]).[29]

The defendant's lawyers downplayed the authority of the code and stated that it and other such guidelines "are not treaties." (In some domestic cases, federal judges have ruled that internationally accepted codes of human subjects protection, in this case the Nuremberg Code and the Helsinki Declaration, cannot be relied on as the basis of civil suits in U.S. courts.) The defense situated Pfizer researchers' activities in the context of a "massive epidemic killing more than 11,000 people," whose outbreak they attributed to "woefully inadequate" sanitary conditions. By suggesting that their experimental treatment could only do good in such a desperate context, the defense obscured the criteria by which to judge the difference between experimental and standard-of-care treatment. Pfizer's defense further stated that it would be "paternalistic" for an American court to adjudicate the appropriate conduct of medical research in a country undergoing a public health crisis, and echoed the ethically relativizing stance already familiar in the African AZT case (*Rabi Abdullahi et al. v. Pfizer Inc.*).

One aspect of this legal parrying is worth stressing. As much as one would like to see the Kano case as an instance of the "dubious" or the "para" (paralegal, pararegulatory, paraethical), an interlocking set of regulatory, commercial, and state interests is at play in such situations that can potentially introduce uncertainty with respect to the observability of international ethics codes in local contexts, or even suspend the relevance of such ethics altogether.[30] In this case, a functional ethical review of U.S. industry–sponsored research might have prevented this tragedy. But from the Nigerian side of things, interests were not on the side of protection but overwhelmingly on the side of making populations accessible to research.

The Trovan case is still being adjudicated, but deliberations so far suggest that knowledge of wrongdoing does not necessarily translate into the ability to regulate or prosecute wrongdoers. The case exemplifies how contextual factors (crisis and its humanitarianisms) and defenses fold into and construct new experimental scenarios and groups. Ethical positions, particularly those revealed by the AZT case, that relativize decision making over appropriate conduct of research to local context inform a legal defense strategy to make acts of experimentation — particularly those enacted in public health crises — either reachable or unreachable by international ethics codes.[31] What appears as scandalous activity with respect to global human subjects research may in fact be seen as legitimate under evolving ethical and legal notions of fair play.

As I noted above, this "expedient" experimentality first caught my attention in the context of the scientific management of the Chernobyl nuclear crisis. Here, too, the language of crisis became instrumental, granting legitimacy to what might be considered questionable experimentation. A public health disaster combined with the state's incapacity to protect the life of citizens, and this combination of circumstances justified a commercially sponsored clinical trial that would have been impossible to conduct elsewhere at the time. Human research whose exploitativeness might have been hard to judge was justified under the rubric of humanitarianism; and this process in itself may lie outside the bounds of what ethical discourse about human subjects research and even legal codes can capture.[32]

Occurring at a time when research priorities in the world of international science were shifting toward biotechnology, Chernobyl afforded a venue for biotechnological research.[33] The Soviet state's response to the crisis is widely documented as having been grossly inadequate, particularly in the first days after the disaster.[34] Under strong pressure to restore the credibility lost by the state's initial inadequate response, General-Secretary Gorbachev agreed to cooperate in an unprecedented Soviet-U.S. scientific venture. He personally invited a team of American oncologists and radiation scientists to conduct experimental bone marrow transplants on workers from the "Zone" (an area thirty kilometers in diameter circumscribing the destroyed nuclear reactor site) whose exposures were beyond the lethal limit and for whom no treatment was available.

In exchange for the credibility garnered from this move, Soviet medical authorities gave in to the American research team's demands to conduct human testing of a genetically engineered hematopoetic growth factor molecule (rhGM-CSF, thought to regenerate stem cell growth and to be useful for treating leukemia). Some animal testing had been under way in the United

States using highly irradiated chimpanzees and dogs, but human testing of the molecule had not been approved by the FDA. The humanitarian ethics to treat in a crisis where there was no other treatment legitimated the transfer and use of unapproved experimental drugs.

The lead scientist on this trial told me that he had no clinical trial protocol but that he had acted consistently "with what was legal."[35] He did not know the exact number of individuals on whom the molecule was tested (he guessed it was over four hundred). During our 1996 interview he described his interests in the Chernobyl cohort as short term. In his view, the accident offered his team a ready-made set of experimental conditions: "The Chernobyl accident for the firemen at the power plant was exactly what we do at the clinic every day. Potentially, there were patients with [leukemic] cancer exposed to acute whole body irradiation." This scientist, who has gained fame and admiration for his humanitarianism, spoke to me about these unregulated trials in a surprisingly confident fashion, suggesting that political arrangements gave him adequate refuge from ethical sanctions. "No one was going to believe what Gorbachev had to say about Chernobyl," he told me. "I convinced them of that [in my negotiations]. They had no credibility."

This scientist's confidence illuminates a political, regulatory, legal, and ethical milieu that lay beyond the procedures governing relations between researchers and their human subjects. Disaster reframed as humanitarian crisis presented a unique scientific and political opportunity. Politically, normal rules of conduct were suspended. Scientifically, the disaster offered a set of negative health circumstances that, because of codes of ethics prohibiting human experimentation, would have been impossible to simulate in normal clinical trial circumstances in the United States. In other words, the crisis provided a ready-made scenario for bioscientific research: it gave researchers liberal access to a pool of highly endangered people. This pool became attractive precisely when a nonhuman model showing the effects of a particular molecule was lacking. Although the results of this trial were deemed largely unsuccessful, both sides gained significantly from their short-term arrangement. The American scientist's team and its major pharmaceutical backer got a valuable jump-start on the emerging biotechnological market in growth-factor molecules, and Soviet officials got a rare opportunity to shore up the state's credibility locally and internationally.

## Biological Citizenship

As the Trovan and Chernobyl cases show, a humanitarian crisis can create a space that appears to be "ethics free" precisely because it is disastrous, beyond the reach of regulation. With the sudden suspension of normalcy, whole groups of people actually or potentially become experimental subjects.[36] Both cases also demonstrate to a greater or lesser extent a breakdown in consent processes and in citizens' ability to trust and rely on state systems of public health and protection. Ethics is used variably and tactically by all actors in a chain of interests involved in human subjects research. Such chains now function in states where lives of citizens are not adequately protected by traditional health or welfare systems. The biological indicators of whole groups, however formed or damaged by social and economic context, are enfolded into regimes of international and local forms of protection in which ethics becomes a "workable document." The issue of human subjects protection thus moves beyond scripted procedural issues of informed consent and into questions of legal capacities and the aggregate human conditions of which they are generative (Marks 2000).

What alternatives are there to counteract abuse and inadequate protection of research subjects? What work can be done locally, scientifically, and administratively to link biology back to regimes of protection? In the Chernobyl context, I documented how, in the newly independent Ukrainian state, radiation research clinics and nongovernmental organizations mediated an informal economy of illness and claims to "biological citizenship" — a massive demand for but selective access to a form of social welfare based on scientific and legal criteria that both acknowledge injury and compensate for it. Such struggles over biological citizenship took place in a context of fundamental losses related to employment and state protections against inflation, widespread corruption, and the corrosion of legal and political categories.[37] Assaults on health became the coin sufferers paid for biomedical resources, social equity, and human rights.

This type of biosocial fabric, in which the very idea of citizenship becomes charged with the superadded burden of survival (also see the chapter by Biehl), is one of many being converted into a model of cost-effective ethical variability in globalized human research. Commercial sponsors argue that clinical trials provide social and material goods to treatment-naive populations where those goods otherwise might not be available; if these populations do not want the goods, sponsors can always go somewhere else. "There are so many places that we can work that we just bypass it altogether," one CRO executive told me. In other words, sponsors are free to bargain down the price and "work the ethics" (in terms of equivalent medications) of any trial.[38]

The circulation of such experimental goods and the relative absence of public scandal over how they circulate do not make the task of gathering more information on the sites and sources of clinical research data any less urgent — particularly while the FDA actively promotes the "search for sites and sources of data" around the world to fulfill its "mandate to determine the safety and efficacy" of new drugs (Office of Inspector General, Department of Health and Human Services 2001:42). In the early 1970s, when the scandal over the use of prison subjects broke, the FDA claimed it had little documentation, citing its duty to protect intellectual property. Today the FDA resists gathering data on the out-migration of human research on the basis that location of testing is proprietary information. One might want to rethink whether anonymity of the sources of clinical research data is a defensible idea anymore.

### Conclusion

In this chapter I have sketched an ethnographic approach to human subjects research — examining its practices and strategies across a variety of international, state, and economic spheres — in the context of an emerging industry of such research. The overriding empirical problem centers on the apparent ease of access to new treatment-poor populations. In the pharmaceutical industry's pursuit of these new global subjects one can observe how deliberations over the ethics of research in crisis-ridden areas are set against — and even eclipsed by — the market ethics of industry scientists and regulators. Rather than leveling the starting conditions in which global human subjects research is conducted, ethical variability itself has become the industry norm, to the point of being consciously deployed in pharmaceutical development. Ethics should protect people from harm. Case-based observation and analysis suggest that the procedural issues researchers rely on in realizing human subjects protection are insulating researchers from the contexts of inequality in which they work.

In contrast, current bioethical commentary on the movement of human trials to developing countries centers on the need to produce better ways of deriving informed consent from human subjects and exporting the IRB model at a quicker pace. The purpose here is to ensure that the autonomy of individuals takes precedence over the demands of science or the interests of society, with the idea that such autonomy can counteract coercion in research wherever it takes place. An exclusive focus on informed consent narrows one's vision of the broad array of factors that are overwhelming ethics. The incursion of procedural norms has not (at least not yet) evidenced itself in the exercise of free will by autonomous agents in human research. Rather, population-wide processes that support reification (and in some cases capitalization) of social and biological difference continue to operate.

This ethnographic assessment of the human subjects research industry brings into focus emergent ethical arrangements around disease and populations where states have collapsed and where the creation of new poverty is a chronic process. Rather than focusing on normative theory of ethics and ideal conditions, I maintain the importance of apprehending the norms that are being propagated and how they are being reconstructed in actual and diverse conditions. Understanding the existing variability in the regulation of ethics and the coinages through which consent, autonomy, and drug markets evolve helps build an ethnographic context that may ultimately provide the basis for a critique of market-driven human research.

## Notes

I thank Arthur Kleinman, Harry Marks, Iris Young, Rayna Rapp, Michael M. J. Fischer, Margaret Lock, Joseph Harrington, Veena Das, and João Biehl for their discussions and clarifying insights. This work was supported by the Crichton Fund (Department of Anthropology of Harvard University) and the National Endowment for the Humanities. The article was revised while I was a member of the School of Social Science of the Institute for Advanced Study at Princeton. A modified version was published in *American Ethnologist*.

1. Business Communication Co., Inc. 2003. This figure is derived from industry surveys, the U.S. General Accounting Office, and the annual reports of seven major philanthropic organizations.

2. The Office of Inspector General, Department of Health and Human Services, states that "among the countries that have experienced the largest growth in clinical investigators [for commercially sponsored trials] are Russia and countries in Eastern Europe and Latin America" (2001:i). Clinical trials typically have been conducted on patients living in major pharmaceutical markets, the United States, and Western Europe (and to a lesser extent Canada, Australia, and Japan). These regions comprise the leading global pharmaceutical markets. By the early 90s, this picture of commercialized drug research began to change. The outmigration of clinical research to so-called non-traditional research areas—countries undergoing demographic shifts or holding a relatively small market share—signals a sea change in a fundamental assumption in clinical trial participation. In the new clinical trials "markets," citizens are not long-term beneficiaries of new drugs. The reciprocal cycle of test subjects typically conceived of as end users/consumers of drugs is being broken.

3. Benatar and Singer 2000; Rothman 2000; Schuklenk and Ashcroft 2000; Benatar 2001; Lurie and Wolfe 2001; Office of the Inspector General, Department of Health and Human Services 2001; Farmer 2002a.

4. For earlier warnings on the dangers of ethics becoming disassociated from the empirical realities it claims to know, see Jonas 1969 and Toulmin 1987. Histories of bioethics and medical humanities approaches speak of the loss of intimacy in medical care as codes and norms (related to informed consent, for example) transform the patient-doctor relationship so that it is "no longer the intimate affair that it once was" (Rothman 1991:4). Intimacy, as anthropologists and historians of colonial and postcolonial settings suggest, is rarely a part of medicine in these settings, where it is the control of populations, rather than of individuals, that becomes the focal point of medicine (see Lindenbaum 1978; Comaroff and Comaroff 1992; Scheper-Hughes 1992; Vaughan 1992; Arnold 1993; Prakash 1999; Misra 2000; Anderson 2003; Briggs and Mantini-Briggs 2003; Biehl 2005; among others).

5. Strathern 1992; Franklin 1995; Cohen 1999; Rapp 1999; Dumit 2000; Biehl 2001; DelVecchio Good 2001; Lock 2001; Petryna 2002; Scheper-Hughes 2004.

6. Rules and regulations for conducting human subjects research have been evolving since the Nuremberg Code was established in 1947. The World Medical Association's Declaration of Helsinki states ethical principles that should guide investigators and participants in medical research. The U.S. Food and Drug Administration (FDA) and other government and professional organizations also issue guidelines. The Office of Human Research Protection of the Department of Health and Human Services (DHHS) and the Declaration of Helsinki follow the ethical principles outlined in the Belmont Report (National Commission for the Protection of Human Subjects of Biomedical and Behavioral Research 1974). Yet these guidelines apply only to companies and institutions receiving DHHS funding. In the United States as well as in other countries, clinical trials are monitored by institutional review boards (IRBs). The number of commercial IRBs is growing.

7. By "government" of human subjects research I mean its ethical codes, the mechanisms of

its growth, and its regulation. One goal of my research is to understand how wider ethnographic contexts inform the design and operation of clinical trials. Harry Marks's (1997) work is particularly illuminating in showing how ethics was incorporated into the design of the controlled, randomized trial in the United States in the interwar period. Elsewhere (Petryna forthcoming) I address the many forms and functions that human subjects research assumes at local and national levels and how the terms of commercialized human subjects research are being challenged so as to redirect economic, moral, and scientific investments in particular contexts.

8. Estimates for the current number of clinical trials range from twenty-five thousand to eighty thousand (see, e.g., CenterWatch 2002). Such ambiguity suggests a global field of experimental activity whose true scope is largely unknown and prone to guesswork and that requires ethnographic attention. Dickersin and Rennie suggest that major barriers to a comprehensive repository of clinical trials include "industry resistance, the lack of a funding appropriation for a serious and sustained effort, lack of a mechanism for enforcement of policies, and lack of awareness of the importance of the problem" (2003:516). I thank Nicole Luce-Rizzo for her insights and generous research assistance here and elsewhere.

9. I interviewed this individual in June 2003.

10. The full name of this initiative is the International Conference on Harmonisation of Technical Requirements for Registration of Pharmaceuticals for Human Use.

11. Testing requirements are typically established by national regulatory agencies and can differ from country to country; duplicate testing threatened to delay foreign market access and affect the global trade in pharmaceuticals. Japan, perceived to be a potential large consumer market for U.S. pharmaceuticals, is famous for its intransigent regulatory system. See the chapter by Applbaum in this volume.

12. Drug development is broken down into four phases (preclinical, clinical, marketing, and postmarketing). Forty billion of the estimated $55 billion that is being invested in drug research and development goes to development. The CEO of one major contract research organization told me, "Probably 60 percent of that $40 billion is spent on phase two and three trials. So big money is there." Hundreds of CROs operate worldwide and employ a labor force of nearly 100,000 professionals (Rettig 2000). The move toward outsourcing increased dramatically in the 1990s. By 2004, nearly 42 percent of all pharmaceutical drug development expenditures had been committed to outsourcing (compared with only 4 percent in the early 1990s). The pharmaceutical industry is outsourcing an increasing number of operations ranging from discovery research to clinical trials operations to manufacturing, final packaging, and distribution as well as sales and marketing activities.

13. For an assessment of the commercialization of ethical review boards, see Lemmens and Freedman 2000.

14. See Jonathan Moreno's analysis of the ethics of human experiments for national security purposes. The focus on standards of consent in a time of international crisis can be read as a means through which a "postwar national security state protects itself from critics of expanded governmental power" (Moreno 2004: 198).

15. Post-Soviet scientists were new to the randomization aspect of modern controlled clinical trials.

16. Geertz's quote continues: "The problem was that the anthros (and the médicos), reduc-

tionist to the core, conceived the object of their study not as a people but as a population. The Yanomami, who indeed had the requisite sorts of brains, eyes, and fingers, were a control group in an inquiry centered elsewhere" (2000:21).

17. This short genealogy points out some reasons why subjects in health resources–poor areas became desirable for recruitment. Not only are they "desperate" and willing to participate in trials (Rothman 2000), they also fit a regulatory framework backed by a particular vision of appropriate scientific evidence promulgated by the FDA.

18. *Health transition* refers to the role that the cultural, social, and behavioral factors of health play in the rising life expectancy at birth (the mortality transition) and the decreasing proportion of all deaths caused by infectious diseases (the epidemiological transition). "Studies of the health transition focus on the institutional aspects that promote such change including public health interventions that control disease and promote modern healthcare" (Johansson 1991:39).

19. The fall of Communism in Poland, for example, marked the beginning of revolutionary changes in the field of cardiology and cardiac intervention. Poland, as the rest of Eastern and Central Europe, was plagued by inordinately high rates of cardiovascular deaths or a "cardiovascular disaster," as the former director of Poland's top cardiology institute (ANIN) called it. Clinicians and epidemiologists in this field were among the first Polish medical workers to participate in multi-nationally sponsored trials. One Polish CRO executive told me in 2005 that by the late 1990s ANIN became a major clinical trial site, "awash in thrombolytics for experimental use, so much so that the Institute had no need to buy them."

20. The placebo control trial typically consists of a placebo arm and a treatment arm. Its alternative, the active control trial, consists of an arm of treatment with known efficacy (active control) and an experimental arm.

21. The Declaration of Helsinki has been modified five times since its first edition in 1964.

22. This statement, of course, does not pertain to instances in which risk from withholding a proven therapy is lacking—as, for example, in the case of analgesics and antihistamines.

23. At stake in the placebo debate was something more than the issue of standard of care and patients' right of access to it. The regulatory weight of the Helsinki Declaration, the ability of IRBs to enforce proper research conduct globally, and the definition of just redistribution (particularly in resource-poor areas of the world) remained unaddressed.

24. CROs and pharmaceutical sponsors tell me that their greatest concern is liability. In Europe, for example, governments require CROs, pharmaceutical sponsors, or both to purchase insurance. As one lawyer who arranges research contracts told me, "What if something goes wrong? What if the patient dies? What if there is some horrible side effect? Who is going to pay? That is big dollars. In the United States we have a legal system that we all understand, and the liability will be divided based upon negligence. . . . But in all of these other countries you really have to think about who is going to be responsible. At one recent conference that brought together representatives of the human subjects research industry from all over the world, I watched as pharmaceutical industry representatives lobbied some developing country officials to avoid "the insurance path" and to rely on systems of universal health coverage to cover costs. Legislation is pending in Brazil that would require CROs to register with the state's national health surveillance agency (ANVISA). According to one Brazilian official, this legislation is being put into place "because often what happens is that big phar-

maceutical companies work through third parties. The CRO comes in and, let's say there is an adverse event, someone needs surgery, and the CRO is not held liable, even though the pharmaceutical company guarantees liability coverage." This official put it very succinctly: "The patient-subject signs the informed consent form but the protection is a fiction. They are not insured."

25. These numbers refer to new drug applications only. In Brazil, for example, the number of clinical investigators grew from 16 in 1991 to 187 in 1999. In Russia, the number grew from 0 in 1991 to 170 in 1999. These countries and others experiencing growth have seen political upheavals during democratic transition and are currently competing to consolidate their clinical trials markets in a neoliberalizing context. In collaboration with the ICH, a harmonizing initiative is under way in the Americas called the "Pan American Network for Drug Regulatory Harmonization." The European Union recently implemented the EU Clinical Trials Directive for EU countries and accession states.

26. The OIG's mission statement is as follows: "The mission of the Office of Inspector General, as mandated by Public Law 95-452 (as amended), is to protect the integrity of Department of Health and Human Services (HHS) programs, as well as the health and welfare of the beneficiaries of those programs. The OIG has a responsibility to report both to the Secretary and to the Congress program and management problems and recommendations to correct them. The OIG's duties are carried out through a nationwide network of audits, investigations, inspections and other mission-related functions performed by OIG components" (Office of Inspector General, Department of Health and Human Services n.d.).

27. I am grateful to Elaine Kusel for providing relevant legal documents, and to Michael Oldani for referring me to this case.

28. Pfizer contracted a CRO, European based at the time, to organize the transfer of blood samples to its laboratory in Geneva to conduct assays on children's spinal fluid samples. The Trovan story illustrates how the political economy of drug development links seemingly disconnected worlds and jurisdictions. At the same time, the legal viability of existing international codes of human subjects protection is being thrown into doubt.

29. The Nuremberg Code was established in response to Nazi medical experiments on prisoners in concentration camps. The code instituted norms of protection for subjects of scientific research experiments in the form of informed and voluntary consent and human rights guarantees.

30. For another instance of lawyers attempting to eliminate ethical limitations, rather than to assert them, see Alden 2004.

31. The domain of international law in remunerating human subjects violations is beyond the scope of this essay. See Das's (1995b) consideration of the Bhopal Union Carbide case.

32. The literature and practice on human rights versus humanitarianism have highlighted this state of affairs over the past decade (see, e.g., Ignatieff 2001 and Rieff 2003). Also see Rabinow 2003.

33. For evidence of the view of Chernobyl as a kind of "experiment" allowing scientists to corroborate or refute biomedical data concerning the long-term health consequences of nuclear exposure, see "Chernobyl's Legacy to Science."

34. Because of government inaction, tens of thousands of people were either knowingly or unknowingly exposed to radioactive iodine-131 — which is absorbed rapidly in the thyroid —

resulting, among other things, in a sudden and massive onset of thyroid cancers in children and adults as soon as four years later. This disaster could have been curtailed had the government distributed nonradioactive iodine pills within the first week.

35. He said he had approval from the FDA.

36. While the rhGM-CSF trials were taking place in a clinic in Moscow, Soviet, European, and U.S. nuclear industry officials met in Vienna to decide how to portray the scope of the disaster to the world. In their press release they announced that thirty-one cleanup workers had died in the course of work in the Zone. As the officials were negotiating over this number, hundreds of thousands of workers were being sent into the Zone in a massive, ongoing effort to contain the flames and radioactivity of a burning reactor. Humanitarianism in the form of scientific cooperation provided the Soviet state some protection in organizing this massive labor recruitment. The number of deaths is not known because of lax monitoring and medical follow-up (Petryna 2002).

37. Social protections include cash subsidies, family allowances, free medical care and education, and pension benefits for sufferers and the disabled. Affected persons, legally designated *poterpili* (sufferers), number 3.5 million and constitute a full 7 percent of the Ukrainian population.

38. In the language of bargaining theory, individual threat points vary globally. A threat point is the level of well-being that could be achieved if bargaining fails. Thanks to Joe Harrington for clarifying this point. Once again, variability seems to be the norm rather than the exception, as access to clinical trial subjects in contexts of minimal or no care becomes easier. And this variability includes a biological component because in some environments states can no longer protect the lives of their citizens.

# The New Medical Oikumene

DAVID HEALY

The third edition of the *Diagnostic and Statistical Manual* (DSM-III 1980) proposed a reorganization of the classification system within psychiatry that in combination with pharmaceutical company marketing was to change the face of psychiatry. DSM-III introduced what critics described dismissively at the time as a Chinese laundry approach to psychiatry—take two symptoms from column A, two from column B, and two from column C. In the case of anxiety, DSM-III broke up what had been a monolithic entity into a number of discrete disorders such as panic disorder, obsessive-compulsive disorder (OCD), social phobia, posttraumatic stress disorder (PTSD), and generalized anxiety disorder (GAD).

   This chapter addresses the role of the pharmaceutical industry in structuring expert and popular understandings of mental illness over the last two decades, specifically focusing on North America and Great Britain. It is based both on historical research and on my own experience as a practicing clinician in Wales and as a clinical psychopharmacology researcher. It elucidates a series of mechanisms whereby industry marketing can both transform the perceptions of physicians and shape the experiences of those seeking treatment and the self-understanding of those not in treatment. Such mechanisms include the standard ploys of company sales departments to increase demand for products, including celebrity endorsements and the sponsoring of educational events. The portfolio of marketing maneuvers has grown, though, by translating educational and celebrity events into the arena of scientific research: clinical trials and ghostwritten scientific articles have increasingly become part of the marketing of disorders and their treatments. The portfolio of marketing maneuvers has also grown to encompass new ways of creating fashion through medical activism by setting up patient groups and disease awareness campaigns. The result is a growth of disorders tailor-made to fit ever more visible drugs.

### The Marketing of Panic

The impact of new *DSM* categories and the marketing of new drugs on the experience of nervous problems can be seen most clearly in the case of panic disorder. Up to the mid-1980s, the average patient presenting in my office with anxiety described periods of feeling tense and stressed, and typically indicated that these states of dysphoria would last between half an hour and two or three hours. By the end of the 1980s, one of the commonest complaints of patients was that they had panic attacks—a term rarely heard before 1980. When asked how long these attacks might last, sufferers would typically indicate a duration of half an hour to two or three hours. This transformation occurred even though by definition panic attacks last for one to two minutes and are rarely much longer.[1]

Coinciding with this transformation in the way people accounted for their dysphoria was a new marketing strategy in which Upjohn sought to market a new drug, alprazolam (Xanax). As part of the development process for alprazolam, Upjohn put this new agent into clinical trials for one of the conditions newly recognized by *DSM-III*—panic disorder. The perception was that panic disorder, first described by Donald Klein in the mid-1960s, was a severe form of anxiety and that demonstrations that alprazolam worked for this condition would lead to it displacing other benzodiazepine drugs from the anxiety marketplace (Sheahan 2000). In the course of the development work for alprazolam, Upjohn sponsored scientific symposia on panic disorder, often in exotic locations, to which the company brought some of the most distinguished figures in psychiatry. The company supported a burgeoning literature on panic attacks and a range of clinical and marketing studies on this disorder (Healy 1990, 1998).[2] When the new drug was finally launched, advertisements geared to physicians featured panic itself more prominently than Xanax. Sales of Xanax followed this marketing of panic, despite the fact that, even in Upjohn-supported trials, panic disorder responded less convincingly to alprazolam than to comparators such as imipramine.

Television, radio, and newspaper editors and journalists, from the BBC to the NBC and from the *Times* and *Guardian* to the *New York Times* and *Washington Post*, became aware of psychiatrists' interest in this new disorder. This led to programs and articles featuring panic attacks. Even though many of these programs and articles recommended behavior therapy as the appropriate treatment, the net result of media exposure was that the way patients understood and expressed their experiences changed, and the way physicians viewed those experiences also changed. This was true even in Britain, where Xanax never became widely available. Pharmaceutical funding strategically placed in academia had leveraged a much wider change in consciousness in society generally.

There is more involved here than a simple change of labels for personal experiences. The term *panic* in the late 1980s connoted a disturbance of biology, whereas *anxiety neurosis* had indicated a psychosocial problem best managed by nondrug means. (A further implication of these changing labels is outlined below in my discussion of the marketing of depression.) Quite aside from the true nature of the problems and their most appropriate treatment, this example of pharmaceutical company marketing gives evidence of a new force at work with capacities to transform some of our most intimate experiences. A few more examples will help indicate the scope of this issue.

In the early 1990s, Roche had hoped to market moclobemide, a monoamine oxidase (MAO) inhibitor, for the treatment of another of this new cluster of disorders—social phobia. In preparation for the launch of moclobemide, Roche commissioned an educational booklet produced, apparently disinterestedly, by a working party of the World Psychiatric Association, aimed at helping clinicians to recognize the features of social phobia. One hundred thousand copies of this were prepared for distribution to clinicians. Moclobemide was eventually licensed in only a small number of markets for social phobia, but the methods of marketing it, which involved selling social phobia, have been documented in some detail (Moynihan 2002) and were subsequently pursued on a much wider scale by SmithKline, the marketers of paroxetine (Paxil), when it was licensed for social phobia. Since then a literature has burgeoned, and even though much of this recommends nondrug treatments for "shyness," sales for Paxil have increased in line with awareness of both shyness and social phobia among physicians and consumers.

What can be seen here is a pattern of marketing diseases that is also evident in the marketing of problems such as osteoporosis, leading to hormone replacement therapy or calcium-enhancing drugs (Berman 1999); elevated lipid levels, leading to the use of lipid-lowering drugs; erectile dysfunction leading to the use of sildenafil; and bipolar disorder by a range of different companies, leading to the use of so-called mood-stabilizers.

### The Rise of Depression

The events that unfolded around the marketing of diseases were shaped by an earlier set of developments that took place within the domain of nervous disorders. In the mid-1980s, the benzodiazepine group of tranquilizer drugs—of which Valium, Librium, and Ativan were among the best known—was linked with the production of physical dependence. Concerns about benzodiazepine dependence rapidly escalated into a crisis that helped establish health as both an item of news and an object of study within the social sciences.[3]

In the late 1980s, the first of the new drugs acting on the serotonin system, buspirone, was marketed as a non-dependence-producing tranquilizer. Buspirone failed in the marketplace, even though its mechanisms of action and treatment effect sizes for both anxiety and depression are similar to the mechanisms of action and treatment effect sizes of SSRIs and other serotonergic drugs for anxiety or depression. This development made it clear that the new generation of serotonergic drugs coming on stream would have to be developed as antidepressants rather than tranquilizers. The idea of a non-dependence-producing tranquilizer had no credibility in the marketplace, whereas antidepressants were not thought to be dependence producing. The SSRIs became antidepressants, and it was predictable even then that companies would seek to branch out from the beachhead of depression into the hinterlands of anxiety (Healy 1991).

Cases that would have been treated by Valium and Ativan were being converted into cases to be treated by Prozac and Zoloft and Paxil. This situation is reflected in data on pharmaceutical sales, which show clearly that sales of antidepressants soared in the United Kingdom and the United States through the 1990s while sales of tranquilizers flattened and dropped, so that by the middle of the 1990s the sales of the antidepressants had overtaken those of the tranquilizers (Rose 2003). The overall volume of sales of drug treatments for nervous disorders remains, however, approximately constant, which indicates that what is involved at least in part is not the detection of new cases of depression but a transformation of cases of anxiety into cases of depression.[4]

The transformation from anxiety to depression in the United Kingdom and the United States is clear in advertisements for antidepressants and tranquilizers during the period. Images of nervous disorders from the 1960s through the late 1980s showed young to middle-aged women in good health after treatment with tranquilizers. In contrast, the image of depression during this period was of older women and occasionally older men. Depression was a relatively rare disorder of middle-aged or older people. In the 1990s, the women featured in advertisements for SSRI antidepressants — such as those for Lilly's Prozac, Solvay's Luvox, and GlaxoSmithKline's Paxil — became progressively younger; by the late 1990s these women appeared to be in their mid-twenties.

By 1996, the World Health Organization was reporting that depression was the second greatest source of disability on the planet (Murray and Lopez 1996). The response from psychiatrists to this news appeared to be satisfaction that the discipline was now the second most important in medicine after cardiology. Nobody seemed to question how a society could have become so depressed so fast. Depression was being touted as a serious illness; but the emergence of a comparable epidemic of any other serious illness on this scale would have led to serious questioning as to what had happened. There appeared to be no such questioning in the case of depression.

Despite the element of skepticism here, it should be noted that many regard this switch from diagnosing anxiety to diagnosing depression as evidence of scientific progress rather than one more instance of disease marketing. The recent rebranding of SSRIS as anxiolytics (outlined below) has, however, considerably strengthened the position of skeptics.

## Marketing Disorders

A more skeptical position also depends on being able to explain how pharmaceutical companies achieve such transformations. With colleagues, I recently tracked reviews of antidepressants used to treat depression in people with *physical* illnesses. This aspect of the literature on depression essentially first appeared during the mid-1980s, even though the antidepressants had been available since the late 1950s. Similarly, when tracking articles on depression from periodicals such as *Vogue*, one can again see a literature on depression and antidepressants appearing in the mid-1980s (Shorter 1999).

The most parsimonious explanation for the emergence of this literature on depression and antidepressants in the mid to late 1980s is that governments, pharmaceutical companies, hospitals, physicians, and the public at large all want good news about treatments, whether drug or nondrug. By the mid-1980s, it had become impossible to write good news stories about the benzodiazepines. The benzodiazepines had been the big trees in the nervous disorder jungle, and their loss provided previously shaded plants with new opportunities to grow. The literature on the antidepressants blossomed from that point, even though drugs to treat depression had been available from the late 1950s. It would appear that this holds as true for the academic as for the lay media.

When a new literature emerges in this fashion — for whatever reason — the coincidence of its claims with those of interested parties can significantly affect the rate of its growth. In the case of psychotropic drugs, pharmaceutical companies provide an extremely efficient distribution system for scientific articles that suit their marketing interests. For example, I have had inquiries from companies about the price of five thousand, ten thousand, and twenty thousand reprints of an article that happens to mention a particular drug; noncommercially based research that doesn't feature a product seldom elicits more than two hundred to three hundred reprint requests.

In addition to supporting research and distributing literature, which they have been doing since the 1950s, pharmaceutical companies use a number of other well-known factors to promote a change in cultures; some have operated for decades and others are more recent. From the 1950s, celebrity endorsements in the lay media have played an important role in the marketing of drugs. More recently, a different form of celebrity endorsement has played an increasing role in the academic media: pharmaceutical companies are commissioning scientific articles from well-known researchers.

## CONTAINING NEGATIVE PUBLICITY: SILENCING CRITICS

In addition to accentuating the positive, pharmaceutical companies have always been prepared to minimize the negative. This has meant providing responses from experts to counter adverse claims made by other experts. Whether well founded or not, there has always been a belief that journals carrying advertisements are at risk of losing this source of revenue if they carry articles detrimental to company interests (Braithwaite 1986). Some recent instances of minimizing the negative that appear to go beyond earlier examples are outlined below.

In spring 2000, the *Hastings Center Reports* published five articles on Prozac (De Grazia; 2000; Edwards 2000; Elliott 2000; Healy 2000; Kramer 2000). Two argued that it was appropriate to restrict Prozac to treating proper clinical depression, and two argued that if Prozac helped people who appeared to be alienated rather than classically depressed, this was a legitimate use of the drug. The fifth article outlined the story covered here: that we have moved from an age of anxiety to an era of depression and we may move back in the near future. The interest in the Prozac story, that paper said, lies in the abilities of pharmaceutical companies to manipulate consciousness, as well as the facts that a key feature in what happens is market share, and that in the interest of market share certain aspects of the data were not entering the public domain in a manner that would be appropriate for science. In response to this article, the firm Eli Lilly, at the time, as I understood it, among the biggest single funders of the Hastings Center, withdrew its funding (Healy 2002b). The clear involvement of public relations agencies in drug marketing and the withdrawal of funds from a bioethical institution point to a new and qualitatively different scale of response to critics. Related examples abound.[5]

## GHOSTWRITING

A 1999 email addressed to me illustrates the scope of pharmaceutical industry perception management. It said: "Dear David, I am delighted you are able to participate in our satellite symposium. . . . In order to reduce your workload to a minimum we have had our ghost-writers produce a first draft based on your published work. I attach it here . . ." The attached article was a recognizably Healy piece, complete with Healy references, saying the kinds of things that I often say. Many people who think they know my work would probably be hard-pressed to pick it out as a fake.

However, I had already mapped out what I wanted to write, and I sent a draft article back to the company that was running the symposium. They were happy with the contents but made it clear that there were some commercially important points in the previous manuscript, adding that they would arrange for someone else to author this. The article I authored finally appeared in a journal supplement (Healy 1999) sitting beside the article that had been authored for me — with, as far as I could make out, only one change in the original ghostwritten article: the name of the author.[6]

A 2002 *Lancet* editorial asks "Just how tainted has medicine become?" One of the examples of the taints the editorial mentions is an article by Thase et al. (2001) on the merits of venlafaxine (Effexor). The article forms the basis for a campaign by Wyeth to try and persuade prescribers that, while SSRIS may get a certain proportion of people better, venlafaxine, Wyeth's drug, will push people beyond better to well. The clinical trial data behind this claim were due to be presented at a meeting held in Laguna Beach, California, in spring 2001.

The Laguna Beach meeting was one to which a large number of clinical researchers were invited. It came complete with travel and accommodation expenses and honoraria, and participants had the opportunity to have their contributions written for them. The organizers of the meeting were keen to have input from me and a colleague on a topic related to the Thase article. A 2001 email communication brought an already written article, making it clear that I was free to edit the article in any way I chose.

Rather than reject this draft, as an experiment I made two changes to it and sent it back. One change pointed to the fact that clinical trial data from mirtazapine, a product directly competing with Wyeth's venlafaxine, appeared to give a message that was very different from the message Wyeth was hoping to put across. The second alteration noted considerable evidence from clinical trial and healthy volunteer populations that personality types may in fact predict suitability to selective agents such as the SSRIs. The same can be expected to hold true for venlafaxine, in which case patients not suited to venlafaxine might become suicidal if they took it (see table 1).

Although I had been told that I was free to edit the original article in whatever way I chose, by return email there was an objection to the mention of mirtazapine. I did not attend the Laguna Beach meeting. The next time I saw this article was after it had been sent to the journal that was going to publish the proceedings of the symposium. The final version had been revised extensively. The reference to the fact that failing to match venlafaxine to patient could lead to problems including suicidal acts was missing. A new ending stated that the current best treatment was with venlafaxine. I objected and removed my name from the article.[7] This chain of events gives the lie to pharmaceutical company claims that the notional authors of these ghostwritten articles check them closely and sign off on them.[8]

## AUTHORING ARTICLES: CURRENT MEDICAL DIRECTIONS

Since the 1980s most of the major pharmaceutical companies have outsourced their medical writing to medical writing agencies (Healy and Cattell 2003). At about that time drug companies also began setting up satellite symposia in conjunction with formerly scientific meetings. Journals began to publish the proceedings of such satellite symposia in supplements. As this happened, concerns grew about the prevalence of ghostwriting of medical articles such as that outlined above. Until quite recently the assumption was that such ghostwriting was confined to review articles and appeared primarily in journal supplements or in obscure journals.

The idea that medical writing agencies would restrict themselves to the margins of therapeutics does not tally with the mission statement for Current Medical Directions (CMD), a medical information company set up in New

TABLE 1. Incidence of Suicides and Suicide Attempts in Antidepressant Clinical Trials

| Investigational drug | Number of patients | Number of suicides | Number of attempts | Suicides and attempts as % |
|---|---|---|---|---|
| *Sertraline* | 2,053 | 2 | 7 | 0.44 |
| Active comparator | 595 | 0 | 1 | 0.17 |
| Placebo | 786 | 0 | 2 | 0.25 |
| Placebo run-in | | 0 | 3 | |
| *Paroxetine* | 2,963 | 5 | 40 | 1.52 |
| Active comparator | 1,151 | 3 | 12 | 1.30 |
| Placebo | 554 | 0 | 3 | 0.54 |
| Placebo run-in | | 2 | 2 | |
| *Nefazodone* | 3,496 | 9 | 12 | 0.60 |
| Active comparator | 958 | 0 | 6 | 0.63 |
| Placebo | 875 | 0 | 1 | 0.11 |
| *Mirtazapine* | 2,425 | 8 | 29 | 1.53 |
| Active comparator | 977 | 2 | 5 | 0.72 |
| Placebo | 494 | 0 | 3 | 0.61 |
| *Bupropion* | 1,942 | 3 | — | |
| Placebo | 370 | 0 | — | |
| *Citralopram* | 4,168 | 8 | 91 | 2.38 |
| Placebo | 691 | 1 | 10 | 1.59 |
| *Fluoxetine* | 1,427 | 1 | 12 | 0.91 |
| Placebo | 370 | 0 | 0 | 0.00 |
| Placebo run-in | | 1 | 0 | |
| *Venlafaxine* | 3,082 | 7 | 36 | 1.40 |
| Placebo | 739 | 1 | 2 | 0.41 |
| All investigational drugs | 21,556 | 43 | 232 | 1.28 |
| All SSRIS | 13,693 | 23 | 186 | 1.53 |
| Active comparator | 3,681 | 5 | 24 | 0.79 |
| Total placebo | 4,879 | 2 | 21 | 0.47 |
| SSRI trial placebo | 3,140 | 2 | 15 | 0.57 |

Source: Data drawn from FDA licence applications.
Note: Companies lodging their data with the FDA have coded data on suicidal acts in the placebo run-in (washout) period under placebo, which minimizes the apparent problem. Comparing investigational drugs to placebo (excluding buproprion on the basis of missing data), using a Mantel-Haenszel procedure, the odds ratio of a suicidal act on new antidepressants compared to placebo is 2.4 (95 percent CI 1.6–3.7). The odds ratio for completed suicides compared to placebo is 4.62 (95 percent CI 1.126–18.953), p = 0.031.

York in 1990 "to deliver scientifically accurate information strategically developed for specific target audiences" (www.cmdconnect.com). Agency employees write studies, review articles, abstracts, journal supplements, product monographs, expert commentaries, and textbook chapters. The agency conducts meta-analyses and organizes journal supplements, satellite symposia, and consensus conferences; it even constitutes advisory boards for its clients. In all this the company "strives to exceed the expectations" of its clients "and to assist them in achieving their strategic objectives."

As of 1998, CMD was coordinating articles on Zoloft (sertraline) for Pfizer. As part of a legal action against Pfizer, I was given on a nonconfidential basis a document that laid out a series of these articles. The document, which lists the progress of articles on Zoloft as of the start of 1999, details a total of eighty-five articles being worked on, of which fifty-five had appeared by early 2001. As might be expected, the CMD articles exclusively cover areas of marketing concern for Pfizer. They are clinical trials or reviews on clinical conditions for which Pfizer had a marketing license for Zoloft or was seeking one.

PTSD was one of the conditions for which Pfizer was seeking a license. In the case of the set of articles on PTSD, the document appears to indicate that the first draft of two articles on PTSD had already been prepared, even though the authors' names were listed "TBD" (to be determined) (CMD 1999).[9] There is no way to know exactly who wrote the articles on PTSD, but the document appears to indicate that an agency called Paladin was actually doing the writing. The document furthermore indicates that the *New England Journal of Medicine* and the *Journal of the American Medical Association* (*JAMA*) were the target journals. The articles actually appeared in *JAMA* and the *Archives of General Psychiatry*.

It is possible to compare CMD articles on Zoloft with non-CMD articles from the same period. Dinah Cattell and I performed such a comparison in three areas (Healy and Cattell 2003: 22–27). First, we searched all CMD and non-CMD articles and established the number of Medline citations for each author. Second, we established the impact factor of the journals in which the articles appear. Third, we determined the subsequent citation rate of all of the articles.

The comparison reveals that the articles on Zoloft being coordinated by

CMD appear in the journals with the highest impact factors in the field, including *JAMA*, the *American Journal of Psychiatry*, *Archives of General Psychiatry*, and the *British Medical Journal*. The authors of the CMD articles are among those with the most Medline citations, with two hundred or more other Medline-listed articles per author. The CMD authors have a three times greater citation rate than non-CMD authors. The CMD articles appear in journals with a three-times greater impact factor than the journals in which non-CMD articles appear. As of mid-2002, the mean citation rate for the CMD articles published in 1998 was 20.2 (95 percent CI 13.4–27.0), while that of the non-CMD articles was 3.7 (95 percent CI 3.3–8.1). Finally, 100 percent of the CMD articles report favorable results for Zoloft, whereas only 44 percent of the non-CMD articles report favorable results.

Our analysis appears to establish that ghostwriting is no longer occurring only in peripheral journals and affecting only review articles. It happens in the most prestigious journals in therapeutics, and it probably happens preferentially for papers reporting randomized trials and other data-driven papers.

An analysis of the published CMD articles reveals some other important points. There are significant discrepancies between at least some of the CMD articles and the raw data underlying them. For instance, six of the CMD articles describe studies in which Zoloft was given in trials to children with obsessive-compulsive disorder or depression. One of these articles published in *JAMA* mentions one child becoming suicidal. The other five articles make no mention of suicidality as a potential hazard of Zoloft given to children. One of these five articles in fact states that the authors are reporting on the side effects that had occurred at a 10 percent rate or more (Alderman et al. 1998). However, it is clear from internal company documents that of the forty-four children who were depressed and went on Zoloft in this series of trials, four, or 9 percent, made suicidal acts.[10]

In an article published in the *British Medical Journal*, Malt et al. (1999) report on a study in which sertraline was compared with mianserin and placebo. Early drafts of the article mention one suicide and three suicide attempts on sertraline, one suicide attempt on mianserin, and no suicide attempts on placebo. The final version does not mention any of these adverse effects.

In summary, our published analysis of the CMD articles allows the following points to be made. First, up to 75 percent of the articles on randomized controlled trials on therapeutic agents appearing in major journals may now be ghostwritten. Second, in terms of citation rates, the most cited articles in therapeutics are now likely to be ghostwritten. Third, the new methods of authorship appear to lead to an omission of negative data on the hazards of therapeutic agents.

Influence has always played a part in science. As Thomas Kuhn (1962) argued, dominant scientific paradigms often act to silence the dissent of critics rather than to stimulate critical thinking. But Kuhn never envisaged the possibility of a dominant paradigm emerging because a writing agency produced an apparent consensus by sprinkling a set of authoritative names on a group of articles.

## Medicalization and the Suppression
## and Marketing of Data

Responding to media concerns about their free meals in the Waldorf and educational meetings in the Caribbean, clinicians say these "freebies" do not influence them. Clinicians claim to be following the evidence. Both the media and clinicians see the free pens, posters, and mugs, as well as meals and hotel rooms, as part of pharmaceutical marketing. But pharmaceutical companies see these trinkets and junkets as part of the gimmickry that stems from the sales department, a subdivision of marketing that comes into play primarily after the launch of a drug.

In contrast to the limited role of a sales division, marketing departments play a large role from the time of discovery of the drug. They determine what clinical trials will be done for what therapeutic indications, and shape, even as early as its point of the origin, the profile this new compound should have in terms of which journals the key articles on therapeutics with this new compound should appear in, with which lead authors. The efforts of marketing departments extend beyond early development to include after-launch support of scientific and educational symposia that are often aimed at selling not the drug so much as the condition the drug will treat. Articles on these drugs such as the CMD articles described above effectively become infomercials masquerading as scientific articles, and are influential because of that form.

The impact of this influence can be seen in the following development. In 2002 *Newsweek* ran a cover piece on teenage depression ("Teen depression"). Pfizer and GlaxoSmithKline either have or are seeking licenses in a range of countries to treat nervous problems such as depression in children or adolescents with Zoloft and Paxil, respectively. Clinicians did not need company trials to treat children with Paxil or Zoloft if this seemed to be clinically indicated, as this could be done based on an extrapolation from the adult data; the same thing is done with anticonvulsants and antibiotics. However, in order to market Zoloft or Paxil to children, Pfizer and Glaxo had to run a clinical trial that in some domain of measurement appeared to demonstrate that their compound has positive effects.

Once the drug is in the market, companies can then draw attention to the misery and discontent experienced by children and adolescents and can claim that this discontent can be mapped onto operational criteria for depression. The fact that adolescent misery can be mapped onto criteria for depression does not mean that all miserable adolescents are classically depressed. Nevertheless, as depression comes with risks, in particular the risk of suicide, pharmacotherapy can be sold not just as a possible treatment but as effectively mandated in order to reduce such risks. This message is too important to leave in academic journals, hence articles in magazines such as *Newsweek*. While clinicians could always treat children with Zoloft and Paxil, before *Newsweek*'s article they may have been likely to reserve pharmacotherapy for more severely disturbed children. But parents who saw the article are much more inclined to seek out and ask clinicians to prescribe drug treatment for conditions that until recently were thought best managed by supportive interventions.

In just this manner a range of intimate childhood and adolescent experiences are at present being actively medicalized. Traditional medicalization is not inevitably tied to drug treatment, but in this case, as with panic disorder, depression rather than its treatments is being sold. The trials of drug treatments, however, are central to the process. Treatment trials do not force medicalization per se, but at present within psychiatry apparent evidence of efficacy is taken to indicate that depression *should* be treated rather than evidence that depression *can* be treated. As in other areas of psychiatry, the effects of treatment on selective outcome measures from clinical trials have become embodied in treatment algorithms and protocols drawn up by experts—many of whom have affiliations with pharmaceutical companies—that rank pharmacotherapy as a leading option for the management of nervousness in children and adolescents.

Apparently missing from this process is any appreciation that except when treating patients moribund from conditions like heart attacks, where ordinarily there will be little disagreement on the need to intervene, treatment in medicine involves value judgments. Other effective treatments are commonly accepted on the basis that they eliminate the condition being treated. But in psychiatry, other than for the use of penicillin in GPI, there are no such treatments, and as a consequence, treatment options ought to be contested.

This is not a matter of some intangible values being pitted against objective data, but rather a question of a disjunction between values and the role of data collection in pushing one set of values. The point is evident in the data from two of the major trials of antidepressants in children. In Glaxo's trials, while Paxil was marginally better than placebo on physician-based measures of outcome, there was a 5 percent rate of suicidal acts on Paxil versus a 1 percent rate on placebo, a measure arguably of great interest to parents (Keller et al. 2001). Despite this, physicians speaking for Glaxo exhort doctors to detect and treat depression because treatment will reduce the risk of suicide. A second major trial, Pfizer's trials of Zoloft in depressed children, produced a 9 percent suicide attempt rate on Zoloft, but the published literature gives no evidence of this.

This recent scenario replays the process that brought SSRIs into the marketplace as antidepressants in the early 1990s. Around 1990, the American Psychiatric Association and the British College of Psychiatrists launched "defeat depression" campaigns that were supported by money from pharmaceutical companies. The campaigns were extremely successful and, as argued above, helped convert cases of Valium and Ativan to cases of Prozac and Paxil and Zoloft. The rhetoric of these campaigns stressed the importance of recognizing depression so that it could be treated effectively.

The central claim of these campaigns, namely that the detection and treatment of severe depression would lower suicide rates, was deeply problematic, however. Just as these campaigns began, data for suicides and suicidal acts from clinical trials of SSRI agents lodged with the Food and Drug Administration (FDA) in the United States demonstrated that SSRIs could not in principle lower suicide rates (see table 1). As of the early 1990s, the complete data sets lodged with the FDA (as opposed to the selected data sets commonly cited by pharmaceutical companies) revealed a statistically significant increased risk of both suicides and suicidal acts for patients on these drugs (Healy 2003). Furthermore, it is now clear that the data submitted to the regulators are misleading on this very important issue. For example, the data on suicides and suicidal acts recorded under placebo in trials of Paxil indicate two suicides and six suicidal acts, when the true figure may in fact be as low as one suicidal act on placebo. The remainder of the suicidal acts occurred during the run-in phase of trials, or sometimes in the case of SSRI trials, up to a year after the trial had ended. This pattern of data management appears common to most SSRI companies.

Other maneuvers seem to include outright suppression of data. Consider the data on suicidal acts with recently licensed antipsychotics lodged with the FDA that are shown in table 2. The source of the data, Khan et al. 2001, indicates that there are no data on nonlethal suicidal acts on olanzapine lodged with the FDA.[11] This is clearly not trivial, as the data on suicides for olanzapine suggest that it has the highest rate of suicides in psychotropic trial history. The fact that these data are missing has been in the public domain since September 2001. During this time there has been no complaint from any scientific group and olanzapine has become the best-selling antipsychotic in North America and Western Europe. It would seem that he who controls the means of data production controls consciousness.

These issues came to a very visible focus in 2004, when, following increasing media interest, the FDA was all but forced to convene two hearings to review the efficacy and safety of antidepressants given to children. As a result of these hearings, it became widely known that in clinical trials with children antidepressants had not been shown to work, and that there was a doubling of the risk of suicidal activity on active drug treatment compared with placebo. It is

TABLE 2. Incidence of Suicides and Suicide Attempts in Clinical Trials of Antipsychotic Drugs

| | Number of patients | Number of suicides | Number of suicide attempts | All suicidal acts as % |
|---|---|---|---|---|
| *Risperidone* | 2,607 | 9 | 43 | 2.00 |
| Comparator | 621 | 1 | 5 | 1.00 |
| Placebo | 195 | 0 | 1 | 0.50 |
| *Olanzapine* | 2,500 | 12 | — | — |
| Comparator | 810 | 1 | — | — |
| Placebo | 236 | 0 | — | — |
| *Quetiapine* | 2,523 | 1 | 4 | 0.20 |
| Comparator | 420 | 0 | 2 | 0.48 |
| Placebo | 206 | 0 | 0 | 0.00 |
| *Sertindole* | 2,194 | 5 | 20 | 1.14 |
| Comparator | 632 | 0 | 2 | 0.32 |
| Placebo | 290 | 0 | 1 | 0.34 |
| *Ziprasidone* | 2,993 | 6 | — | |
| Comparator | 951 | 1 | — | |
| Placebo | 424 | 0 | — | |
| *Totals*: | | | | |
| New Antipsychotic | 12,817 | 33 | (72 | 1.0)[a] |
| Comparator | 3,434 | 3 | (10 | 0.6)[a] |
| Placebo | 1,351 | 0 | (2 | 0.3)[a] |

Source: Khan et al. (2001).

Note: The data obtained by Khan et al. (2001) are supplemented with data for suicidal acts on quetiapine provided by the company; in contrast to Khan's scrutiny of FDA medical reviews for olanzapine, my scrutiny suggests that the true figure for suicides on placebo in these trials was zero; data from sertindole trials were provided by the Lundbeck pharmaceutical company; data on ziprasidone trials were taken from FDA medical reviews for ziprasidone obtainable from the FDA site. Analyzing the data on suicides using an exact version Mantel-Haenszel procedure and a one-sided test for significance yields an odds ratio with a confidence interval of (1.0825, infinity), $p = 0.03955$, for new antipsychotics compared to placebo.

a. Parentheses indicate provisional totals because some data for olanzapine and ziprasidone were missing.

now clear that the gap between what the data from these clinical trials had in fact shown and the claims made in "scientific" articles purporting to represent the outcomes of these studies is the greatest known divide in medicine between a set of data and its literature (Healy 2004).

Given this divide and company documents indicating plans to publish only the positive results from studies, New York State's attorney general filed a lawsuit against GlaxoSmithKline for fraud in May 2004. The company settled. Later in 2004 a bill making it mandatory to make clinical trial results available was introduced in Congress. Such a development has considerable potential to transform healthcare. In the meantime, other aspects of our current situation need scrutiny for what they reveal about the dynamics of the current medical marketplace.

## Aspects of the Sociology of Clinical Trials

The developments outlined here point to three issues in need of detailed social scientific analysis. First is the centrality now accorded clinical trials within the medical marketplace. Second is the emphasis on marketing compounds by selling diseases and the risks associated with diseases. Third is the role of social institutions such as the regulatory apparatus and institutional review boards in containing problems that drug development makes almost inevitable.

On the first issue, there is a general perception that clinical trials prove that treatments work. Philosophically, however, clinical trials are set up on the basis of a null hypothesis—namely that a putative treatment in fact does not differ from placebo. They were designed to stop therapeutic bandwagons. If the treatment appears to differ from placebo in short-term trials (six to eight weeks) undertaken in conditions that may last months, years, or decades, all that can be said is that the treatment does something and there is a basis for further research. This is not the same as saying that treatments work. To establish that would require studies that demonstrate long-term benefits and also control for hazards such as physical dependence that appear on discontinuation.

Far from being treated as a basis for further research, however, the data resulting from clinical trials have now become the fuel of therapeutic bandwagons (Healy 2001) on the road to globalization. A key to such pharmaceutical globalization is the universality claimed for scientific methods. The results of trials conducted in what may be a small subset of volunteers recruited by advertisement are held to apply universally—in Japan as well as America, for children as well as adults, for all ethnic groups, ages, and sexes. This claim underpins transitions such as that from anxiety to depression, but it also leads to an extension of the psychopharmacological reach that can be seen in globalization (see the chapter by Petryna in this volume). The same mechanisms that have been employed to transform the intimate experiences of many Westerners can be expected to lead to a homogenization of experiences on a global scale—while at the same time, as the contributions to this volume indicate, social differences and structures of inequality between diverse sites pose challenges to such homogenization.

Within psychiatry in the United Kingdom and the United States, the current evidence-based medicine bandwagon is as hegemonic as the Freudian paradigm ever was. The results from trials are incorporated into algorithms and protocols which increasingly define a supposedly rational medicine. Critics of the system who offer sociological or qualitative analyses are ignored. Evidence-based medicine sees itself as building a value-free, timeless, ahistorical science. One of the current challenges facing the history and sociology of modern medicine is to outline the origins of this belief system and the factors that maintain it.

This is particularly important in the face of good evidence that treatment outcomes within mental health are deteriorating. While the absolute number of patients occupying beds in asylums up to the 1950s began to fall thereafter, the numbers of both voluntary and involuntary admissions per annum have been rising steadily since then in both Europe and North America. We were able to quantify this increase in a study recently undertaken in North Wales which systematically compared mental health service utilization over the course of one hundred years in a unique service delivery system that, owing to population, financial, and geographical constraints, allows such comparisons to be made in a manner that should hold for services in both Europe and North America. In line with other data, this study demonstrated that we now compulsorily detain three times more patients than were detained before modern psychotropic drugs were first developed, that we admit fifteen times more patients than were admitted before the present psychotropic era began, and that patients now on average spend more time in the course of a psychiatric career in a hospital than they did before modern drugs came on stream (Healy et al. 2001). In part this situation has arisen because psychiatry began to manage community nervousness differently after the 1950s. Based on these findings, there would seem to be a major disjunction between the results of short-term clinical trials and the longer-term effects of using treatments endorsed by such trials.

**Back to the Future**

Establishing what is happening within the scientific, social, and corporate domains of mental health is of great importance, especially in the wake of the events of 9/11. The discontents associated with globalization have been closely linked to the events of that day.

By that date Pfizer had obtained a license for Zoloft for post-traumatic stress disorder (PTSD), Wyeth had obtained a license for venlafaxine (Effexor) for generalized anxiety disorder (GAD), and GlaxoSmithKline was about to license Paxil for both GAD and PTSD. Articles about the anxious times we live in began to appear in broadsheets and tabloids. Some of these articles were full of references to these drugs and the companies that produced them and gave detailed operational criteria for GAD or PTSD. These articles may not have been written by the public relations agencies of the different companies. Perhaps the editors of newspapers simply realized that anxiety was in the air. Regardless, it is another example of pharmaceutical company money leveraging broader changes in consciousness.

At present up to $100 million is being spent per year selling SSRIs as anxiolytics or anxiolytic antidepressants. Wyeth has set up a campaign to teach general practitioners to recognize anxiety, worried apparently that they can no longer do so on their own. The Wyeth promotional material for Effexor contains two important commercial messages which reappear in material for Pfizer's Zoloft and Glaxo's Paxil.

The first is that Paxil/Effexor/Zoloft works to "correct the chemical imbalance [supposedly a lowering of serotonin] that causes the disorder." In fact, there has never been any evidence for a lowering of serotonin levels in those exhibiting any nervous disorder, or indeed anything wrong with the serotonin systems in anyone affected with nerves or moods.

The second commercially important message is to "talk to your doctor about non-habit-forming Paxil today." The other way that this is expressed is that anxiety can be treated with a benzodiazepine or with Paxil/Effexor/Zoloft. Benzodiazepines, however, cause dependence. The clear implication is that it will be easy to stop taking these SSRIs.

These claims are being made even though Paxil withdrawal problems were so clearly recognized in the mid-1990s that Lilly could run symposia on the issue and run advertisements telling clinicians that Prozac is less likely to cause withdrawal problems than Zoloft or Paxil. These claims are being made even though the rates at which withdrawal from and dependence on Paxil and related drugs have been reported to regulators and other bodies worldwide greatly exceed the rates for reporting either withdrawal from or dependence on benzodiazepines or even therapeutically used opioids (Medawar 1997; Medawar et al. 2003).[12] These claims are being made even though twenty years ago, several years ago before Paxil was launched, the company in question had undertaken clinical trials on healthy volunteers that gave clear evidence of withdrawal problems, including a suicide.[13]

These developments see the closing of a circle. Paxil and other SSRIs came on board as antidepressants in great part because of the withdrawal problems linked to the benzodiazepines. The business designation of these drugs as antidepressants deflected concerns about their dependence-producing potential, which now seems as great as anything associated with earlier drugs.

As of 1990, it was relatively clear that a post-SSRI generation of psychotropic drugs would be targeted at anxiety and sold as anxiolytics. This simple switch of terminology — from tranquilizer to anxiolytic — was all it would take to allay the concerns of the public regarding the risks of dependence. No one would make the connection to Valium, Librium, and Ativan, even though these drugs are also anxiolytics. However, companies have been slow at bringing the next generation of drugs out and hence have needed to rebrand the SSRIs as anxiolytic antidepressants. In 1990, the SSRIs became antidepressants because it was thought unlikely that branding them as anxiolytics would convince academic psychiatrists. As of 2002, it was clear that marketing departments have decided that rebranding SSRI drugs as anxiolytics and avoiding use of the term *tranquilizer* is all it takes to bring academic psychiatry onboard. This development offers some measure of the degree of control pharmaceutical company marketers now have over the consciousness of a profession.

This essay has attempted to outline some of the mechanisms by which this control is achieved. These involve a set of relatively new departures within marketing, such that companies now sell diseases rather than just drugs. To do this they have abandoned endorsements for celebrity academic endorsements. Where articles were placed in the lay media by PR companies before, academic articles are now increasingly written by medical writing agencies and placed in the leading journals in the field. Where company products were previously judged on the basis of independent research and research publications were distributed by companies if they coincided with company interests, companies now design and conduct their own studies for indications that suit their commercial interests. Clinicians meanwhile continue to believe they are not unduly influenced by pharmaceutical companies.

## Notes

1. I base the frequency estimate here partly on personal clinical experience, but the fact that transformations like this "mistake" were happening is attested to by Don Klein, the creator of the concept (see Klein 1996).
2. The first series of Upjohn studies can be found in volume 45 of the *Archives of General Psychiatry* with an overview by Klerman (1988). An early critique of these studies is Marks et al. 1989. A response to this critique came from Klerman and colleagues in Klerman 1989. These studies were also published in the *Journal of Psychiatric Research* (1990) 24 (suppl. 1). A second series of Upjohn studies can be found at Klerman et al. 1992. Again these were critiqued by Marks et al. (1992) with a reply from Klerman (1992). A subsequent "anti-Upjohn" study of interest can be found in Marks et al. 1993. This drew a response from investigators working with Upjohn. See Spiegel et al. 1993 and a reply, Marks et al. 1993a and 1993b. This series of exchanges offer a no-holds-barred set of comments on the merits of industry support of research.
3. Bury and Gabe 1990; Gabe and Bury 1991; Bury 1996.
4. This switch did not happen in Japan, where benzodiazepine dependence had never become a crisis. The Japanese pharmaceutical market is a high-volume market with many fea-

tures in common with Western pharmaceutical markets. In both Japan and the West, the antidepressant market had been a much smaller one than the tranquilizer market through the 1980s. For every person put on an antidepressant, three or four were put on tranquilizers. In Japan this distribution of sales continued: the market for tranquilizers remained robust through the 1990s while sales of antidepressants remained what they had been during the 1980s. There were no SSRIs on the Japanese market until 1999, when fluvoxamine was licensed for the combination of OCD and depression. In 2000, Paxil was licensed for the combination of social phobia and depression. As of 2003, Prozac is still not on the Japanese market. Far from being anomalous, the Japanese were closer to the global norm. It was the United Kingdom and the United States that proved the exception. Figures from South America and elsewhere during this period show comparable trends to those found in Japan. See Rose 2003 and the essays by Applbaum and Lakoff in this volume.

5. In April 2000, a book entitled *Prozac Backlash* appeared (Glenmullen 2000). A series of reviews apparently authored by a number of senior figures in U.S. psychiatry were sent to a number of media outlets shortly afterward. These reviews have a consistent theme which dates back to Lilly's first defense of Prozac in 1990 against charges that it might provoke suicide in some patients, namely that Prozac is one of the most researched drugs in history and that the problems stem from the disease depression and not its treatment with Prozac. These reviews went to Jamie Talan of *Newsday* in New York with a covering letter from Robert Schwadron of Chamberlain Communications, a PR agency working for Lilly in New York. In his cover letter Schwadron offers to arrange for interviews on this book with members of Eli Lilly as well as with "independent researchers from the medical community." The Chamberlain logo features a target. It will come as no surprise therefore to find that Chamberlain had listed Dr. Glenmullen as someone to manage. Chamberlain also appears to have targeted me. The views I have expressed in recent years are entirely consistent with views expressed in *The Antidepressant Era* (Healy 1998), which were reviewed favorably by clinicians as well as by investigators and others working with the pharmaceutical industry. Yet a few years later the same views were being described as controversial. I was receiving phone calls from Canada, the United States, Japan, and elsewhere telling me that I was being described as trouble and was soon to be criticized by American psychiatrists who neither knew me nor had heard me talk.

6. Articles available from author on request.

7. All copies including the published article in the *Journal of Psychiatry and Neuroscience* are available from the author.

8. As Spilker of the Pharmaceutical Research and Manufacturers of America put it when the issue was raised in the *Washington Post*, "Academic researchers participating in studies 'are given every opportunity to review, make suggestions and sign off on manuscripts [and] except for some very, very rare exceptions . . . [the process] is working very well'" (cited in Okie 2001). In practice, as shown in the litigation surrounding Redux, senior figures are prepared to incorporate any changes suggested to them by companies or agencies and to sign off on articles without suggesting a single change. See Mundy 2001.

9. This document is available on request from the author. See Lagnado 2003 for a response from a medical writer to these issues and analysis.

10. These figures are drawn from a public domain document available from the author: Pfizer

Expert Report, "Sertraline hydrochloride for obsessive-compulsive disorder in paediatric patients," approved 20 October 1997.

11. Data for suicides and suicidal acts for antipsychotics can be accessed from medical reviews posted on the FDA website: www.fda.gov/. My scrutiny of the records confirms that the FDA does not appear to have the data. Requests to the company for the missing data have been rebuffed. Requests to the relevant departments of government in the United Kingdom have gone unanswered.

12. Adverse reactions lodged with the Adroit database in Britain, which are corroborated by the World Health Organization database.

13. This material was made available to me on a confidential basis when I served as an expert witness in *Tobin v. SmithKline Beecham*, case no. 00-CV-0025-BEA, heard in Cheyenne, Wyoming, starting 21 May 2001, and all that is available in the public domain is my testimony in this case, which returned a verdict against SmithKline. The transcript is available on request.

# Educating for Global Mental Health
## The Adoption of SSRIs in Japan

KALMAN APPLBAUM

> *Rational foundations of modernity are cunningly accepted by*
> *man as the launching platform of ever wilder irrationalities.*
> SAUL BELLOW, *MOSBY'S MEMOIRS*

Does the process by which the new antidepressants (selective serotonin re-uptake inhibitors, or SSRIS) are being adopted around the world represent a global evolution of medical treatment or an agent-driven enlargement of global markets? In either case, must medical, commercial, and ethical dispositions toward the drugs be compatible before they can be implemented in healthcare? These two questions are mutually revealing in the analysis of rhetorics engaged and actions taken by transnational pharmaceutical corporations seeking to "launch" these drugs in diverse locations.

Global evolution in this analysis denotes progress toward superior medical treatment, based upon scientific advances coupled in localities with increasingly enlightened healthcare policy that recognizes and adopts medical innovations. Most laypersons and pharmaceutical company managers as well as many psychiatrists share this optimistic supposition. Its significance as a model lies in this triple backing. A theory of an agent-driven enlargement of global markets, by contrast, ignores the hypothesis of improvement in medical technology, focusing instead on the agencies (and the history of these) behind standardization in patterns of testing, adoption, and use. In what follows I separate global evolution from global expansion. I analyze the role of a few key players in the pharmaceutical industry whose efforts are helping to bring about the global convergence of psychopharmacological practices in general, and the recent and emergent adoption of ssris in Japan in particular.

As regards the compatibility of science, commerce, and ethics, I use the term *ethics* not to describe the contrasting sets of moral principles or values of American pharmaceutical companies and the Japanese mental healthcare milieu, the exploration of which may be a separate and worthy undertaking. Instead, I wish to show how foreign pharmaceutical industry actors employ what Sally Falk Moore (1993) might refer to as "moralizing strategies" in their attempt to (re)structure Japanese social institutions in an advantageous direction. The characteristics of this aim to create consensus on key issues across cultural differences in order to bring about the sharing of compatible grounds for professional practice and social action are evinced in the ethnographic details that follow. Here I wish to leave off by qualifying my assertion about the commercial deployment of ethical discourse with the observation that the success of this strategy depends not upon the force of commercial or political influence applied, but upon the ability to engender consensus over the principal issues concerning biological and medical clinical science, patient care, and the respective roles of business and government in providing for these. This is why moralizing rhetoric receives favored — but not exclusive — attention in the evidence cited below.

The effort to launch ssris in Japan is more than just another case study in export marketing or adaptation to medical cultural particularities in a given locale. The foreign firms endeavoring to introduce this and other psychopharmaceuticals to Japan are no longer seeking to merely adapt their drugs and marketing programs to local situations, the more common practice until perhaps ten or fifteen years ago. Instead, firms are working strategically and in some regards cooperatively to alter the total environment in which these drugs are or may be used. Effectively, we are seeing a new synergy being created by the combination of the familiar medical conception of universally definable diseases; patients' right to receive up-to-date treatment for such diseases; and a global strategy for testing, registering, and distributing drugs. The synergy emerges as a "naturalized" product of the metaphorical coincidence of universal medical needs, on the one hand, and the marketing presumption of globally pertinent needs, on the other. Upon the subsequent (marketing) supposition that universal medical needs can most effectively be treated within a deemed appropriate structure of treatment that operates to a global standard, the roadmap for what needs to be accomplished in a given locality is ready for implementation. (The marketing profession sees itself as having a special position vis-à-vis needs; therefore, marketers give themselves the moral high road here.)[1]

The universal need in this case encompasses depression, anxiety, and related syndromes, which are referred to as "diseases" by most of my informants: pharmaceutical company managers and industry experts, clinical researchers, marketing representatives, and psychiatrists.[2] The instruments of remedy are SSRI or Prozac-type drugs, which were introduced in the United States in 1988. By 2001 SSRIs had been prescribed to tens of millions of people worldwide, accounting for over $9 billion in annual sales. In the face of obstacles to their adoption in Japan, drug companies recognize that they must apply a comprehensive program. I will outline sites in Japan that several SSRI manufacturers have targeted in the attempt to alter the total sales environment for their drugs. More definitively, I will show that this program conforms to a new paradigm in pharmaceutical marketing: the "global drug-marketing platform."

The elements of the program include (1) rhetorical strategies that refer to purported deficiencies in the treatment of Japanese sufferers from mental disorders, to political cronyism and clinical testing incompetence in the drug registration procedure, and to the inequities of reward disbursed for pharmacological innovation; (2) companies' recognition that it takes a whole industry's combined exertion to break into and make a market for a new product category; (3) a metaphorical linkage, which presents to some as actionable self-evidence, between biomedical universalism with its ideas of universal diseases, on the one hand, and commercial globalism with its idea of global needs, on the other; and (4) the use of transnationally mirroring institutions as a base for hammering out common agendas for solving what are proposed to be deficiencies in Japanese healthcare. These "mirroring" institutions include the International Conference on Harmonisation (ICH, considered below), patient advocacy groups, government-to-government pressure (*gaiatsu*), and foreign agencies seeking to raise the power on internal debates about healthcare reform and Japanese drug company competitiveness. These are each specific locations at which ethical appeals can be made in the attempt to influence Japanese healthcare policy overall. Finally, I describe the programs the pharmaceutical companies in question undertake to educate patients and their families, doctors, hospitals, and other relevant publics to the prevalence of mental disorders, the linkage of these to suicide, and the efficacy and safety of SSRIs in their effective treatment.

Let me conclude this introduction with the caveat that I do not wish to be interpreted as attempting an evaluation of the pharmacological or clinical science entailed in the production and use of SSRIs. I am not a psychiatrist or a clinical pharmacologist, and I cannot assess the professional medical literature that seeks to grade the efficacy and safety of SSRIs. I am an anthropologist with a background in Japanese studies and transnational marketing management culture and practice. My aim in this chapter is to illuminate one aspect of the process of globalization of pharmaceuticals.

## Pharmaceutical Industry Globalization and the Reconsideration of the Japanese Depression Market

In focusing on the agency of specific players in the drug adoption process, one must begin with the recognition that a given actor's agency can fulfill itself only within a preexisting context of practices, attitudes, and other constraints. A drug company attempting to launch a new drug program perceives this context in terms of obstacles and opportunities, which in managerial thinking are always concurrent. Companies employ market assessment analyses, such as the popular "Strength Weakness Opportunity Threat," or SWOT matrix, as a first step to measure feasibility of a proposed product launch.[3] The first launch of

SSRIs in Japan occurred in 1999, eleven years after the rather precipitous adoption of these drugs in the U.S. market. Though some of the delay is attributable to holdups in testing and registration procedures in Japan, which until recently were notoriously slow, both Japanese psychiatrists and pharmaceutical company representatives told me that the principal reason for the delay was that in 1989, when the largest SSRI manufacturer went to Japan to test the waters, they were told by local experts that Japanese barely suffer from depression. The company in question decided that the opportunity side of the opportunity/obstacle equation was too small to be worth the effort and went home. The smaller manufacturers did not waste resources investigating the matter for themselves, but simply followed the industry leader.

A number of factors, some intrinsic to the situation in Japan and some extrinsic, led to a reassessment of the opportunity/obstacle equation, and three American companies and one Euro-American company came to Japan in the mid to late 1990s to initiate the registration and launching procedure there. The intrinsic factors included an increased rate of diagnosis of depression and anxiety by Japanese psychiatrists. Perhaps the gradual adoption of the International Classification of Diseases (ICD-10) and the *Diagnostic and Statistical Manual of Mental Disorders* (vols. 3 and 4) through the 1990s in Japan were the most visible contributors to this change.[4] Other factors, such as Japanese psychiatrists' enhanced awareness of medical practices abroad, were not intrinsic in a clear-cut fashion. This is so because once the foreign drug companies arrived and could place themselves in a position to influence the environment for mental health care, the internally driven and externally catalyzed factors became more difficult to distinguish. This flattening of the internal and external dimensions is a key feature of globalization in general.[5]

Several changes took place within the pharmaceutical industry itself during the 1980s and 1990s that prompted the four leading SSRI producers to reconsider Japan as a viable investment. The first of these changes was the heightening of competitiveness in the pharmaceutical industry coupled with the consolidation of the industry into a few very large players who jockey with each other for stakes in markets worldwide. Industrial competition impels firms to expand their market base for products and product lines geographically, and to deepen each existing market through a variety of marketing-inspired techniques. At the same time that competition was broadening to a global scale, the estimated cost of developing new drugs rose from $231 million in 1987 ($302 million in 2000 dollars) to $802 million (not including marketing costs) in 2002.[6] As research and development leading to new product development thus became a fixed rather than a variable cost, pressure shifted to amortize the investment over a larger market base. This also prompted firms to rely more on marketing, since the most profitable way to minimize marginal contribution to fixed costs is to boost sales.[7] Finally, a factor often cited by drug companies is the diminishment of differences in healthcare practices around the world, which increases the share of hospitable environments in which to conduct business.

Regarding the SSRIs in particular, the range of diseases and disorders approved for treatment by SSRIs had expanded during the ten-year interim, conveying more segments of the pie chart describing the Japanese mental disorder market into commercial relevance for these products. The newly prevalent awareness of and proposed SSRI treatment for disorders not much considered in the late 1980s — panic, bulimia, posttraumatic stress disorder (PTSD),[8] social anxiety and phobia, and premenstrual dysphoric disorder (PMDD) among them — is a trend of apparently global proportions. It is transmitted as much by medical publications as by drug company advertisements, in combination with other pharmaceutical company programs to fund relevant research, underwrite nongovernmental health organizations, and other activities mentioned below.

### The International Conference on Harmonisation and Good Clinical Practice

The first step in introducing a new drug into a given market is to seek approval from the national regulatory body (the equivalent of the U.S. FDA), which in Japan is the Ministry of Health Labor and Welfare (MHLW, *koseirodosho*).[9] Specialists hired to negotiate the approval process at one of the firms where I conducted interviews deplored the bureaucratic sluggishness and political subjectivity of the approval process, as well as of the implementation of randomized clinical trials (RCTS) by Japanese physicians. Some of these grievances, I came to discover, pertained more to conditions in the past than since 1997, when the pharmaceutical sector became included in the U.S.-Japan Enhanced Initiative for Deregulation and Competition. The outcome of this initiative has been the shortening of the approval process for new drug applications through the elimination of various stages in the process. Most significant for opening the door to global activity in the industry is the move to accept foreign clinical data as based on the International Conference for Harmonisation (ICH) E5 guidelines and consistent with Good Clinical Practice (GCP), a proposed worldwide (but as yet realized mainly in the United States, European Union, and Japan) "standard for the design, conduct, performance, monitoring, auditing, recording, analysis and reporting of clinical trials."[10] This means that rather than having to repeat Phase III clinical trials in Japan, as had previously been the case, the MHLW will now accept foreign data supplemented by small specific studies, called "bridging studies," carried out on Japanese patients to determine ethnic dosage particularities.

Although the implementation is still incomplete in a number of regards, outside researchers evaluating the new initiative have no doubt, as Tsutani Kiichiro and his colleagues concluded in the 1997 workshop on clinical trials and GCP in East Asia, that adoption of the ICH guidelines has drawn Japan into the global pharmaceutical community.[11] It has by the same token sped up the marketing of new drugs there.[12] In this light, I regard pharmaceutical company managers' criticisms partly as an artifact remaining from past attempts to alter the Japanese environment. The persistence of the rhetoric, however, also suggests an ongoing relevance to the complaints within the overall framework for actions taken to achieve the desired result of establishing relations of correspondence and confluence between global business and universal science.

## Working Jointly to Establish a Market Beachhead

Most readers will be familiar with at least some of the strategic measures used by businesses in the course of their competition with firms selling similar products. Branding, promotions and advertising, pricing, service add-ons, and calculated distribution channel selection are common measures firms take to differentiate themselves from competitors. We may be less observant of the process by which new categories of products are introduced. Coke and Pepsi are competitive social facts; they were here when we were born. But how did they gain a foothold in society at their outset? I condense greatly but not speciously when I say that the initial introduction of a new product tends to occur by means of either collective or cooperative action on the part of the purveyors of the new category.[13] Sometimes the collective action results from the competitive, homogeneous field effect of several firms simultaneously backing comparable products through corresponding marketing channels; sometimes these firms actually work in concert to establish the groundwork — the trade structures — for future sales which will eventually proceed on a more purely competitive basis.

It thus came as no surprise to me that the four principal foreign pharmaceutical companies promoting SSRIs in Japan could to some reasonable extent be seen as working jointly rather than competitively to broaden the horizons for the adoption of these medications into the Japanese market. In the words of a manager at one of the pharmaceutical companies in question, "It takes a whole industry to make a market. . . . It's going to take all of us." The most observable locus of this joint effort is PhRMA (Pharmaceuticals Research and Manufacturers of America), the primary advocate for the American pharmaceutical industry.

Managers at two pharmaceutical companies I approached suggested that I might get a clearer picture of events in Japan from the PhRMA representative. I went to visit him in a small office in Chiyoda-Ku, Tokyo. Michael (not his real name) is a British national who began his career working for Upjohn in the United States in 1966. He stayed with that company through its various mergers until 2000, in the interim having been country manager in Nigeria, Portugal, Holland, and Mexico, and then vice president for operations in Japan between 1989 and 1994, followed by a similar stint in Europe. He began his current appointment on a five-year contract in 2001. PhRMA represents the healthcare interests of American companies to the Japanese government by lobbying the Japan Medical Association (JMA), the Japanese Pharmaceutical Association, and so on.[14]

Michael wasted no time in telling me that the contemporary Japanese healthcare system is less discriminatory to foreign pharmaceutical manufacturers than it is to innovation and adequate pharmacological treatment of Japanese patients. In fact, in all his years working with people at the ministry, he never once heard anyone there use the word *patient*. Michael meant to demonstrate by this that care receivers in Japan are deprived of certain choices because the system is provider- rather than consumer-driven, and the provider, which for present purposes is effectively the government, acts mainly from conservative impulses to limit risk exposure associated with new medications and to combat rising healthcare costs.[15] PhRMA's true task, he explained, is to lower barriers to the evolution of a free market, or, in his words, to help create "a market based upon competition, customer choice, and a transparent pricing structure that supports innovation." Psychopharmaceuticals, he continued, are particularly susceptible to retrograde thinking because mental illness is stigmatized in Japan and because procedures for clinical testing are less precise and thus require greater scrupulousness on the part of testing supervisors—a state of affairs that has not yet been reached.

What measures is PhRMA taking to induce this transformation? Michael explained that PhRMA must convince the Japanese government that not just Japanese patients but Japanese firms themselves are suffering under the present regime. Global pharmaceutical practices represent the objective market and innovation-driven ideal to which excellent and competitive Japanese firms also aspire. But they are stunted by the present system's inability to accommodate innovation. Poor clinical trial habits lingering from the pre-1997 accords likewise impede the registration process of good new drugs because, he claimed, in the absence of regularized channels and procedures for testing, political cronyism steps in. Once ICH guidelines are fully and honestly implemented, the bar for efficacy and safety of new drugs will be raised to "global, objective, scientific standards." "No longer," Michael continued, will "a Tokyo University professor with a friend in the MHLW leverage that friendship to get his drug approved." Other interest groups will likewise be routed: "To a certain extent, smaller local industry resists the ICH because it disadvantages them: they don't have the R&D power to produce innovative drugs; they haven't the ability to train and carry out clinical trials according to GCP standards. ICH standards come at a high cost to such firms because it is harder to prove efficacy of their drugs. The current situation favors the existence of scores of nonefficacious drugs that are only shown not to do harm."

## Clinical Trials, Pricing, and "Junk Science"

I am not in a position to evaluate claims by the PhRMA representative and drug company managers that clinical trials in Japan continue to be influenced by incompetent or fraudulent practices. My initial data on the recent history of trial procedures, and the reports of Japanese academics I have interviewed on the topic, suggest far more parity in Japanese RCT protocols and practices with American and European standards than my foreign informants seem to be suggesting. The foremost concern, and the area where the most effort is devoted, is pricing — an "issue" for pharmaceutical companies in Japan because drug reimbursement rates are set solely by the government and subsidiary bodies. This is of course true to some degree everywhere; there may be no place where drug reimbursement schedules through insurers are completely unregulated. But Japan's nationalized health insurance system, in the words of the pricing specialist at one of the firms, is "a command economy in the classic sense: dark, opaque, and impenetrable." For the drug company, pricing is the goose that lays the golden eggs.

The following accounts drawn from my field interviews show how the issues of the standards for scientific practice in clinical testing and methods used to determine drug reimbursement prices meld into one another. Company personnel are predisposed to embrace a common standard of value determination for both. I will elaborate on the larger implied framework below.

In the first phase of this research, in November 2001, I visited the U.S. headquarters of a leading SSRI manufacturer. My first meeting was with six managers involved with the Japanese SSRI program. Two of the six were psychiatrists, one was a research scientist involved in clinical trial design and evaluation, and two were business–government relations experts, one of whom focused specifically on the firm's attempts to negotiate advantageous price reimbursements for the company's drugs. The managers had each spent varying amounts of time in Japan, ranging from a couple of months to several years, and they are in the practice now of traveling back and forth to Japan to handle current projects, including the introduction of their SSRI drug. We sat around a conference table. I explained who I was and what my research is about, concluding by saying that I had come prepared with a list of questions, but that I was fairly new to their point of view on the subject and would appreciate their guiding the discussion in the directions they felt were most apposite.

No sooner had I completed my self-introduction than the clinical testing experts declared that the scientific standards for clinical testing in Japan are "quite poor." There is no "evidence-based medicine" in Japan, they said, no "good clinical practice" (referring to GCP). Instead, the Japanese have "do no harm medicine." When I asked what they meant by this they explained that drugs are tested not so much for efficacy in Japan as for side effects. Fluvoxe-mine, for instance (a competing drug), was not approved for treating depression in the United States, but in Japan, "because it happened to test successfully for few side effects, it was approved."

"What sorts of testing deficiencies are common?" I asked. Patients in Japanese clinical trials sometimes miss doctor visits, one responded, yet researchers deny this as having been a factor when a study goes awry. Japanese researchers are unable to account for and thus respond to the nebulousness of psychiatric drug clinical trials. "If a patient marks off their experience as being between a 3 and a 4, the [doctor] researcher in Japan will arbitrarily decide that it is a 3, for instance." The managers interpreted this as a culture-bound discomfort with uncertainty. "Their hankering for precision may pay off for making cars or electronics," one of them said, "but it fails them in medicine." Other deficiencies included the following: "Various sites along the RCT are not rationally supervised"; there is no central "study coordinator," no "Case Judgment Committee," no "IVRS [interactive voice response system, for participants to call in case of problems]," no "information technology person"; "there are fewer checks and balances in the system." For example, "In the U.S., [we] deliver kits to the [test] sites. The kits are closed so that the doctors giving the medicines are unaware of which are the placebos and which are the live medicines. In Japan, the investigator knows which patients get the placebo."

The discussion proceeded in this somewhat emotive fashion. "You ought to write a whole book and not just an article about this," cried one of the managers. I dispensed with my questions for a time and let the conversation flow according to their inclinations. I will not reproduce many of the details of the ensuing discussion except to note the sequence of topics, which went from drug approval and randomized clinical trials to the difficulties of doing business in Japan, and finally to a résumé of the state of Japanese science, medicine, and psychiatry. I paraphrase their conclusions: The Japanese practice poor clinical science—"junk science," in fact—resulting in inferior treatment of Japanese patients since excellent drugs that would under objective testing conditions become available are instead delayed and not approved. In place of superior new drugs a plethora of nonefficacious "do no harm," "me-too," and generic imitation drugs flood the market, making it difficult for new drugs to edge their way in, and to break even when they do.

Embedded in this litany against "junk science" are, I believe, three collateral claims that in their evaluative framework managers see as contingent upon one another. The core claim is a condemnation of the state of Japanese science. Concomitant with this appraisal, however, is a moral assertion that poor clinical trial procedures conceal the efficacy of excellent drugs, thus delaying or withholding from Japanese sufferers the truly efficacious therapies. "There is no sense of urgency about patient need in Japan," said one. The third issue for the managers is that junk science prevents them from profiting from their efforts. Nonrationalized testing procedures make it necessary to repeat costly trials. More damaging (to the company), the registration process contains within it an MHLW subcommittee determination of the drug's insurance reimbursement price, what the company will be paid for each pill prescribed. These two issues—the cost of doing science in Japan and government-controlled pricing—emerge more clearly from two following interview contexts in which the term *junk science* was discussed.

I visited the headquarters of a drug company in Japan and spoke with the director of research, a former professor at a leading British university who said he had quit in frustration over how Britain was handling its clinical treatment of mental illness. This time I raised the expression *junk science*, mentioning where I had heard it. William, I shall call him, explained the junk science phenomenon first by referring to reasons trials fail that would be familiar to a medical anthropologist. "There is the unthinking use of not well validated ratings. The adherence to protocols is okay, but there still exist validity problems. For instance, in OCD [obsessive compulsive disorder], ADHD [attention deficit hyperactivity disorder], and especially as regards mania the scales are unclear, their cross-cultural applicability is based on uncertain grounds." Junk science, in this articulation, refers to the resistance of cross-cultural scales or measures for what are held to be objective definitions of disease.[16]

As William considered my question further, he expressed disapproval of his American colleagues' purported connotation of *junk science*, saying that while there is a certain tendency for clinical research to not be rewarded as much as biological research in Japan, it would ultimately be unfair to characterize Japanese research as junk science. "Perhaps more at issue in the matter of junk science," he said, "is that one has to pay a price to have drugs approved. You are just buying a ticket. Drug testing in Japan is 'science in Japan for the sake of doing science in Japan.' The bridging agreements have not yet had real results in how things are done. The IRB and GCP will eventually reduce the junk science effect, as the improved scientific environment since 1997 has shown. But the culture of practice must be improved before the theory can be converted to implementation."

In William's rationalization, junk science is less a matter of inferior standards and practices than the implementation of bridging agreements, a focus much closer to the source of frustration of pharmaceutical company actors. In the view of the pharmaceutical industry, SSRIs have been in use for fourteen years and have proven to be safe, effective drugs for people all over the world — even genetically Japanese users. Why, they ask, should the drugs have to be retested intensively in Japan? Such testing is expensive, risky (insofar as standards for testing in Japan are considered uncertain, and hence liable to error), and superfluous. The requirement for such tests, they conclude, is the result of arbitrary policy decisions motivated by interest group donations and pressures. An example showing the arbitrariness of the drug approval procedure was raised several times by different managers — Japanese and foreign nationals. Viagra, I was told, was approved in a mere six months because of what one manager referred to as "the dirty old man factor." This rapid approval galvanized women's groups to lobby for the immediate approval of the birth control pill, which had been waiting in line for approval for much longer than had Viagra. "The pill had been delayed for ten years. No new data was introduced, but suddenly the pill got approved." The introduction of political considerations in the practice of science, in sum, "junkifies" it.

Finally, in a conversation with a corporate affairs executive of the same company, an American whom I shall call Terry, the term *junk science* surfaced in connection not primarily with science or the politics of approval, but with pricing. This manager was moved to give me a two-and-a-half-hour lecture on the vagaries of price determination and the ways this subjective procedure constricts the activities of his firm and the development of what he called "First World medicine" generally. The following emphasizes the institutionalization of a scheme in which scientific advancements and drug efficacy are wedded to price.

Terry's segue into the discussion of junk science was his expansion upon what PhRMA is trying to accomplish. "PhRMA is seeking to change the system so that innovation is recognized. In the current system, scientific innovation is not recognized by price." The characteristics of the pricing system were explained to me by Terry and by the pricing experts at both his firm and at another Japanese pharmaceutical company that has been shepherding a different American company through the SSRI approval process. Their views coincide with an interested version of the system. A healthcare economic perspective, not to mention that of the government bureaucrats in charge of overseeing the process, would undoubtedly view the matter in a different light.

Apart from the overall fact that drug prices are set by the MHLW and associated bodies, there are four germane attributes — seen as obstacles and inadequate solutions to the inequities — of the pricing system. First is the "comparator system," which determines the price of a new drug by comparing it with a similar existing medicine. The shortcoming of this approach, according to the drug companies, is that when no comparator from the same pharmaceutical class is available, drugs from a different class are used instead, resulting in unanticipated variability in the price assigned. This interferes with the anticipated return on investment calculations that drug companies rely on to conduct long-term business.

The second bugbear of the system is progressive price reductions. Once a drug price is set, the price is not guaranteed through the patent life; there is a gradual lowering of drug prices due to inflation. Price reductions were purportedly instituted to correct for *yakkasa*, or reimbursement discounts to prescribers, but they end by shearing manufacturer profits over time. Likewise, if a manufacturer sells more of a drug than it originally forecast, the government lowers the price. Another purported corrective to inequities in the system is the foreign price adjustment rule, which takes into account the calculated average price of the new drug in France, Germany, the United Kingdom, and the United States. It is intended to mitigate distortions caused by the other two factors. Pharmaceutical company pricing experts point out that the averages are distorted because they do not account for varying dosage levels, indications, and cost of approval and marketing. Finally, there are price premiums. Price premiums were established to reward drug companies introducing innovative new drugs, but it is said that the criteria are too vague to allow appropriate application. PhRMA claims that since 1996 only one premium has been awarded for true innovation.

Terry likened the comparator method of drug pricing—the "Do we have any similar molecules?" approach—to the mindset of one walking through a bazaar looking for a teacup similar to one's collection at home. He gave examples of drugs from his company that suffered in the comparison, including its drug for schizophrenia, which is known as belonging to the "atypicals" class. In Japan, it was classified with drugs from an earlier released class and assigned an undeserved low price.[17] Moreover, because therapeutic use is one of the factors considered in classifying a drug and determining its price, the nationally subjective question "will Japanese doctors find this drug useful in their practice" is given play. The difference between "will Japanese doctors . . ." and "should Japanese doctors find this drug useful in their practice," Terry claimed, is established upon habits grounded in factors other than medical excellence. He again referred to the example of the atypicals class of drug for schizophrenia. "At present," he continued, "the average M.D. is prescribing maybe seven different pills on each patient visit. We are arguing that the M.D. can switch to monotherapy, and then you can even discharge the patient from the hospital. The doctor . . . is not motivated to do this because he will lose money on empty bed days in his hospital — remember that the private hospital owner, which is 80 percent of them, is also the M.D. in charge. In the case of [his company's drug], because it is not an Olympic gold medal winner [i.e., the first in its category, as determined by the MHLW], the reimbursement price is low and the doctor is even more disincentivized from prescribing it."

The assumed interpolation of flawed or nonscientific yardsticks for meting out rewards for scientific innovation is the basis for Terry's recurrent use of *junk science* to describe the Japanese system of drug approval and registration overall. The best therapy, he thinks, should be reflected by the best (highest) price. The source of the companies' indignation, in turn, is the deprivation of the Japanese sufferer, who receives belated and inferior drug treatments. In the perfect market world, the amoral techniques of science are globally (that is, cleansed of cultural peculiarities) harnessed in the service of a moral cause — that of shifting the focus of healthcare provisioning from the care provider to the care receiver. This eventuality is seen by the drug companies to guarantee a democratic outcome in a number of respects, the two most important of which are as follows. First, it decontaminates the care-giving process from the impurely interested or deluded institutions who corrupt it, such as interested hospital owners, ignorant government bureaucrats, and noninnovative but influential Japanese pharmaceutical companies. Second, the market solution is seen to provide free choice to patients who, if they are properly educated regarding the choice of drugs available, can be trusted to eventually select the best product. Patient education, one manager added, will also in time erode the archaic paternalistic character of doctor-patient relations in Japan. That "will help [patients] get out of that relationship and take their treatment more into their own hands. . . . If they come in with knowledge about their condition — and especially about the medication they think they ought to be taking — then matters are improved." What the pharmaceutical companies are less willing to acknowledge (or perhaps do not recognize — or *misrecognize*, in Bourdieu's terminology) is that their wish to privatize pharmacology by unfettering the existing institutional provisioning structure of it and by converting Japanese patients into informed, free-ranging consumers of medicines merely replaces one systematizing, moralizing, and perhaps hegemonic set of overseers with another.

Beyond the moralizing rhetoric, the persuasive metaphorical associations, the enjoining of international agreements, and the pooled efforts to establish the legitimacy of their claims to Japanese authorities, the most visibly effectual area of corporate ingenuity and exertion to establish the market lies with what the companies refer to as the education campaign. The goals of this campaign are epitomized in the conceptual framework of the inevitable evolution of the Japanese market, to which marketers in particular are providing the encouraging push.

### "Speeding the Evolution" to Global Standards: The Mega-marketing Challenge

I have elsewhere described how in their endeavor to resist the loss of unique identity for and control over their products, marketers act on much more than merely the materiality, aesthetics, and signification of the objects of their manufacture. Marketing, I argue, more greatly concerns itself with a science of consumer consciousness, experience, and total environment.[18] The tapestry of influence being exerted in Japan to create a hospitable environment for the propagation of these medicines is likewise elaborate. These practices closely resemble the actions of pharmaceutical companies in the United States,[19] and thus do not require full depiction here. However, it is the *similarities* of these marketing programs that best demonstrate how disparate markets are seen as analogous and are approached as though they exist on an evolving continuum. In our discussions, managers (American as well as Japanese) constantly emphasized that with respect to several key issues — public recognition and acceptance of mental illness in scientific terms, progressiveness of the insurance system, infrastructure for the distribution of SSRIS, national or personal income to pay for them, and so on — Japan may be five years ahead of China, which is in turn ahead of Brazil, which lags perhaps fifteen years behind Britain, and so on. The U.S. market is the standard against which other markets are measured, and SSRI marketing managers prefer to use it as an example because of the prescriptions per capita there. If it were possible, a manager would reproduce all the reported elements of the U.S. market in Japan: phenomenal brand recognition and high rate of prescription on demand to patients; (relatively) free market pricing; 70 percent prescription by nonspecialists— a particularly fervent ambition in Japan, where there are comparatively few psychiatrists;[20] and on and on. However, the challenge is not so much how to make the Japanese market like the U.S. market, a senior marketing manager explained, as how to "speed the evolution along. It is only a matter of time before Japanese patients [sufferers of depression, anxiety] rise up and demand to be treated the way patients are treated in the rest of the world." The targets for action are not restricted to patients, but also include physicians, government bureaucrats, journalists, and hospital administrators.

What are the obstacles these companies face in their challenge to establish the market? First are public attitudes toward mental illness: there is considerable stigma attached to it (particularly schizophrenia), which itself stems from and contributes to the entrenched practice of long-term hospitalization of mental patients in underfunded, segregated mental hospitals.[21] One prominent psychiatrist whose efforts to reduce the stigma of mental illness were noticed and subsequently sponsored by one of the four companies explained: "Until a generation ago there was a great shame to go to clinics or mental hospitals for treatment. . . . The term *seishinka-i*, or psychiatrist, still rouses some apprehension in people's minds. This is the result of the association of mental illness with the hospitalization for it. A person might be reluctant to go to a mental hospital even on an outpatient basis because of this association. Parents say to small children who cry too much, 'Do you want me to call the yellow car to come and take you to the mental hospital?' "

The poor amenities of mental hospitals and the low status of psychiatrists result in continued underinvestment in the field from both research and health insurance perspectives. The campaign to destigmatize mental illness in Japan is spearheaded by the efforts of the foreign pharmaceutical companies introducing drugs that affect the central nervous system (CNS). This activity is taking place in cooperation with several well-situated Japanese psychiatrists and is backed by PhRMA and supported in parallel by the overseas activities of the World Health Organization's Nations for Mental Health program,[22] which is itself sponsored by one of the aforementioned companies.

The destigmatization campaign is coupled with another directed toward increasing *recognition* among the public of how widespread depression, anxiety, OCD, panic, bulimia, social phobia, and related disorders are. This enterprise is facilitated by the cooperation of concerned medical practitioners, public officials, and journalists who purportedly recognize the underdiagnosis of depression and anxiety as a social ill that can be remedied by awakening public consciousness to the symptoms and treatability of these disorders. Newspaper features on this topic have reportedly increased manyfold in recent years. People told me of this or that celebrity's "coming out" about their own depression as having been a watershed point for this trend, much as occurred in the United States in the late 1980s after Prozac was first introduced into the market.

Pharmaceutical companies use a number of techniques to reach potential end consumers of SSRIS; these include clipping, reproducing, and disseminating newspaper articles on depression, especially when it is reported being treated by SSRIS; advertising for clinical trial volunteers (direct-to-consumer ads are illegal, but full-page ads for trials, bearing the branded imprint of the drug, are permitted); encouraging the growth of patient or illness advocacy groups that can pressure the government for the early approval of new drugs; distributing glossy waiting-room brochures explaining depression and SSRIS' purported mode of action in the brain (in fact a scientific uncertainty of the highest order); supporting research and scientific and professional congresses concordant with company goals;[23] sponsoring the translation of a couple of best-selling books from the United States that acclaimed SSRIS among the public when they were first introduced; and developing Internet sites "where patients can get educated about depression and about [our drug]," as one marketing manager at an American pharmaceutical company in Tokyo explained. When I inquired about Japanese restrictions on direct-to-consumer (DTC) advertising, he replied:

The best way to reach patients today is not via advertising but the Web. The Web basically circumvents DTC rules, so there is no need to be concerned over these. People go to the company website and take a quiz to see whether they might have depression. If yes, they go to the doctor and ask for medication. [Our company] doesn't push anyone. I believe it is crass to advertise antidepressants. . . . If someone has a problem and [our Product Z] is a solution to that problem, then they ought to buy it. . . . [Such a] system moves us toward patient choice and [Product Z] wins in such a case because [Product Z] is a brand name and consumers will be inclined to take it up on that account.

Observe the subtle reassignment of connotation to the idea of education here. The "educated" customer is one who knows and is therefore inclined to the brand, Product Z. The empowerment or perhaps authorization of the layperson to provisionally self-diagnose, using the company's web-based instrument (the Zung scale), is a step on the route to the person approaching his or her doctor and asking for Product Z by name.

Complementing the crusade to raise the Japanese public's awareness about depression and thus to soften sufferers' presumably culturally characteristic reluctance to take antidepressants is a corresponding campaign, described by the same manager: "You have to educate the doctors." The effort begins with research backed by the company. Pharmaceutical companies in all therapeutic areas in Japan fund medical research in topics in which they have a stake (*jutaku kenkyu*, or research with a purpose). They also invest in individual researchers whose results best coincide with the given drug company's interests. For instance, in their effort to associate the rising suicide rate with clinical depression, pharmaceutical companies, according to Emiko Namihira, a medical anthropologist, fund research showing such a linkage. They print leaflets summarizing the research and distribute them to physicians and also induce the national newspapers to report the research as breaking news.[24] Contrary evidence is given no such boost. The result is a shift in professional and public attitudes favoring the approval of the new antidepressants and their expedited adoption increasingly by nonspecialist physicians who lack the training to evaluate the validity of the original research. By these means, the investigations of medical specialists are commandeered into a kind of market research by pharmaceutical companies. The research simultaneously serves as publicity for the essentially predetermined consumer need.

Pharmaceutical companies employ public relations specialists, often people with substantial media backgrounds and connections, to promote tendentious science in this way. In addition to organizing professional conferences pertaining to SSRI use and conveying influential, preferably young, Japanese doctors — since these are targeted as the most amenable to adoption of innovation — to overseas conferences where they will be exposed to "global" standards in the treatment of mental illness, public relations and marketing managers expend great energy and expense generating scientific brochures intended for consumption by psychiatrists and other professionals interested in psychiatric disorders (there is not the same specialization in Japanese medicine as in the United States). SSRI-sympathetic researchers at leading universities are asked to contribute research summaries for publication in pamphlets that the sales representatives of the company will then distribute to practitioners in hospitals nationwide. Alternatively, suitable research found in professional journals is excerpted and reproduced in the booklets. Quoting medical research supporting the use of a particular medication is an effective device for a drug company to promote its products because the average doctor respects the credentials of the high-powered specialist cited and has too little time to collect a wider sample of opinions to cross-check against the claims made in the brochures. A study quoted to me by an industry expert estimated that psychiatrists obtain approximately 70 percent of their information regarding medications from brochures distributed by sales representatives of drug companies.

Further strategies that would carry us more specifically into the state of affairs in Japan would be deserving of analysis were there space to enter into it. I shall leave that discussion, as well as one concerning particular marketing practices and strategies (segmenting, branding, positioning, targeting; getting primary care physicians to prescribe SSRIs; company scientist involvement in market research and strategies for testing, dosing, and labeling, for example) for another occasion.

## Conclusion: Covering Up the Tracks
## of Global Market Expansion

At the outset I placed global evolution in opposition to agent-driven global expansion. I postponed spelling out the full significance of this dichotomy because I wished first to demonstrate the extent and bearing of the pharmaceutical companies' agency in this case study, particularly as evident from the details of their mega-marketing program. At this point I can specify the duality a bit further, situating it within a larger framework for thinking about globalization in pharmaceuticals and in general. I said that "global evolution" implies progress and enlightenment (political, scientific, moral), while "global expansion" highlights the agent-centered and historical dimension of globalization. This description of evolution is commonplace; it appeals to a kind of background-noise common sense that has traditionally been applied to thinking about scientific or technological complexification. Yet, it is increasingly shared as a folk model for thinking about the development of markets as well, whether by means of some derivative of modernization theory or that of the scaled ascent to "modern lifestyles."[25] The correspondence between the two is an additional peg in the as-yet metaphorical linkage between science and commerce, as earlier discussed. However, it is important to recognize that marketers also assume this folk theory. In fact, I wish to argue that it is more than merely tacit knowledge—which, as Bourdieu argues, has generative properties. The global evolution of the markets model is a crucial element in marketers' own "theory of practice."[26] This is why the discourse about the Japanese market being X years behind the American market and so on is not idle chatter. It forms the basis for specific marketing plans based upon "learnings," as marketers call it, from other experiences. Firms such as the large pharmaceutical manufacturers discussed in this chapter circulate internal instructional materials regarding experiences with the same product in what they consider similar markets. Managers fly about the world to training conferences where such archetypes are hardened. And old advertisements and communications strategies from the earlier stage of more "advanced" markets are imported. In Japan, the marketing director for one of the SSRIs showed me his marketing plan and explained that it was a boilerplate reproduction of the plan that had been used in Great Britain a number of years earlier. I add that this highly placed manager had joined this firm after having spent ten years working as a marketing manager for Unilever on personal care products with no relation to pharmaceuticals — demonstrating in yet another way that much of the motivating logic behind the dissemination of these medicines derives from marketing and not from psychopharmacology. The extent to which company scientists are also subsidiary to the marketing directives of the firm began to be evident to me in initial inquiries made to that purpose at two companies near the end of my research visit. What is significant to note is that particularly with regard to SSRIS, which are either protean or messy (depending on how one construes the psychiatric evidence), the latitude for the reinterpretation of their value back to the consumer through brand positioning is somewhat flexible.

If evolutionary globalism is a theory of practice among marketers, it is also a self-naturalizing ideology that can mask the actual agency that has historically (rather than evolutionarily) brought about the present situation of global relevance in the pharmaceutical industry. The applicability of this framework is particularly acute in the case of psychopharmaceuticals, I believe, because laypersons might unsuspectingly slot these drugs in the same scientific, commercial, and ethical container as antibiotics or hypertensives, whose mechanism of action and efficacy are more substantiated. This is precisely the understanding the commercial purveyors of these drugs are seeking to promote. "The challenge for us," a PR manager for one of the companies explained to me, "is how to put the brain on a par with other organs such as the liver, the kidney, the heart." She specified no particular target at this point, such as doctors, bureaucrats, or the public. It was understood to be a blanket interpretation of Japanese resistance to dealing with depression medically.

Will the Japanese establishment be persuaded to the marketers' point of view? To some extent this question is meaningless because it is not for evidence of a single, visible agreement that one would look to determine whether the moralizing rhetoric and mega-marketing engineering program have achieved their goals. As Moore comments, "The work of establishing public meanings and legitimizing social action is continuous, never achieved once and for all and never undertaken in toto, for a whole 'system,' but rather situationally."[27] It may not be inconsistent with Moore's theory to observe that moments of crisis — such as Japan perceives itself to be experiencing in the face of a decade-long recession, an escalating suicide rate, and the looming healthcare crisis of the "aging society" (*koreisha shakai*) — are more susceptible to grand experimentation and change. But even as is, Moore's insight can inform the present case by drawing our attention to the manner in which corporations in general go about achieving their goals of influencing public opinion, morality, and ultimately policy. Namely, their successes tend to come at the cumulative end of many small pressures. And perhaps it is not even pressures placed so much as numerous innocuous-seeming instances of "troubleshooting." The largest and most ethically exposed corporations parry unfavorable trends by creating conferences where people are given the opportunity to learn the "correct" outlook from experts or other role models; by founding institutions for arbitration, research, and guidance leading to the negotiation of the short distances necessary to reach harmonious viewpoints; by lending succor to internal scientists and pundits whose "right vision" for the future has been denied proper airing; and finally by copiously backing already legitimated organizations that intercede on behalf of public welfare. In this manner, through a kind of moral bridging, shared foundations for a global healthcare model emerge as though from a naturally occurring consensus.

## Notes

My thanks to Ingrid Jordt, Joshua Breslau, and Sally Falk Moore for their constructive comments on an earlier draft of this paper. Glenda Roberts, Eguchi Shigeyuki, Arthur Kleinman, Paul Talcott, Namihira Emiko, and others who might wish to remain anonymous helped me carry out the research in Japan. Michael Crichton generously funded the research through a grant to the Department of Social Medicine, Harvard Medical School.
1. See Applbaum 1998, 2004a.
2. For a discussion on the difference between syndrome and disease, see Kleinman 1987.
3. For a generic discussion of SWOT analysis, see Kotler 2000:76–79. More specific examples relating to the pharmaceutical industry are available on the Internet.
4. See Someya et al. 2001.
5. See, for example, Giddens 1990:64.

6. According to the Tufts Center for the Study of Drug Development. See the center's website, http://www.tufts.edu/med/.

7. Applbaum 2000a:258.

8. On Japan, see Breslau 2000.

9. Numerous subcommittees and external evaluative boards participate in the drug registration process. For the sake of simplicity I refer to the MHLW or the ministry throughout.

10. Electronic document at the FDA's website: http://www.fda.gov/oc/, accessed 2 May 2002.

11. Tsutani 1997.

12. Ueda 1997.

13. Tales of initial consumer resistance to new product categories outnumber those of eager adoption, but in either event a concerted producer "push" rather than a consumer "pull" force is entailed, as the history of cola drinks, for one, would substantiate.

14. PhRMA maintains a website for its Japan office, but the site at present writing contains no information; see http://www.phrma.org/.

15. For an analysis of similar rhetoric against Japan during the Structural Impediments Initiative of the early 1990s, see Applbaum 1998b.

16. As a material aside in considering this matter of scale validity and cross-cultural translation, Emiko Namihira, a medical anthropologist and president of the Japanese Ethnological Society, observed to me (personal communication, 11 January 2002) that the Hamilton Depression Rating Scale (HAM-D), even when properly translated, is far more operative on people under forty than above it.

17. I believe there is reason to qualify this argument, but I cannot do so without revealing the name of the drug and hence the company. In any event, the pricing decision was considered unsatisfactory by the manufacturer, and the comparator pricing method is, using the logic they bring to it, certainly responsible.

18. "Marketing informs and configures a total provisioning system that does not merely cater to needs and desires but seeks to define and render self-evident what these might be in relation and proportion to sponsored product categories. . . . This activity is sustained by the efforts marketers take to modify the conditions for sale and distribution at the sites surrounding the objects themselves; to expand the zone of existing commodities by incorporating new populations as well as by target inventing new commodities; to assert through the production of advertisements and educational promotions an influence over the environmental conditions in which use, meaning, requirement and desire are to be defined; and to project to the individual or population segment the necessity or desirability of the object as constituting a part of their personal code of distinction according to which consumption and taste are to be defined as classificatory actions in the construction of 'lifestyle'" (Applbaum 2000b:120).

19. For a highly critical account, see Glenmullen 2000, chap. 5; see also Healy 2003c.

20. Approximately ten thousand.

21. See Kawabuchi 1998.

22. "Nations for Mental Health" is a World Health Organization Action Programme initiated by the United Nations in 1996 following the presentation of the Harvard Report to the secretary general of the UN in 1995. It works mainly at country level to address key

mental health issues such as stigma, human rights violations, accessibility to services and effective treatment, prevention strategies, and promotion of mental health. It aims to (see http://www.profbriefings.co.uk/events/partmh.htm): stimulate political will internationally on mental health; promote alliances between policy makers, the scientific community, health professionals, mental health service users and their families; encourage technical support between countries; and promote good practice.

23. See Applbaum 2004b.

24. Personal communication, 11 January 2002.

25. See Applbaum 2000a.

26. Bourdieu 1999.

27. Moore 1993:2.

# High Contact
## Gifts and Surveillance in Argentina

ANDREW LAKOFF

This chapter seeks to analyze the generation of demand in the global pharmaceutical economy by looking at a specific case: the apparent rise in antidepressant sales during the Argentine financial crisis of 2001. Observers of
recent mutations in global capitalism have noted an increasing emphasis on
consumption rather than production in its operations.[1] In turn, social analysts have turned to strategies for shaping consumer demand as a source of
insight into contemporary forces of social regulation and identity formation.
But in the case of "ethical" pharmaceuticals (drugs whose consumption is restricted to physician prescription), identifying the actual consumer is a complex problem. Professional and state regulation of the pharmaceutical market
means that consumption is based not directly on patient need or consumer
desire but is mediated by medical expertise. The problem for pharmaceutical
marketers is to link doctors' selection of their products to the practice of authorized knowledge. The boundaries between capitalism and science seem to
blur: the generation of demand must be at the same time an appeal to professional authority. This merging of domains can inspire either denunciations on
the grounds of impurity or celebrations of the benefits of entrepreneurialism

to health.[2] In this chapter I take a different approach based on research into the psychopharmaceutical market in Argentina. My argument will be that the mutual imbrication of science, regulation, and business in the circulation of pharmaceuticals is best seen not as a contamination of pure science but rather as part of a distinctive and emergent regime for authorizing knowledge claims and expert action.

The essay has two parts. I first look at the use of audit data by pharmaceutical firms as a means of regulating expertise and as a way of constituting the market as a domain of practice. Such techniques of regulation are particularly salient in places like Argentina, where the role of the state has receded in the wake of neoliberal reforms. I then consider recent shifts in the Argentine psycho-pharmaceutical market. Specifically, I ask whether rising antidepressant sales revenue should be attributed to the country's ongoing economic and social crisis or to the techniques of regulation described in part one.

## Neoliberal Contraband

"The history of Argentina is the history of contraband," said Daniela, a pharmaco-epidemiologist employed at a pharmacy benefits management firm in Buenos Aires, by way of explaining the structure of the country's pharma-ceutical industry. While the statement implies a more general analysis of the trajectory of capitalism in the Río de la Plata, her specific reference was to the sanctioned prevalence of unlicensed copies in the domestic pharmaceutical market.

To understand the central role of copies in the Argentine pharmaceutical industry, it is useful to begin with some background on changing forms of po-litical rationality in Argentina and their relationship to innovation and indus-trial policy. The domestic pharmaceutical industry was founded according to a logic of import-substitution, producing copies for the internal market in a climate where patent rights for pharmaceuticals were not recognized. This was part of the broader strategy of the postwar Argentine welfare or "planning" state, which constituted its citizens as subjects of need and the state's task as provider of basic services. The developmentalist program was based on state-led industrialization that, it was hoped, would not only lead to independence from external powers but would also provide work and affordable goods for the population (Sikkink 1991; Waisman 1987). But mounting debt crises and hyperinflation eventually led the government to abandon this model and embrace IMF-designed structural adjustment policies oriented toward reducing the role of the state.[3] In the late 1980s and early 1990s, after more than a decade of fitful attempts to shift away from the planning state, the Peronist government of Carlos Menem began a radical experiment in market liberalism through rapid privatization of state-owned entities such as electric utilities, railroads, and the oil company, and the deregulation of protected markets.

The goal of such reforms was to limit the role of the state in overseeing human welfare and to extend market rationality to areas that had not previously been seen as economic — such as education, health, and security (Barry et al. 1996). The premise was that market competition rather than state planning was the most efficient and effective way to provide such goods: given a space of ideal competition entrepreneurs would quickly step in to offer the best service at the best price, whereas states were hampered by bureaucratic inertia, corruption, and inflexibility — the inability to deal with rapid change.[4]

The pharmaceutical industry provides a good illustration of the uneven and contingent effects of such "liberalization." Under neoliberal reform in the early 1990s, price controls were dropped, the protection of local markets was eliminated, and the process of registration and authorization of medications was eased by giving automatic approval to a new drug if it had been approved by regulators in a "leading country" — that is, in Western Europe or North America. The idea was to regulate prices not by state-imposed controls but through competition structured by the free choices of consumers.

Argentina agreed to comply with the TRIPS accord on intellectual property that emerged from the 1986 Uruguay Round of the General Agreement on Tariffs and Trade (GATT). Multinational pharmaceutical companies were encouraged to expand their efforts in the market through their local subsidiaries. This was obviously bad news for the domestic industry, which controlled most of the market but depended on the absence of an effective patent regime. To continue its operations the domestic industry had to be able to freely expropriate intellectual property, and during the 1990s it was able to repeatedly delay implementation of the patent regime. Under these circumstances, many domestic firms thrived in the neoliberal transition by making exact copies of multinational drugs and selling them as local brands. This strategy should be distinguished from generic production: these products were marketed brand names sold at prices comparable to those of the multinationals. In other words, domestic firms took advantage of the value structure of the transnational pharmaceutical industry, which is based on patent protection, while at the same time defying such protection.[5]

As of 2001, the Argentine pharmaceutical market was thus in an unlikely grouping with the United States, Germany, Switzerland, and Japan as the only countries whose domestic producers had a greater market share than foreign ones. But it was unique in that this thriving domestic production was founded on high-priced brand name copies. For example, among the fifty-four antidepressants marketed in 2001 there were fourteen brands of fluoxetine (Prozac) and six brands of paroxetine (Paxil).

During the 1990s, Menem government's deregulation policies produced a striking change in the Argentine pharmaceuticals market. Drug prices rose sharply despite the lack of enforcement of patent protection, and while overall pharmaceutical consumption declined by 13 percent in the first five years after the reforms, drug revenues increased by 70 percent (Fundación ISALUD 1999). This was in part the result of informal collusion between drug firms and insurance providers and the systematic blockage of the emergence of a generic industry. But it also had to do with the role of doctors as gatekeepers to consumption. In this sense, the model of rational consumer choice is clearly an inappropriate one for the pharmaceutical market, which is inherently "imperfect" in economic terms: the one who chooses the drug is not the one who consumes it, and the one who consumes it is not (or often is not) the one who pays for it (Fundación ISALUD 1999). Doctors' prescription practices are not shaped by price competition.

Given the presence of so many copies (and the continued prohibition on direct-to-consumer advertising), there was intense competition among both domestic and multinational firms for the loyalties of doctors. At the same time there was an oversupply of medical professionals, who had difficulty finding enough patients to maintain private practices and received abysmally low salaries in public hospitals or social insurance–based clinics. With no research costs, domestic firms could reinvest their earnings directly back into marketing—and the key strategy was building relationships of reciprocity with doctors through gifts of access. In this environment major gifts were common: at the American Psychiatric Association (APA) meetings in New Orleans in 2001, the largest foreign contingent was from Argentina. Of the five hundred Argentine psychiatrists who attended, the vast majority had received sponsored trips from pharmaceutical firms, both domestic and multinational.

## Pharmaceutical Relations

The ubiquity of gifts from pharmaceutical firms to doctors has drawn increased scrutiny in American professional and ethical discourse. The practice provokes concerns about a "conflict of interest" between the doctor's duty to the patient and a reciprocal obligation to the pharmaceutical company that might compromise doctors' professional integrity. At least two problems with this framing of the gift relationship are particularly acute in understanding the Argentine context.[6] First, it assumes that a clear distinction can be made between "rational pharmacology" and marketing. However, as David Healy and others have shown, marketing and expertise cannot be so easily disentangled: pharmaceutical companies are producers not only of pills but also of knowledge about their safety and efficacy, and their gifts to doctors provide access to the latest information (Healy 2001). The fortress that is supposed to guard against the crude logic of profit—biomedical expertise—is itself ensconced in the market.

This issue points to a second problem with the "conflict of interest" framing. It assumes that the gift is a terminal exchange rather than the strengthening of an ongoing relationship (see Appadurai 1986). Rather than a direct transfer of goods, however, I would argue that pharmaceutical gift relations involve something more like *reciprocal access to guarded resources*. This will become clearer as I describe the structure of relations between doctors and pharmaceutical companies in the Argentine context. From the vantage of the firms, these relations obviously enable access to patients—either as drug consumers or as subjects of clinical trials. From the perspective of Argentine psychiatrists, the kinds of gifts that are offered — email accounts, computer equipment, travel to international congresses — represent the possibility of engagement with centers of knowledge production and professional authority. Given the lack of other means of accessing cosmopolitan systems of expertise, pharmaceutical relations become portals to the global biomedical infrastructure. In their relations with pharmaceutical companies, it is not so much that doctors are faced with a conflict of interest between science and the market as that they are embedded in an atmosphere of *interested knowledge.*

This analysis does not in itself delegitimate knowledge produced and disseminated about pharmaceutical safety and efficacy. Rather, it directs us to consider how doctors come to invest authority in the information that comes to them via pharmaceutically mediated circuits.[7] This requires the investigation of the structure of the relationships between pharmaceutical companies and doctors. While such relations are strengthened through exchange, the form of trust involved is deliberative: there are structures of accountability on each side (Sabel 1997). Let us begin by looking at how firms monitor the effectiveness of promotional strategies focused on shaping the behavior of doctors.

## Postsocial Regulation

The goal of the sponsored conference trip and other major gifts is to forge a relationship of loyalty between the doctor and the firm. Two kinds of doctors are particularly sought after for such relationships: prescription leaders and opinion leaders. The basic strategy of building brand loyalty among doctors takes different form depending on whether the doctor is an opinion leader or a prescription leader. The delicate work of forging ties with opinion leaders is the job of the sales director or product manager. The key figure in relation to prescription leaders, on the other hand, is the sales representative ("rep"). The Argentine pharmaceutical industry devotes 15 percent of its total revenue ($3.6 billion in 2000) to the reps. There are ninety thousand physicians and eight thousand reps in the country.[8] The rep's task is to work within an assigned territory to increase the market share of his or her company's products. Strategies for gaining loyalty also differ somewhat between domestic and multinational firms. Multinationals rely on their links to prestigious knowledge centers and regulate themselves (at least in appearance) according to transnational norms; domestic firms tend to invent tactics based on knowledge of the local terrain.

Argentina is by no means unique in terms of the centrality of gift relations between doctors and drug companies. However, a number of distinctive characteristics of the milieu in Argentina give these relations a particular form. The country's peripheral position in the global biomedical knowledge economy means that experts have few opportunities to participate in cosmopolitan scientific interchange other than on conference trips provided by pharmaceutical companies. The large number of underemployed professionals, the highly competitive characteristics of the domestic pharmaceutical industry, and weak regulation by the state all make these gift relations especially important in the Argentine context. At the same time, the details of how these relations work provide insight into structures that are present in multiple sites (see the chapters by Applbaum and Healy in this volume). Here I will focus on pharmaceutical audits as techniques for modulating professionals' prescription behavior.

The pharmaceutical audit industry provides data that enables pharmaceutical companies to gauge the results of their marketing campaigns as well as to monitor their relations with individual doctors. I first became interested in the uses of pharmaceutical sales data through a well-known psychiatrist who edits a leading Argentine journal of psychiatry. He had complained at one of the journal's editorial meetings about sales reps from Lilly who had rebuffed his request for sponsorship of his journal, saying: "Why are you asking us for help, when you only prescribe Foxetin?" Gador's Foxetin, a copy of Prozac, was at the time the leading antidepressant on the Argentine market while Lilly's patented original languished in sixth place.[9] The editor, a militant leftist activist during the early 1970s, was outraged: first at the extortionary tactics of the reps, and second at their in-depth knowledge of his prescription practices. How did they know what he prescribed? It turned out that there are database firms that microfilm individual prescriptions in pharmacies, collate the data, and then sell the information to pharmaceutical companies. I was impressed at the detail of this private-sphere knowledge — especially in a country where it is nearly impossible to find any epidemiological data on the prevalence of mental illness in the population or information on rates of pharmaceutical use.[10]

The gathering of detailed knowledge about prescriptions that the editor had stumbled upon is a window into a more general set of practices that have to do with the regulation of contemporary expertise, and which are particularly salient in sites—such as Argentina—where other forms of knowledge and regulation typically associated with the state or with professional organizations are not present. The "avalanche of numbers" about the population's health status and practices produced by pharmaceutical audit firms, and its stark contrast with the lack of data available elsewhere, shifts attention to the role these numbers play in governing expertise.[11]

In his genealogy of governmental rationality, Michel Foucault showed that sciences concerned with gathering knowledge about public health first appeared as an element in an art of government whose aim was to improve the health and welfare of populations, in the service of increasing the strength of the state (Foucault 2000). Understanding and fostering the well-being of subjects understood as living beings gradually became a central task of state administration. Forms of knowledge about the health of populations—from statistics (which first referred to "the science of the state") to demography to epidemiology—have since been linked to a variety of modern state-building projects, as well as to efforts to modernize colonial and postcolonial territories (see Rabinow 1989). The gathering of detailed data about the condition of the population is thus crucial to modern forms of government, in that these numbers constitute the domains that become sites of its intervention—economy, society, and population (Rose 1999).

If sciences such as epidemiology emerged in the context of regulating the health of collectivities within a territory, how should we understand new forms of knowledge such as audit data with respect to the problem of government? It might be said that the role of the social scientist in the welfare or planning state—to constitute and intervene in the collectivity understood as a national population—finds an analogue, in a post-"social" order, in the contemporary market strategist (see Rose 1996a). Gilles Deleuze hinted at this shift in his "Post-script on Control Societies" (1990), describing the importance of marketing to the new form of capitalism oriented toward "meta-production" (see Deleuze 1995). "Marketing is now the instrument of social control and produces the arrogant breed who are our masters," he remarked darkly. Deleuze argued that predominant forms of power relations have shifted as well: disciplinary power has given way to control, the problem of confinement to the problem of *access*. This new form of power operates through constant modulation and transmutation rather than surveillance or confession, he argued. But where and on whom does it operate? In the case of pharmaceutical marketing, the figure who is being modulated through the question of access is not the patient but the doctor. This complex, interactive control is made possible by audit data, the information collected by private companies about pharmaceutical sales volume and doctors' prescription behavior.

The numbers generated by audit firms make the pharmaceutical market palpable as an entity that can be both a target of strategists' intervention and a source of rectifying "feedback." As a form of knowledge about health practices that is used in guiding expertise, pharmaceutical audit data emerge as a kind of "neoliberal epidemiology." These numbers provide a vision of the territory as containing a market rather than a population. While the notion of a sales territory is not new, information technology now makes possible immediate and detailed knowledge that changes the character of territory management.[12] During my research, a veteran psychopharmaceutical marketer told me how he used such data to find prescription leaders, referring to an upper-middle-class neighborhood of Buenos Aires: "You know that Palermo's postal code is 1425 and so you say, 'I want anti-psychotic prescriptions from Palermo.' You find the five best prescribers, and how much they prescribe of what. These are often doctors who are affiliated with high-volume insurance plans." The strategist can then target his marketing effort. Older places devoted to clinical encounters can be used as sites of encounter and transaction: thus in Buenos Aires, public hospitals provide important opportunities for access to prestigious doctors who commute to private practices in places like Palermo in the afternoons — and to patient populations for use in clinical trials.[13]

### Bringing the Market to Life

As I explored this milieu, my specific interest was in recent changes in psychopharmaceutical sales, but it was quite difficult to get hold of the actual numbers and trends. I was sometimes allowed to surreptitiously glance at the huge IMS binder listing monthly sales figures that each sales division receives, but not to make copies. One sales director I met with in a café had written them down on a piece of paper before coming. He let me look at them quickly and then tore up the piece of paper. Sales data are private numbers. They are quite valuable: it costs pharmaceutical firms up to $150,000 per year to subscribe to the IMS service, which is only one kind of audit. The other service, Close Up, which collects prescriptions from pharmacies, provides a different and complementary set of data that are equally difficult to access. Both come with software that allows one to move through their databases and break down the information into significant components: For what pathology do doctors generally prescribe a given drug? Who are the leaders in a given therapeutic class over the last twelve months, and what is the pattern of change? And more impressively, how do sales break down by region—by city, neighborhood, or even postal code?

IMS Health, a multinational firm headquartered in Britain with a subsidiary in Buenos Aires, is the leading collector and distributor of pharmaceutical sales data in the world. The firm's "primary material" is standardized information on overall sales and specific therapeutic classes in terms of units and value at the level of regional and global markets. IMS information can also be specified down to the level of the zip code of the pharmacies where drugs are sold. In Argentina IMS buys this information from wholesale drug distributors. As an executive at IMS Argentina told me, IMS provides only the "pure information"; it is up to the companies themselves to figure out what the data mean.

The practices of market strategists illustrate how a specific market is both constituted and transformed through the use of audit data. Information from IMS makes it possible to grasp the market as a kind of living entity evolving in unpredictable but measurable ways. With it the market's evolution becomes visible. Gabriela, product manager for a new antidepressant whose sales grew 33 percent in 2000, told me how strategists distinguish between markets according to therapeutic class. Pointing at the figures in the IMS binder, she explained: "Studying the market in the past, we deal with the sales statistics to see what specialties use our products, and seeing, for example the *evolution of the numbers* I was just talking about: *which are the markets that evolve most rapidly or which are the markets that are growing?* I have a general market that is shrinking and this market is growing; this one is attractive."

The IMS executive explained how to use the company's database of qualitative information gathered from interviews with panels of experts to plan a campaign: "So—I'm thinking of launching a tranquilizer. The first thing I'm going to do is enter [the database] by pathology, and what am I going to see? From my information, which products do doctors use, which brands, what do they associate it with, in what cases do they use them?" The market is that which directs strategy as well as that which strategists try to reshape. It can also be seen as a foe, an antagonist. Martín, CNS sales director at a multinational firm whose antidepressant is struggling in the overcrowded field, talked about how he uses audit information to design a market strategy: "First you analyze the market. . . . What volume it has, how it is evolving, who are the companies that participate, what percentage that company has in sales of its products in the market . . . this means: *whether I'm going to attack it, whether it's going to react or isn't going to react, how it's going to react*, what is the age of the products, what is the index of penetration of the new products that were launched onto the market, what differentiation do you have with what is already there, who are the doctors that prescribe the products in this market, how many there are."

### Integrated Control

An executive at Close Up, the Argentine firm that audits prescriptions, told me why IMS's data on territorial sales alone are not enough—one must also have individual doctors' prescription numbers: "It's sort of an integrated control. We don't claim that the pharmaceutical companies don't have to see the territorial sales, but they also have to see the prescriptions. [These] . . . have to be analyzed at the same time, to be able to have more coherent and more precise explanations of what is going on in the field." With a subscription to Close Up's databases, you can look up which doctors prescribed your products, which prescribed competitors', and how much each doctor prescribed. To get this information, Close Up buys or barters microfilmed copies of actual doctors' prescriptions from pharmacy chains. They claim to cover 18 million (out of an estimated 300 million yearly) prescriptions and to have profiles on the behavior of over ninety thousand physicians, including nearly two thousand psychiatrists in the city of Buenos Aires. Their data, in the hands of Lilly reps, had been the source of the journal editor's ire.

Close Up's promotional material advises: "Success, for a pharmaceutical company, depends on a primary factor: The physician's prescriptive behavior." How do pharmaceutical companies use these numbers to guide that behavior? The audit company's literature provides a rather sinister vision of government by surveillance targeted specifically at doctors. It seems to confirm recent analyses of audit cultures in terms of the prevalence of "technologies of mistrust" — means of monitoring and shaping behavior that otherwise cannot be checked (Power 1997; Strathern 2000). If you use Close Up, you will know "what the doctor does, not what he says he does." The company's "Audit Pharma" database can be loaded onto hand-held computers that sales reps consult while in the field. As one psychiatrist told me, "You feel like you're being watched by the CIA."

Why would doctors lie to the medical reps? To keep the gifts coming. The numbers give the reps a way to check whether or not the company's gifts are actually paying off. As Gabriela told me, "So if [the doctor] says, 'Why don't you pay for my trip to the APA because I'm prescribing a lot of this product,' [we check] to see if it's true or not . . . because the doctor can tell all the laboratories that he's prescribing a lot of every product." And thereby get a lot of trips. Sometimes this negotiation between the firm and the doctor is quite direct. The rep might say, "Doctor, if you get me twenty more prescriptions a month, I'll send you wherever you want to go." But usually it is more subtle — "How can I help you?" the rep asks.

### Territory Management

Doctors are not the only parties subject to audit surveillance. While detail men (reps) track doctors' behavior armed with knowledge of their actual prescription practices, sales managers monitor how their reps are doing. Gabriela pointed to another number in her IMS binder and explained: "This statistic shows the 'market share' of each visitor [rep] in each zone. So you know that you have a visitor in Santa Fe and you see the market share of each product in this zone, so you see how this visitor is doing in the zone. And you are doing what is called 'territory management,' you are seeing the profitability of each zone or how each visitor is doing."

This constant monitoring of sales performance colors the interactions of doctors and reps. Reps, who try to form relationships of "friendship" or at least mutual obligation with doctors, sometimes plead for help from doctors in raising their territorial sales figures. By keeping track of reps' performance, the audit becomes a reflexive technique for the firm, a way of directing intervention but also a means of self-modulation in a precarious market. Close Up claims that its service for measuring reps' productivity, called "Feedback," allows the sales manager to know exactly what is happening in the territories: "Measure the prescriptive productivity of each one of the representatives and their supervisors, through prescriptions captured from the visited doctors. Eliminate the deviations of productivity measurement according to territory [this is a dig at IMS]. An objective and valid measure of the results from promotion with visited doctors. Feedback is the only technical report that makes it possible to make precise decisions to identify market opportunities."

How well is a given campaign—of samples, information diffusion, symposia—going? The reflexive loop provided by the audit database allows for self-evaluation and transformation. As Martín said upon getting the disappointing results of his new campaign: "We thought we would grow 15 percent this year, and we're getting there, we're doing pretty well. But *one has to be permanently monitoring what's happening.*" The "market"—here, the accumulated prescribing decisions of Argentina's ninety thousand physicians—is a semicontrollable entity that one wants to act upon but which itself reacts—reinforcing successful decisions and throwing unsuccessful ones into question. The modulation is interactive—pharmaceutical marketers regulate doctors, but doctors, as a collectivity represented in the market's monthly evolution and the inevitable bell curve of any specific product's "life cycle"—shape the actions of marketers as well.

## Opinion Leaders

While directly surveying prescriptions helps to manage relations with prescription leaders, with whom one can make arrangements of exchange, a more subtle set of dynamics occurs with opinion leaders. Explicit negotiation and direct exchange are not typical qualities of the relationship between the opinion leader and the firm. In fact, it can be counterproductive to bring sales numbers into these relationships. Here the main technique is to develop trusting relationships. This task is not left to the reps in the field; it is the responsibility of the sales director or product manager. Audit numbers play a role in the process, but in a more complex way. Gabriela, who was CNS product manager at an upstart European firm, told me how the firm decides with whom to develop contacts: "We work with doctors with high prescriptive power, very prestigious doctors who can establish some trend in the use of psychopharmaceuticals, either because they have a lot of patients or because they are well known. . . . or they decide on purchases, for example in hospitals, or they participate in some important institution or in the psychiatric associations. So these doctors are those that enable us — through a good, fluid contact and relation — to get the message we need out to the doctors who follow his trends."

In the case of opinion leaders, it is a question not of monitoring prescriptions but of developing alliances — of having these respected figures available for seminars, symposia, the authorship of "scientific literature" to be disseminated. The role of the opinion leader is something like a brand spokesman — although you will see opinion leaders allied with multiple firms. There is a hierarchy of opinion leaders, and of firms. Market strategists know as well as anyone who the key players in the field are — and in fact can play a major role in making them opinion leaders. It is a reciprocal relationship: companies ally themselves with experts who command respect and have the trust of other doctors, and the experts reaffirm their authority and disseminate their knowledge through their relationship with pharmaceutical firms — such as one well-respected leader whose book on "practical psychopharmacology" was sponsored by Organon and introduced by the head of Pharmacology at the University of Buenos Aires. Another technique for forging ties with opinion leaders is to offer them a "Phase IV" clinical trial — a marketing-oriented trial of an already approved medication, whose results are pretty much known beforehand. The ostensible study results in a poster presented at an international scientific congress, with travel expenses paid for by the company. For young doctors, this is one way to begin to appear in circuits of expertise as an emerging opinion leader. In Argentina such opportunities for circulation at the international level are rare.

Firms must tread lightly with opinion leaders. A veteran strategist told me that if he is putting on an event, he makes sure to invite all the most important opinion leaders. If you leave someone out, they will be upset and won't prescribe your product. The opinion leaders are very sensitive, he said: "They want to feel important." In this respect multinational firms have an advantage given their ability to link local opinion leaders to their transnational networks of prestigious experts. Companies strive to develop a reputation for taking good care of their opinion leaders. Gabriela, the product manager, said of her company's efforts at conferences: "If there is something that distinguishes us it's that we don't make huge investments of money but we do make high-quality investments, we are with them all the time; it's not that we invite them and then they go alone. *We are very careful with the relationship of the doctor with the laboratory*, because we don't have such a big [sales] force." And the psychiatrists care about how they are treated. At an editorial meeting of the psychiatry journal mentioned above, two members of the editorial board talked about their upcoming trip to the APA meetings in Washington, D.C. The younger of the two was going early to attend a Lilly course on antipsychotics and depression. "Oh, it's marvelous," enthused the more experienced one, "you're going to love it, and they look after you so well."[14]

Opinion leaders will tell you that they never endorse a specific product and accept offers only from reputable companies whose products they believe in. The reputation of the firm then becomes a means of ethical self-regulation. In other words, firms that wish to ally with prestigious opinion leaders must maintain a reputation for propriety: they do not give out samples ("like the others do"); they provide access to information, sponsor studies, help patients. A former Janssen marketing director described a campaign he ran for Risperdal that won a prize from an international patient organization. Its theme was "reinsertion"—an attempt to go beyond medication to resocialization. Ten patients from a schizophrenic patient support group were hired at Janssen for short periods to do simple tasks like photocopying; they were paid small salaries and then received scholarships for training and certificates confirming their work experience. The program showed that these patients needed less medication and had fewer relapses—that they could be successfully "reinserted." More than being directly about sales, the marketing director said, the campaign was about shaping the image of the company as one that was interested in the "quality of life" of patients.

## Local Knowledge

The Risperdal campaign was ingenious in its awareness of the importance of questions such as social reintegration to the epistemic milieu that it targeted: Argentine mental health. Psychiatry is distinctive from other fields in biomedicine in the multiple forms of expertise that coexist within it, each of which has a distinct model of the cause, site, and optimal modes of treatment of mental disorder. While in the United States psychiatry has recently shifted toward a "neuroscientific" approach that locates illness in the brain of the patient, in Argentina social and psychoanalytic explanations remain predominant. This poses a challenge for pharmaceutical marketers accustomed to campaigning in terms of serotonin levels and synaptic receptors. How, for example, might one appeal to former activists like the journal editor, a staunch critic of globalization who associates neuroscientific psychiatry and the extension of DSM-IV with American imperialism, and who says of neoliberal policies more generally that "in the same way that they open the market to foreign products and liquidate the state, they liquidate the forms of hospital care, the training criteria, training institutions, and the public university as the center of knowledge production."

Here we can distinguish between the kinds of knowledge about the market that strategists gather. One is quantitative and gridlike; it evolves, displays trends, and provides a long-term picture of the market—this is what IMS and Close Up provide. The other form of knowledge is local, qualitative, picked up gradually through interactions with doctors. It shows an awareness of the ethos of the market. This distinction might help answer the question of why Gador's generic fluoxetine was the leading antidepressant in 1998 while Lilly's Prozac remained far behind. The sales director of CNS disorders for Gador, a longtime veteran of marketing psychiatric medications, is something of a legend in the field. In an interview he told me that audit data are necessary only if one does not already know the market—"they are orienters, but they are not [so] important. . . . We don't apply some of the tools that other companies do because our strength, in the case of the sales force, is very different; this is a totally atypical company." In what sense? "In the average seniority of our men . . . in each of their zones . . . our man has a lot of stability and is someone who inspires trust."

Given his knowledge of the terrain, he intuited that lock-and-key illustrations of neurotransmitter reuptake inhibition might not be the most effective technique for pitching psychopharmaceuticals to Argentine psychiatrists. In the late 1990s a critical social psychiatry actually became the basis for Gador's marketing campaign, which used globalization and the anxieties it provoked to promote the company's large anxiolytic and antidepressant line. One ad featured a series of grim figures traversing a map of the world and suffering from symptoms of globalization: "deterioration of interpersonal relations," "deterioration in daily performance," "unpredictable demands and threats," "personal and familial suffering," "loss of social role," "loss of productivity." Gador's explicit use of pharmaceuticals as a means to alleviate social suffering indicates how medication can operate in distinctive ways according to its milieu of use.[15]

I asked him how he came up with the "Globalization" campaign. "For as long as Gador has been putting together molecules," he answered, "the work has been, in some way, to establish clearly the niches to which each one of these molecules is directed and, in this sense, globalization as a cultural concept—it is too strong not to use it." He told me about the next phase of the campaign: "Right now we are in a later stage; we realized that the medical audience and even the users are absolutely conscious that globalization brings all these problems and we are in a campaign that is in the next stage: . . . *vulnerability*." Martín, envious of Gador's success, noted the cleverness of this word choice, pointing out its resonance with a popular television series called *Los Vulnerables* about an eclectic group of patients involved in group therapy. The Vulnerability campaign was kicked off by a symposium in October 2000 called "Stress, Anxiety, and Depression: A Progressive Clinical Sequence," at which a number of important local opinion leaders spoke. Among the organizers of the symposium was the journal editor: Gador had succeeded where Lilly had failed—by approaching the opinion leader on his own terrain.

## High Contact

How do the relations described above operate to manage doctors' prescribing behavior? The recent shift from anxiolytic (or tranquilizer) sales to antidepressant sales in Argentina provides a glimpse into the work of transforming a market. But it is a complex story that intersects with recent events in Argentine political and economic life. I began this chapter by asking how to explain a dramatic rise in antidepressant sales revenue over the past few years. While the Argentine pharmaceutical market as a whole shrank over the years of hyper-recession between 1998 and 2001, income from antidepressant sales jumped: 16.5 percent from June 2000 to June 2001 alone.[16]

I asked market strategists and database managers why they thought antidepressant sales were rising so much while the rest of the industry was in recession. The Close Up executive suggested a couple of reasons: on the one hand, older anxiolytics were losing market share to antidepressants; but also, a tremendous increase in panic attacks, especially in Buenos Aires, was driving up antidepressant sales. Why were there more panic attacks? He answered: "Because there is a totally confusing situation in this country . . . a very stressful situation; there's a huge amount of unemployment, there's underemployment, and on the other hand we Argentines are in a dead end. It seems like we don't have or *we can't find the way out.* . . . *You're an anthropologist, you understand well.* Problems of social relations are being added to personal problems."

The overwhelming sense of insecurity linked to the ongoing economic crisis was generally the first answer members of the pharmaceutical industry gave to the question of why antidepressant sales were increasing. When I asked the IMS executive in his Puerto Madero office, he said: "You've been here for a month. You must know by now . . . the socioeconomic situation and the politics of the country make it so that people are consuming more anxiolytics all the time and are going to the psychiatrist more all the time. . . . Imagine a man who works, who has . . . who had a decent quality of life and has an income around a thousand or twelve hundred dollars a month. A few years ago he could live on this, now it's not enough to live on, so he becomes anxious. Don't forget that everyone in Argentina, everyone, has a tremendous fear of being left without work."

In August 2001, announcements of "Anxiety Disorders Week," an information campaign designed to bring patients to hospitals where they could consult with experts, appeared in a number of Buenos Aires newspapers. "One of every four Argentines suffers from them," one article proclaimed: "panic attacks, phobias. Specialists say that they are increasing; factors such as insecurity or incertitude with respect to the future can influence them" (Cecchi 2001). The reference to uncertainty and insecurity was apt: the country was entering its fourth year of recession, the unemployment rate had reached 20 percent, the widely tracked index of *riesgo-país* (country-risk) was spiking to record levels each day. And the campaign was successful beyond the expectations of its sponsors: the city's hospitals were inundated with patients complaining of symptoms of stress. The articles did not mention that the campaign had been co-sponsored by the domestic pharmaceutical firm Bago, makers of the alprazolam brand Tranquinil. Since in Argentina it is still against the law to market a drug directly to the general public, an alternative is to "grow the market" by making general practitioners and patients more aware of the illness the drug is supposed to treat. In an article that appeared two months later in the daily *Clarín* on the role of the growing economic crisis in increasing tranquilizer sales, a Bago sales manager reported that August had been a month of record sales for Tranquinil. The piece was subtitled "Illnesses Brought on by the Crisis Are Increasing Medical Visits and Anxiolytic Use."[17] What might have been seen as evidence of the success of the Bago information campaign was instead cited as a sign of the nation's social and psychic crisis.

In the months that followed, as the crisis in Argentina reached its zenith with the fall of two presidents and a record default on the $132 billion national debt, the apparent increase in psychopharmaceutical sales became a subject of increasing interest to the press. A Spanish-language *BBC Online* article from late January 2002 cited reports from the pharmaceutical industry that while overall sales had decreased 10 percent in the previous year, antidepressant sales had increased 13 percent and tranquilizer sales 4 percent.[18] The *Observer* cited similar statistics in a piece called "Argentina hits rock bottom," again linking the crisis to increased symptoms of anxiety and increased suicide rates (Arie 2001). Audit numbers extended their use here. Not only did they provide a map for strategists' efforts to regulate doctors' prescribing practices, they could also serve as evidence of effects of the crisis on the mental health conditions of the population. After mentioning an increase in stress-related medical visits in the wake of the crisis, the BBC article quoted an Argentine psychiatrist: "Argentines feel devalued. People feel lost. The rules of the game have changed. Working hard for many hours doesn't mean economic security any more."[19]

It was not clear, however, whether the primary cause of the dramatic change in the psychopharmaceuticals market was the crisis or the promotional strategies that harnessed its effects. These articles at first seem to provide evidence of the medicalization of social disorder in a time of crisis, but it is important to differentiate between actual data on transformations of the market and the stories that were being told about this data.

While mass media attention to psychopharmaceutical consumption seemed to increase toward the end of 2001, it was not a wholly new phenomenon. In 1996 — at the height of the mid-1990s economic boom in Argentina — a piece called "The ranking of remedies" appeared in *La Nación* (Palomar 1996). In it, the president of the Argentine Federation of Pharmacies tied the consumption of psychopharmaceuticals to social conditions: "Perhaps what is most notable is the boom of the antidepressants, whose massive consumption took off in our society at the beginning of the seventies. And not by chance. . . . Of the five products most sold annually in our country, one is an antibiotic and the rest are a faithful reflection of the two great maladies of our time: stress and *nervios.*" More pharmaceutical industry representatives added their interpretations: "Who isn't *nervioso* in Argentina today?" asked the executive director of the CAEME, the council of multinational laboratories. The president of the College of Pharmacists gave a sociological reading of the sales data: "Life conditions are getting worse . . . and we live in a permanent state of alteration. In 1994 alone more than 16 million boxes of psychotropics were sold."

Such social analyses of psychopharmaceutical sales patterns were common among market strategists. A veteran of the industry told me his theory of the relation of social change to drug consumption: "In the seventies you had the cold war, and a heightened sense of tension and nervousness—so Valium sold well. Then in the eighties with the phenomenon of the yuppies and their emphasis on career success, the drugs of choice were anxiolytics. In the nineties antidepressants became popular, for two reasons: first there were those who had failed to meet their expectations in the eighties and so they were depressed. But pharmaceutical marketing strategies also had to do with it."

To analyze increased psychopharmaceutical sales as an instance of the medicalization of suffering seemed somehow redundant in this context: it was a part of assumed knowledge that increased symptoms of anxiety and depression were linked to social and political phenomena. So much so that the very salience of social accounts of suffering served not as a *critique* of the role of pharmaceutical marketing but as its *basis*, as we saw in the case of the Gador Globalization and Vulnerability campaigns. The Gador campaigns had captured a more generally prevalent explanatory model of mental disorder as grounded in the social.[20] Even CNS product managers did not have a neuroscientific model of mental illness. Thus Martín, discussing the question of the sources of depression, protested the predominance of psychoanalytic explanations in Argentina—in favor of a social one. He could have been describing one of the figures on Gador's *globalización* map: "It's not necessarily the case that the current modification, which is the cause of the depression, has its origin in what happened to me during my infancy. It's very likely that this marks us, but also the context and this sense of feeling ever more vulnerable before change. . . . The world is changing very fast, too fast for all of us. Today I was talking with someone about this issue and how we're *stuck* now—the deficit, the default or not, devaluation or not, it's such an uncertain horizon."

Media pundits, sales directors, and database firm executives agreed: insecurity linked to the economic crisis was driving up psychopharmaceutical sales. But in fact it was not clear that actual consumption had changed significantly. Martín told me: "The quantity of patients treated with antidepressants hasn't increased that much; what has changed is the average price of antidepressants."

This would make sense given the pattern in the early 1990s in the rest of the pharmaceutical market—an increase in revenue generated not by an increase in consumption but by the use of newer, more expensive drugs. In this case the explanation for increasing antidepressant sales could be a gradual switch, among nonspecialists, from anxiolytics—still used far more than antidepressants—to the new SSRIS.

In fact, Martín thought that the market was still relatively untapped. "I think it's the tip of the iceberg, what we have today. Today the antidepressant market, even though as you said it's growing, I think that the potential is easily ten times more than what it is now." How did he know this potential since there were no data available on the prevalence of depression in Argentina? He used transnational epidemiology, combining it with audit data: "If you take the index of the prevalence of depression in any country in the world, which is around—let's take a conservative number, 3 percent—you would be talking about a million or so people. . . . In reality that would be pure depression, but if you begin to take the different types of depression, dysthemia, we're talking about three million people, more or less. And *today you have treated patients, 350,000, more or less*." I was impressed by the number—not because it was low, or because it was right, but because I hadn't been able to get even an estimate from anyone before—not from the health ministry (which did not have such data) or the database firms (which would not give them away) or health insurance managers.

Martín's argument that higher prices more than the actual number of patients treated were driving up sales revenue was substantiated by a study I initiated—given the paucity of other available data—with a group of pharmaco-epidemiologists affiliated with a Pharmacy Benefits Management (PBM) firm in Buenos Aires and the University of Belgrano. The study compared the pattern of anxiolytic (tranquilizer) and antidepressant use over the period from 1997 to 2000 among members of four separate health plans comprising a population of about 600,000 people (Gattari et al. n.d.). It turned out that over this period there was a sharp *decline* in anxiolytic exposure, from 21 to 14 percent, and a slight increase in antidepressant exposure, from 3.6 to 4.5 percent of affiliates. These results are striking in comparison with the steep rise in psychopharmaceutical sales revenue cited by the media as evidence of the effect of the economic crisis on the population's mental well-being. They are confirmed by data obtained from the IMS on changes in psychopharmaceutical unit sales volume in Argentina over the last five years, which indicate that overall anxiolytic unit sales declined by 5 percent between 1997 and 2001 while antidepressant unit sales increased by 9 percent.[21] While the gap was narrowing, anxiolytics were still sold at nearly six times the rate of antidepressants. In other words, the increase in the use of antidepressants was offset by a decline in the use of anxiolytics.

If we add to the results of this study another piece of illicitly obtained information we can be more precise about what was happening in the market: it turned out that the impressive growth in antidepressant sales revenue between December 1998 and June 2001—from $45 million per year to $54 million per year (20 percent)—could be mostly accounted for by sales of Paxil and Zoloft, which leapfrogged Gador's Foxetin to become the market leaders.[22] This was due to "high contact" between the companies' sales reps and doctors, and to the enviable position of these drugs over this period within the product life cycle. Thus GlaxoSmithKline and Pfizer had apparently been successful in getting generalists to switch from anxiolytics to their SSRIs—which were now indicated for anxiety disorders as well as for depression.

Rather than a precipitous increase in overall psychopharmaceutical consumption due to the economic crisis, the increase in antidepressant revenue can best be explained in terms of a specific tactic: the work by sales reps and opinion leaders to convince doctors to prescribe the newer SSRIs instead of tranquilizers for symptoms of stress, anxiety, and depression. It is worth noting that such a shift is in accord with the recommendations of leading health authorities, who have expressed alarm at high rates of anxiolytic use (often tied to addiction and self-medication) in countries such as France and Argentina. In other words, "high contact"—the intensification of relations between pharmaceutical companies and doctors—worked in this case to shape prescription habits more or less along the lines that officially sanctioned expertise would authorize. It does not make sense, then, to speak of the contamination of pure science by the kind of illicit pharmaceutical relations I have described. Rather, these relations are part of a larger structure of interested knowledge that links marketing to science at the deepest levels of the biomedical economy.

## Notes

The research for this essay was made possible through the generous assistance of the Crichton Fund, Department of Social Medicine, Harvard Medical School. I would like to thank Arthur Kleinman for his support and encouragement of this project. I am also grateful to Jean Comaroff, Byron Good, Mary Jo Good, and Susan Reynolds Whyte for their comments and suggestions on an earlier version.
1. Deleuze, "Post-script on Control Societies," in *Negotiations* (1995); for a wide-ranging description of the experiential implications of new forms of global capital, see Comaroff and Comaroff 2000.
2. For the description of the practice of denunciation as the uncovering of impurity within regimes of action, see Boltanski and Thevenot 1991. Paul Rabinow (2003) shows that as early as Pascal's plan to sell transportation infrastructure to the Parisian bourgeoisie, truth seeking has coexisted with enterprise. On the "impurities" that patient activism introduced to clinical research into HIV/AIDS, see Epstein 1996.
3. Martin Hopenhayn (2001) provides a lucid account of this process from the perspective of Latin American intellectuals and policymakers.
4. Despite the extremity of its reform measures, the Argentine state was not completely stripped away. In fact, per capita spending on health (40 percent of which is public funds) increased from 1990 to 1999 by 50 percent and in 2000 was 10 percent of the GDP. In 1999, about one quarter of the health budget was spent on pharmaceuticals — $6 billion. Per capita health spending went from $827 to $1,291 in this period according to the World Bank's standardized units of calculation. See World Health Organization 2001a. In 2000 the Argentine GDP was $285 billion.
5. The brief submitted by the lobbying group PhRMA claimed, as part of the U.S. case against Argentina that appeared before the WTO, that "Argentina is widely recognized as the worst expropriator of U.S. pharmaceutical inventions in the Western Hemisphere, as local firms dominate over 50 percent of the pharmaceutical market currently estimated at almost U.S. $4.1 billion. Substantial and continuing loss of market share, in the range of hundreds of millions of dollars, is directly attributable to Argentina's defective intellectual property regime."
6. Here I am following the critique of a decontextualized bioethics discourse raised in Kleinman et al. 1999 ("Bioethics and Beyond"). Jeremy Greene's ongoing research into the history of the detail man in the United States has been very helpful in my thinking about the forms of relation at play between doctors and the pharmaceutical industry.
7. In *A Social History of Truth*, Steven Shapin (1994) shows that relations of trust and socially sanctioned authority have underpinned scientific knowledge from the earliest moments of what came to be known as the Scientific Revolution.
8. Fundación ISALUD 1999. Data on the number of reps comes from the union of *agentes de propaganda médica* (APMs). Their website, which features a suitcase-bearing rep, can be found at http://www.apm.org.ar.
9. IMS Health, December 1998.

10. As the Pan American Health Organization reports of Argentina, "information on the prevalence of mental illness is very scant" (Pan American Health Organization 1998). As for spending, in its "Atlas" of global mental health, the World Health Organization notes of Argentina: "Details about expenditure on mental health are not available" (World Health Organization 2001a:148).

11. Ian Hacking describes the "avalanche of printed numbers" produced by nation-states beginning in the Napoleonic era in *The Taming of Chance* (1990).

12. For the history of the use of "territory" measures in sales management, see Spears 1995.

13. I describe this dynamic in more detail in *Pharmaceutical Reason* (Lakoff 2005).

14. The course was part of Lilly's efforts to promote Zyprexa as Prozac went off patent.

15. Van der Geest et al. (1996:166) make this point in their important survey of the anthropology of pharmaceuticals: "Pharmaceuticals are often recast in another knowledge system and used very differently from the way they were intended in the 'regime of value' where they were produced."

16. IMS Health.

17. "El Consumo de Tranquilizantes creció entre un 8 y un 9 por ciento" (*Clarín*, 3 October 2001). The article also cites IMS figures: "the total sales of prescription medications declined in the last year by 5.63 percent. But this number isn't the same for all remedies. The sales of anxiolytics grew 3.86 percent and that for heart ailments grew 1.31 percent. The data does not seem coincidental."

18. "Los Argentinos se sienten devaluados" (*BBC Online*, 24 January 2002).

19. "Devaluation" here referred to the uncoupling of the dollar-peso peg, which for ten years had provided Argentines with a tenuous sense of economic security while at the same time hampering the government's capacity for macroeconomic intervention to promote growth.

20. For the concept of explanatory models in psychiatry, see Kleinman 1988.

21. I am very grateful to Nikolas Rose for obtaining and sharing this most valuable data.

22. Unofficial data: over the two-and-a-half-year period Paxil sales revenue had gone from an annual $6.2 million to $11.5 million. Unit sales of Paxil and Zoloft also increased markedly.

# Addiction Markets
## The Case of High-Dose Buprenorphine in France

ANNE M. LOVELL

In 1996, France became the first nation to introduce buprenorphine, a synthetic opiate, as the major modality for the long-term treatment of problem opiate use. In a novel setup, the national commission on medicine authorized high-dose buprenorphine (HDB) as a medicine that could be prescribed in general medical practice—an almost unheard-of practice for a treatment usually provided in highly regulated specialized centers or hospitals. Currently, HDB dominates treatment for heroin dependency and problem heroin use in France, although medicalized treatment of heroin users in other Western countries primarily involves methadone.[1] Yet until the mid-1990s, the notion of a pharmaceutical drug to treat addiction met vehement opposition in France. How did an addiction pharmaceutical come to be marketed there, and to constitute the main source of revenues in that country for a major pharmaceutical multinational?[2]

During that same year, 1996, drug users in Indian cities like Calcutta, Chandigarh, and Chennai, their heroin supplies cut off by the Tamil rebellion, shifted to injecting buprenorphine sold commercially for the treatment of severe pain (Kumar et al. 1998). And across the Indian border, drug users in

Nepalese cities like Pokhara and Kathmandu consumed buprenorphine purchased in India (Dixon 1999). But except for occasional experimental use for withdrawal, buprenorphine remained outside the realm of treatment for opiate addiction.

To analyze addiction pharmaceuticals in a global context, one must examine two addiction markets simultaneously. The status of an opiate antagonist and partial agonist like HDB changes as it travels from one market to the other. In the doctor's office or hospital, it may be a full-fledged medication (to alleviate pain or to treat opiate dependency), or merely a chemical tool, a commodity or gift in the form of samples from the pharmaceutical company's *visiteur médical*. As it moves along the networks constituted through everyday drug use, the addiction pharmaceutical changes into an object of desire and danger, and into a commodity of another type, loosened from formal market regulations and state control and bound up in flows outside the pharma sector. As I will suggest shortly, these two markets are necessarily intertwined.

## Addiction Markets and the Particularity of Addiction Pharmaceuticals

The pharmaceuticals market is one of the most profitable sectors in the global economy. The movement from development (whether biopirating, lab experimentation, or testing) through marketing, acquisition, and consumption of pharmaceutical products, however, involves various relationships to numerous local situations, practices, and actors. The trail of buprenorphine used in addiction treatment delineates particular global-local configurations, particularly compared with other pharmaceuticals, including the psychotropic medications with which it is sometimes classed.[3]

Using the example of France, I will examine where and how a global industry that produces pharmaceuticals for addiction medicine intersects with local practices and illness etiologies, preexisting concerns, and dispositions. A different side of globalization creates the demand for addiction pharmaceuticals or justifies their existence: the illegal flows of drugs, one of the largest markets globally and one that mimics in many ways the economic logic and organizational structures of multinational corporations. Wars, economic development and economic crises, institutionalized forms of inequality, drug enforcement policies, and government health and welfare policies both halt and hasten the flow of opiates from world region to world region, affecting local drug consumption practices and health, and hence the justification for one type of addiction treatment instead of another.

These two global addiction markets are joined through the process of pharmaceutical leakage, the movement of an addiction pharmaceutical from the site that legitimizes it (the treatment context, in which its commodity status is downplayed before its status as a pharmaceutical tool or a medicine; see below) to an informal, illicit network (the drug economy, where it morphs into a symbolically charged "dirty" commodity that escapes market and state regulatory mechanisms). Through this process the pharmaceutical object transforms itself from one type of commodity into another one of a radically different rationality and symbolic nature, yet one not normally discussed in the "social lives" of pharmaceuticals.[4] In keeping with the biographical metaphor, I would suggest that pharmaceutical leakage and diversion mark the *secret life* of addiction pharmaceuticals.

The history of buprenorphine, like that of psychotropics more generally, is a narrative of effects in search of an application. Buprenorphine is a synthetic molecule derived from one of the active alkaloids in opium; it blocks two of the three opioid receptors in the brain, the kappa and mu receptors, hence deactivating the effect of other opiates such as heroin. As a partial agonist, it has a ceiling effect; that is, an increase in dose increases effects only up to a finite level. Thus, unlike heroin, it is less addictive and less likely to depress the respiratory system (a major safety issue with opiates). It is considered less toxic and less likely to cause mortality from overdose (unless combined with benzodiazepines and/or alcohol) than full antagonists like methadone.

Like methadone, buprenorphine was originally developed as an analgesic and was used as such before it was recognized as potentially useful in the treatment of addiction.[5] But like all pharmaceuticals used to treat opiate addiction or alcoholism, it presents the paradox of being applicable to a large potential patient population but having only a small potential market. For example, persons diagnosed as dependent or as problem drug or alcohol users are over four times as numerous as persons diagnosed with schizophrenia.[6] And within the neuroscientific paradigm that currently serves as the basis for developing psychotropic medications, addiction is better understood than depression or schizophrenia (LaPiazza 2002). Yet, sales of all antiaddiction drugs are much smaller than those of even a single drug for schizophrenia.[7] A high dropout rate from clinical trials and the social stigma associated with the figure of the addict are cited as reasons why the pharmaceutical industry prefers to keep away from addiction medicine.[8] At the same time, once identified as a synthetic opiate, a drug may be difficult to market for uses other than drug treatment or pain control, as may have been the case when buprenorphine was recognized as possibly useful in treating drug-refractory depression.[9]

Interestingly, buprenorphine in the form commercialized in France (buprenorphine hydrochloride, or Subutex) is designated an orphan drug (Center for Drug Evaluation and Research 2002) although it does not meet the criteria for this status: the U.S. Department of Health and Human Services reports a "currently untapped population of at least 610,000 people with untreated or under-treated opioid problems."[10] In practical terms, this means that the pharmaceutical company receives direct and indirect government subsidies and other incentives for developing it: seven-year marketing exclusivity, tax credit for the product-associated clinical research, research design assistance from the FDA, and grants of up to $200,000 per year. Such government-sponsored inducements indicate not so much the rarity of the disease (opiate abuse is not rare) but the disincentives from a market perspective for developing it. The particularities of addiction pharmaceuticals suggest why a European country like France might become a stake in the development of such a product. Hence, while HBD constituted only about 6 percent of total global revenues for Schering-Plough when Subutex was its best-selling product in France, the French experience with commercializing HDB through private, general health-care delivery generated symbolic capital and either a model or a trial-by-error experiment for future addiction pharmaceutical markets.

In this chapter I will show how the marketing of buprenorphine required not only the collaboration of the pharmaceutical industry and local actors, but also a shift in the way problem heroin use was conceptualized. While the introduction of high-dose buprenorphine has shaped the way the French think about and treat problem heroin use as an illness, certain transformations were necessary before that could happen: the conceptual and practical shift from toxicomania to addiction; the embeddedness of toxicomania addiction treatment within a social-medical framework of harm reduction; and the travel of buprenorphine, before and after the commercialization of HDB, through the everyday "pharmaco-associative" practices of drug users. Then I will show how the French experience has been reinterpreted to promote the same pharmaceutical product in the United States in an inversion of the position each country originally held in relation to the other in addiction medicine.

## Before Addiction

Until the mid-1990s, addictive drugs did not exist "in and of themselves" in France (Bergeron 2001). Drugs — synthetic or natural substances compulsively consumed — constituted a particular kind of illness. To understand this we must trace the ways in which drugs and problematic drug consumption were — and to a great extent still are — conceptualized in contemporary France. At least three movements constitute this history: the development of a specialized sector for drug treatment, the centralization of regulation and management of this sector, and the dichotomization of drug treatment into a dominant psycho-analytically oriented approach and a secondary somatic one.

The preferred designation for problematic drug use in French is a late-nineteenth-century psychiatric category, toxicomania (*toxicomanie*). The two national drug agencies, MILDT and OFDT (respectively, the Interministerial Mission to Fight Drugs and Toxicomania and the National Observatory on Drugs and Toxicomania),[11] designate their mission by that term, and it is still used by drug users, healthcare providers, and policymakers. Even neuroscientists are prone to slippage between *addiction* and *toxicomanie*.

The attribution of the suffix -*mania* to the name of a mind-altering substance first appeared in French medical writings in 1885. It refers to a "modality" (the use of the intoxicating substance: morphine in morphinomania, opium in opiomania, etc.) in response to an underlying illness, the "more or less irresistible" need for artificial excitement, for sensations that range from simple euphoria to dreams, hallucinations, and "artificial paradises." The term *mania* implies at once mental aberration and obsessive passion (Yvorel 1992).

The term has long resisted attempts to replace it (for example, with the DSM language of "substance abuse" or with the category "addiction" more common to contemporary neurosciences).[12] The reason lies less in the original positive meaning of *toxicomania*, which is largely forgotten, than in the assumption that alternate terms imply a biological model.[13] In contemporary France, drug treatment emerged as a particularly French specialty, in opposition to biologically based treatments.

While problematic drug users had long been treated in psychiatric hospitals, only in 1970 did drugs emerge as a felt social problem. It entered the public sphere through the dramatization of heroin (the widely publicized death of a young woman from an overdose in the hip resort of Saint-Tropez; see Lovell 1993). The "Law of 1970" that resulted from the public outcry reformed earlier legislation from the turn of the century. The new legislation continued the criminalization of drug use (though broadening the criteria from use in public to any use) but also added a new option: court-ordered treatment instead of imprisonment (Lovell 1993). However, most drug users whom service providers encountered in those first fervent years were not *héroïnomanes*, but "soft" drug users, middle-class citizens or temporary dropouts.

The first drug treatment services emerged in the wake of the post–May 1968 "libertarian ethic" (Bergeron 1999).[14] Influenced by French antipsychiatry, radical Lacanianism, the new political and countercultural values of May 1968 (Lovell 1980), and public intellectuals like Michel Foucault, the social workers and psychiatrists who set up these street outreach and drop-in centers for drug users mistrusted much drug treatment, considering it an instrument of medical oppression or the normalization of forms of deviancy that threatened public order. They opposed medicalized approaches, whether with psychotropic medication or methadone, as simply another form of social control. Like radical Lacanianism, and following the more general tenets of psychoanalysis dominant in France at the time (Turkle 1978), the early drug treatment movement focused on the "subject who hides behind the drug." Treatment providers, they claimed, should aim to restore to the subject the freedom to cure him- or herself.

By the 1980s, this social movement had crystallized into a highly professionalized sector. The loosely defined treatment approaches, characterized largely by street work, short-lived encounters, the staff's "good intentions," and empathy with the *toxicomanes* (using drugs together was not unheard of), gave way to longer-term, one-on-one treatment provided at specialized drug treatment centers (CSSTs), codified treatment techniques based on psychoanalytic tenets, and a professional society, the ANIT (the Association Nationale d'Intervenants en Toxicomanie). The romantic rebel was replaced by the toxicomane patient, spontaneous interventions by psychoanalytic knowledge production about toxicomania. Drug dependence was acknowledged as the real problem, abstinence as the treatment goal, and psychoanalytical psychotherapy as the ideal modality. While addiction does appear as a category at this time, it provides only one theoretical approach. Most of the specialized drug treatment sector understood the compulsion to use drugs as the symptom of an underlying psychopathological structure rooted in childhood trauma. Drug abuse could be likened to any other defense mechanism. The toxicomane was normalized and destigmatized by being redefined as neurotic (or, more rarely, psychotic). This view allowed the libertarian ethic of the post-1968 social movement to survive by giving the toxicomane the same status as other "sufferers" (suicidals, anorexics, etc.), whose freely expressed demand for treatment was the only guarantee against the pressures of the outside world (Bergeron 1999). Thus, until the introduction of high-dose buprenorphine in 1996, drug treatment in France was dominated by psychiatry and psychology.

### The Slow Uptake of Medicalized Treatment

Two alternative approaches, widely diffused in North America, Great Britain, and, later, other parts of Europe, existed at the time. Both — the therapeutic community and methadone substitution — were rejected, often with vehemence, by the French specialized drug treatment sector. The reasons for this rejection lie in the structure and ideology of the French public health sector and, one might hypothesize, in the professional interests of the drug treatment sector service providers.

Alongside professionalization, the drug treatment sector was consolidated through the establishment of a toxicomania bureau in the national General

Health Department (DGS) of the Ministry of Health. (Drug treatment policy, like that for all epidemics, was the mandate of the French state rather than of local or regional government.)[15] In fact, these were coterminous processes, as major professionals from the sector were named to the bureau. Centralized management of the entire drug treatment sector based on a single model, the CSST, replaced local experimentation. In the years that followed, innovations designed in response to the changing population of toxicomanes were rejected, as was local control of the drug treatment issue. Thus the DGS essentially rejected any projects other than the by-then-familiar CSST.

Nor was the drug treatment sector open to these alternatives. With one exception, therapeutic communities were not tolerated.[16] French psychiatrists, after visiting Synanon, Phoenix House, and similar "ideal small societies" in the United States, criticized their behavioral conditioning and authoritarian, prisonlike social organization. And just as years earlier Jacques Lacan had lambasted American ego-psychology as part of a psychological Marshall Plan, French psychiatrists and psychologists criticized methadone as uncritical American pragmatism. Methadone not only depended on a biological explanation of opiate dependency as a metabolic deficiency in the endorphin system due to long-term use of external morphine substances, it also replaced one drug with another. Major figures among treatment providers considered methadone a form of social control preventing critical reflection on the relationship of the subject to the chemotherapeutic object.[17] Dependence on a drug that would do the work for the patient also flew in the face of a cultural stance toward pain management. French physicians had refused for many years to treat pain adequately, often well below WHO standards for diseases like cancer, until the legitimization of pain management in French medicine (see Baszanger 1995).[18]

Given the widespread use of methadone in drug treatment in other countries, the Ministry of Health did eventually fund two research teams, both in Paris, to test the substance on héroïnomanes. Contrary to both the libertarian ethic and the characteristics of methadone à l'Américaine, the French experimental patients were under strict surveillance and highly selected. Only those who had been heavy heroin users for at least five years and had unsuccessfully tried every other available treatment were eligible. In her comparison of two emblematic clinical trials of methadone—Dole's and Nyswander's in New York and the one at St. Anne's Hospital in Paris—Gomart argues that in the latter trial, methadone came to be conceived of not as a *medication* for treating addiction, but rather a *tool* that allowed the clinician to determine whether the "apathy" of the drug user was indeed a symptom of a psychiatric diagnosis or defective personality or the temporary effect of long-term narcotic use (Gomart 2002). Methadone, that is, was administered for only a short period. If, at the end of it, the patient still showed a compulsion to use drugs, then there was an underlying pathological psychic structure that had to be addressed.[19]

For fifteen years both French centers remained isolated from the mainstream drug treatment sector, which was reluctant to use any medication, and neither center ever held more than twenty patient beds at any one time. The Pelletier Report mandated by President Valéry Giscard d'Estaing in 1978 decreed the experiment a failure while legitimizing the French psychotherapeutic model.[20] The centers continued to operate. The center researchers themselves never really pushed their modality (Bergeron 1998). But they rejected "American methadone" as a biological modality for a nonbiological illness and as a mass-produced, sloppily administered treatment that resulted in diversion of methadone to street use (Gomart 2002).

### The Local Invention of Substitution Treatment

The missing pieces in this analysis of the pre-buprenorphine era are the general practitioners. The irony of buprenorphine is that the drug existed as an object of pharmaceutical leakage long before it was first marketed as a treatment for drug addiction in France in 1996. In fact, buprenorphine for substitution treatment was "invented" by drug users and their primary care physicians.[21]

Along with the professionalization of the drug treatment sector came segmentation of service providers into essentially two groups: the new "psy" specialists (psychologists, psychiatrists, social workers in the CSSTs) and the increasingly isolated general practitioners (GPs). Psychologization of problematic drug use had limited the role of the nonpsychiatric physician to either supervision of the center or somatic treatment of drug-related and other conditions. Many retreated into their free-standing medical offices. But their role was not contradictory to psychoanalytically oriented treatment, for the psy specialists saw themselves as working with the symbolic realm and leaving to others the realm of the "real" (the somatic, the social). Bergeron argues that this setup allowed specialists to maintain their normative practice by relegating to GPs those needs (social, medical) that might have challenged their model (Bergeron 1999). In sociological terms, we could say that specialists let GPs do the dirty work. The drug treatment centers became hermetically sealed worlds, both through self-selection (choosing motivated patients who knew what to expect) and by excluding difficult cases.

By the 1980s the drug scene had changed radically, but the specialists, catering to choice patients, remained oblivious, unlike GPs. Middle-class experimentation subsided; *héroïnomanes* became the real losers (*paumés*) among an already marginalized youth in the low-income neighborhoods. The *Trente Glorieuses*—France's postwar economic boom—eroded before high unemployment, particularly among young adults; deindustrialization; job insecurity (half of all new jobs created were temporary); and an eroding *état providence*. Second-generation immigrant children faced discrimination regardless of their education level (Tribalat 1995) as the spatial segregation of the *banlieues* reproduced the growing economic divide. *Toxicomanie* was increasingly associated by the French public with poverty, violence, and immigration.

Without the possibility of obtaining medication from drug treatment centers, heroin injectors turned to inexpensive over-the-counter codeine-based cough medicine when their opiate of choice was unavailable. According to a pharmacy survey, on a given day, 94 percent of this medicine was used for conditions other than what was legally indicated—the implication being by drug abusers. (That drug treatment specialists tolerated this practice is suggested by their opposition to a government attempt to designate this medication a controlled substance.) And the great majority of toxicomanes seen by general practitioners (with no training in the dispensation of psychotropic medication) were requesting psychotropics (Binder 1994).

General practitioners began prescribing, clandestinely and against medical indications, morphine products to their toxicomane patients. Jean Carpentier, an activist and general practitioner who was later appointed to the national narcotics commission, claimed to have used opiates to treat symptoms and "addictive behavior" of toxicomanes since the early 1970s (Carpentier et al. 1994). These practices can be considered a form of pharmaceutical leakage: prescription for uses other than those authorized. Doctors were pursued in court by the French state. Some hospitals also used synthetic opiates to treat withdrawal and symptoms of drug use without the knowledge even of the specialists. When a low-dose version of buprenorphine marketed as a post-operative, injectable analgesic (Temgesic) became available in the late 1980s, it, too, was prescribed to toxicomanes. With status of Temgesic as an ethical drug having now shifted from hospital prescription only to outpatient use (but under strict regulation as a narcotic), many doctors protested the absence of medicalized treatment for opiate dependency, especially for methadone. Later, sales of Temgesic dropped and heroin users switched to long-acting analgesics like morphine sulfate (Groupe de Travail de l' INSERM. 1998, no. 32). By the time HDB was officially introduced in 1996, many heroin users were already familiar with the leaked low-dose version.

## A French Exception?

By the end of the 1980s, the epidemiology of drug use was changing in two major ways. Social workers, community workers, GPs — in short, those social actors not locked into the self-reproducing, relatively hermetic world of specialized treatment centers — encountered a new type of drug user: socially marginalized, in extremely poor health, living in densely populated low-income peripheral areas of large cities (euphemistically called *les banlieues*, connoting at once immigration, youth, and poverty).[22] By 1989 the AIDS epidemic affected drug users disproportionately. Over one-third of intravenous drug users were HIV-positive, and 18 percent of AIDS patients were intravenous drug users. But both the French state and the specialist drug sector were slow to respond. French officials and professionals greatly underestimated the severity of the AIDS pandemic (Setbon 1993).[23] And the simplistic equation according to which the AIDS epidemic brought about drug treatment reform is contradicted by detailed media analyses revealing the inertia of psychiatrists and health officials in the face of sick and dying heroin users at the time (Coppel 1996).[24] Not until 1992 did the Ministry of Health release methadone from its experimental status, and until 1995 rigid eligibility criteria more or less inhibited its treatment use. Similarly, over-the-counter purchase of syringes without the presentation of ID cards was officially decreed in 1978, but for various reasons became effective only after 1993 (Feroni and Lovell 1996).

Ultimately, the conception of substitution treatment that activists promoted from the trenches, coupled with "foreign influences," challenged the dominant French opposition to medicalized drug treatment. GPs and hospital doctors, some aware of harm reduction practices (needle exchange, low-threshold methadone, etc.) elsewhere, joined AIDS and drug treatment activists and nongovernmental organizations such as Doctors of the World to promote substitution—as HIV prevention, not as long-term treatment. Advocates drew on the results of dispersed "natural experiments" whereby physicians in Belgium and certain parts of France had, mostly illicitly, successfully used buprenorphine for withdrawal and dependency management. Noting France's "backwardness" (*retard*) in the area, the World Health Organization's Europe section and the European Union began lobbying France in 1988 to introduce methadone and prevention measures. Yet practically no centers were developed for several years. Early proposals from NGOs and others to implement low-threshold methadone (as a risk reduction tool, with liberal inclusion criteria) were rejected by the Ministry of Health. ANIT came around to supporting risk reduction in 1994. After years of activism (see the first-person account by the sociologist and activist Anne Coppel [2002]) and the personal involvement of two cabinet ministers,[25] the strict criteria for methadone clinics were dropped in 1995.

Approval for commercializing HDB (the *autorisation de mise sur le marché*, or AMM) for opiate addiction treatment was authorized in 1996, before the completion of Phase III clinical trials mostly held in the United States.[26] The French laboratory commercializing buprenorphine had already been in contact with the National Institutes of Health. Also, problems concerning leakage of buprenorphine onto the illicit market and its injection, particularly in Great Britain, were already published in the scientific literature. The authorization indicates HDB as a "global treatment" — that is, for "major pharmaco-dependency on opiates within a framework of medical, social and psychological care." It is deemed appropriate for two types of heroin users: those for whom detoxification has failed and those already being treated with 0.2 mg sublingual tablets of buprenorphine (precisely the dose of the illegally prescribed Temgesic) (Schering-Plough n.d.:41). Emphasis is placed on noncoercive treatment (the patient's participation should be voluntary, urine tests are useful but should not be imposed, and so on). But why buprenorphine and not methadone? Methadone is cheaper, at least in the European Union, and inhibits parallel heroin use (but not use of other drugs, like cocaine), but it carries the risk of overdose. Most medicalized drug treatment elsewhere in the European Union involved methadone ("Deux médecins" 2002).

One explanation for the choice of buprenorphine is rejection of American models. To many drug treatment specialists, methadone reeked of American pragmatism and consumerism, although the experimental centers did develop a "French methadone" (Gasquet et al. 1999; Gomart 2002). (Later, harm reduction methods were also criticized as "American pragmatism"; see Lovell and Feroni 1998.) A second possibility views HBD as a "gift" extended to French GPs for their early role in treating heroin users in the midst of the AIDS epidemic, at a time when public authorities continued to view drug users as delinquents rather than as objects of public health policy. Several of my informants specifically stated that the AMM was intended either to satisfy conditions posed by the GPs (an *exigence*) or as a "gift" offered in return for their years in the trenches. A government-mandated random telephone survey conducted in the four regions most affected by drug problems in 1992 estimated that general practitioners — about half the total for France — were seeing 200,000 toxicomanes a year (Charpak et al. 1993).

Another hypothesis for the way HBD treatment came about in France lies in the particular status of French GPs and in citizens' accessibility to healthcare. A brief explanation of the French healthcare system may clarify this. France benefits from a national health insurance (NHI) system, the Sécurité Sociale, that covers the working population and their dependents. In accordance with the principle of *solidarité* (mutual aid) that underlies much of French policy and politics, the nonworking poor receive universal health coverage (CMU), which was implemented in 1999 to replace local health insurance arrangements for the economically marginal. A solidarity tax on income from wages and capital, the Contribution Social Généralisée, covers about 30 percent of government healthcare expenditure.

Unlike patients in the national health systems of Great Britain and Denmark, for example, French patients are theoretically free to choose their physicians.[27] But while the CMU theoretically guarantees healthcare to everyone, the lack of complementary insurance (which 8 percent of French subjects lack) for outpatient care limits accessibility to physicians willing to accept state-set rates of payment for services and hence creates social inequalities in healthcare.

Outpatient healthcare is mostly private, and private practice physicians are reimbursed per medical act. Health economists note that in such a situation, physicians tend to multiply the number of medical visits as a means of increasing their income (Palier 2004). Medical visits also involve high levels of prescriptions for medicine. The pharmaceutical industry does not control pricing, but it encourages high prescription levels through its company representatives and the usual gifts to physicians (paid conferences, free computers, etc.). France ranks first in the world in the number of prescriptions per inhabitant (Palier 2004). Finally, French physicians, who consolidated an unusual amount of authority during the early twentieth century, have until now successfully resisted any threat to that authority, including through computerized micromanagement and monitoring.[28]

Currently one out of five GPS prescribes Subutex ("Un généraliste sur cinq" 1999). HDB provides GPS with an opportunity to increase their clientele—the only way of increasing their income. Regardless of why it is prescribed, HDB prescription builds in the multiplication of medical visits because it must be renewed at regular intervals (at most, twenty-eight days). The way HDB has been introduced in France also transforms drug dependency from an acute disease model (the medicalization of drug withdrawal, the response to emergency situations) to a chronic disease model. In fact, French healthcare administrators deliberately chose the term *substitution* over *maintenance* to differentiate long-term use of buprenorphine or methadone to control the craving for heroin from short-term use to manage withdrawal. This economic reasoning is reinforced by the fact that French physicians are paid less than their European counterparts (including British). They are acutely aware that their salaries rise more slowly relative to other socioprofessional categories in France and that their economic power has eroded (Hassenteufel 1997).[29]

But lest we be tempted to interpret the development of HDB in private office–based medical practice as mere neoliberal tinkering—a strategy to shift costs from state-funded (methadone) centers to the market-driven private health sector—it should be pointed out that what changed is the part of the state machinery that foots the bill. GP visits, and most of the cost of medication, are covered by the state medical fund. On the other hand, GPs, it seems, presented (to extend Claude Bernard's metaphor) a "favorable terrain" for buprenorphine. In 1995, before the commercialization of buprenorphine, a random telephone survey of GPs cited above estimated that almost two-thirds of GPS saw toxicomanes in their practice, and 14 percent treated at least ten a year (Charpak 1993). Almost half of them prescribed low-dose buprenorphine (Temgesic), although that was illegal (not indicated in the AMM).[30] Another study found that GPs with little experience in treating toxicomanes discriminated against them (Moatti et al. 1998).

Another explanation for the French HDB program lies in Schering-Plough's proactivism. Observers insist that the pharmaceutical industry's symbiotic relationship with the French public health system is (again) a French exception. As might be expected, medical visitors (reps) are implicated in France's status as the highest consumer of psychotropics, and of all medications, in Europe.[31] Until recently, continuing medical education in France (not required for physicians) was offered by the pharmaceutical industry. The industry is heavily represented on the expert committees that approve the marketing of pharmaceuticals (because, experts claim, there is so little expertise to go around, and publicly funded researchers are "necessarily" funded by the industry);[32] the complicated negotiations with the industry have until recently involved trade-offs between approval of a product, substitution of high prices, or refusal to schedule a potentially dangerous medication, on the one hand, and the establishment of production sites—jobs—in France, on the other (Cahuzac 1999).

Schering-Plough was able to acquire approval for marketing HDB following limited clinical trials, which prompted the DGS to name, in collaboration with the company, a commission shortly afterward to propose research questions.[33] In the late 1990s, a period of continued deindustrialization for France and loss of jobs in the service sector, food industry, cosmetics, and other nonindustrial areas to global competition, Schering-Plough continued to add new jobs in France ("Un généraliste sur cinq," 1999). The jobs-for-authorization process must be interpreted in relation to France's activist medical profession and the fear that pharmaceutical companies would simply move abroad (Kervasdoué 1999).

## Pharmaco-association: Incorporating Buprenorphine into Everyday Practices

Between the newly legitimized context in which HDB is prescribed and purchased and the everyday social spaces in which it is consumed lie mediating processes. Both medical prescriptions and pharmaceutical leakage, the one sometimes facilitating the other, allow buprenorphine to move into these new spaces. But the consumption of this pharmaceutical is not an automatic act of compliance with a medical order. It is incorporated into a preexisting nexus at once material, symbolic, and social.

Materially, buprenorphine can be distinguished from street drugs such as heroin, which it replaces, or cocaine, with which it is combined. The modern pharmaceutical, synthesized and sized for maximum efficacy, contrasts with the indeterminacy of the effects of these so-called street drugs. Part of the risk involved in illicit drug consumption is the difficulty with determining such qualities as pureness, strength, and toxicity of the substance. But even the effects of the modern pharmaceutical are never perfectly harnessed, in particular once it circulates outside the laboratory. Its real efficacy is an abstraction whose truth can be arrived at only by factoring out the symbolic, psychological, environmental, and other factors from the overall effect, or remedy—a virtually impossible task.[34] (In purely material terms, think of the litany of side effects that accompany powerful pharmaceuticals.) Hence, the material and the symbolic are inextricably bound together.

In a social sense, the work of drug consumption is enabled by a particular type of relationship, which it in turn contributes to building and perpetuating. These social ties are not necessarily the only or defining ones for drug users. They are not equivalent to the coming together of users in self-help groups and drug use advocacy groups. While these practices became particularly visible in France in connection with issues of harm reduction (they surfaced earlier in other countries), they touch a minute proportion of drug users. A closer look at the work of drug consumption will clarify the differences in social ties.

The placing of a used syringe in a needle exchange automat in Marseille to procure a sterile injection kit, the dissolving of a buprenorphine tablet so that it can be injected, the awareness of how much a substance costs in which neighborhood and for whom — all mobilize bits of knowledge and experience appropriated by drug users through their interactions with others. In these acts, Becker's (1973) well-known observation that the consumption and experience of drug effects depend on skills acquired through shared learning exhibits its full force.[35] But despite his constructivist interpretation of drug use, Becker ultimately adopts the essentialist position that the effects of "hard drugs" like opiates override the possibility of constructing their use (Becker 2001). In contrast, I claim that bodily bricolage — the alteration of mental and physical states, of pleasure and pain with the toolkit of substances, sounds, instruments, atmosphere — involves competencies arrived at interactively. I call this social harnessing of bodily knowledge around the consumption of a specific type of substance and through specific social relationships, which enable and permit its effects, the *pharmaco-associative*.

The notion of the pharmaco-associative is grounded in a basic sociological distinction. In the first part of *The Theory of Social and Economic Organization*, Weber opposes "association" (in French, *sociation*) to communal sociability.[36] The latter emerges from a preexisting identity or sense of belonging to some whole. The "associative," on the contrary, emphasizes the *rational* dimension of ties. This abstract opposition is useful in allowing us to differentiate between the two ideal types of social relationships alluded to. The first are preorganized through a commonly felt identity — drug user — and adherence to a belief, such as the right to consume mind- and body-altering substances (activist drug groups such as ASUD in France and Junkiebond in the Netherlands) or, for older groups (like Narcotics Anonymous), the importance of confrontation among users in moving toward abstinence. The second type of social relationship operates through mutual consent or conventions between social actors concerning the different steps involved in drug acquisition and consumption (what I am calling work, which implies at once the work of culture and of social interaction).[37]

*Pharmaco-associative* draws also on insights attached to one of the term's roots, *pharmakon*. I am suggesting that the particularity of the social relationships is linked to the very nature of the substances involved in both medicines and in the passions, risks, annihilation, and numerous other possibilities of nonmedical use. In a recent discussion on illicit drugs, François Dagognet, a philosopher of science and a physician, elaborates on the well-known Platonic idea of the endless variants, manipulations, and uses to which the material substance opens itself (Dagognet 2000). The Greek root *pharma* refers to remedy and poison, medicine and drug, a substance that can both alleviate and kill, excite and calm.[38] What distinguishes a good substance from a bad one is not inherent to the substance itself; it depends on the effect sought, the quantity taken, the means of administration, the frequency of the practice, the context, individual vulnerability, all of which are highly symbolized.

The ability to differentiate between poison and remedy, to generate a dialectic between these two poles of the pharmakon, depends upon the lay knowledge and scientific knowledge that circulate among drug users. Indeed, it is a necessary foundation of their consumption practices. They may know that buprenorphine is prescribed to counter the craving for heroin, but they also know that it gives one a "*petite défonce*," a safer high than heroin, when taken in small enough doses; or that it helps "come down" after injecting cocaine. Cocaine will be sniffed or injected to get high, but can also be inhaled before going to the dentist, much as someone might take a tranquilizer. Prozac circulates in local drug markets for its short, "speedy" effect, but will be requested from a doctor by someone stuck in a tunnel of depression. "Rups" (Rohypnol, a nervous system depressant) helps one man sleep at night while his former injecting partner gobbles forty at once.[39] Knowledge and value judgments about the multiple uses of a given substance emerge through trial and error as well as through the indigenization (Kleinman 1980) of pharmaceutical knowledge, the interweaving of the expertise of health practitioners and information from the *Vidal* (the physicians' desk reference of medications) into popular realities. And both illicit substances and medical ones are highly symbolized. Buprenorphine is reputed by drug users to be a highly addictive drug associated with marginality; ex-users sometimes see those on buprenorphine as "weak" (as compared with, say, those who go through the highly regulated methadone treatment protocol). "Rups" is looked down on as "poor man's heroin" (buprenorphine sometimes has this name) and as a rape drug. Heroin and cocaine come and go as chic. The "natural," or *bio* (in French), reputation of a drug, or the machismo associated with it — its hardness or gentleness, its aggressiveness or generosity — are also linked to other highly symbolically charged phenomena: places, music, visuals, syringes, gender play, style.[40] Knowledge of the pharmakon is largely tacit, passed on from one user to another verbally, through modeling, and otherwise.

The work around drug consumption in the context I have studied resembles the largely tacitly learned skills of cooking. In fact, some of the same terms are used in both: "cooker" (English) or *gamate* (Marseillais) for the container in which the substance is heated, for example. Users sometimes refer to the preparation of the drug as "*ma cuisine.*" The buyer or consumer of heroin relies on color, taste, feel, and smell to indicate how good the drug is, just as a skilled cook feels, weighs in her hands, or smells the fresh produce she will work with. The injector complains about the way HDB coagulates or "brown" heroin smells, just as the seasoned cook finds that light cream heats to a different consistency than thick cream or that ready-made mixes have an aftertaste that foods made from scratch lack. Drug injectors, like cooks, eyeball amounts of ingredients that are mixed together. A drug injector in the know estimates how much the heroin should swell once water has been added, just as a cook knows what dry rice will yield once it is boiled.

This savoir-faire is passed on from user to user. Just as parents might (at least traditionally) transmit cooking skills to their children, an older drug user usually initiates a novice.[41] Of course, cooking can be learned from books and videotapes. In the same way, novels, music, video, film, and even the packaging and advertising of consumer products expose drug users to the pleasures and dangers of various substances. Knowledge about drugs, even among users, is unevenly distributed, of course, but then not everyone is familiar with food preparation.

The pharmakon and its circulation thus emerge as a central operator "tying" individuals to one another; that is, building the pharmaco-associative. In the *longue durée*, the same psychotropic moves in and out of grace, now valued for its appeasing qualities, now demonized as illicit pleasure; now domesticated in the family medicine cabinet, now smuggled into dens and dance halls (Bachmann and Coppel 1989; Courtwright 2001). And at a global level, the same substance is incorporated into very different regimes of meaning.[42] But at any one moment, the frontiers between "good" and "bad" substances are blurred, subject to diverse economic and moral interests and political climates (Ehrenberg 1998).[43] These boundaries, too, are already embodied and voiced by drug users themselves.

This moral status of drug consumption is affected by the pharmaco-associative, including through the means of procuring and using drugs. Illegal drugs, because of their cost and the secrecy and stigma that lawbreaking imposes, require users to band together around a "plan" to obtain them. Each user is necessarily caught up in a network of exchanges with other users. Energy must be expended to avoid being caught. Furthermore, the composition of illegal street drugs is rarely certain, as testers realize.[44] Hence, "trust" and one's "word," built through social interaction, are necessary dimensions to drug purchasing.[45] Of course, trying the drug is the ultimate test, and many relationships of trust are breached, in public displays of conflict, when the "word" or recommendation of a go-between or friend contradicts the actual experience. Buprenorphine, on the other hand, as we shall see, depends less on these contingencies: its purity is guaranteed, its accessibility requires fewer drug network members if any, and its legality can be argued. But the illicit market into which it leaks is not a *tabula rasa*.

## The Secret Life of Pharmaceuticals:
## Leakage, Diversion, Dirty Commodities

Let us return now to the substance that is circulating: the molecule become commodity become ethical drug in the doctor's office and legitimate remedy in the family medicine cabinet. But it has a secret life as well, a Mr. Hyde for its Dr. Jekyll.[46] The two lives are linked through leakage from the legitimate market of addiction pharmaceuticals to illegitimate addiction markets. Leakage happens through the prescription of the medicine for nonindicated conditions, the diversion of licitly prescribed medicine to others than the patient, or both. It connects the doctor's office or the pharmacy with networks of drug users who can diffuse the product and knowledge about it. The leaked substance travels thanks to the pharmaco-associative: the indigenous transmission and elaboration of knowledge about psychoactive substances and the ongoing interaction and ensuing social organization of the drug users themselves. When diverted from the pharmacy or the holder of the prescription to the market where drugs are sold illegally, an ethical medicine becomes a dirty commodity.[47]

Field observations and interviews in Marseille illustrate how the leakage from substitution treatment has further embedded injection drug use within an isolated behavior set.[48] Drug users paradoxically incorporate HDB into their lifestyle, along with other legal and illegal substances. Some practice "medical nomadism" (the French term translates as "doctor shopping," a practice that has been attributed to the freedom to choose one's physician; hence it is not limited to HDB) to obtain large quantities; it is not unusual for a spouse or parent to seek out HDB prescriptions s/he will then pass on to the partner or child. But nomadism is a far more complex phenomenon than first meets the eye.

An example illustrates how an addiction pharmaceutical travels from the treatment setting to the local drug market, where it becomes a (relatively precious) illegal commodity. Zé told the doctor he and Akim go to that Akim had stolen his supply of HDB, a typical ruse. Akim and Zé compete in the same neighborhood selling their prescription drugs. The doctor stopped Akim's prescriptions of HDB and other medication, effectively eliminating him as Zé's major competitor on the small-time local drug market. The next doctor Akim sought out took precautions, trying to explain how HDB affected Akim's hepatitis C, but Akim lacks the cultural capital to understand such abstractions. After all, prevention and the panoply of care that precedes downright emergency treatment are luxuries he never experienced while growing up. A third doctor would not see him because he was late for his appointment. Still another doctor sent him to a social worker, but following through on an application for disability benefits was beyond Akim's (and probably the social worker's and doctor's) psychic energy level. And so returns to the first doctor. He doesn't understand why his body is swollen like that of the old alcoholic man next door, or why doctors keep cutting off his HDB (surely they know how easily he can get it) or why he can't get a straight story on his abscesses and infections and why women avoid looking at him. He is caught up in a vortex of HDB injections and cocaine injections, spending more and more time in his room. His mother just spent hard-to-come-by money to put bars on the windows so he couldn't sell pills out of the house. Unable to stop up the holes in his life or get adequate responses to his problems, Akim burrows further and further into isolation. The irony here is that HDB does indeed reduce harm — the harm he experienced before as a small-time heroin *rabatteur* and big-time injector constantly fearing withdrawal, going to prison again, incertitude, and precariousness even beyond what he lives with now.

Observing and listening to how drug injectors think about and use HDB reveals different ways in which users incorporate it into their private lives. Whereas the product is a molecule conceived as a substitute for heroin, for the drug user it must replace much more than a neurophysiological mechanism. Someone who is dependent on heroin may feel that neither the methadone nor the HDB prescribed for her makes her feel really better. Perhaps something else is lacking. He or she may not be receiving the desired time or attention from a physician. Akim's lack of cultural capital makes it next to impossible for him to understand what the doctor says about his tri-therapy, substitution with buprenorphine, and treatment of hepatitis C.[49] He may not be capable of completing the application for assistance that the social worker gave him, which the social worker and most ordinary citizens find mind-boggling as well. His poor living conditions or strained personal relations with family and neighbors may make him depressed and less accepting of substitution. The immediate risk here is "not feeling better." He may then smoke joints, sniff cocaine, use a prescription drug such as benzodiazepine, or inject (as opposed to orally consume) buprenorphine, for example — to buffer the "bad feelings" or to give a *"petite chaleur"* or to more effectively reduce his opiate craving. Reducing the risk of feeling bad, then, is somehow balanced against the other risks incurred, such as the psychological dependency on "the needle" or the abscesses caused by buprenorphine injection.

On the other hand, some inject HDB in an attempt to "normalize" or "mainstream" their private life. Persons who self-medicated with injected HDB mostly injected the product by themselves, while heroin injection had been part of a group act. (There were some exceptions. For example, a woman normally injected HDB with her partner, who shot up heroin.) They might inject HDB at work or in the family bathroom or in other everyday spaces, whereas heroin injection was most commonly done in cars, cellars, or other hidden quasi-public spaces, and less commonly in apartments or at work. HDB injectors reported a more limited number of reactions: "I felt normal"; "I was no longer craving" (*en manque*); "I felt nothing special" (*y'a pas de montée, y'a rien, hein*), whereas they described their responses to heroin with a broader array of terms that included "wasted" (*défonce*), "the best feeling I had ever had," "great," "sick," and so on. Buprenorphine injectors described what they did after injecting in terms of everyday routine: "I watched TV"; "I was with the family, you know"; "I went to work" *"la télé, puis le lit"*; and so on.

But the social uses of HDB also break down the social dimension of the pharmaco-associative. In recent years HDB has become a drug of choice for injection as cocaine has replaced heroin in the streets. (Did heroin disappear from the market as HDB was introduced? Or did introduction of HDB make heroin less attractive? HDB, as was mentioned earlier, is injected for the "*de-scente*" from cocaine, just as heroin and other drugs used to be.) When HDB is transformed into a commodity in the local drug market, it often bypasses the social dimension of earlier drug exchanges. HDB, like Rohypnol, is a far easier drug to sell than heroin or cocaine, with fewer harmful side effects. The standardization of the dosage and the assurance provided by commercial packaging reduce the need for harm reduction work to avoid bad effects; the purity better ensures the drug's efficacy. Hence, a user's dependence on pharmaceutical knowledge tacitly transmitted or on the seller or intermediary's "word" that before him is the real thing becomes less important. Obtaining the product, even on the street, involves little effort. The seller and the buyer are often protected against arrest because they can claim to have a prescription. Buprenorphine, like methadone, also enjoys a special legal status in France, in that it is not classed as a narcotic (and hence not illegal). With less fear of the police and little need to pool enough money or think up a "plan" to purchase an expensive drug, group cooperation among buyers loses its importance. In other words, the user can consume a product such as buprenorphine (or benzodiazepines, Rohypnol, or any number of other commonly illicitly used medications) with relatively little mediation from other people, making the consumption an individual affair rather than a part of the *pharmaco-associative*.

To what extent is the secret life of this commodity known to the pharmaceutical industry, the physicians, and the state health agencies? The national health fund (CNAM), which pays for most prescriptions, estimates that 21 to 25 percent of these directly supply the illicit market, and 6 percent of patients receiving prescribed HDB engage in important trafficking of it (Cadet-Taïrou and Cholley 2004). The national surveillance center on drugs and drug abuse (OFDT) suggests that one-fourth of all HDB patients are receiving "irregular prescriptions" (Cadet-Taïrou et al. 2004). In our own street study in Marseille, 41 percent of ninety-one currently injecting drug users stated that they "self-substitute" with HDB, a practice highly associated with risky injection practices that lead to contamination with HIV or hepatitis viruses (Lovell 2002). More recently, the OFDT has identified, from a number of studies, problems it claims are linked to the lack of an adequate regulatory framework for prescribing HDB: injection of what is theoretically a noninjectable drug (11 percent of patients receiving prescribed HDB and 54 percent of those who use it to get high inject the product) and primo-dependency on HDB (i.e., developing a dependency on the product without ever having used heroin or another opiate) (Costes and Cadet-Taïrou 2004).

Clinicians are aware of leakage; in fact, the treatment manual distributed by the pharmaceutical company assumes a "demand" on the part of the patient for HDB (sometimes over other alternatives), which can only have been created through leakage and circulation of pharmaceutical knowledge.[50] How users have responded to oral or injected HDB obtained illicitly affects their decision to seek out treatment with HDB. Users who experienced unpleasant or no effects from illicitly obtained HDB sometimes turned to methadone treatment. Others did not seek treatment. Still others "self-treated" with HDB, either prescribed or bought on the black market, varying the doses. For perhaps one-third of HDB consumers, experience with the drug in the illicit market became what administrators and clinicians term "the gateway" to treatment (Costes and Cadet-Taïrou 2004). In other words, the ecological experiment of making HDB easily available pays off as "global" or "social" treatment by bringing highly marginalized individuals into the general health system.

The company that markets HDB sponsors training to help doctors identify patients who "divert" their medicine (assuming that doctors are never complicitous). The cost of potential misuse was not factored into the cost-effectiveness study of HDB in France financed by the company (Kopp et al. 2000). While the monetary value of diverted HDB would probably not affect the results of cost-effectiveness analyses because heroin use is so expensive, misused or diverted buprenorphine is certainly a nonnegligible source of revenue for the pharmaceutical maker of the product and loss for the national health fund that foots the bill—and hence a potential tension between pharmaceutical sector and public sector.

### Biopolitics of Buprenorphine

What are the implications of the adoption of high-dose buprenorphine within the tolerant and loosely regulated context of private medical practice in France? While the logic of the pharmaceutical industry may fit with the neoliberal economic logic of the pharma sector more generally, I have argued above that the "gift" of this addiction pharmaceutical to French general practitioners does not represent a shift from public- to private-sector responsibility for healthcare. The financing of visits to general practitioners is made possible through a virtually universal national health insurance system, itself financed by a mix of mandatory payroll taxes, government general-revenue funds, and a small share of consumer coinsurance. There are no deductibles, and pharmaceutical benefits are extensive compared with other countries' systems (Rodwin and LePen 2004).

In another way, however, the degree to which HDB is officially prescribed within a harm reduction perspective reflects neoliberal consumerism. Like the French healthcare system in general (Rodwin and LePen 2004), it embraces principles of solidarity at the same time it espouses certain principles of liberalism; at least this is implied by the harm reduction perspective within which it was promoted.[51]

Harm reduction has evolved into a highly *individualized* set of bodily practices and discourses that are resonant with the individually focused "new public health" (Peterson and Lupton 1996), which locates responsibility in the lifestyle of the individual as purely an individual decision.[52] What is presented as a choice for the consumer is an indeterminacy that reverses the role of the drug consumer-as-patient in the expert-client treatment relationship. The health practitioner now calls upon the client to act reflexively. By presenting the drug user with a hierarchy of risk in a menu of possibilities (continuing to inject, but with sterile material; sniffing rather than injecting; and so on), the work of risk reduction is left up to the drug user her- or himself. Hence, the drug user is no longer simply the target of a risk reduction intervention; the user is also the *decision maker* who rank-orders his or her own practices in terms of the level of risk he or she "chooses" (to inject "safely" rather than to stop injecting, to sniff rather than to inject, to use "soft" drugs rather than "hard," and so on). While the message that accompanies harm reduction efforts such as needle exchange may disapprove of continued drug use, the apparatus itself and the autonomy to hierarchize risk taking send another message implying that addiction is an individual "choice." Risk is disembedded from the original conditions that produced it, including the life conditions of poverty, dead-end jobs or unemployment, discrimination, disrupted families. Individual responsibility is reinforced by shifting harm reduction practices away from a particular site (treatment center) and into the private sphere. The only moral entrepreneur left, in the end, is the person who consumes the drug.

The result, however, is not simply benign neglect or the surveillance attached to methadone delivery. Rather, the body treated with addiction pharmaceuticals has become the major site of social and political intervention for a "problem" population: a problem as much because of its social precariousness as for its illicit practices. To understand this we need to examine more closely how the drug is prescribed.

The addiction pharmaceutical is not prescribed — at first — with an eye to abstinence, or even as treatment of toxicomania (Gibier 1999). Rather, high-dose buprenorphine is meant to lessen the *effects* of heroin use and dependence: the imminent danger of infection with HIV and the more newly discovered hepatitis C virus, which touch a part of the citizenry beyond drug users themselves; *and* the risk of socioeconomic marginalization. For public health actors, the objective of substitution is not purely therapeutic, in the medical or psychological sense of the word. It is meant to alleviate suffering — medical, "psychic," and "social."[53] This is in keeping with a larger tendency in France during the 1990s — the biolegitimization of poverty and social precariousness. As a number of case studies in the development of local public health indicate (Fassin 1998), psychic and physical "suffering" became a primary target of service providers, elected officials, and the array of local actors. The *écoute* (empathetic listening and hotlines) and *pointes-écoutes* (drop-in centers where this takes place) have proliferated for youth, drug users, and other "hard-to-reach" categories all over France. Poverty is acknowledged more and more through the mediation of sick or suffering bodies, and not through actions directed at the social conditions of drug users, migrant families, clandestine migrants, unemployed and precariously employed, and many other social groups affected by the mechanisms that preclude equality of chance (Maurin 2002).

High-dose buprenorphine provides an explicit medicalized response to social suffering and exclusion.[54] According to the president of the French drug agency, the MILDT, a goal of substitution treatment is to access medical care. By attracting the drug user to a noncoercive form of treatment (with the current mode of methadone delivery from specialized treatment centers held up as the coercive opposite to unmonitored care by the GP), substitution is supposed to ease the way into the healthcare system. And by providing a licit opiatelike pharmaceutical with effects similar to but less addictive and shorter-lasting than those of heroin, it attracts and "loyalizes" ( *fidéliser*) people who have been excluded from or have avoided the healthcare system. In this way, substitution helps prevent or halt marginalization and social precariousness

(Maestracci 1999; Cholley et al. 2001). This biolegitimization appears less a form of surveillance than an abeyance mechanism, a holding pattern in the management of flows.

## Americanizing French Buprenorphine

How does the pharmaceutical industry capitalize on the marketing of an addiction pharmaceutical in France? How is it generalizable to other nations? Most HDB is paid for through the national medical fund, as are the bulk of healthcare visits. And the price of HDB is probably lower than in countries such as the United States because of the negotiating power of the French state: it purchases, through the health fund, the pharmaceutical product directly from the manufacturer.

Just as in the 1970s French experimenters aimed to make French methadone "safer" than American methadone by transforming its form (from pill to syrup, so that it could not be easily hidden by the patient and sold as a "drug"), developing a monitoring system, and limiting its use to a diagnostic tool (Gomart 2002), currently American addiction psychiatry, in collaboration with industry, is making American buprenorphine "safer" than French buprenorphine by transforming the assemblage to which it will be attached and ensuring greater controls on physicians; higher doses; and a combination with naloxene, which causes withdrawal or a diminished effect when the buprenorphine is injected. French data on deaths associated with buprenorphine, mostly in combination with alcohol, benzodiazepines, or both, were taken into consideration, as were other data on outpatient use of buprenorphine.[55] The National Institute on Drug Abuse also commissioned two of the anthropologists most expert in the drugs field to study buprenorphine's potential as a street drug (see Agar et al. 2001). They concluded that buprenorphine has always had and will continue to have great potential as a street drug.

Meanwhile, Titan Pharmaceuticals has developed a mechanism for long-term controlled release of buprenorphine that shifts the site of surveillance, literally embodying it in the patient. It combines buprenorphine with a co-polymer, ethylene vinyl acetate. The combination is then shaped into a tiny, flat rod that can be placed under the skin. According to Titan's press release, "as body fluids absorb the drug, a steady dose is maintained in the blood in a fashion similar to intravenous administration, thereby avoiding the peak and trough levels seen with oral dosing."[56]

### Conclusion: Addiction Pharmaceuticals and Their Sites

To what extent is the commercial success of the sale of high-dose buprenorphine — like all addiction pharmaceuticals a "difficult" one to market — shaped by local and transnational interests of the pharmaceutical industry concerned? The "French experience" — itself being marketed elsewhere as a medical response to addiction epidemics — reveals the circumstantial overlapping of multiple processes framed by multiple actors around particular stakes and at different levels.

In sum, at least two aspects of this convergence stand out. First, a social movement arose from the professionals (who prescribe pharmaceuticals) themselves that was consonant with a transformation of the discourse that coats the pharmaceutical; this discourse shifted from being a mask for underlying psychiatric problems to being a multilayered response (medicine, lure, etc.) to marginalization and poverty. Such a discourse enables the passage from a hegemonous psychoanalytic model to a sociomedical one: the legitimation of "substitution" with its implicit recognition of addiction. These circumstances enabled the widespread diffusion of "French buprenorphine" despite the failure of its predecessor, "French methadone."

The second aspect concerns heroin users themselves, who quickly recognized the value of the new commodity and the ease with which it could be handled on the local informal markets. Through both pharmaceutical leakage and normative prescription-consumption practices, the incorporation of high-dose buprenorphine into the practices of both groups — prescribers and consumers — coupled with harm-reduction principles produced highly individualized regimes of practice.

The French experience may prove to have been a new laboratory, in the industrialized and postindustrial world, producing evidence of "what can be accomplished" — even if that evidence is shaky. And this is perhaps where the pharmaceutical industry comes in, in its partnership with the French state and the general practitioners, and a post-hoc research arm. Translated into the discourse currently generated in the United States, French buprenorphine was a test case — though the results of the test are greatly lost in translation.

## Notes

My gratitude goes to Susan Makiesky Barrow and Samuel Bordreuil for their helpful suggestions. An early version of this essay was written under sponsorship of the CNRs (France's national scientific research council), which supported my leave from the University of Toulouse-le-Mirail and residency at the Centre de Recherches Psychotropes, Santé Mentale, Société, University of Paris V. The street ethnography observations presented here were made possible by a grant (MILDT 98D12) from INSERM, MILDT, and the CNRS.

1. The French Center for Surveillance of Drugs and Addiction (OFDT) puts the number of patients prescribed HDB at between seventy-two and eighty-four thousand, versus eleven to seventeen thousand on methadone (Cadet-Taïou et al. 2004). In the European community the tendency is the opposite, with methadone being the most widely used form of medically assisted drug treatment. In the newer European states, however, drug-free treatment continues to be the major modality available (European Monitoring Center for Drugs and Drug Addiction 2004).

2. Schering-Plough-France. Until recently, Schering-Plough, present in 135 countries, was what financial analysts call a "major player" in the pharma sector. While still in the top ten pharmaceutical industries ranked by *Fortune* in 2003, its inability to gain revenues in the last year separated it from better performers such as Merck, Johnson and Johnson, Abbott Laboratories, and the "up-and-coming" player Amgen.

3. By global-local I do not mean Western/non-Western, modern/traditional, developed/developing, or other such dichotomies.

4. For example, the commodification I discuss is absent in the review by van der Geest et al. (1996), which applies Kopytoff's biographical metaphor to pharmaceuticals. See Kopytoff 1986.

5. World War II spurred the development of opiatelike analgesics, but only in the 1970s was their application to treatment of opiate addiction fully explored. Buprenorphine was "discovered" by John Lewis, a chemist at Reckitt-Colman, a British company best known for its dry mustard product. Reckitt-Colman, which mostly produces home care products, contracted with Schering-Plough for the commercialization of HDB. (Through merger, Reckitt-Colman is now Reckitt Benckiser).

6. A diagnosis of severe psychiatric illness, however, does not necessarily imply treatment, including with psychotropic medication. For example, at any given time in the United States almost half of the patients with schizophrenia are not receiving any type of treatment for their illness. See Lovell 1993. A business report (Moukheiber 2001) evaluates drug dependency at seven times that of schizophrenia and twice that of cancer.

7. A drug for treating bipolar depression, such as Zyprexa (Lilly), could earn $2 billion in sales in 2000. All antiaddiction drugs together made only $170 million, mostly from naltrexone for heroin and alcohol dependence, buprenorphine for heroin, and acamprosate for alcohol (Moukheiber 2001).

8. "Treating crackheads doesn't quite fit the wholesome image pharmaceutical companies want to project," notes Zina Moukheiber (2001).

9. According to an editorial published in *Biological Psychiatry*: "One handicap BPN [buprenorphine] has had as an antidepressant was the absence of any interest in that application on the part of the manufacturer. The idea of selling BPN as an OTC analgesic was not an unreasonable one, but it did not lead R&C [Reckitt & Colman] to pursue work on the psychotropic properties of their drug. . . . BPN's use in treating addicts, plus the ominous '-orphine' suffix in its name, have been even more of a deterrent to BPN's exploitation as an antidepressant than has R&C's narrow focus on its analgesic applications" (Callaway 1996).

10. Buprenorphine hydrochloride and naloxone hydrochloride dihydrate (Suboxone), the combination available for office-based physician prescription in the United States, are also orphans as of March 2004. An orphan drug is defined as a product that treats a rare disease affecting fewer than 200,000 Americans. The Orphan Drug Act, signed into law in the United States in 1983, is intended to stimulate research, development, and approval of products that treat rare diseases. Various financial mechanisms, mentioned above, are used to this end. A U.S. government health report case study criticized the seven-year exclusivity as too short, arguing numerous market barriers for LAAM (levo-alpha-acetylmethadol), a synthetic opioid analgesic marketed under the trade name Orlaam by Roxane Laboratories. Although an expensive antipsychotic medication such as clozapine also encountered market barriers, for the addiction drug they were more formidable, ranging from the oft-mentioned noncompliance of the patients, provider resistance to change and competition from methadone. See the website www.aspe.hhs.gov/.

11. In French, Mission Interministérielle de Lutte contre la Drogue et la Toxicomanie (MILDT) and Observatoire Nationale des Drogues et de la Toxicomanie (OFDT).

12. As substance abuse became incorporated into the "brain diseases." See Leshner 1999 (Leshner was at that time the director of the National Institute of Drug Abuse).

13. Yet various other manias populate everyday French language, from the passionate forms of the *mélomane* (music lover) to pathological ones of the *érotomanes*, *dromomanes* (compulsive walkers), and so on.

14. This section draws in large part on Bergeron's (1999) excellent analysis of the constitution of a specialized drug treatment sector in France. Space constraints do not allow me to do justice to the conflicts and complexities behind its making. My purpose is to discern possible relationships between this larger process and the buprenorphine narrative.

15. On the centralized model of French public health, see Ramsey 1994.

16. For many years, a major drug treatment modality was the chain of state-approved and funded therapeutic communities run by a charismatic figure, Lucien Engelmayer, known as *le Patriarch*. But after an initial enthusiasm, the specialized drug treatment sector demonized both the centers and their leader. These survived through private funds and Engelmayer's strategical genius until accusations of embezzlement and, probably, a general public and political reaction against "cults" (loosely defined) did them in.

17. In 1992, President Jacques Chirac called substitution the first step to decriminalization of drugs (Ehrenberg 1995:112).

18. In 1995, the Code of Medical Ethics allowed the Order of Physicians to sanction doctors who do not provide pain management. This French stance toward pathos needs to be explored in relation to the country's rate of medicine consumption, the highest in the world.

19. This critical view of methadone's utility did not prevent the St. Anne group from using

psychotropic medication to treat the underlying psychiatric disorder, as contradictory as that may seem. The French methadone experiments were in fact conducted by the forerunners of French biological medicine.

20. "After a four year trial, the research teams at both centers have come to similar conclusions: they reject the model of prescribing methadone that is practiced in the United States and Holland, and they express caution about extending this method" (Monique Pelletier, cited in Bergeron 1998:92–93).

21. French practitioners prefer the term *substitution* to *maintenance* as a way of differentiating short-term use of buprenorphine in withdrawal from opiates from its longer-term use to control the craving for heroin. The shift in terminology needs to be explored.

22. Decentralization, a major sociopolitical transformation of French society in the 1980s, allowed "local actors" such as social workers and humanitarian NGOs to play a major role in developing a hybrid discipline and field of action, that of *sida-toxicamanie*. See Lovell and Feroni 1998.

23. Michel Setbon and Henri Bergeron analyze a Crozerian perspective of institutional dysfunction in bureaucracies, the difficulties of establishing an adequate response to AIDS or to the drug crisis within. It is useful to recall that Crozier considered his sociology of bureaucracy the ethnography of a particular kind of bureaucracy—the French system! See Crozier 1963. Bergeron weighs two hypotheses: the unawareness of a psychologized drug treatment sector turned in on itself, and the corporatist interests. While he evokes some of the same factors found in Setbon's analysis of the contaminated blood scandal, he also suggests that that scandal may have spurred the DGS to finally implement methadone and other AIDS prevention techniques.

24. This equation is implied in Bergeron's otherwise excellent study.

25. The conservative Simone Weil, a concentration camp survivor open to humanitarian arguments, and the socialist Bernard Kouchner, himself a health activist, media figure, and former president of Doctors of the World.

26. Schering-Plough acquired this authorization before the end of the clinical trials process and trials on outpatients. Studies showed that subjects taking the molecule in certain doses reduced their injection of opiates during the first ten weeks of treatment, but the follow-up period was limited to twenty-six weeks. The FDA extended the trials to fifty-two weeks (excluding subjects who had already dropped out), but in France the molecule was approved before those results became available (Groupe de Travail de l'INSERM 1998).

27. That may change. As this essay goes to press, the French health system is moving toward a form of state-managed care which will impose the general practitioner as a gatekeeper to specialized care and require patients to pay one euro toward the cost of medical visits.

28. Despite its excellent healthcare system and general access to care, France has some of the most severe health inequalities in the so-called developed countries, with far lower life expectancy for workers than managers, and higher death rates among manual workers than nonmanual workers, to cite only two examples. Furthermore, these health inequalities increased in the 1990s. See Leclerc et al. 2000.

29. This certainly explains the wave of strikes by GP unions in the past few years; only in 2002 did the cost of a visit rise from 17.53 euros to 19 euros.

30. See also Clary 1999; Carpentier 2000. Leakage of Temgesic was tolerated, although police

often confiscated the medicine from patients during identity checks, and the Order of Physicians sanctioned Carpentier.

31. Twenty per year per person per annum, versus eight in Great Britain and fourteen in Germany (Kervasdoué 1999).

32. Patrick Lemoine, a leading French biologist specializing in psychotropics, responded thus to the question of independence of experts on the AMM commissions: "The place and independence of experts and members of the commissions (AMM, Transparency) including, for a long time now, myself—all of us are voluntary—are never guaranteed. The only security is a declaration made to the agency of possible ties to the laboratories; it is also forbidden for the presidents and vice presidents of the two commissions to have financial ties to the industry, which for them is equivalent to suicide, as far as the possibility of research in their department or laboratory goes. You can understand why no one rushes to volunteer and why the position of vice president of the Transparency Commission has been vacant for many months. Otherwise, it is the ethic and morals of each member that constitute what you call a guarantee [of independence]. The position is hard for experts who need financing for their [groups] and have hardly any alternative to industry financing because the official public organisms, like INSERM, rarely finance pharmacological studies. The only solution is to create a new national agency financed by industry and mandated to carry out studies in total independence. That would be a revolution" (Lemoine 2001).

33. *Evaluer la mise à disposition du Subutex® pour la prise en charge des usagers de drogue.* Rapport réalisé sous l'égide de l'INSERM dans le cadre d'une convention avec le Secrétariat à la santé, Direction Générale de la Santé et le laboratoire Schering-Plough. June 1998.

34. The modern pharmaceutical shares, though to a lesser degree, this indeterminacy with the older remedies, which were taken directly from flora and fauna rather than synthesized chemically. François Dagognet expresses this relationship as $a = x - y$, where $a$ stands for the global effect of the remedy, $x$ for the real effect, and $y$ for symbolic, psychological, and other nonmaterial effects (Dagognet 1964). To $y$ we can add such variations as temporality, the physical body that receives the remedy, and the imaginary. Even the sophistication of modern psychopharmacology (for example, through the use of statistical reasoning that allows for unknowns) can only reduce the degree of indeterminacy. In Dagognet's words, the alleged remedy corresponds "to a 'nonexistent' and an authentic fiction. It is but the remainder after subtraction; it cannot be presented as a veritable remedy because, were it administered or injected, it would give effects that are superior or inferior to those expected, for the simple reason that he who gives it just as he who receives it would charge it either with their distrust or with their redemptory enthusiasm. Once a remedy is given out, it necessarily loses its beautiful neutrality, its clear objectivity" (42).

35. See Gomart's (2002) commentary on Becker's 1973 essay.

36. In other words, the French term *sociation* and the English term *association* are both used to translate Weber's notion of *Vergesellschaftung*. Talcott Parsons, the editor and one of the translators of Weber's volume, notes that neither "society" nor "association" translates adequately the German term (see editor's footnote in Weber 1964). For this reason, I have chosen to use the less awkward "associative" in English.

37. I am aware that *pharmaco-associative* bears a family resemblance to Paul Rabinow's notion of biosociality (Rabinow 1992). But the latter, in my reading, pertains more to the "communal" side of solidarity. When biosociality becomes adherence to groups whose members

"have" similar conditions, it seems to trade nature (a common bodily affliction or genetically transmitted risk) for culture (social groups founded on different types of social action).

38. Dagognet quotes Claude Bernard, for whom this principle is fundamental to modern medicine. In his 1883 treatise, *Leçons sur les effets des substances toxiques et médicamenteuses*, Bernard writes: "that substance which is a medicine when it comes in a small dose can become a poison in a higher dose or because of an untimely administration."

39. Publicized as the "date rape" drug because of its amnesic effect. French physicians sought to have this medication withdrawn from the market, without success.

40. Older male users in Marseilles refer to the syringe as "my woman." Some explicitly describe injection in the same terms as sexual penetration. During the period of my fieldwork, synthetic drugs like ecstasy and MMDA were considered middle class by poorer heroin and buprenorphine users. Buprenorphine was nevertheless consumed in the rave and free party atmosphere dominated by synthetic drugs.

41. But in Marseille, according to drug users I interviewed in largely Magrebin neighborhoods, *grand frères* never used to initiate *petits frères* to hard drugs. Brotherhood here should be taken in the large, often fictive kin sense. Older heroin users deplore the disappearance of this code among the younger ones.

42. Throughout history these substances are caught up in much larger relations of power, economy, and the social imaginary (Courtwright), but that history seems to have been written mostly from the Western point of view.

43. Or, as Joe Dumit pointed out in response to the oral presentation of this paper, enhancement is the site of ethics, prompting scientists and policymakers to declare pharmaceuticals safe and illegal drugs dangerous and neurotoxic.

44. Various voluntary associations test street drugs, particularly at raves, free parties, and other collective events where synthetic drugs are present. Testing fits the harm reduction paradigm in that it reduces the risk of unwanted effects from cut (impure) drugs; critics claim it increases the risk of drug consumption by banalizing if not medicalizing it.

45. Amina Haddoui, unpublished manuscript.

46. Thanks to Ilana Lowy reminding me of the Robert Louis Stevenson analogy!

47. Leakage is neither new nor limited to opiates. Agar and Stephens (1975) described the phenomenon in relation to methadone clinics in the 1970s but attributed the illicit sale and use of methadone to the street scene around the clinic.

48. I am not concerned, here, with patients who use buprenorphine in keeping with the tenets of "good practice." My observations included such patients, but my point here is to examine the less often studied underside of medication consumption.

49. Luc Boltanski long ago introduced the notion that cultural capital reproduces, along with other forms of capital, social and bodily inequalities in health. More privileged patients share with their physicians both the same bodily habitus and the language and everyday knowledge for describing it. Poorer patients' lack of this cultural capital creates poor doctor-patient communication, with negative effects on treatment and thus health; see Boltanski 1971.

50. Gibier 1999. All the HDB injectors I interviewed had come into contact with that substance *before* contacting a doctor. Some learned about it in prison, but many "happened" upon it by chance. Again, as mine was a street ethnography, not a treatment-setting study, it is "biased" away from successful buprenorphine substitution.

51. The French term *réduction des risques* translates as both "risk reduction" and "harm re-

duction." Generally, it is harm reduction that is being referred to, specifically the reduction of the possibility of physical harm from viruses. In fact, an argument today for moving away from *réduction des risques* is that it ignores addiction and other harms from the drug itself (as opposed to harm from the tools of administration of the drug, such as syringes, filters, etc.). Buprenorphine in general practice was promoted alongside more classical harm reduction approaches such as low-threshold services, liberal regulations governing syringe sales in pharmacies, needle exchange programs, and so forth.

52. For an extended argument, see Lovell 2001.

53. According to an epidemiologist deeply involved in the introduction of Subutex, "One can hypothesize that the social problems associated with drug use are aggravated by [the] social crisis and that the older hegemonous models centered on psychological needs were insufficient for dependent drug users to find a new social integration [insertion]; one can also imagine that for the persons concerned, social integration, even without drugs, remained problematic in the context of the crisis" (Lert 1998:7).

54. The manual, distributed free of charge by the pharmaceutical company, emphasizes partnership and networking as well as the social, economic, and relational aspects of drug addiction and treatment (Gibier 1999).

55. See, for example, the recommendations of Substance Abuse and Mental Health Services Administration's (samhsa) Center for Substance Abuse Treatment (csat) National Advisory Council. The csat's report does not mention that the French researchers cited received financing from Schering-Plough for their buprenorphine research.

56. Titan states this "drug delivery system" is aimed at situations in which compliance with oral drug delivery would be problematic. The rod could provide six months' continuous therapy, following just one physician visit, for "patients with opiate dependence." Titan Pharmaceuticals, Inc. "Titan Pharmaceuticals, Inc. announces preclinical study for results demonstrating long-term drug delivery for treatment of opiate dependence." March 27, 2001. http://www.titanpharm.com/press/Drug_Delivery.html.

# Pharmaceuticals in Urban Ecologies
## The Register of the Local

VEENA DAS AND RANENDRA K. DAS

Our aim in this chapter is to interrogate the routine and unproblematic use of terms such as *self-medication* in biomedical and anthropological discourse. The "self" of this compound expression is often seen in the literature as a bearer of disease whose "noncompliant" practices endanger not only her own health but also the health of the social body.[1] Further, as Paul Farmer (1999) forcefully argues, it is the poor and the marginalized who are stigmatized and blamed for "noncompliance." The impressive case material Farmer has presented in his various papers over several years shows the overall conditions of poverty that make it difficult for patients to comply with a prescribed therapeutic regime, especially for illnesses that require prolonged therapy. Though we agree that the patient's agency is often exaggerated in many accounts of noncompliance in the literature on social and health sciences, the wider problem of understanding how pharmaceuticals are consumed cannot be understood by setting up stark oppositions between agency and structure or between the patient's beliefs, on the one hand, and the (biomedical) expert's knowledge, on the other. The problem is compounded by the fact that there is on one side the problem of noncompliance, and on the other the problem of unnecessary or inappropriate use of drugs. A recent review of public health interventions to improve patients' compliance and to decrease unnecessary use of drugs states the issues succinctly: "Modern pharmaceuticals are now part of [the] armamentarium of all families and healers. Physicians and health workers, the pharmaceutical industry, retailers, pharmacists, peddlers, traditional practitioners and patients themselves are responsible for the high consumption of medicines. International organizations and some governments have invested substantial resources to promote a more rational use of medicines. In spite of the efforts, in most developing countries there continues to be widespread use of drugs that are not essential to recover from illness, are not acceptably safe, and are not affordable" (Homedes and Ugalde: 2001:100). In a 1996 paper on inappropriate distribution of medicines by professionals in developing countries, Trostle had noted a relative dearth of studies on physician practices and prescribing patterns compared with thousands of studies on compliance.

Instead of opposing physician practices to patient beliefs we provide an ethnography of the intricate connections between households and practitioners in urban neighborhoods in Delhi and argue that what is at stake in local worlds is constituted through the articulation between medical practices, formations of belonging, and informal regimes of labor. We then go on to show that the medical environment of urban neighborhoods may be an unintended outcome of global and national processes of health policies with regard to how the health of the poor is imagined. The geography of blame that is enabled by such expressions as *self-medication* deflects attention away from the roles of global and national policy, regional markets, and livelihoods, and toward pathologizing the behavior of the poor. One way of reading this essay, then, is to see that to render an account of the use of pharmaceuticals in the register of the local is also to construct a different genealogy of biopower than the one located in Western modernity.[2]

A typical depiction of the social factors explaining the practice of "self-medication" in India puts together the supply-side factors (such as protection offered by the government for the production of generic drugs, especially in the small-scale sector, and expansion of the number of drugstore outlets) with the increasing demand for allopathic drugs. Saradamma, Higginbotham, and

Nichter (2000:892) explain the demand-side factors in the following terms: "On the demand side it is well documented that medicines in India are attributed powers beyond their active ingredients. The public at once desires the fast relief that 'strong' allopathic medicines deliver and at the same time fears the potential long-term side effects. . . . Consequently people are less inclined to take long-term courses of medicines particularly when symptoms subside. . . . Medicines are often not used as intended." The evidence for the practices of this generic public that "desires" strong medicines and at the same time "fears" the long-term consequences is taken from household surveys that document the prevalence and frequency of the use of antibiotics (but rarely relate it to the history of the illness episodes) and from exit interviews in pharmacies in which patients can often be seen buying drugs without current prescriptions.[3] Thus, it is assumed that self-medication is a result of the easy availability of drugs and the decision of the patients to self-treat their illnesses. We argue that these results are in fact artifacts of the survey designs; because the therapeutic practices deployed by practitioners are not built into the investigation, researchers have assumed that they are witnessing practices of self-medication. Saradamma et al. (2000) summarize the results of several surveys to say that these studies document that antibiotics were self-administered and often taken in inadequate doses for too few days. We wish to tell an alternate story. It concurs with the finding of widespread and harmful use of antibiotics, but the terms in which we understand these practices point toward a different configuration of factors than "desires" and "fears" of a generic public.

## Ethnographic Sites and Sample Households

We used a sixteen-week panel of 1,621 individuals located in seven localities in Delhi. We chose four neighborhoods through initial research contacts and three neighborhoods through a school health questionnaire. After the initial selection of the neighborhood and the streets within the neighborhood, we contacted every fourth house until we had the requisite number of households. We explained the project to any adult member who was present in the household. The rejection rate to our request to join the survey was less than 4 percent.

Our aim is to build longitudinal data on health-seeking processes and to collect information on social support networks. At the time of this writing we have completed two years of survey and ethnographic interviews. Weekly morbidity surveys were conducted in two cycles of sixteen weeks each, carried out from August to December 2000 (first wave in four localities) and January to April (second wave in three localities); each household was visited every week on the same day by the same researcher. During the first wave of data collection we had to add two additional weeks because widespread disturbances in the city prevented data collection one week and made for patchy collection the subsequent week. In addition, our research team has surveyed 500 healthcare practitioners in these neighborhoods.[4] The practitioners were identified by a field researcher mapping the practitioners located within fifteen minutes' walking distance of the sample households. Intensive fieldwork was conducted with a subsample of 245 practitioners including observation of one full day in the clinic or dispensary of each practitioner (see Das and Hammer 2004).

The seven localities exhibit considerable internal variation in economic, social, and demographic characteristics. How representative is this sample for urban households? We compared our sample data with the National Family and Health Survey of 1993 and found it to be in agreement with the survey in terms of age distribution, mean household size, literacy, and household characteristics such as sources of light, water, and sanitation. We use a tripartite classification of the sample households on the basis of consumption and income to carve out the notion of social vulnerability. It is well known that both of these variables are subject to measurement error. We attempted to address that problem by estimating consumption expenditure using household assets and amenities as explanatory variables.[5] For one of the measures we therefore obtained the value of predicted consumption from a regression of the log of reported consumption deflated by the square root of the household size on the tangible assets of the household and household amenities. Thus we considered the following three measures using the data aggregated over all the localities:

1.  Measure 1 (CONS) based on reported household consumption expenditure deflated by the square root of the household size
2.  Measure 2 (ASSET) based on the predicted consumption expenditure
3.  Measure 3 (INC) based on reported household income

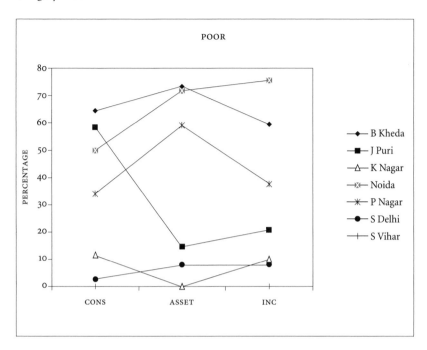

We obtained the thirty-third and the sixty-sixth percentiles as the cut-off
points of the cumulative distribution of income for measure 3, of logarithmic
transformations of deflated consumption expenditure for measure 1 and predicted consumption expenditure for measure 2. The households falling below
the thirty-third percentile are classified as "poor," those between the thirty-
third and sixty-sixth percentiles as "middle," and those above the sixty-sixth
percentile as "rich." Though the profile maps of the localities depicted in figures 1, 2, and 3 show considerable variability, it is possible to conclude that
Bhagwanpur Kheda, Noida, and Patel Nagar belong to the same cluster of poor
localities. Jahangir Puri is at a different level from this cluster, but within a
strictly dichotomous classification we assign it to the first cluster.

Figures 1–3 show how the different measures described above lead to differences in the classification of households as poor, middle, or rich. In each
figure the vertical axis represents the percentage of households that can be classified as poor, middle, or rich according to the three classification schemes.

FIGURE 2. Sample Households on the Basis of Consumption and Income, Category "Middle."

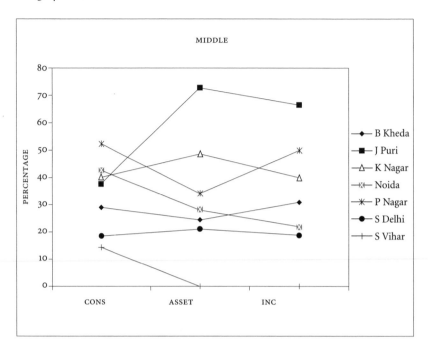

The horizontal axis shows the differential effect of using these three measures to classify households. Thus, for instance, if the consumption measure or the income measure in figure 1 is used for Patel Nagar, approximately 30 percent of households are classified as poor. If we use the asset measure instead, this increases to 50 percent, primarily because households in Patel Nagar typically have asset levels lower than their consumption aggregates would lead us to expect.

In our discussion of acute diseases in the low-income localities we will use Bhagwanpur Khedra as the representative site. We submit that the therapeutic strategies found in this locality are similar to those of the other three low-income localities that cluster together. The type of medical care available in all four localities is similar and can be easily differentiated from the strategies deployed by households in the wealthier neighborhoods.[6] We now take up the features of the medical environment in these neighborhoods by looking at how biomedicine is embodied in these local worlds.

FIGURE 3.   Sample Households on the Basis of Consumption and Income, Category "Rich."

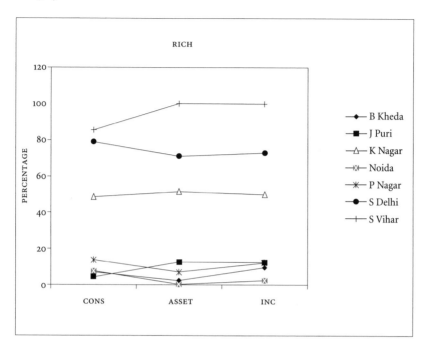

## Biomedicine Embodied

Writing on the quest for competence in American medicine, Mary Jo DelVecchio Good (1995) draws attention to the intricate relations between medical knowledge and power, cautioning us against presenting an overly unified picture of the profession or of professional discourse. Byron Good (1994) has similarly argued that an anthropological understanding of biomedicine consists not in proposing a series of propositions to which claims of truth or falsity can be attached, but rather in describing how medicine functions in various institutional settings such as in clinical or pedagogic encounters. We would like to add that these encounters are in turn driven and shaped by many sites that lie beyond the bedside of the patient. Especially important are the processes that shape both medical and household understandings of what constitutes therapy; these generate a specific ecology of care in low-income neighborhoods in urban sites.

TABLE 1. Distribution of Practitioners by Qualifications

| Code | Type of practitioners | All localities | Four low-income localities | Three middle-income and higher-income localities |
|------|----------------------|----------------|----------------------------|--------------------------------------------------|
| 1 | No formal qualifications | 16 | 11 | 5 |
| 2 | RMP | 37 | 29 | 8 |
| 3 | BAMS/BUMS/BIMS | 120 | 102 | 18 |
| 4 | MBBS and higher degree | 189 | 47 | 142 |
| 5 | BHMS/DHMS | 47 | 14 | 33 |
| 6 | Others | 82 | 60 | 22 |
| Total | | 491 | 263 | 228 |

Source: Survey conducted by ISERDD and World Bank, 2002.
Notes
1. Practitioners who have no formal education but may have acted as apprentices to a practitioner or may have simply set up shop.
2. Registered medical practitioner.
3. Holders of degrees (BAMS or BUMS) in alternative medicine (ayurveda and unani) given by state-certified institutions.
4. Degrees in biomedicine (MBBS/MD) that follow a standard curriculum.
5. Degrees in homeopathy (BUMS) comparable to BAMS or BUMS.
6. A mixed bag of practitioners including holders of degrees in correspondence courses offered by private institutions without state certification or with a general degree in a nonmedical subject.

To understand the specific features of the medical environment in which low-income families function, let us first examine the distribution of practitioners by qualification in the four low-income localities compared with the overall distribution in the total sample, as shown in table 1.

### WHAT DO THE SPATIAL PATTERNS TELL US?

What does this distribution of practitioners imply about health in low-income localities? Before we address this question, it may be useful to give a brief account of the debates in the policy arena on the role of different types of medical practitioners in the healthcare system in India. Each category of practitioner encountered in the locality lends itself to a fascinating genealogical analysis of how knowledge and institutions have been aligned in the shaping of the health system. Our specific concern here, however, lies in demonstrating how policies come to be *mapped onto localities.*

The wide variation in their training reflects a struggle between the state and organized groups of practitioners over the pedagogy and practice of medicine (see Jeffrey 1981). The state's attempt to control medical practice and training can be traced back to the Medical Registration Act of Bombay enacted by the colonial government in 1912, which legislated strict fines on anyone pretending to be a registered medical practitioner (RMP). Similarly, the Indigenous Medical Inquiry Committee (Punjab) set up in 1938 stated that it was "imperatively necessary that the Practitioners of Indigenous systems of Medicine should be controlled." However, the colonial state also had to confront the fact that such control was not easy to implement and that it had the potential to destabilize existing economic arrangements and thus create resentment against the government. Thus the 1938 report went on to add the following qualification: "We have also taken in view the economic aspects of the matter, the present day need of the public and the profession, and are of the opinion that an embargo on practice by persons who hold no diploma or degree but have been in practice for a number of years now will throw out of employment a large number of practitioners who will find it too late in the day to embark on a new career. We, therefore, recommend that there should be three classes of Registered Practitioners" (cited in Government of India 1948:50–51).

The proliferation of degrees and diplomas thus reflects the regulations effected by state practices and the contests and adaptations of practitioners to these regulatory provisions. It is significant that the households we studied did not use the distinction between biomedicine and traditional medicine as much as the distinction between practitioners with certification and those without it, or between government facilities (*sarkari*) and "private" practitioners.[7] The genealogical chart in figure 4 tries to introduce some order into the classification of practitioners when viewed from this perspective.[8]

Table 1 shows a concentration of practitioners trained in alternate medicine in the four low-income localities. Out of the random sample of 263 practitioners interviewed from the low-income localities, only 47 had a degree in biomedicine. It is important, however, to note that trained practitioners have

FIGURE 4. Classification Scheme for Practitioners in Delhi

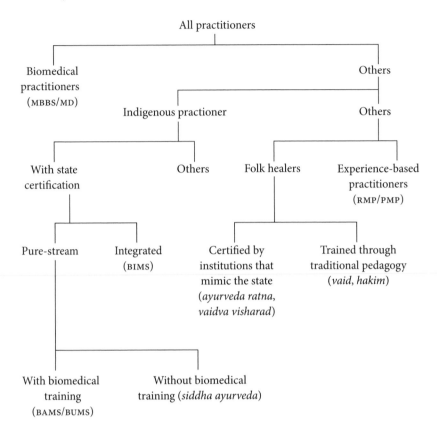

Key:
*Ayurveda ratna*: degree by correspondence given by various literary societies—literally, "jewel of ayurveda."
BAMS: bachelor in ayurvedic medicine and surgery.
BUMS: bachelor in unani medicine and surgery.
BHMS: bachelor in homeopathic medicine and surgery.
BIMS: bachelor in integrated medicine.
MBBS: bachelor of medicine and bachelor of surgery.
PMP: private medical practitioner or practitioner in experience-based medicine (title assumed by those without formal training).
RMP: registered medical practitioner; most lack a formal degree but do have a state license to practice.
*Siddha*: a form of ayurveda found primarily in Tamilnadu.
*Vaidya visharad*: degree offered in ayurveda from various organizations.

replaced those with no formal qualifications even in Noida, the area with the lowest average reported income. This spatial spread is consistent with reports of the spatial patterns of practitioner distribution in other urban areas. For instance, Ramesh and Hyma (1981) found that high-class and upper-middle-class neighborhoods in Madras city did not seem to attract IMPs (indigenous medical practitioners). They note that in the "informal sector of the city, many of the IMPs seem much more secure and confident and continue to offer a useful public service in the city." And further, "A number of favorable factors support them: they charge less for their services; they are located in centers where effective demand for their services still exists; they provide many dietary prescriptions which are expected by people of Indian culture when they are ill" (1981:78). This claim echoes the policies of the World Health Organization and the Indian government premised on the notion that medical care for the poor is best supplied by training practitioners in indigenous medicine to serve them. A well-known statement from the UNICEF-WHO (1975) study on alternative approaches to meeting basic healthcare needs in developing countries states: "It is now becoming clear that the ultimate solution to the health problems of the developing nations is a fully integrated type of training embracing the essential principles of both indigenous systems of medicine and modern medical science, so that practitioners can serve the rural populations effectively and understandingly and at a relatively low cost."[9] Thus the poor are not only seen as resource-constrained but also as able to absorb medical care more easily from indigenous healers because of the imagined comfort of a shared culture. If we consider the growth in pharmaceutical markets along with the legitimacy accorded to practitioners of various streams of medicine to use their biomedical training in their therapeutic strategies, we begin to get a particular assemblage of state imaginaries, markets, and household economies that have shaped therapeutic strategies that we call self-medication. It is to this facet of our study that we now turn.

## Illness and the Life World

In our weekly morbidity survey we collected information from each household about sickness, visits to practitioners, medicines used, and costs incurred. In addition, fieldworkers kept a regular diary on events that were reported and conducted detailed ethnographic interviews with the members of the households. The data they collected offer a unique opportunity to determine how illness trajectories intersect with household or individual decision making regarding healthcare. On the basis of this database we suggest the following.

First, practitioners and patients shared categories for symptoms and diagnosis, but the various terms used by both showed that ideas about what constitutes pathology were drawn from a variety of sources. Starting from experiential terms such as cold (*sardi*) or pain in knees (*ghutnon mein dard*), the lexicon could move to diagnostic terms derived from biomedicine such as BP (blood pressure), TB, or pneumonia.[10] Despite the concentration of practitioners from the alternate streams of ayurveda and *unani* medicine, the diagnostic categories were invariably drawn from the biomedical lexicon.[11] Use of such categories as *vata, pitta,* or *kapha*[12] was absent, but it is possible that more folk understandings of the body were operative behind the use of words like *gas*. We did not find a neat distinction between words that have a soul derived from indigenous understanding and a pure pragmatics that reflected the effort to communicate these in the language of the biomedical practitioners. In other words, people used such concepts as "low BP" as frequently in their interactions within the context of family and community as they did in reporting their illnesses to the practitioner.

Second, all practitioners in low-income localities, regardless of the type of training they had received, showed a similar pattern for dispensing medications. First, the preferred mode was *dispensation* (rather than prescription) of medicines from the practitioner, usually to cover one to two days with the proviso that the patient should report back if she did not improve. The charge paid by the patient covered both the fee for consultation and the cost of medications. Prescriptions for medicines were given only if these were expensive and the normal fee charged by the practitioner would not cover their costs. Similarly, pharmacists in the government dispensaries where the patients had the prescriptions filled dispensed enough medicines for two to three days in accordance with the names of medicines entered on the patient's OPD (outpatient's department) card by the attending practitioner. Only in cases when the medicines were not in stock in the dispensary did the physician in charge write out a script with names of medicines to be bought by the patient at his or her own expense. There was no charge for either consultation or medicines dispensed in the government dispensary, but the overcrowding made it difficult for people to find the time to access these facilities routinely. We offer the example of a government dispensary in Bhagwanpur Kheda in which one of us (Veena) recorded in the month of July 2002 that the attending physician saw 105 patients in two hours, spending less than one minute on each patient and routinely writing out the same set of medications (in this case tetracycline) for patients with a wide range of symptoms such as colds, coughs, or intermittent episodes of fever. The patients then queued up to get these medicines from the pharmacist in the dispensary. This case was not exceptional; other government dispensaries in all the localities showed the same pattern. We would like to clarify that the physician in charge had to manage a large crowd and was constrained by the complete lack of basic facilities such as a washbasin in which to wash his hands. The expectation of the patients was that they would receive something in exchange for their long wait; what is more, the attending physician could not write a script for free medicines if these were not in stock.

Third, our data show that the pattern of employment, the nature of cash flows in the households, and the therapeutic strategies deployed by practitioners molded the local ecology of care. It is this complex that determined the use of medications rather than any steadfast beliefs about the power of modern medicine as an undifferentiated entity. This is not to say that our informants never mentioned the efficacy or side effects of medicines; but such remarks were like building blocks for experimentation with therapeutic choices rather than definitive statements about belief and knowledge.

## PATTERNS OF ILLNESS

We start with an account of the magnitude of illness in the sample population and its implication for therapeutic choices made by households. We used two measures of morbidity. Because of our sampling design (weekly interview) we recorded as "sick weeks" the number of weeks that an individual reported sick, while an illness that spanned a period longer than a week would constitute a single episode. For instance, if an individual recorded headache for the first week and fever for the two subsequent weeks over a three-week period, this was recorded in the data as *three sickness weeks* but *two episodes of illness*.

TABLE 2. Individual Episodes of Acute Illness During the
First Survey Period

| | Frequency (percentage) | |
|---|---|---|
| Number of Episodes | All localities | B. Kheda |
| 0 | 23.72 | 11.48 |
| 1 | 21.62 | 18.52 |
| 2 | 17.42 | 19.26 |
| 3 | 12.91 | 13.33 |
| 4 | 8.4 | 6.3 |
| 5 | 6.49 | 10.37 |
| 6 | 3.83 | 8.52 |
| 7 | 3.15 | 8.15 |
| 8 | 1.48 | 1.48 |
| 9 | 0.43 | 1.48 |
| 10 | 0.43 | 1.11 |
| 11 | 0.06 | 0 |
| 12 | 0.06 | 0 |
| Total | 100 | 100 |
| Total individuals | 1,619 | 270 |

The first measure helps us to track illness and decision making as it developed, while the second measure is important for determining the severity of an illness (in terms of duration, cost, and so on). Table 2 gives the percentage distributions of individual episodes of acute illness during the first survey period for all localities and for Bhagwanpur Kheda. Thus 23.72 percent of the individuals in our entire sample did not suffer any illness in the first survey period, versus 11.48 percent of those in Bhagwanpur Kheda. Table 3 gives the percentage distributions of acute episodes by duration. Thus, considering all localities, 69.65 percent of such episodes lasted one week or less; for Bhagwanpur Kheda the same figure is 68.49 percent. Figure 5 represents the kernel densities for number of episodes (*numepi*) fitted to the data in table 2. This provides a statistically smoother picture of the underlying distributions.[13]

There are two important points here. First, about 52 percent of the sample population experienced one to three episodes of illness in a four-month period; second, a large proportion of illness episodes (nearly 70 percent) were of less

TABLE 3.  Duration of Episodes of Acute Illness

| Duration (weeks) | Percentage of all Episodes | |
|---|---|---|
| | All localities | B. Kheda |
| 1 | 69.65 | 68.49 |
| 2 | 18.16 | 17.79 |
| 3 | 5.32 | 6.63 |
| 4 | 2.31 | 2.33 |
| 5 | 1.44 | 1.05 |
| 6 | 1.03 | 1.51 |
| 7 | 0.52 | 0.81 |
| 8 | 0.22 | 0.12 |
| 9 | 0.27 | 0.12 |
| 10 | 0.11 | 0.23 |
| 11 | 0.22 | 0.12 |
| 12 | 0.14 | 0.12 |
| 13 | 0.08 | 0 |
| 14 | 0.11 | 0.12 |
| 15 | 0.05 | 0 |
| 16 | 0.38 | 0.59 |

than one week duration. Only 24 percent of the population reported no illness. It is important to observe that the pattern of duration for Bhagwanpur Kheda follows roughly the same pattern as the general population, but there is a cluster of individuals who suffered five to seven episodes in this period. Our narrative interviews show that these are cases of individuals who reported repeated short-duration illnesses that later turned out to be undiagnosed tuberculosis, or individuals suffering from continuing allergies or wounds who reported a decline in signs and symptoms as a measure of "cure" and saw an increase in these as fresh episodes. What does this tell us about the ideas of the normal and the pathological in low-income localities? We explore these questions specifically with respect to Bhagwanpur Kheda.

Recent work on illness narratives has shown that complex ideas of the normal and the pathological inform people's reflections on the nature of illness. Many of these studies, however, privilege accounts of chronic or life-threatening ill-

FIGURE 5. Kernel Densities of Number of Episodes

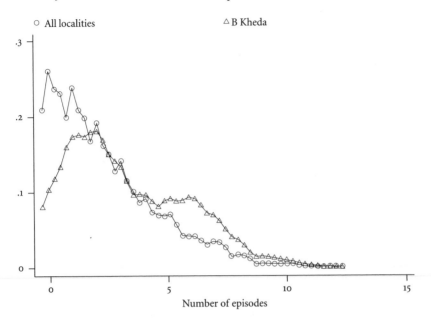

nesses since the boundaries between sickness and health, and hence between pathological and normal, are not clear in these cases (see Morris 1998). Others have suggested that there is a culturally standardized point at which one can locate the break between health and illness (Johansson 1991). Given that nearly 70 percent of acute illnesses lasted less than one week and that only 20 percent of the sample population reported no sickness in the survey period, can we say that the people we interviewed consider illness to be simply part of ordinary life?

It is interesting to observe that under different kinds of conditions *the same set of symptoms* could be treated either as "normal" to that age or that season or as something that required medical attention. For instance, we recorded cases when a baby was taken to a practitioner for loose bowel motions and irritability one week, but in another week the mother would report that the same set of symptoms did not require medical attention because it was "probably just teething." This explanation was often qualified further by a discursive form of "where do we poor people have money for running to doctors? Such ups and downs are part of life [*chotti moti taklif to lagi hi rehti hai*]."[14]

These discursive forms point to the blurred boundaries between health and illness, normal and pathological, and to the experience of illness as split between days when the person had access to small amounts of money and hence could consult a practitioner versus the days when symptoms were endured because money had run out. Thus, the idea of the normal was powerfully mediated for low-income families by conditions of poverty and precariousness of income flows, rather than being a standardized break in the continuum of health and illness. Among the low-income families in our sample, only 20 percent of the adults had jobs in the public or private sector; 30 percent were engaged in the informal sector working as hawkers, rickshaw pullers, housemaids, or unskilled labor in factories and shops; and 44 percent were outside the labor force but sometimes engaged in household production doing piecemeal jobs for household industry in the area. The dominant experience of work, then, was of intermittent employment, of being on a threshold, of being in danger that one will not get work or that a serious illness will throw one into debt, or that the nexus of relations through which one maintains one's job or raises debts or finds a doctor in a public hospital could somehow collapse. Cash flows to the household were irregular. While even the poorest households had some disposable income, any large expenditure propelled the family into debt. Thus the typical pattern of health seeking related to the availability of cash: if there was some money available, then treatment for diseases that were not considered severe or life threatening was sought from a practitioner in the locality; otherwise attempts were made to absorb the illness within the notion of the normal.[15] As we saw, a mother may take a child with diarrhea to the local practitioner if she has some cash in hand, but in the absence of money the same symptoms can be absorbed within the idea of the normal by attributing them to teething. Let us consider another example.

P, a woman in her early thirties, reported ten sick weeks; the duration of her illness episodes varied from two days to fourteen days. In the fourth, seventh, and thirteenth weeks she visited a practitioner with a bachelor in ayurvedic medicine and surgery (BAMS) degree who dispensed a cocktail of medicines. In the other weeks when she reported sickness she did not consult a practitioner, but instead bought one tablet of dispirin or went without medication. Her symptoms included fever, toothache, body ache, cold, and recurring boils. Every week that she visited the private practitioner she spent ten rupees on consultation and medication. In the fifteenth week she went to the government dispensary for the treatment of a boil that was oozing, because she did not have even the ten rupees necessary to pay the private practitioner. In addition to a medicine that was dispensed she was given a prescription for an antibiotic, but she had only enough money to buy two tablets. In her explanations she tilted between complaints that the local practitioners were of no use in dealing with her frequent illnesses and the idea that the illnesses were part of her life.

The interviews point to a constant search for relief in low-income households, but also show that people had to improvise by combining visits to private practitioners with the use of the government dispensary and deciding how much or which of the prescribed medicines they could afford to buy. Let us now look at the general picture in the locality with regard to decisions regarding therapeutic choices.

Table 4 shows the distribution of various types of actions taken in case of a reported acute illness in any week for Bhagwanpur Kheda.[16] Subsequent to a reported illness *that week*, in 21.75 percent of the cases no action was taken. People generally consulted a practitioner (35 percent of total actions) rather than a pharmacist (3.27 percent) for diagnosis. Further, there are 389 illness weeks in which patients bought medications without a current prescription; if we add the weeks when such self-medication was combined with other actions (that week), we find 592 illness weeks when patients bought medications without a prescription. The figures, at first glance, appear to suggest a high level of self-medication. However, when we disaggregated these cases, we found that a previous prescription was used in 207 cases, and that in 184 cases the person bought a medicine that he or she had taken earlier with good effect. In the other cases, either a person was on maintenance dosages for ongoing aches and

TABLE 4. Patterns of Action Consequent upon Illness Reported in a
Particular Week in B. Kheda

| Action | Frequency | Percentage | Cumulative |
|---|---|---|---|
| No action taken | 319 | 21.75 | 21.75 |
| Only practitioner visit | 508 | 34.63 | 56.3 |
| Consulted pharmacist only | 48 | 3.27 | 59.65 |
| Medicine bought without current prescription | 389 | 26.52 | 86.16 |
| Two or more actions | 203 | 13.84 | 100 |
| Total | 1,467 | 100 | |

Source: Data collected by ISERDD.

pains or, in a few cases, the person bought a medicine on the recommendation of a family member or some other person.[17]

Let us look at the 207 cases in which a medicine was bought on a previous prescription. In 37 instances the person bought an antibiotic; in the other cases the medicines were analgesics, tonics, skin ointments, and so on. The typical scenario in which the person used a previous prescription was in the middle of an episode that lasted longer than one or two weeks. For example, a patient might be receiving medications from a DOT (Directly Observed Therapy) center free of charge, but a family emergency might make it impossible to go to the DOT center that week, in which case the person might buy medicines from a local pharmacy with a script already on hand. When symptoms recur, some patients buy medications with the prescriptions they were given in previous consultations because they feel that they can predict the behavior of the practitioner. K, for example, a woman in her thirties, had complained of recurrent episodes of cold, cough, loss of appetite, and fever; she reported sickness for eleven of the sixteen weeks and consulted a practitioner five times. She was diagnosed alternately with flu and then with pneumonia, and along with dispensed medications she had also received a prescription for antibiotics.[18] In this entire period she was not offered any diagnostic tests. Thus, she bought antibiotics on a current prescription three times and used the previous prescription in two of the other weeks. There is a certain temporal rhythm in her experience of illness: fever diagnosed as flu — dispensed medications — patient feels better first then feels sick again — goes back to practitioner — is told she has pneumonia and is given prescription for antibiotics — buys a few tablets — gets better — feels sick again — uses the same prescription to buy another round of antibiotics — goes back to the practitioner — and so on. The intermittent use of the practitioner interspersed with self-medication is indicative of the fact that individuals with multiple episodes like those described for Bhagwanpur Kheda simply do not receive a correct diagnosis and treatment and hence report what may be a single episode of sickness such as TB as repeated episodes of one or more diseases.

In many cases, especially for illnesses of long duration such as TB, patients who were accessing private practitioners used a prescription to buy medicines in small quantities rather than a full course at one time because that is all they could afford in that week. Further, for diseases such as allergies with recurring symptoms, patients may mix strategies, consulting the practitioner some weeks and buying medicine from the pharmacists in other weeks. Such patterns of use reflect the character of medical practice in the locality as well as the inability of households to buy a full course of medication at one time. They are also indicative of the failure of many practitioners to recognize that recurring episodes are part of the same illness that requires a different line of treatment rather than dispensation of antibiotics or analgesics for symptomatic relief.

Most of the medicines that were consumed by Bhagwanpur Kheda patients were either dispensed by practitioners or were bought under some medical supervision, even if a current prescription was not being used. In interviews practitioners were asked to give names of up to five medications that they regularly dispensed or prescribed. Most practitioners from the low-income localities named only two or three, most frequently analgesics followed by antibiotics. Interestingly this pattern of dispensation was consistent across all practitioner categories with the exception of those trained in homeopathy.[19] This information, along with our ethnographic observations in the field, seems to make it clear that medications dispensed by practitioners are the major source of the analgesics and antibiotics consumed in low-income households. Our analytical strategy of combining household interviews with practitioner surveys allows us to see this pattern of therapeutic strategies where others have seen only self-medication.

Finally, our data show no differences in the pattern of dispensing or pre-scribing regardless of the type of training the practitioner received. Consider the cases seen by Dr. S, who holds bachelor of medicine and bachelor of sur-gery (MBBS) degrees from a premier university and practices in Bhagwanpur Kheda. He was the most frequently visited private practitioner in the category of physicians trained in modern medicine. In the eighteen survey weeks Dr. S received 53 visits from members of the sample households in B. Kheda for a variety of complaints ranging from fever, rashes, and tuberculosis to weakness and pain. There was only one case in which he did not dispense or prescribe any medicine, even though many patients saw him for coughs, colds, and short-duration fevers. He gave a prescription in 9 cases and dispensed medicines in 43 cases. When the packaging of the medicines was intact, we found that these included antibiotics such as ampicillin, gentamicin, and ciprofloxacin. He also dispensed medicines that had been withdrawn from the market by some phar-maceutical companies in the United States for possible adverse impacts such as the various compounds of cisapride.[20] There did not seem to be any correla-tion between the severity of a disease and the medicines that were dispensed. In the same period, Dr. L from the same area, who has a BAMS degree, re-ceived 108 visits. In 3 cases he did not prescribe or dispense any medication; two of those patients reported that they had leftover medicine (such as Sep-trin) from their previous visits and were advised to use it for their complaints such as colds, coughs, and flu. In 14 cases Dr. L gave prescriptions for such mediations as ciprofloxacin, neomycin, ampicillin, and Bludrox. In all other cases he dispensed medications. Once again, the medicines were dispensed or prescribed on a symptomatic basis without any clear correlation between the diagnosis and the treatment. For instance, Bludrox, a medicine for severe skin or respiratory infections, was prescribed in one case for a cold and cough and in another case for a septic wound.

It seems that in general, practitioners dispense or prescribe antibiotics for short durations and are frequently unable to diagnose serious diseases. Our data show that the short-term therapeutic patterns that have become established in these localities are the result of a complex assemblage comprising poor regulation by the state, the pattern of cash flow to the households, and the mutation of both biomedicine and traditional medicine to create a specific local ecology of care. What is at stake in local worlds with regard to the use of pharmaceuticals can be comprehended only within this complex ecology.

## The Traffic in Categories

Related to the pattern of consumption of pharmaceuticals was the way in which the local ecology mediated the categories that were deployed to refer to several kinds of illnesses. Neither practitioners nor patients tried to make any clear distinction between symptoms and diagnosis. The lexical terms they used were heterogeneous and ranged from terms that were close to experience, such as *fever* or *pain*, to diagnostic terms derived from the lexicon of Western medicine. Yet the pattern of use of these terms by both practitioners and patients showed the traffic between the "expert" culture as embodied in the local and the so-called folk categories. We offer two examples of the way such terms as *a mild case of* TB, *double pneumonia*, or *low* BP can circulate and become part of the everyday lexicon used by patients.

B, an old (possibly in her late sixties) widowed woman in Bhagwanpur Kheda who lived with her son, his wife, and their unmarried children, constantly complained of stomach ache, feelings of weakness, and lack of appetite, and insisted that she had a "heart condition" or "perhaps TB" (*dil ki bimari, ya shayad teebi*). B's husband died a year before our survey commenced, and no one was clear about the cause of death. He had been admitted to the TB hospital for a short period, so he could have been a case of untreated TB. The family also said that he might have had a heart condition. In the eighteen weeks of the survey, B was reported as sick for eleven weeks. Precise information on her illness was missing for seven weeks: one week because the household could not be surveyed and for six weeks intermittently because she went twice to visit her married daughter in a village on the outskirts of Delhi to "get treatment." She was taken to a local practitioner trained in biomedicine with an MBBS degree. She showed us a couple of prescriptions that the practitioner had given her; the diagnosis entered on these was "old Koch." Throughout the survey period her son bought medicines from the local pharmacist by showing him the old prescription. The medicines that were bought included Refka, for acute or chronic viral hepatitis, three capsules for three days; Liv 52, an ayurvedic tonic for improved liver function, intermittently for the period; and Pyrazinamide, a first-line anti-TB drug, for two weeks intermittently. Underlying the history of intermittent drug treatment ranging from powerful anti-TB drugs to drugs for improving liver function was B's demand for more attention from her son and daughter-in-law. Whenever the daughter-in-law was interviewed she would say, "*Budape ka sharir hai aisa to hota hi hai par amman mein sahan shakti kam hai*" (this is the body of old age; such things happen but *amma* [mother] has no capacity to tolerate). To show her displeasure with her son, B went off to her daughter's village and stayed there for four weeks, pronouncing herself to be much better after she returned. She was receiving some medicines from the practitioner in the village that were sent by her daughter intermittently through the agency of a Delhi Transport Corporation bus driver who lived in that village and happened to be a relative. He would occasionally divert the usual route of the bus to deliver the medicines to her. The entry next to her name for the last week of this survey period records her as having "mild TB" as diagnosed by the village practitioner. During the eighteen-week survey period this family spent a total of 350 rupees that represented an expenditure of approximately 1 percent of their annual income. This was not an exceptional case; using the same database, Das and Sanchez calculated that expenditure on short-duration morbidities constituted 3.3 percent of the annual total expenditures for low-income families (Das and Sanchez 2002).

B's own representation of her illness was made up of complaints that she had picked up from previous encounters with the medical system. During the second year of the survey she was examined by a physician who had volunteered his services to our project. On the basis of a sputum examination and an X-ray, she was told that she had not TB but a mild gastric disorder.[21] She nevertheless continued to think of herself as having a "little bit of TB." Although B did not suffer from a serious disease, her case raises the question of whether within both the medical system and the distribution of power and resources within the household there operates a patterned nonrecognition of severe disease that helps to absorb serious pathology within the notion of the normal. The next case shows how serious symptoms of disease may be treated as "minor" illnesses for prolonged periods.

J, with undiagnosed TB, reported symptoms of fever, headache, and body ache for twelve weeks in the first phase of the survey period. She visited the same practitioner five times in this period and each time her illness was treated as a new episode. She was not asked to take any diagnostic tests. The volunteer physician examined her toward the end of the first phase and recommended a chest X-ray, which showed a lesion in her right lung. She was then advised to take treatment from the DOTS center, where she was found to be sputum-positive and hence could be placed in a treatment regime that was free.[22]

In an influential paper on the cultural inflation of morbidity during decline in mortality, S. R. Johansson suggests that high morbidity may be a function of the availability of categories in which suboptimal states of health can be re-classified as disease. "In general," she notes, "social scientists cannot or should not attempt to relate morbidity and mortality during the health transition be-cause morbidity is made up of phenomena of several different kinds, each of which relates differently to sickness and death." Further, "the more diseases there are, the more likely are individuals to think of themselves as sick or to be diagnosed by a professional as sick. In this way the incidence rate is a func-tion of the culturally recognized stock of diseases, along with the propensity of *ordinary people* to classify biologically suboptimal states as sickness accord-ing *to culturally standardized breakpoint* on the health continuum" (Johansson 1991:44, emphasis added).

We agree with Johansson that the availability of categories may expand the possibilities of how to think of bodily discomfort, but we have interro-gated such generic categories as "ordinary people" and "culturally standard-ized breakpoint" on the health-sickness continuum. We suggest that it is rather the concrete experience of illness in the family and local community, the na-ture of the clinical encounter, and the availability of such medicines as antibiotics in an imperfectly regulated market that become the stock of knowledge through which illness categories are represented and therapies sought. There is a tremendous struggle to authorize the "real": are these symptoms to be interpreted as indicative of "mild TB" or old age; are these experiences of repeated different episodes of illness or are they the same illness? The notions of normality or pathology are deployed in this struggle within a set of family dynamics, as the two cases presented above show.[23]

Terms such as *low BP* are sometimes used to refer to feelings of sadness, weakness, or inability to engage with everyday life. Patients and practitioners in the low-income neighborhoods used this category without necessarily measuring the patient's blood pressure. Medications for low BP, thus diagnosed, might include an intravenous drip given in the doctor's office or analgesics and vitamins. We want to emphasize that patients do not use this term to convey certain feelings of ill-being to practitioners as a device for translating experiences for which they would have used a different set of terms outside the clinic. Rather, the transactions between the tensions they encounter, the therapeutic strategies they use, and the legitimacy these terms acquire through their interaction with practitioners make them think of these as experiential categories. We feel that this is relevant for contesting the view that patients resort to self-treatment because they have clear-cut beliefs about the causes of their illnesses and the efficacy of different types of medications (allopathic versus ayurvedic) for different kinds of illnesses. Instead, what we find is that terms for illness acquire meaning through use — patients are trying to learn language and world together but are repeatedly thwarted in their quest to understand the real. In the next section we show how these frustrations come to the fore when the strategies devised within the local world fail.

## When the Local Fails

Though 70 percent of the illness episodes reported in Bhagwanpur Khedra lasted less than one week, more than 6 percent of the episodes lasted three or more weeks. In such cases, with a family member faced with a life-threatening illness, families began to despair of the therapy within the local context. While chronic conditions that are not life threatening can be absorbed within the idea of the normal, the worsening of illness to the point that it becomes life threatening always leads to a search for therapy outside the local in the world of specialists and hospitals. It is not possible to describe this journey in terms of any straightforward model of vertical or horizontal resort (see Kleinman 1980). The households did not act with a coherent explanatory model of which illnesses were best treated through which kind of therapeutic system (for example, allopathic for acute diseases and homeopathy for chronic diseases) but rather which networks of information and influence they could activate.[24] The practitioners in these localities generally reported that they provided a service to patients by referring them to private, but more expensive, medical facilities when the disease could not be managed through the resources they had to offer. Intrigued by the fact that the billboards outside the offices of some practitioners displayed rates for various kinds of diagnostic tests when we could not find any sign of such facilities in the office of the practitioners, one of us (Veena) asked, "How do you do these tests?" This particular practitioner, an active member of the National Association of Practitioners of Integrated Medicine, told us that he knew a good diagnostic laboratory in the area and received a small commission for referring patients there. Not all practitioners displayed billboards, but many acted as brokers between patients and providers of more sophisticated facilities or specialists. If the disease was seen to worsen in the sense that the practitioner began to fear that death might result, households were advised to take the patient there. Sometimes the family was able to raise or borrow enough money to deal with the emergency; in other cases they accessed such facilities for a few days, decided they could not sustain the expense, and tried to find someone who could get the patient treated in a government hospital. The other route for patients was to access a public hospital; 30 percent of all visits to practitioners were to public hospitals. In such cases the capital required to sustain treatment might include a "contact" — often a relative working in a hospital as an orderly or janitor who could push the file ahead so that the patient was able to access the doctor without very long delays. We found several variations in the way patients reported their treatment in the public hospitals. In the lower-middle-class area of Jahangir

Puri, many households had learned how to access the Jagjivan Ram Hospital located in the area, but with the exception of treatment for TB they could rarely sustain long-term treatment because of the time demands. In other areas such as Noida, the distance to the nearest public hospital made access very difficult. In Bhagwanpur Kheda, the first hospital to be accessed was the nearest government hospital (GTBH Hospital). We are struck by the element of contingency in patients' accounts of how a disease becomes an "emergency" (to use their own expression) or how the trajectory of the therapeutic choices comes to be determined. We offer two accounts here of how a "normal" pregnancy became a life-threatening condition and how two patients dealt with this emergency. The first interview was conducted by one of us (Veena), the second by Rajan Singh, a member of the Institute of Socio-economic Research on Development and Democracy (ISERDD) team.

### DANGERS OF AND IN MEDICAL SPACES: KAMLA'S PREGNANCY

Kamla had two children at the time of her third pregnancy. Her older children had both been born at home and childbirth had been attended by a trained *dai*. During the course of the weekly surveys we learned that unexpected complications had developed at the time of the third delivery and the *dai* had been unable to handle the case. Kamla was moved to the nearby government hospital where a caesarian section was performed and a baby daughter was delivered. Initially mother and daughter did well, but within days Kamla's stitches became infected; her condition deteriorated and she was moved to a private hospital. The family was unable to tell the fieldworkers who visited every week the precise nature of the complications, but on every visit we were told that her condition was "serious." Meanwhile, the baby, who was in the nursery of the government hospital, contracted an infection and died. After a two-month stay in the private hospital Kamla was released. The family had incurred a huge debt during her hospitalization. Her husband had to sell the three-wheeler motorized rickshaw he owned and subsequently had to hire one to ply his trade. The family's income dropped considerably because Kamla's husband had to pay interest on the debt he had incurred as well as rent to the owner of the rickshaw. I (Veena) was away at the time of these events. When I returned to Delhi in the summer, I went to meet Kamla to express my condolences. Over several visits, including one in which I accompanied her to a cardiac specialist to get a second opinion on her line of treatment, I constructed the following understanding of her illness experience.

Throughout her pregnancy Kamla had a sense that she was not well, but her husband and his mother dismissed her complaints. "You are fine and fit," they said; "after all, this is your third child." The reports of the weekly survey showed that she went to a local practitioner and was given analgesics for pain and sometimes a tonic for weakness. From the medical reports of the private hospital I gleaned that she had developed an infection of the heart valves. Though her medical records do not say it, I inferred that this was in all likelihood because the instruments used during her caesarian section were not sterile. She told me that the delivery room in the hospital was dirty and that the instruments were not properly cleaned. She feels that the shift to the private hospital saved her life, but the debt it generated is like a load on her head. She knows that at some time she will require a heart valve replacement but would like to avoid it as long as possible because the hospital scares her terribly now and also because there is no money. She needs expensive medicine on a daily basis and an injection every six weeks. We managed to raise some money to pay for part of her medicines. At the time I accompanied her to the cardiac specialist, I could feel her visceral fear and doubted that she would agree to the surgery, but she and her husband are now firmly convinced that treatment is necessary and that the prescribed medicines have to be taken regularly. "*Pehle idhar udhar dolte rahe—isi liye halat kharab ho gayi—logon ki batein sunte rahe—par ab samajh aa gauyi hai*" (initially we kept moving from here to there—that is why the condition deteriorated—we kept listening to what people said—but now we have understood). Kamla blames the government hospital for its lack of cleanliness, her family for its neglect during her pregnancy, and some malign persons who, she suspects, reside in the neighborhood and have performed some kind of magic or sorcery out of envy.

## WHAT IS IT TO BE CURED?

### SANGEETA'S ENCOUNTER WITH TUBERCULOSIS

We describe the second case using a transcript of an interview on the experience of tuberculosis with a person who has been cured. The interview was conducted in Hindi in her house.[25]

**How did you discover you had TB?**

*I had many problems, a lot of weakness, so much so that it was difficult for me to sit.*

**So you had weakness. Did you have any other problem?**

*No, brother, but I did not feel like eating, nothing seemed to interest me, my heart did not engage.*

**And fever?**

*Yes, there was constant fever, there was also coughing.*

**For how long did you have this?**

*Some days, some weeks. First I started to take medicines—[then] private [in English] was started.*[26]

**So, which practitioner did you go to first?**

*See, first [I took] medicines from here and there. The local doctor gave medicines. I was not getting better. Then my daughter was born. Because I was feeling quite sick, they took me to hospital for the birth (it was my time).*[27] *I would feel great pareshani [trouble] in my throat—so they took me to hospital for my throat. . . . First they took me here and there [idhar udhar le ke dole]. Then my daughter was born. Still I could not eat anything—so then I had gone to my mummy's place. I still could not eat anything. So Mummy took me to sarkari hospital where X-ray happened. . . . Then it was known. So then in the government hospital they said I had TB. They told us to go to this TB hospital for medicines.*

**So you did not have to take any private medicines?**

*No, first Mummy thought that the private medicines will be better. See, there were problems with my throat—there was swelling, difficulty in swallowing, no appetite—so we also had it seen by a private doctor in Mayur Vihar [an upper-middle-*

*class neighborhood], but there the doctor said, don't worry—it is just a cold you will get okay. So he gave some medicine but it was very expensive and anyway there was no improvement.*[28]

As the interview progressed, she described how some people said that it was magic or sorcery and they should have it blown away through a diviner or a healer, and others recommended other private doctors.

*Then my mummy said she would just take me to the sarkari hospital—the TB hospital where they had told us to go. She said that she would not listen to anyone.*

**You mean you decided to go to the TB hospital—the one where doctors from the hospital where your daughter was born asked you to go?**

*Yes, that is the one. People said go here, go there, but Mummy said whatever anyone says I will take her to that government hospital.*

**What happened there? Did you get medicines? X-ray?**

*Yes, they gave medicine—two tablets a day. The doctor there said that the medicines must be taken. He said you can forget to eat your food but you cannot forget to take your medicine. So my husband did not have time to take me there to get medicines—so I stayed with Mummy.*

Sangeeta's interview indicates that she received free medications from the government hospital for two years, though the family also had to buy tonics from a private pharmacy. She stayed for long periods with her mother in the course of her illness. At the time of the interview she pronounced herself to have been fully cured after two years. Rajan and she discussed whether she had experienced any hostility from other family members—whether the stigma of the disease had affected her—and she said that her husband did not believe in such things. Toward the end of the interview Rajan asked, as a matter of courtesy, "So your daughter who was born at the time that your TB was discovered—is she okay?"

*No, she died when she was two years old. Everyone said I should not feed her my breast milk—she became weak. She hardly spoke. See, you have to listen when people say things. I became pregnant again and had a son but he too could not survive.*

Did the doctors in the TB hospital advise you not to feed your daughter breast milk? Did the doctors tell you anything about what to do when you became pregnant?

*No, the doctors did not tell me anything, but everyone said that my milk was not good because of the disease.*

We can see that the space surrounding therapy is crisscrossed by possibilities. Suggestions and countersuggestions come from all directions. You do not know whom to trust. In this case the medicines dispensed by the local doctor did not cure the symptoms. Sangeeta was taken to the hospital because of a difficult birth, and the TB was discovered accidentally. Her family, especially her mother, played a major role in her therapeutic choices. As a senior woman the mother could take the decision to ignore the advice of relatives and neighbors — the voices (somebody said one thing and somebody said another) had to be resolutely set aside. And though Sangeeta managed to complete the anti-TB regime of medication, she could not ignore the advice to withhold milk from her newborn child. The deaths of her two children do not seem to belong to the narrative of TB, which is not to suggest that she does not mourn for them. Yet the overall affect of the story is about the care she received from her mother and the success of the therapy. We suggest that her identification of therapy as *successful* is premised upon a certain deletion: the death of her children, to whom she may have transmitted TB. The failure of the medical system to take the overall condition of the patient into account — the concentration instead on the strict protocol of the DOT center and the poorly regulated medical practice that allowed local practitioners to treat symptoms of TB as if the patient had a simple cough or fever — is writ large in this story but never pointedly mentioned. Sangeeta is happy that her social relations endured through the course of her illness. Such is the face of success.

There are other cases in which the illness is cured but the social relations are not cured. While we cannot draw out the full implications of this entanglement of illness and forms of sociality here, it is important to note that forms of belonging in the urban context are fraught with tensions. The relation of the individual to her kinship network, her community, or her neighborhood is not one in which one can be said to belong to it as, let us say, water belongs to the bottle or clothes belong to the wardrobe. The "voices" of the community, the repeated quests for therapy for illnesses for which only temporary relief seems possible, and the constant need for brokers through which the outside world can be accessed: these make up the experiences of the body. The dependence on the medical system goes along with a tremendous distrust of the services people are receiving. The "self" in self-medication is a composite of these experiences in which the real seems to constantly elude attempts by the poor to establish a hold on it. Unlike Johansson (1991), we believe that the high rate of morbidity is not simply a function of the availability of more categories or of discursive forms alone. It is also a matter of how the institutions of the state and market interact to produce the local ecologies we have encountered in Bhagwanpur Kheda. As against the generic desires and fears of a public that propel patterns of therapy (with which we started this chapter), we hope to have shown that experiments with categories and medicines take place in specific worlds in relation to concrete questions about the problems of life, labor, and language that confront people in *a* rather than *the* world. We have tried to show how the local ecology mediates experiences of illness and the therapies that are sought. Outside the local world lie hospitals and specialists who are available only through brokered forms of sociality. The experience of illness and cure and the patterns of pharmaceutical use take place predominantly within local worlds, though the hospitals and the specialists to which patients are taken in states of emergency are never absent from the consciousness of people. These are the worlds of the poor—produced through complex configurations of policies and programs shaping medical realities that lie beyond the bedside of the patient.

The concept of local ecologies helps us to analyze the interaction between discursive and nondiscursive patterns (including but not restricted to strategies of everyday tactics) within neighborhoods. It shows how such material processes as household cash flow, patterns of disease burden, and the availability of pharmaceuticals are integrally tied to the way that linguistic diagnostic categories come into being within specific local worlds. Within these local ecologies, everyday life is about both securing access to context and being in danger of not quite securing it. Thus, local ecologies do not produce contexts for *transparency* of experience but rather for the struggle over the real.

## Notes

We are extremely grateful to the team of researchers at ISERDD, to the Centre for Livable Futures for partial financial support, and to participants in the seminar on Global Pharmaceuticals for their comments. We especially thank Susan Whyte and the editors for their help in clarifying many points. Jishnu Das and Arthur Kleinman have given intellectual support to this project which we truly value. To our households in the project and the practitioners, we will be forever indebted.

1. The concept of "self-medication" is not identical with the concept of "compliance," but they overlap to the extent that they raise questions about the power of biomedical authority. Conrad's (1985) distinction between a practitioner-centered and a patient-centered orientation to prescribed medications tries to break away from the simple opposition of compliance and noncompliance. However, the discussions around medical authority and patient autonomy generally pay somewhat less attention to the variations in the medical environments in which patients have to function. Further, most of the discussion on patient-centered strategies takes the management of chronic diseases, especially psychiatric disorders, as the privileged site for posing questions about medical authority and patient autonomy. The case of therapeutic strategies for infectious diseases in the context of urban poverty, we argue, alters the perspective from which one poses these issues, bringing in the *intertwining* of practitioner and patient practices in the creation of therapeutic strategies.

2. Even in the Western context the attitude to self-medication has varied historically according to the general cultural milieu in which commercialism, the rise of the professional power of trained physicians, and the ideology of self-reliance operate. For a brief review of these issues, see Pincus 2002.

3. For example, many of the contributors in two important volumes on the use of pharmaceuticals based their studies on household practices (see Etkin and Tan 1994; van der Geest and Whyte 1988). These volumes also include papers on the use of pharmaceuticals by traditional healers. Nichter and his colleagues have published several papers on the way that drugs are acquired, using data obtained by placing fieldworkers in pharmacies (see Kamat and Nichter 1998; Saradamma et al. 2000).

4. The project on medical markets and practitioner visits was conducted under the direction of Jishnu Das and Jeffrey Hammer and is anchored to the household survey.

5. We obtained the value of predicted consumption expenditure by estimating a regression model. In the model the reported consumption expenditure deflated by the square root of household size is regressed on the tangible assets of the households and household amenities.

6. The variations between health-seeking processes in high-income and low-income neighborhoods are important. For the purposes of this chapter, though, we are interested in the specific ecology of low-income neighborhoods.

7. The failures of medicine were often attributed to *uppari chakkar* (which refers to accusations of magic and sorcery), and specialists were deployed to deal with this through various practices of magic and exorcism.

8. We hope it will become clear later that one cannot assume a sharp separation between the classifications of the people and those of the state, in that the state categories carry traces of struggles in the civil arena and also because these categories become part of people's own repertoire of practices.

9. This particular theme is found in practically every government report on indigenous physicians since 1919.

10. Davis (2000) makes a distinction between primary terms and secondary terms depending upon how categories are combined in reference to illness in her work in Central Africa.

11. If we consider the meaning of these terms to lie in their uses, then the local context invested them with a different sense than their scientific usage would imply. Examples of this are offered later in the chapter.

12. According to Ayurvedic principles, disease occurs when there is a disturbance in the balance of the three qualities of *vata*, *pitta*, or *kapha* in the human body. Each quality is made up of a combination of two of the five elements of space, air, fire, water, and earth.

13. The estimation of kernel density fits a frequency curve to a frequency distribution without making any assumption about the nature of the underlying probability distribution.

14. The expression literally means "such small-big discomforts cling to one." Putting together two contrasting terms such as *small* and *big* to create vagueness in boundaries of expressions is a common form of speech.

15. It is important to note that practitioner access for short-duration morbidity was higher for those members of the household who were outside the labor force than those who were in it. For a detailed analysis, see Das and Sanchez 2002.

16. We note that the magnitude and pattern of visits stand in sharp contrast to the findings in the literature that suggest that number of doctor visits increases with household income (Peabody et al. 1999).

17. As stated earlier, we are not considering chronic diseases here, but even for some acute conditions, such as ongoing allergies or gas, patients reported buying medicines as maintenance doses. The number in Bhagwanpur Kheda for this pattern of use was very small (only seventeen cases).

18. Pneumonia is a category frequently used by practitioners and patients to describe severe cold or respiratory distress, and it is impossible to tell whether the diagnosis would correspond to the disease, biomedically defined. We discuss this case in greater detail later but note here that she subsequently received a diagnosis of TB and began the anti-TB regimen at the DOT center.

19. Practitioners trained in homeopathy were consulted much more in upper-income localities. A brief comparative study that we conducted in Calcutta, West Bengal, showed that there was far greater trust in homeopathy among the poor in that city. Thus, specific regional historics must be taken into account when one describes therapeutic strategies of the poor.

20. The following cautionary note is found in *CIMS* (*Current Index of Medical Specialities*), which gives drug profiles: "Cisapride has been voluntarily withdrawn in the US by Janssen Pharmaceutical. However, it was available in the US till July 14th, 2000, and for a limited period thereafter, for people meeting specific criteria. The background of this development points to certain adverse effects of concern caused by Cisapride. The Regulatory authorities in India have not voluntarily announced the discontinuation of Cisapride from

the Indian market. We, however, urge doctors in India to use Cisapride on patients based on their judgment and experience" (*CIMS*, 2001, vol. 24, no. 3: 59). Debates on the ethics of using drugs that have been withdrawn from North American and European markets in low-income countries with weak regulation are often based on the idea that such drugs are being used for life-saving events at lower costs, and that makes it permissible to tolerate a higher risk of adverse effects. Our data, however, show that in low-income neighborhoods such drugs are being used either for trivial complaints or in inappropriate fashion.

21. Dr. Saumya Das from Massachusetts General Hospital spent one month in the field conducting medical examinations with the individuals in the area who reported multiple short-duration episodes, and on the basis of his clinical judgment tried to connect these individuals with existing medical resources in the city that were better equipped to deal with their illnesses.

22. The trajectory of TB cases shows considerable variation. In this case the woman was able to access the TB center herself, whereas in the case of B, her old age would have been a major impediment to visiting the center regularly, since the family had only one earning member and the strained relations between her son's wife and her could have made it difficult for her to find someone to accompany her. Though many fresh cases of TB have developed among our contacts, there is no program of routine surveillance of contacts in the city.

23. For an excellent analysis of the way in which sickness gets entangled in the continuous reframing of one's social relations, see Davis 2000, which uses the extended case study method developed by the Manchester School for the analysis of law to the study of illness experience.

24. We found households in upper-income groups engaging in such discussions, but this was not how the poor thought of therapeutic choices.

25. The translation from the original is by Veena Das. We have retained the Hindi usages as well as the jerky character of the informant's speech. Smoothing the character of the speech would make all informants sound like professors.

26. When patients described various treatment options, the major division they used was between *private* (the word circulates in English) and *sarkari* (government). This was the dominant classification for all kinds of services ranging from health providers to schools to liquor shops to grocery stores. It is an interesting reflection of how the opposition between state and market pervades everyday categories.

27. "*Mera time aa gaya tha*" (my time had come).

28. It is difficult to respond to the question raised by some as to how the doctor could "get away with this" because a careful answer would involve documenting the nature of pedagogical practice in medical schools, the decline of institutions, the rampant corruption in admissions and examinations, and the absence of any serious monitoring of medical practice. This is what allows a high level of competence in the elite hospitals to be maintained along with unacceptable levels of incompetence in the practice of medicine in low-income neighborhoods.

# Pharmaceutical Governance

JOÃO BIEHL

## Treating AIDS in Brazil

Brazil's groundbreaking AIDS Program combines safe-sex prevention and harm reduction campaigns with the free distribution of antiretroviral therapies (ARVs). In 2005 some 170,000 people were taking anti-HIV drugs funded by the Brazilian government.[1] According to the Health Ministry, both AIDS mortality and the use of hospital services have fallen by more than 50 percent in Rio de Janeiro and São Paulo, the most affected areas of the country (MS 2002). Mother-to-child HIV transmission is said to have been reduced by two-thirds, and Brazil's initiative is widely touted as a model for stemming the AIDS crisis among the poorest (Galvão 2000; Farmer et al. 2001; Rosenberg 2001:28).[2]

Of the more than 40 million people living with HIV worldwide, 95 percent are in the developing world. More than 44 million people in thirty-four of these poor countries, mostly in sub-Saharan Africa, will have lost one or both parents to AIDS by 2010.[3] In the face of the devastation brought about by AIDS, the unlikely availability of a vaccine in the near future, and the relatively few interventions that seem replicable, Brazil's is a most welcome success story. The Brazilian response to HIV-AIDS challenges the perception that treating AIDS in resource-poor settings is economically unfeasible, and calls our attention to the possible ways in which biotechnology can be integrated into public policy even in the absence of an optimal health infrastructure. It also opens up the political and moral debate over delivering life-extending drugs to countries where patients are poor and institutions have limited capacity, and the immediate and long-term medical implications of doing so.

In this chapter, I discuss how this life-extending policy came into existence through an inventive combination of activist forces and the interests of a reforming state, transnational organizations, and the pharmaceutical industry — all in a context of deeply entrenched inequality. I then assess the policy's medical and social reach, particularly in impoverished urban settings where AIDS is spreading most rapidly. Among the questions my ethnographic and social epidemiological work addresses are: Which political institutions and technological practices make this large-scale drug rollout possible, and what guarantees its sustainability? What networks of care emerge around the distribution and use of ARVs among the poor and marginalized? What makes them visible or invisible in their communities and within this pharmaceutical regime? How do individual sufferers fare in the long term as they engage with AIDS treatments? Which models of public health and of citizenship are unfolding?

Throughout the chapter I show that the development of the AIDS policy dovetails with former president Fernando Henrique Cardoso's efforts to internationalize Brazil's economy. Drawing from research I carried out among people working in state, corporate, scientific, and nongovernmental institutions, I was able to identify some of the practices and means through which the AIDS policy materialized and yielded change: AIDS activism within the state; international partnerships (e.g., World Bank); centralized and businesslike management of an AIDS expert community; regional AIDS programs and epidemiological monitoring making some AIDS populations visible; revitalization of the state-run pharmaceutical sector, which was in ruins; a decentralized universal care system facilitating drug distribution; a well-orchestrated mobilization for drug price differentiation in favor of developing countries.

The medical accountability at stake in this innovative policy has drastic implications for Brazil's fifty million urban poor (some 30 percent of the population), who are either indigent or make their living through informal and marginal economies. Despite the alleged universal reach of the AIDS policy, these people have not been explicitly targeted for specific governmental policies related to housing, employment, and security, among others. They gain some public attention during political elections—even then only in the most general terms—and through the limited aid of international agencies. However, through AIDS, new fields of exchange and possibility have emerged.[4]

Medication has become a key element in the state's arsenal of action. As AIDS activism migrated into state institutions, and as the state played an increasingly activist role in the international politics of drug pricing, AIDS became, in many ways, the "country's disease." While new pharmaceutical markets have opened, and anti-HIV drugs have been made universally available (the state is *actually* present through the dispensation of medication), it is up to individuals and communities to take on locally the roles of medical and political institutions. This redefinition of governance and citizenship, obviously efficacious in the treatment of AIDS, also crystallizes new inequalities.

In sum, this chapter illuminates the political and social implications of a shift that the Brazilian AIDS policy represents: from a crumbling welfare state to an activist state; from international and public health understood as prevention and clinical care to access to medication; and from political to biological rights as a new and selective form of patient citizenship takes form.[5]

These are not straightforward realities with predetermined outcomes. I approach the AIDS policy as a contemporary "form/event," to use Paul Rabinow's terminology, through which novel political rationalities and infrastructures of care are actualized. Mobilized individuals and groups must continuously maneuver this particular form/event to gain medical visibility and have their claims to life addressed. "Analytic attention to forms/events," writes Rabinow, "brings us closer to the shifting practices, discursive and otherwise, as well as to the shifting configurations that both shape and are shaped by such practices" (1999:179; also see Rabinow 2003).

### AIDS and Democratization

With a population of more than 170 million, Brazil is the most populous country in Latin America. While HIV prevalence is estimated to be below 1 percent nationally, this low prevalence hides serious local epidemics. In certain cities, for example, some 60 percent of injecting drug users are infected with HIV (UNAIDS 2004).

HIV/AIDS emerged in Brazil in the early 1980s concurrently with the demise of the military state. Its growth coincided with the country's democratization amid a ruined economic and social welfare system (Parker and Daniel 1991; Parker et al. 1994; Galvão 2000). Epidemiological surveillance services registered the first HIV/AIDS cases in 1982: seven homosexual or bisexual men (later, one HIV/AIDS case from 1980 was found in São Paulo). In 1984, 71 percent of all HIV/AIDS cases were among men who have sex with men; injecting drug users and hemophiliacs were also affected. The virus was most prevalent in urban centers—as of 1985, 89 percent of the reported cases came from São Paulo and Rio de Janeiro (Castilho and Chequer 1997). But over the following two decades, this epidemiological profile would rapidly and dramatically change (Bastos and Barcellos 1995, 1996).

For example, in May 2000, the homosexual/bisexual mode of transmission accounted for less than 30 percent of the total number of AIDS cases registered since the beginning of the epidemic; and transmission through intravenous drug use accounted for 20 percent (MS 2002). By the late 1980s and early 1990s, heterosexual transmission had become predominant, and the number of women infected grew considerably. In 1985, there were 25 men for every woman with HIV/AIDS; by 1990, the ratio had reached 6:1, and in 2000 it arrived at 2:1. The feminization of the epidemic also led to a gradual growth of mother-to-child HIV transmission. In 1990 vertical transmission was responsible for 47 percent of HIV infections among children; and in 2002 this number had risen to 90 percent.

The epidemic has also rapidly spread among the poor and disadvantaged. In 1985, for example, 79 percent of the reported HIV/AIDS cases involved individuals who had at least high school education; by 2000, 73.8 percent were illiterate or had only finished elementary school (Fonseca et al. 2000).

By 1985, all regions in Brazil had reported AIDS cases. The Ministry of Health and the media, however, continued to stigmatize HIV-AIDS and treat it as an issue confined to homosexuals and posing no threat to the "general population." According to pioneer AIDS activist Herbert Daniel, since its beginnings AIDS in Brazil was thought of as "something foreign and strange," as well as "something inevitable, almost a kind of price to be paid for the modernity of our cities" (1991:542). The National AIDS Program was put into place in 1986, but the minister of health made it clear that while the government considered AIDS "a serious disease . . . [it] is not our priority" (in Parker and Daniel 41991:77). The government's initial refusal to seriously address the particularities of the spread of AIDS in the country and systematic nonintervention would play a determinant role in the unfettered course of the epidemic among most vulnerable populations (Scheper-Hughes 1994; Parker 1994).[6]

In those early years of AIDS — amid fear, stigma, and lack of national and international support — effective responses sprang from grassroots movements, most notably from gay activist groups that pressured municipal and regional health services for information and treatment, and that also carried out their own prevention campaigns. Founded in 1980, GGB, the Gay Group of Bahia was already actively at work during Carnival 1982, distributing brochures that alerted people to the "gay plague" or "pink cancer." In São Paulo, groups like Outra Coisa and Somos also distributed information on the disease and played a key role in creating a province-wide public health HIV/AIDS program in 1983, the first of its kind in Latin America. Its supervisor, Dr. Paulo Teixeira, would bring his know-how to the National AIDS Program and later also to the World Health Organization (WHO; see Teixeira 1997). Here grassroots and local-state interventions were not antithetical to each other. Already, a mutual implication of activism and state — that is, activism within the state — becomes characteristic of AIDS mobilization. The local activists and governmental actors had a common progressive political commitment; both understood the need to integrate information and care, as well as to pragmatically establish alliances with health professionals and philanthropic and religious institutions — these interventions proved to be quite efficient (Galvão 2000:59).

The HIV/AIDS epidemic also occasioned the creation of several new nongovernmental organizations (NGOS) throughout the country, bringing together AIDS patients, progressive intellectuals, and activist migrants from other social movements on the decline. In 1985, the first GAPA (Group of Support and Prevention Against AIDS) was created in São Paulo; it soon set up affiliates in Porto Alegre and Salvador. The GAPAS worked on prevention and also mediated the treatment and legal demands of AIDS sufferers. In 1986, Herbert Daniel created ABIA, the Brazilian Interdisciplinary AIDS Association, which played a key role in the production and dissemination of HIV/AIDS knowledge. ARCA (Religious Support against AIDS) was created in 1987 to mobilize response in religious institutions. In 1989, the group Pella Vida (another important outgrowth of Daniel's work) was formed in Rio de Janeiro and São Paulo, mostly composed of HIV-positive persons and aimed at addressing their medical and treatment concerns. A language of solidarity and citizenship punctuated the various initiatives of these NGOS.

These organizations played a decisive role in shaping AIDS prevention policies; they also helped to shape legislation that made the registration of AIDS cases compulsory in 1986 and to reform dangerous blood bank practices (Galvão 2000:73).[7] The groups galvanized demands and actions aimed at securing AIDS patients the rights to healthcare mandated by Brazil's new progressive constitution. "Health," the 1988 constitution reads, "is a right of every individual and a duty of the state, guaranteed by social and economic policies that seek to reduce the risk of disease and other injuries, and by universal and equal access to services designed to promote, protect, and recover health" (Constitution of the Federative Republic of Brazil 1988). The principles of universality, equity, and integrality in health services were supposed to guide the new Brazilian health care system known as Sistema Único de Saúde or SUS (Fleury 1997). In practice, however, the right to healthcare would have to be realized amid fiscal austerity, decentralization, and community- and family-centered approaches to primary care. In 1989, for example, the federal government spent $83 on health per person; in 1993 this amount plunged to $37.[8]

Representing socially vulnerable groups such as homosexuals and sex workers, AIDS activists developed a strong public voice in the dispute over access to ever-scarcer public and medical resources. In 1988, for example, activists successfully lobbied the Congress to extend disability status and pensions to all people with AIDS (Law 7670; see Teixeira 1997:61). As the underfunded and understaffed state public healthcare services were increasingly incapable of addressing the growing complexities of AIDS, grassroots and pastoral spaces of healthcare began to emerge — until today the so-called *casas de apoio* ("houses of support") bear the medical and social burden of the AIDS crisis among the poorest.[9]

## Transnational Policy Space

Amid major political changes (including the impeachment of President Fernando Collor de Melo), the National AIDS Program was restructured in 1992. That same year the Brazilian government and the World Bank approved a $250 million aid package for the creation of a new national AIDS program designed to reverse what international experts were already calling the "Africanization" of AIDS in Brazil.[10] Experts were predicting that by the year 2000, Brazil would have 1.2 million people infected with HIV. The country's epidemic was neither "nascent" (as in Chile or Morocco) nor "generalized" (as in Sub-Saharan Africa), the experts said. Rather, it was "concentrated" — meaning that HIV was found in more than 5 percent of the so-called risk groups and in less than 5 percent of all women undergoing prenatal care — and was thus technically manageable.

In the 1990s, with the IMF and World Bank figuring prominently into policy decisions, fiscal austerity was on the rise and the social contract was on the decline. The well-known "Washington Consensus" — with all its support for structural readjustment, market deregulation, and trade liberalization — was developed specifically in response to Latin America's problems (Williamson 1990). According to the international financial institutions, governments had let budgets get out of control, loose monetary policy had led to rampant inflation, and excessive state intervention in the economy had thwarted sustained economic growth.

Alongside these policy shifts, AIDS became increasingly cast as a development problem, prompting social mobilization and demands for public intervention. Various circumstances and actors met in an empty "space of policy" (Hirschman 1995:179). According to Dr. Paulo Teixeira, one of the key articulators of the changes in the national AIDS program, "There was a strategic convergence of interests. . . . Of course, the World Bank was interested in the country's overall economic restructuring, but Brazil was also a concrete site for the Bank to test the financing of such an abstract area: the control of an epidemic through prevention, in the absence of a vaccine" (personal communication, June 2005).

With new national and international funds available, both mobilized citizens and governmental institutions were to infuse this policy-space with specific rationalities, technologies, and claims of human and medical rights. Activists gave up their antagonism toward the state and organized, together with politicians, social scientists, and public health professionals, an impressive apparatus of HIV/AIDS control. The infrastructures and networks previously developed by NGOs and afflicted communities became a key asset in the development of a centralized and efficient AIDS program, dealing with international monitoring and regional demands for intervention. Epidemiologists, demographers, and statisticians working within both the program and local health systems were also beginning to make the human scope of the epidemic legible.

Just as in other policy areas, the World Bank attempted to shape the Brazilian AIDS program. But this time, according to Dr. Teixeira, "The Bank's team included experts that had very progressive views, very similar to those we defended. They supported actions compatible with our national needs—for example, work with injecting drug users. They also agreed that NGOs would have access to the financial resources and would execute the projects. . . . Of course, our view of the NGO was more of a grassroots type, and they had in mind something much more institutionalized" (personal communication, June 2005).

The main disagreement between the World Bank and the Brazilian AIDS policy-makers was over treatment, states Richard Parker, who also participated in the first meetings with the Bank's experts: "In this negotiation process, the Bank's pressure not to have free dispensation of medication was always in the air. There was pressure for the resources to be used mainly for prevention, because within a neoliberal logic of costs and benefits, it is prevention that would bring more economic benefits. This was the logic that guided the Bank's work to a certain degree, and in spite of some changes, continues to guide the Bank's investments in health and in AIDS in general" (Parker 2001).

The politically progressive and socially minded activists and health professionals that now run the AIDS program kept open the possibility of medical assistance being part of the government's response to the epidemic and, in many ways, fought for it to happen on a larger scale. In 1988, medications to treat opportunistic diseases were already available, if on a limited basis, in the public health care system. Then in 1991, the government signed into law the free distribution of AZT and medication for opportunistic infections, but in practice, the supply and dispensation remained irregular (Galvão 2002:214).

The majority of new AIDS funds were allocated to prevention, mostly through NGOs (which grew in number from 120 in 1993 to more than 500 in early 2000) and to the institutional development of regional and municipal AIDS programs that operated like NGOs. Massive, community-mediated prevention projects sought to contain the epidemic's growth, with a particular focus on safe-sex education, condom distribution, HIV testing, behavioral change and harm reduction (CN 2000a; Galvão 2000; World Bank 1999).

In my work in several regions of Brazil, I documented how the local implementation of HIV/AIDS prevention projects corroborated at least three cultural processes: (1) the individualized ingraining of a health-based concept of citizenship mediated by risk and vulnerability assessments; (2) the management of subjectivity in public health sites through testing technologies; and (3) the shaping of an ideal form of communitarian sociality. Social ties were being recast in nongovernmental sites, anonymous epidemiological clinics, and in short-term community initiatives (Biehl 2001b; see also Larvie 1997).

At any rate, at that moment in the AIDS policy's existence, NGOs represented afflicted populations within the state, and at a local level, the NGOs themselves were ruled by what the anthropologist Jane Galvão calls "the dictatorship of projects" (2000). Also at local levels, religious and philanthropic institutions were triaging AIDS patients' access to welfare and medical goods.

After researchers presented the combined antiretroviral therapies at the Eleventh International AIDS Conference in Vancouver, in 1996, Brazilian AIDS activists and patients—together with politically progressive technical specialists working within the National AIDS Program—were able to mobilize public opinion and to garner the support of various political parties in guaranteeing the right to these new technologies.

In November 1996 Brazil became the first developing country to adopt an official policy of universalizing access to life-extending drugs. President Fernando Henrique Cardoso signed a law (proposed by senator and former president José Sarney) that made antiretrovirals available to all registered HIV-AIDS cases. The law obliged the public health system to freely dispense these drugs. Technical specialists at national and regional levels generated criteria for identifying AIDS patients and for implementing this intervention through SUS, the universal healthcare system. Doctors were required to report cases to the Ministry of Health in order for patients to be able to obtain the medication from their local public health services.

The immediate results of this pharmaceutical policy were striking: as of June 1998, fifty-eight thousand AIDS patients were taking ARVs. By the end of the previous year, the National AIDS Program was already reporting that the therapies were decreasing the number of AIDS deaths and treatment costs (CN1997h). In São Paulo, the number of reported AIDS deaths during the first three months of 1997 was 35 percent lower than the numbers of deaths in the same three-month period in 1996. The reported death decrease for the same period in Rio de Janeiro was 21 percent (Oliveira et al. 2002). In considering these shifts, the Program emphasized that the decrease in AIDS deaths paralleled a substantial reduction in hospitalization rates among AIDS patients for diseases such as tuberculosis and pneumonia. Use of emergency services and day-hospitals was also said to be on the decline: "In São Paulo, the demand for treatment in day-hospitals decreased 40 percent. The reduction of the demand for this kind of service led to the closure of one of the two floors of the AIDS Unit of the Hospital das Clínicas" (CN1997c). The economic gains were reported to be immense. Although the National AIDS Program and the Ministry of Health had spent some $300 million on anti-HIV medication in 1998, the policy saved the government at least $500 million.

"This drug-policy increased self-reporting and as a result, we have achieved near universal registration," epidemiologist Pedro Chequer told me in an interview at the Health Ministry, in August 2000. He had been director of the AIDS program since 1996 and played a key role in the implementation of the drug rollout. Indeed, antiretroviral therapies were now available, but the claim of universal access and demand sounded like a strategy to bolster the success of the policy, and thus add political value to it, as a way to ensure sustainability. As I will show later, the supply of AIDS services in public hospitals in poorer regions remained precarious, and many AIDS victims were left without adequate care. All this technical infrastructure and medication "is not a gift," added Chequer, "it is the governmental response to a very well organized social demand. . . . The state has to continue to invest in pharmaceutical production, and it will."

One of the National AIDS Program's chief pharmacists noted: "It is social mobilization that gives us the political legitimacy to make the medication available. We are an instrument of social mobilization; we give it rationality and make it work. Politicians give priority to this kind of social pressure. It is time now for AIDS to transfer this experience of both social mobilization and treatments to other pathologies, like TB and Hansen's. We have to revolutionize the health sector" (personal communication, January 2000).

These committed health professionals/activists are well aware of how to maximize demands for equity within the reforming state. With an agenda of social inclusion, they defend national autonomy and a productive state (at least to account for medical needs). At the same time, they also articulate an awareness that social policy should be cut to fit the logic of international market institutions. "Now we have concrete data on the decline in mortality, showing that the investment has been worthwhile," Chequer told me: "The talk on rights and ethics is nonsense for people in the economic area of the government. . . . You must say [to them] we spent that much, we saved that much, the policy is valuable because of this. We demonstrated that even though the investment is high, the indirect savings are higher in terms of treatment of opportunistic diseases, less family disruption and loss of productivity. . . . The AIDS experience also challenges other disease-areas to work from this management perspective and use us as a template" (personal communication, August 2000).

Given this innovative management and apparent HIV/AIDS containment associated with the first World Bank loan, a second loan, "AIDS II," was approved and implemented in 1998. By 1999, the World Bank was reporting that its joint project with the Brazilian government, NGOs, and regional and municipal AIDS programs had led to "an estimated 30 percent decline in morbidity levels among the leading risk groups" (World Bank 1999; Garrison and Abreu 2000). The new estimate had 600,000 people infected out of a population exceeding 170 million. That same year, UNAIDS named the Brazilian program the best in the developing world (CN 2000a).

José Serra, an economist and Brazil's former health minister (see Serra 2002), told me in an interview in June 2003 at the Institute for Advanced Study at Princeton, where he was spending the year: "The [World] Bank's loan is small if compared with what the government has spent on the AIDS Program. But the bank presents it as one of its most important success stories." Serra had run for president the previous year, and the AIDS policy played an important role in his campaign. In spite of its traditional "nonuniversalistic and focused approach, the bank never limited the scope of our action," said Serra. "Overall, the bank's participation was positive, as it obliged us to do something well organized, to manage things efficiently, to have a transparent accounting of all projects."

The World Bank, along with the International Monetary Fund (IMF), had been harshly criticized in the mid-1990s for the negative impact that structural readjustment plans were having, particularly on the ability of local governments to reduce the spread of HIV infection (Lurie at al. 1995). The Brazilian success story came at a time when the bank was seriously reconsidering its mission to eradicate poverty and was exploring the need to more directly involve governments in the design of policies (Stiglitz 2002). As Serra (currently the mayor of São Paulo) noted, "Informally the bank's leading figures told us that we were doing the right thing with medication distribution and challenging the pharmaceutical companies to reduce prices." Evidently, the state does not completely compromise its regulatory functions as it negotiates loans and adjustment plans with international agencies. Nevertheless, acts of governing and concepts of development are definitively recast in the process.

### AIDS Markets

Most accounts by social scientists explain the Brazilian "antiretroviral revolution" in terms of the strength of the country's social mobilization. Gay activist groups, AIDS activists, and experts on the disease all played a critical role in forcing the federal government to fulfill its constitutionally mandated health obligations. "If the decision to distribute medication can be seen from the technical-political angle," Jane Galvão writes, "the mobilization of civil society has been key to its maintenance" (2002:16). Galvão cites the 1999 and 2000 public mobilization that forced the Ministry of Economics to continue importing medication in spite of the devaluation of Brazil's currency. In 2000, at the World AIDS conference in Durban, a manifesto from the AIDS program demanding treatment for all in need and offering aid to other developing countries stirred international debate. Brazil also coordinated efforts that led the United Nations to pass a resolution in June 2001 that recognized access to medication as a fundamental ingredient for the human right to health. The success of these events, argues Galvão, is due to local activists' alliances with international organizations that have politicized patents as a question of fair global exchange and social justice.

Indeed, much of the inventiveness and success of the AIDS policy is due to the encroachment of social mobilization within the state and its transnational ramifications (CN2002). Other political, technological, and market forces have also been determinants of the AIDS policy's form and course, and I will briefly consider their contributions below. I will also elaborate on the *pharmaceutical form of governance* that comes out of these new configurations of collective action, a neoliberalizing state, and the pharmaceutical industry.

Let us consider first how the antiretroviral law fits into former president Cardoso's plan to internationalize Brazil's economy. It was no coincidence that just a few months before the antiretroviral law was approved the government had given in to industry pressures to legalize patent protection. Brazil had signed the Trade-Related Aspects of Intellectual Property Rights treaty, known as TRIPS, the previous year, and because the government was eager to attract new investments, it allowed a quicker change in legislation than other countries such as India, China, and Argentina (Sell 2003). Brazil's new intellectual property legislation became effective in May 1997. Meanwhile, parallel to the new legislation, pharmaceutical imports to Brazil have increased substantially. Between 1995 and 1997, the trade deficit in pharmaceutical products jumped from $417 million to $1.277 billion (Bermudez 2000:6).

"Brazil bet a lot on the World Trade Organization [WTO] and dove into it, body and soul," former health minister José Serra told me in an interview in June 2003. "We adopted all trade rules that the developed world wanted." The U.S. government always put patents on the negotiating table, said Serra: "They had a few hanging things with Brazil, the nuclear thing, human rights, indigenous people and patents, these were always on the agenda in the early 1990s." Middle-income countries were offered a very strong "developmental" justification for adhering to TRIPS, as is often the case in the call for neoliberal reforms. You provide patent protection in your country, the logic goes, and we, the investors, feel confident in investing there, which translates to more foreign investment and development for you.

According to Serra, neoliberalization developed "abruptly; it anticipated events. In one or two years Brazil changed commercial policies in place since the 1930s. From a closed and protected economy we went to the opposite. Today, Brazil is an economy that is much more open and unprotected than the American one. This openness was unilateral. It was not a negotiating process through which the country gained something in return. The developed countries didn't make any concessions with textiles and agriculture, for example."

Serra suggested that the early and mid-1990s was a transition period that left little time to critically reflect on the wide-range implications of the terms of economic readjustment — "Things were not so clear." The long-term effects of TRIPS did not generate a great deal of public debate, for example, other than recognition that it marked countries' conformity to global trade reforms. In particular, there was a lack of discussion over the impact of pharmaceutical patents on drug prices and accessibility. The president and his team took hasty and legally binding decisions. And from this new landscape defined by globalization, government was built. "We did not hesitate to abolish all taxes for the import of medication," Serra recalls. "Many in the national industrial sector complained, but we did this to hold the impact of exchange rates on inflation and to increase competition, to stimulate the production of generics."

Brazil is among the ten largest pharmaceutical markets in the world (Bermudez 1992, 1995). In 1998, approximately fifteen-thousand drugs were sold in the country, with sales reaching $11.1 billion (Cosendey et al. 2000; Luiza 1999). Some seventy pharmaceutical multinationals compete for a slice of Brazil's lucrative market. The Brazilian case is much in line with global trends; by 2010, the developing world is expected to account for approximately 26 percent of the world pharmaceutical market in value, compared with 14.5 percent in 1999. The majority of growth is estimated for Latin America and Asia, specifically Brazil and India. As a Brazilian infectious disease specialist and adviser to the World Health Organization explains: "Pharmaceutical companies had already recouped their research investment with the sell-off of AIDS drugs in the United States and Europe and now with Brazil, they had a new fixed market; and even if they had to lower prices they had some unforeseen return. If things worked out in Brazil, new AIDS markets could be opened in Asia and perhaps in Africa" (personal communication, August 2000).

An executive of a pharmaceutical multinational that sells anti-HIV drugs to Brazil and whom I shall call Dr. Jones does not put things so explicitly, but he asserts, "Patents are not the problem. The problem is that there are no markets for these medications in most poor countries. Things worked out in Brazil because of political will" (personal communication, May 2003). Here "no markets" dovetails with local governments' lack of a holistic vision of public health, in which the public and private sector work in tandem: "We see an evolution in countries which have coordinated efforts, a strong national AIDS program, partnership with private sectors, and the country's leader supporting intervention."

Brazil recognized the impact of the disease immediately, this pharmaceutical executive claimed, and "it also approached the problem from a multisectoral perspective." In Dr. Jones's recollection (which bypasses the national government's initial disregard of AIDS), campaigns for education and destigmatization led to public dialogue, coupled with a changing vision of public health: "Health is not an area that the Brazilian government allowed to deteriorate anywhere near the degree of what we see in other developing countries. You had an existing structure of STD clinics and World Bank funding helped to strengthen the infrastructure." In this rendering, Brazil's "political will" to treat AIDS coincides with the country's partnership with both international financial institutions and the pharmaceutical industry: "Different than in Africa, in Brazil we had a successful business with our first antiretroviral products. And we will continue to have tremendously successful businesses based on our partnership approach with the government. Brazil continues to be an example of how you can do the right thing in terms of public health, understanding the needs of both the private sector and the government and its population. The government was able to take advantage of existing realities. There was no intellectual property protection for our early products, and given Brazil's industrial capacity, they were able to produce the drugs."

I asked Dr. Jones how the pharmaceutical industry reacted to this strategy. "We were angry," he said. But rather than withdraw from Brazil, the company used the incident over pricing and generics to negotiate broader market access in Brazil. "The down side could have been 'why bother and continue to invest in Brazil?' But anti-HIV products are not the sole bread and butter of most companies. So from a portfolio perspective, any private company balances its specific activities vis-à-vis the entirety of what it is doing. This one sector was being affected but our company had been in Brazil for a long time and we continued to be ranked as a top company there. So we had to look at it in a much broader perspective than an action taken in one product category."

The industry's capacity to neutralize and redirect any form of counterreaction to its advantage is indeed remarkable. In the last few years, following the consolidation of the Brazilian policy and other successful treatment initiatives (by organizations such as Partners-in-Health and Doctors Without Borders), an international consensus has emerged over the feasibility of delivering antiretroviral therapies to the neediest in resource-poor settings. The industry is again exercising its flexibility and turning these unexpected fields of medical action into market opportunities.

As I continued the interview, I told Dr. Jones that I had recently read a pharmaco-economic report on emergent HIV/AIDS pharmaceutical markets—namely Brazil, Thailand, India, China, and South Africa—that argued that if these governments were to provide the simplest version of the "AIDS cocktail" to 30 percent of the affected populations at 10 percent of the current U.S. price, the industry would still profit an additional $11.2 billion. He refuted this idea of emergent AIDS markets in the developing world, evoking Africa and corporate philanthropy once again: "We will supply ARVs to Africa at low cost, there will be some demand, there will be increase in volume of products sold, but by definition it is not a market for us. . . . We know that the more we sell the more we lose."

As I engaged the pharmaceutical executive's arguments and juxtaposed them to those of policymakers such as Serra, I was able to sketch the logic of the form of pharmaceutical governance represented in the Brazilian AIDS policy. Global markets are incorporated via medical commodities. This process is mediated by international public organizations (WHO, UNAIDS, the World Bank, for example) and has crucial ramifications for the nature and scope of national and local public health interventions. More specifically, once a government designates a disease like AIDS "the country's disease," a market takes shape — a captive market. Here, political will means novel public-private cooperation over drugs. As this government supposedly addresses the needs of its population, which is now (unequally) refracted through the "country's disease," the market possibilities of the pharmaceutical industry are taken in new directions and enlarged, particularly as older lines of treatment (generic ARVs) lose their efficacy, necessitating the introduction of newer and more expensive treatments (still under patent protection) that are demanded by mobilized AIDS patients. Patienthood and civic participation are thus conflated in an emergent market. As Dr. Jones puts it:

> We are seeing changes there where governments try to find out the role they can play in the field of health, health as a fundamental issue they need to deal with. At what point does it get to the government that today citizens put a huge premium on access to health? And it is not just a matter of guaranteeing access to the available medications but of the new ones being developed. If you don't have the capacity to produce this new medication, then you have to find a way to align yourself and partner and trade with those who are doing it. With a global disease like AIDS you must play together and not on your own.

### The Pharmaceuticalization of Public Health

This pharmaceutical logic implies a magic-bullet approach in international health (that is, delivery of technology regardless of immediate attention to health care infrastructures). In Brazil, this logic was deeply involved in the health policies that Cardoso's administration devised. The antiretroviral law was immediately implemented across the country through the ailing universal health care system. The new AIDS policy was aligned with a pharmaceutically focused form of health delivery that was then being put into place: Brazil has indeed seen an incremental change in the concept of public health, from prevention and clinical care to community-based care and drugging—that is, public health is increasingly decentralized *and* pharmaceuticalized.

As part of Brazil's decentralization and rationalization of universal healthcare, the government recast the costly and inefficient Basic Pharmacy Program whereby municipalities distributed state-funded basic medication to the general population. Provinces and municipalities were urged to develop their own specific treatment strategies and to administer federal and local funds in the acquisition and dispensation of basic medication (Ministério da Saúde [MS] 1997, 1999; Yunes 1999; Wilken and Bermudez n.d.). The localized policy should contribute to cuts in hospitalizations and to making families and communities stronger participants in therapeutic processes. This program took root in key states, which then became models for other regions (Cosendey et al. 2000).

Overall, however, as I discovered in my fieldwork in the southern and northeastern regions, the universal availability of essential medication has been subject to changing political winds; treatments are easily stopped, and people have to seek more specialized services in the private health sector or, as many put it, "die waiting" in overcrowded public services (Acurcio et al. 1996; Arrais et al. 1997). Local services can rarely plan alternative treatments, for their budgets are as restricted as their pharmaceutical quotas. State plans and medical demand are uncoordinated. The flow of this universal and pharmaceutically mediated health care delivery is discontinuous.

But the problem is not universal. Even though the responsibility for distributing medication is being increasingly regionalized, the lobbies for patients and the pharmaceutical industry have kept the federal government responsible for the distribution of medication classified as "exceptional," as well as medication for diseased populations which are part of "special national programs," such as the AIDS Program. A federal decree on pharmaceutical dispensation was approved in 1995, as was a list of drugs that were officially part of the Health

Ministry's budget. The content of the list was most likely based on interest groups' demands. The fact is that an increasing number of patient groups — many funded by the pharmaceutical industry — are legally forcing the government to keep importing their extremely expensive medication. According to Jorge Bermudez, a public health expert, what is being consolidated is "an individualized rather than collective pharmaceutical care" (Bermudez 2000). An understanding of the success of the AIDS policy must keep in sight this mobilization and lobbying over inclusion and exclusion as new markets and regulations, and certain forms of "good government" are being realized. In the last part of this chapter I will show that on the ground, these new mechanisms of governance are mediating the emergence of *local triage states* and selective forms of *patient citizenship*.

"This new phase of capitalism does not necessarily limit states; it also opens up new perspectives for states," former president Cardoso told me in an interview in May 2003. "The old producing state had no ways to capitalize and compete. As we broke monopolies we also had to create new agencies and rules to oversee the market for you cannot allow the state not to have voice in these areas." The AIDS policy evolved within this paradoxical space of a downsizing of the role of central government and the need to create, in Cardoso's own words, "new rules for the political game." During Cardoso's two administrations, centralized decision making, clientelism, and corruption, as he sees it, were replaced by combined state and community actions and the "work on public opinion." These actions are fundamental for the maximization of equity and social well-being in the face of the market's "inevitable" agency in resource allocation and benefits. The work of nongovernmental organizations and their international counterparts gave voice to specific mobilized communities and helped to consolidate actions that were wider and more efficacious than state action alone. "I always said that we needed to have a porous state so that society could act in it. The case of AIDS is the maximum: the state and the social movement practically fused," Cardoso told me. In retrospect, Cardoso sees himself as the articulator of an "activist state."[11]

Empowered by the National AIDS Program, activists forced the government to draft two additional legal articles that would allow compulsory licensing of patented drugs in a public health crisis, and this legislation created a venue for state activism vis-à-vis the pharmaceutical industry. As Cardoso put it: "All the nongovernmental work, [the] change in legislation, [and the] struggle over patents are evidence of new forms of governmentality in action . . . thereby engineering something else, producing a new world."

I asked José Serra whether the state had the capacity to address other large-scale diseases pharmaceutically. "Without a doubt. But the problem does not lie in government," he said. "The government ends up responding to society's pressure, and with AIDS, the pressure was very well-organized. You must have a huge mobilization. See the case of TB. It is easier to treat than AIDS, and much cheaper. The major difficulty lies in treatment adherence. But you are unable to mobilize NGOs and society for this cause. If TB had a fifth of the kind of social mobilization AIDS has, the problem would be solved. *So it is a problem of society itself*" (personal communication, June 2003).

For Cardoso, too, the management of AIDS is clear evidence that politics have definitively moved beyond the control of parties and ideologies: "There is no superior intelligence imposing anything . . . a party, a president, an ideology . . . but there are assemblages, alliances, strategies," he stated in the interview in May 2003. "Today, Brazilian society is much more open than people imagine and very mobilized. In reality, people do not live in a state of illusion as intellectuals and journalists generally think of them; they have learned to mobilize and know how to make pressure and activate those in Congress with whom they have affinities."

This is also true for the pharmaceutical industry and its powerful lobby, I added. Cardoso replied: "Indeed, they also mobilize because there is a struggle going on. A bet on democracy leads to this kind of diversity. The government has to navigate amid all these pressures. It must set some specific objectives and develop directives to that end amid this confusion. It cannot just be on this or that side, it must more or less pilot."

### Public Sector Science

Brazil's AIDS policy is fueled by a politicized science sector.[12] The strengthening of the country's scientific infrastructure and pharmaceutical industry has been key to its realization of the antiretrovirals law and the sustainability of the distribution policy. Dr. Eloan Pinheiro, a chemist and former manager of a British pharmaceutical subsidiary, was until early 2003 the director of Far Manguinhos, Brazil's main pharmaceutical company and the one producing many of the generic antiretrovirals that are being dispensed (see Cassier and Correa 2003). In an interview in August 2001 she told me that public laboratories accounted for some 40 percent of Brazilian ARV production, and that her Technological Development Division had already reverse-engineered two drugs that were under patent protection and were "ready to go into production if the government deems it necessary."

Dr. Pinheiro views Brazil's patent legislation as simply "wrong." "It makes the country dependent on imports and hinders local scientific and technological development." In the years following the country's 1996 new industry property law, Brazil has requested only seventeen pharmaceutical and biotechnological patents, representing 1.4 percent of the world's total requests (the USA had 46 percent, Great Britain 13 percent, and Germany 10 percent; Bermudez et al. n.d.). Dr. Pinheiro is adamant in her support for state industry: "Nobody can negotiate price without challenging a patented product. We don't want to compete with richer nations, but we hope to reach a stage of independence."

Given the fact that the production of medication in Brazil "has been a multinational business" since the 1950s, says Dr. Pinheiro, she was not totally surprised when she learned that the state's top laboratory had reduced production to three basic drugs by the time she took over as coordinator of Far Manguinhos in the late 1980s. In her work with the British multinational, she had learned much about drug engineering and production, "particularly, how to integrate adequate local materials into the drug's manufacture." She also developed a keen understanding of the market maneuvers that keep drug prices high: "I saw how much fat was put into the products and that the final prices didn't correspond to research expenses at all. It was huge profit, period." After mentioning her student militancy against the military government, Dr. Pinheiro said that she had always wanted to see Brazil "a stronger country, incorporating technology."

As Dr. Pinheiro denounces unfair market tactics, she also speaks of the social-mindedness and creativity of local scientists: "the multinationals must become flexible, and we must all deal with the question of whether new technologies are going to benefit man or exclude him from the possibility of surviving. Justice and equity ought to be defended amid globalization." She dismisses criticisms that her way of doing science is sheer copying: "We had to develop our own methods of analyzing the drugs. I traveled to China and India to learn techniques and to buy salts from them. . . . Sometimes, if we want the species to survive, we have to regress from some advanced logics that are in place." Far Manguinhos thus plays a key role in the acquisition of knowledge on anti-HIV drugs, which, Maurice Cassier and Marilena Correa note, "it can then transfer either to Brazilian public-sector laboratories or to private-sector pharmaceutical laboratories in Brazil and, in the future, in other countries in the South" (Cassier and Correa 2003:91).

Interestingly, Dr. Pinheiro does not speak of social mobilization as being key to the country's antiretroviral initiative. She credits "efficient managers," both in government and in science, and the mobilization of experts as foundational. Already during Cardoso's first presidential term, Dr. Pinheiro had been called to Brasília to discuss strategies for drug development. She immediately noted "seriousness and signs of efficiency." In her negotiation with the state she ensured that Far Manguinhos would become "a center for technological development": "We wanted to produce, to sell to the state, and then reinvest the profit in technological development with an eye toward endemic diseases." In 2001, Dr. Pinheiro had 600 people working for her, of whom only one quarter were paid by the federal government. Under her administration Far Manguinhos increased its production to sixty-eight drugs, most of them for diseases such as TB and Hansen's disease, "which are treatable but are of no economic profitability to the multinationals." The AIDS Program is to a large extent responsible for generating this development by integrating demand for medication for other patient groups into the fight for anti-HIV medications.

The antiretroviral policy is emblematic of a new kind of "state-market integration," added Dr. Pinheiro during our interview. It is the realized vision of Minister Serra, "a fearless economist with the ability to make the right decisions." Serra championed the entrance of generics in the Brazilian market and gave incentives to their local production. This was the only way of keeping the policy going, the former health minister told me, "giving extreme budget constraints and the impact that the forthcoming currency devaluation would have on imported medicines" (personal communication, June 2003). In 1999, 81 percent of the money the government spent for AIDS drugs went to multinationals and only 19 percent to Brazilian companies; in 2000, 41 percent was going to national laboratories, both public and private (Cassier and Correa 2003; CN 2001a; Galvão 2002). As the Brazilian policy created a market for generic drug components, it also raised international competition that led to an overall decrease in drug prices. In 1999, for example, 2.2 pounds of 3TC, an anti-HIV drug, cost $10,000; in 2001 the same 2.2 pounds sold for $700.

On several occasions in the past few years the minister of health has deployed the country's generic antiretroviral know-how to politicize the practices of big pharma and negotiate better prices (Paraguassú 2001). Pharmaceutical patents have not been broken yet. But the strategy of having the technology and threatening to issue compulsory licensing has proved successful. In 2002, for example, Brazil was able to obtain 40 to 60 percent cost reduction on purchases of patented components from Merck and Roche that are essential to the production of the AIDS cocktail.

The United States threatened to bring sanctions against Brazil at the World Trade Organization in 2001, but in the end the two sides reached an agreement: Brazil would not export products resulting from broken patents, and it would officially notify the American government before breaking patents. Here, out of constraint and imagination, global market logics and the politics of science and technology are forced into explicitness, and this produces a new field of tension and negotiation. Inside the Brazilian state, this pharmaceutical activism has occasioned the creation of a strong and autonomous government regulatory agency along the lines of the FDA. The agency replaced a department within the Ministry of Health that was ripe with corruption and the target of unceasing political pressure; it became, according to Serra, "an essential ally in the tug-of-war with the pharmaceutical industry" (personal communication, June 2003).

In sum, at the intersection of a "technological surprise" (the HIV antiretroviral therapies), social mobilization and the restructuring of both state and market operations, the following is taking form: a new political economy of pharmaceuticals with global and national agencies and particularities, a pilot population through which a reforming state realizes its vision of scientifically based and cost-effective social action, and a contingent of mobilized groups articulating a novel concept of patient citizenship. As Dr. Paulo Teixeira, the former national AIDS coordinator, states: "In the past years, 234,000 hospitalizations for opportunistic diseases have been avoided, saving us more than $700 million in medical assistance." In Brazil, human rights are biomedical rights that the state has to fulfill and through which the pharmaceutical market is moralized. Teixeira explains: "In the international economic field there is a prevalence of unjust and restrictive rules, but nationally we see the universal values that ground public health and also the defense of the individual's right to life." These statements resonate with Cardoso's view of "a solidarity-based globalization," a concept he developed in his pursuit of a new strategic position for Brazil internationally and which the new president, Luis Inácio Lula da Silva from the Worker's Party, is taking further under the banner "Not just free but also fair trade." The AIDS policy reflects a sense of political responsibility, national and transnational, and has become an efficient vehicle shaping a perception of the reformed state as open to the public, rational and coherent, efficient, and ethical. Interestingly, however, the country's computerized register of individual viral loads and medication distribution does not include data on income, education, or any other social indicators. As a result, it cannot yet give us a detailed profile of who this population whose rights are biotechnologically realized is and how it lives.

The transformations of the state and of the concept of public health that my political, scientific, and activist informants emphasized look rather differently at the margins. In my ethnographic work in the northeastern city of Salvador, I observed many poor AIDS patients extending their lives with free access to antiretrovirals. These patients worked hard to keep philanthropic, nongovernmental, and medical support in place to guarantee the effectiveness of the antiretroviral therapies. Fighting for food and housing is concurrent with learning new scientific knowledge and navigating through laboratories and treatment regimes that now coexist with scarcity. However, although some marginalized AIDS victims exercise their "will to live" and acquire a form of patient citizenship, many others remain epidemiologically and medically unaccounted for and die in abandonment. In what follows, I show that their dying in apparent invisibility is part of a pattern of local nonintervention that coexists with the national AIDS policy and the country's overall reform.

## A Hidden Epidemic

The data I discuss in this section are from a social epidemiological study I did with local scientists in the northeastern state of Bahia (Dourado, Barreto, Almeida-Filher, Biehl, Cunha 1997). We analyzed AIDS death certificates in the AIDS unit of the state hospital in the capital, Salvador, which is where the poorest and the homeless are sent for treatment. We counted 571 AIDS deaths at the unit between 1990 and 1996. Only 26 percent of these cases were actually registered with the epidemiological surveillance service. Among these AIDS patients, 297 (52 percent) died during their first hospitalization. One can argue that when these people finally had access to the hospital it was largely in order to die.

The categories traditionally used by epidemiologists and social scientists to map and interpret the impact of social and economic realities on health-disease-death processes (such as age, race, and individual risk factors; or gender inequalities, sexual culture, and social representations of risk and safety) are insufficient to account for the rational-technical dynamics at work here. In his book *The Taming of Chance*, Ian Hacking identifies scientific and technical dynamics that mediate the processes by which "people are made up" (1990:3; see also Hacking 1999). Categories and counting, he argues, define new classes of people, normalize their ways of being in the world, and also have "consequences for the ways in which we conceive of others and think of our own possibilities and potentialities" (1990:6). Hacking views categories and statistics as making up people, but I am concerned with how technical and political interventions make people invisible and affect the experience, distribution, and social representation of dying. As I found out in my ethnography, bureaucratic procedures, informational difficulties, sheer medical neglect, moral contempt, and unresolved disputes over diagnostic criteria mediate the process by which these people are turned into absent things. During the course of my study I began to call these state and medical procedures and actions "technologies of invisibility." These technologies routinely intersect with patterns of discontinuous medical care and dispensation of medication.

Interestingly, the AIDS protocols we worked with had no social indicators such as level of education. But, as the unit's social worker put it, "These are the patients who live in the gutter. Sometimes strangers send them here in a taxi; others are brought in by the police. They come in dying; they have bad skin lesions. The ones who recover just return to the streets, where they die. They seldom come back for a follow-up. It is unrealistic to demand that a person who lives on the street adhere to treatment. They never heal. There must be thousands of people in the same situation." This medical invisibility is not restricted to the AIDS epidemic and its local and regional management. Local epidemiologists affirm that during Salvador's 2000 dengue epidemic only one of every one hundred cases were registered; that more than 40 percent of deaths in the state of Bahia have "no known cause"; and that maternal death, which is very high among the poor, is 200 percent higher in the northeastern region.[13]

Specialized health care is provided only to those who dare to identify themselves as AIDS patients in an early stage of infection at a public institution, and who autonomously search (they literally have to fight for their place in the overcrowded services) for continuous treatment—those whom I call patient citizens. While the national AIDS policy does help some of them, local and state medical professionals and communities allow others to die unaided.[14] The poorest and most marginal AIDS patients are in a sense blamed for their own deaths.[15] They are referred to as "drug addicts," "robbers," "prostitutes," or "noncompliant." It is difficult for individuals burdened by these labels to self-identify or be identified as AIDS victims deserving of treatment and capable of adherence. At best they are at the margins of nongovernmental interventions. In the end, there are no records tracing their individual and social trajectories, and the complex economic and technical causes that exacerbate infections and immune depressions remain unaccounted for. Most likely, a large group of potential users of AIDS public health services do not even look for assistance, medical or pharmaceutical. The short-term care of these dying marginal patients is relegated to a mostly sporadic street charity.

My physician-collaborators and I wrote a report to the Bahian Health Division informing them about the existence of this hidden AIDS epidemic. I learned later that this report was simply shelved. It was within this kind of unreformed and publicly discredited regional politics that the antiretroviral policy came into effect; it is in these local force fields that the sustainability of the AIDS model remains in question, that a triage-like state gains form, and that social death continues its course.

### Life-Extending Mobilization

Some of the poorest and homeless AIDS patients abandoned by local government organizations self-select for social and medical regeneration in community-run "houses of support" (*casas de apoio*). To learn more about this different destiny I undertook a long-term study at Caasah, a grassroots care center in Salvador. Caasah was founded in 1992 when a group of male and female prostitutes, transvestites, and intravenous drug users moved into an abandoned maternity ward in the outskirts of this city of 2.5 million people. City officials and local AIDS activists helped Caasah to gain legal status, and by 1993 it had become a nongovernmental organization. With thirty inhabitants, Caasah then successfully applied to the National AIDS Program for funds for two projects involving technical upgrading. The core maintenance of the institution was thus closely tied to the funds channeled from the World Bank loan. Indeed, Caasah and similar initiatives were actually being incorporated by the state and qualified as health services. The question of where to put the diseased poor had fallen out of the state's purview and had become a philanthropic and nongovernmental undertaking (by 2000 at least one hundred of the five hundred or so registered AIDS NGOs were houses of support). By taking over the task of immediate care of patients and overseeing their medical treatment, Caasah became a venue of triage as well. It mediated the relationship between AIDS patients and the haphazard and extremely limited public AIDS services and selected the patients who could benefit the most from the scarce resources (the state's AIDS unit only had sixteen beds, for example).

Caasah provided a means through which these marginalized individuals could accede to a distinct (and tentative) form of political and medical accountability previously unavailable to them. This late-born democratic practice of citizenship via patienthood (or at least a claim to it) would transform in the next few years into a focused and sophisticated practice of pharmaceutical well-being. These individuals and their AIDS community became less confrontational with political forces, local and national; less a part of street life; and more integrated into the mechanisms and technologies associated with the AIDS program, local and national. Beginning in 1994, strict disciplinary measures led to the expulsion of "unruly" patients. The reduced group passed through an intense process of normalization coordinated by a therapist sent by the National AIDS Program in 1995. By the end of that year, concerns about internal violence, aggression, and drug selling and consumption were replaced by concerns for hygiene and house maintenance. The next move involved medical treatment under the guidance of a newly hired nurse who established a reasonably consolidated infirmary post and pharmacy.

Thus Caasah had dramatically changed by 1996–1997, the year I carried out my long-term fieldwork there. The main corridor was now crowded with nursing trainees and volunteers wearing white lab coats carrying trays of medicine to their patients. The marginal patients had either left or had died, and more working poor and white people were now living there. Over the past five years, the face of AIDS in Caasah has altered. According to Caasah's Vice President Naiara: "In the beginning there were mostly homosexuals in here; you only found a few women and one or two heterosexuals. Now, at the most we have four homosexuals in here. . . . There is the same proportion of men and women. Most of the men got contaminated through drug use; and most women say they got AIDS from their partners." There were now less people "from the streets," added Celeste Gomes, Caasah's president: "The patients who wanted to attend to the norms stayed, the ones who did not want to submit had to leave. They went back to the streets. Many were really from the street, true marginals." What also changed is the "consciousness of the residents": "With time, we domesticated them. They had no knowledge whatsoever and we changed this doomed sense of 'I will die.' We showed them the importance of using medication. Now they have this conscience, and fight for their lives."

Caasah's inhabitants are now focused on their biological condition; their disease has become an entity and a personal foe. Many refer to the HIV virus as "my little animal." Some patients say, "I want to let the little animal sleep in me." I frequently heard comments such as, "The moment you fall back into what you were and stop taking your treatment, the virus occupies your place. And the virus only occupies the place because you let it." Many live, in their own words, "in a kind of a constant battle." They know they are trapped between two destinies: dying of AIDS like the poor and marginal, that is, *animalized*; and the possibility of living, aided by ARVs, into a future, thereby letting the animal sleep and preventing it from consuming the flesh. Irene, the first Caasah patient to have successfully taken the combined therapies, knows that she is now "another person." "I have been born again," she says; "it is not such a bad thing to have HIV. It's like not having money. And in Brazil everybody experiences that."

In houses of support such as Caasah former noncitizens have an unprecedented opportunity to claim a new identity around their politicized biology, with the support of international and national, public and private funds. Here, immediate access to the language and goods of biomedicine and the administration of health, the politics of patienthood, has priority over the making of "metasocial guarantees of social order" or over political representation (Alvares, Dagnino, Escobar 1999).[16] For the moment, let us think of Caasah as a *biocommunity* in which a selected group of poor and marginal diseased people have access to a novel social and biomedical inclusion. This citizenship is articulated through biotechnology, pastoral means, disciplinary practices of self-care, and monitored treatment. At work are new arts of extending life, of being medically treated, and of surviving economically as a diseased but cost-effective citizen.

The new medical and political reality lived by Caasah's inhabitants adds to Hannah Arendt's insights on what determines the public sphere and the human condition these days. Arendt identified a modern political process that progressively eliminates the possibility of human fulfillment in the public realm, excluding the masses and reducing them to the condition of *animal laborans* whose only activity is that of biological preservation (1958:320–325). This preservation is an individual concern; it is superfluous to the state and to society at large. "They begin to belong to the human race," Arendt claims, "in much the same way as animals belong to a specific animal species" (1973:302).

Brazilian scholars have been using some of Arendt's insights to problematize the operational logics of Brazil's crumbling welfare state. Sarah Escorel (1993), for example, argues that fragmented and stratified concepts of citizenship legitimate a political order in which social policies are unequally distributed according to the citizen's participation or exclusion from the production processes. Escorel identifies the continuous social exclusion of the poorest masses as a trait of a totalitarian state. For the excluded, she says, there are no social policies, "the only social policy is the police" (1993:36).

I am telling a somewhat different story. In Brazil's current structural readjustments, novel forms of biosocial inclusion and exclusion are being consolidated. What is distinctive in Caasah is that AIDS is not simply an embodiment of marginalization and exclusion to be policed; it is also a technical means of inclusion. While these people learn new scientific knowledge and navigate through new laboratories and treatment regimes, they constitute themselves as patient citizens and force their inclusion into a very sophisticated form of pharmaceutical governance (Biehl 1999; Rabinow 1999; Rapp 1999; Knorr Cetina 2001; Petryna 2002). Processes of social and medical regeneration legitimate marginal patients' demands to be governed and redistribute the scope of the state's authority. Against an expanding discourse of human rights, we are here confronted with the limits of the official structures whereby these rights are realized, biologically speaking, on a selective basis, and also with the emergence of a new political economy of pharmaceuticals.

It was within this interrelated context of local, national, and transnational forces shaping an AIDS response that I became interested in how the project to extend life informed institutions and individual agency, particularly at the margins. As I have been arguing, both the technical extension of life and death in social abandonment are elements through which the state, medicine, community, family, and the citizen empirically forge their presence. Nongovernmental, sociomedical, and pastoral networks link, through AIDS response, the marginal world and the state. An ethnographic analysis of these linkages or their lack can broaden our understanding of bureaucratic and technological determinants of disease and health among these individuals and groups, as well as the everyday medical and political practices that give form to the line between inclusion and exclusion; it can also reveal the extent to which people in the margins learn to use technology and medicine to enhance their claims for social equity and human/biological rights. In my work at Caasah I could also see how the death of the other actually reinforced a rather individualized and depoliticized existence. As Rita, one of Caasah's founders, a former prostitute and intravenous drug user, put it: "I know what I have to do to live. If they still die with AIDS in the streets, and there are many, it is because they want it."

## Conclusion

Brazil's policy of biotechnology for the people has dramatically reduced AIDS mortality and improved the quality of life of the patients covered. This policy has become an inspiration for international medical activism and a challenge for the governments of other poor countries devastated by the HIV/AIDS pandemic. Brazil is now sharing its know-how in a range of ways, among them taking on a leadership role at the WHO's "3 by 5" program, helping to rebuild a state-owned pharmaceutical plant in Mozambique, and providing Doctors Without Borders with ARVs for a pilot treatment program in South Africa. In past years, within the limits imposed by international trade agreements, the Brazilian government has exerted its own force through AIDS, as it has been leading developing nations in WTO deliberations over a flexible balance between patent rights and public health needs.

The Brazilian response might not have achieved international justice in the realm of AIDS, but it has at least helped to expose the fallacies of reigning paradigms of public-private partnerships in the resolution of social problems and the limits faced by international development agencies to truly act on behalf of the poorest. Practically speaking, it has opened channels for horizontal south-south collaborations and devised political mechanisms (as fleeting and fragile as they may be) for poor countries to level out some of the pervasive unevenness in international power relations and in disease and health outcomes.

But as with all things political and economic, the reality underlying the policy is twisted, dynamic, and filled with gaps. On the other side of the signifier "model policy" there is a new political economy of pharmaceuticals with international and national particularities. As the AIDS policy unfolded, Brazil attracted new investments, and novel public–private cooperation over access to medical technologies ensued. While Brazil experimented with new modes of regulating markets for life-extending treatments, pharmaceutical companies took the incidents over drug pricing and the relaxation of patent laws at the WTO as opportunities to both negotiate broader market access in Brazil and to open up unforeseen AIDS markets in other countries. The industry has also been able to expand clinical research in Brazil, now run in partnership with public health institutions. American pharmaceutical companies have also successfully downplayed the WTO as they lobbied for strict bilateral and regional trade agreements that made local production of generic drugs unviable.

As ways of mobilizing and extending life are shaped, ethnography takes on the task of illuminating the trajectories that determine these forms and approximating the paths through which people become the physicians of themselves and of their world amid the growing tension between health as public or private good. By keeping these interrelated aspects in view—political economy and activism, biotechnology and public health, population and individual, medicine and subjectivity—one orchestrates a more effective discussion concerning changing political cultures and ethics in a time of unprecedented crisis.

As I outlined shifts in the concept of the state (from a crumbling welfare state to an activist state), in the substance of human rights (from political to biological), and in strategies of public health (from prevention and clinical care to access to medication), I also opened space for people missing in official data, policy decisions and accounts, reflecting on the work necessary to address this void. All this said, it is encouraging that this time, discussions about Brazil have shifted to the maintenance and advance of a life extending policy already well under way.

# Notes

I want to express my deepest gratitude to the people of Caasah for allowing me to observe their daily activities, and to the health professionals who collaborated with this research. I am also very grateful to Albert O. Hirschman, Ada Gropper, Leo Coleman, Tom Vogl, and Adriana Petryna for their help. I want to acknowledge the generous support of the John D. and Catherine T. MacArthur Foundation, the Wenner-Gren Foundation, and the Committee on Research in the Humanities and Social Sciences and the Program in Latin American Studies of Princeton University.

1. ARVs and laboratory testing are estimated to cost approximately $2,000 per patient.

2. There is by now a very significant body of activist and social scientific research and literature on the evolution of the Brazilian response to HIV/AIDS, particularly vis-à-vis political forces and cultural influences, as well as vast documentation of the unfolding of the policy and its programs that the National AIDS Program itself has made available. See Parker and Daniel 1991; Parker 1994; Parker et al. 1994; Bastos and Barcellos 1995, 1996; Castilho and Cherquer 1997; Bastos 1999; and Galvão 2000. My work has unfolded in dialogue with this highly relevant literature.

3. See the report Consensus Statement on Antiretroviral Treatment of AIDS in Poor Countries (Boston: Harvard School of Public Health, 2000).

4. See Caldeira 2001 for a discussion of democratization and human rights in Brazil, and Paley 2001 for a discussion of health movements and democratization. See Das 1999 for a critique of the measures, practices, and values related to international health interventions; and Appadurai 2002 for a discussion of the urban poor and new forms of activism and governmentality in India.

5. My discussion of patient citizenship is informed by Adriana Petryna's work on "biological citizenship," a concept she developed in the context of people's struggle for care and accountability in the Chernobyl aftermath (Petryna 2002).

6. The government's delayed attention to the epidemic followed patterns of slow development of anti-AIDS policies at international levels: only in 1986 did the United Nations, for example, recognize AIDS as an important problem to be addressed (see J. Galvão 2000: 92).

7. In 1988, activist mobilization also helped to defeat a congressional resolution to restrict the entrance of HIV-positive people into the country.

8. Conferência de saúde possibilita intercâmbio, *Jornal NH*, 7 November 1994.

9. In 1985, transvestite Brenda Lee founded the country's first *casa de apoio* (house of support) in São Paulo.

10. See O sexo inseguro, *Isto É/Senhor*, 21 November 1991:52. See also Galvão 2000.

11. See Ferguson's and Gupta's (2002) discussion of new forms of neoliberal government and Nancy Scheper-Hughes's (2003) discussion of changes in the concepts of bodily integrity, sociality, and human values in the context of the global market in human organs for transplantation.

12. In *Global Responses to AIDS*, Cristiana Bastos argues that without state incentive and money, and without the technical know-how to develop original protocols, Brazil's complex AIDS clinical practice "could not be converted into scientific knowledge that would be accepted by the international system" (1999:150). Global pharmaceuticals have recast the workings of this local AIDS science.

13. Naomar de Almeida Filho, personal communication, August 2000.

14. In *Seeing Like a State*, James Scott illustrates why some of the major projects to improve the human condition in the twentieth century failed and produced tragedy: "The lack of context and particularity is not an oversight; it is the necessary first premise of any large-scale planning exercise" (1998:346).

15. I am here rethinking one of Michel Foucault's maxims that biopower dominates mortality rather than death: "power does not know death anymore and therefore must abandon it" (1992:177; 1980; see also Agamben 1998).

16. See Ana Maria Doimo's discussion of Brazilian social movements: "that indiscriminate posture of negativity *vis-à-vis* the institutional sphere . . . gave room to selective and positive relations with the political and administrative sphere" (1995:223).

# Treating AIDS
## Dilemmas of Unequal Access in Uganda

SUSAN REYNOLDS WHYTE, MICHAEL A. WHYTE,
LOTTE MEINERT, AND BETTY KYADDONDO

Differential access to AIDS medicine exemplifies global inequalities between wealthy and poor countries. Price cuts by the big multinational pharmaceutical companies, production of cheaper generics, action research programs, and donor support for treatment offer ways of remedying these inequities. Yet even in countries that have benefited from such developments, equal access to treatment is still a long way off. The Uganda AIDS Commission estimates that only 10,000 of the 157,000 people who should be taking the drugs are actually doing so (Uganda AIDS Commission 2003).

The fall in price has been dramatic: triple combination therapy cost about $500 per month in mid-2000; in March 2003, the same treatment using the generic drug Triomune from the Indian firm Cipla cost $28. But to put that price tag in perspective, the combined public and private spending on healthcare in Uganda is only $38 per capita per year, as opposed to $4,499 in the United States (United Nations Development Programme [UNDP] 2003). The vast majority of Ugandans cannot afford $28 each month (and that figure is a minimum; it does not include consultation, monitoring, and drugs for other infections). The drop in price has created dilemmas for a minority who would never have considered treatment at the old price but have just enough resources to make the cheaper drugs an almost realistic option.

Solutions shape the way we see problems. In principle, affordable treatment will change the meaning of AIDS (and of life!), as it has done in wealthy countries, where AIDS is something you live with — if you can tolerate the drugs — and where mortality from the disease has fallen sharply. If treatment were available in poor countries, people would likely be far more willing to be tested and to identify themselves as having the disease. Perhaps we are entering such a new phase in the cultural and social history of the disease in Africa. But the process is a rough and inequitable one — well suited to the kind of work ethnographers can do at the crossroads between historical forces and the complications of social agencies, be they local institutions, families, or individuals. As drugs for AIDS become more common, they expose the nature of healthcare in countries like Uganda — its dynamism, its unevenness, and the order in its disorder.

In this chapter, we explore the dilemmas that AIDS treatment poses as people learn about options, make painful choices, and imagine the possibilities open to others as well as to themselves.[1] Who should have the drugs and who can get them? Our theme is that AIDS medicine is socially as well as pharmacologically active in that it occasions reflections on social relations and distinctions. This happens within families who are in a position to consider paying for treatment; and it happens as people experience programs that offer treatment to some but not others. Healthcare workers and ordinary citizens are more and more often confronting the reality of unequal access. For some this is a matter of moral concern; for others it is the normal order of things; and for yet others it is a practical problem to deal with or to overlook while taking on more immediate difficulties. Our ambition is not only to document pharmaceutical policy and inequality (Farmer et al. 2001), but also to show their significance for differently positioned Ugandans as they work out a vernacular view of social pharmacy. This chapter should be read in conjunction with chapter 8. Biehl's analysis of biomedical citizenship in Brazil and of the processes of inclusion and exclusion that are at work in AIDS treatment and care programs provides another approach to the issues of inequality with which we are concerned.

## The Social Lives of AIDS Medicines

Adopting a framework proposed by Appadurai (1986) and used as an expository device for following the movement of pharmaceuticals (Van der Geest et al. 1996; Whyte et al. 2002), we can set the scene by tracing the life courses of antiretroviral drugs (ARVs) as they enter Uganda and flow through alternative channels to sick bodies. We must enter a caveat, however. This is an account from one moment, mid-2003, in a complex and rapidly changing situation.[2] Although we attempted to interview a wide range of actors—from people responsible for information, research, and treatment programs to health workers and pharmacists—our view is inevitably partial and incomplete, like the views of the sick people, family members, and colleagues whose concerns are presented in the sections to follow.

The ARV drugs available in Uganda are born as brand name products from five multinational pharmaceutical firms and as generics from several Indian companies. Under an initiative from UNAIDS, the multinationals set up an autonomous organization, Medical Access Uganda Limited, in 1999 to ensure a steady supply of AIDS drugs to gazetted treatment centers, with a small profit margin to cover costs. When Indian companies entered the market with generics in 2000, they did not come in through this initiative, but set up distributorships at Kampala pharmacies. Two of the multinationals, Bristol Meyers Squibb and Merck Sharp & Dohme (MSD) followed suit, establishing sales representatives dedicated to AIDS products at a Kampala retail outlet. In addition to the drugs imported through these established channels, others find their way from Europe through the hands of individuals who bring them in for themselves, friends or family, or perhaps to sell again.

Once in the country, ARVs flow out to sick people through four kinds of channels, some well demarcated, and others less so. One way in which they are made available is through treatment and research programs funded by donors and provided for free. These include Prevention of Mother to Child Transmission (PMTCT) projects (integrated into maternity services at selected health units); a Centers for Disease Control research project that will treat one thousand adults and their eligible children in Tororo, eastern Uganda; the Developing Antiretroviral Therapy (DART) trial at two sites in the Kampala area, funded by Rockefeller, to provide drugs to two thousand people; a Medicins sans Frontières project treating one hundred patients in Arua, northern Uganda; and the Uganda Cares Initiative in Masaka, also with one hundred patients as of early 2003. There are other smaller projects as well, like the larger ones localized and with strict eligibility requirements. Most of the drugs used in these projects are brand name pharmaceuticals from the big multinationals that enter through Medical Access. Because they are donor funded, supply is ensured for the life of the project at least, and there is fairly good control over the provision of the treatment.

A second channel provides drugs through gazetted treatment centers such as Nsambya and Mengo hospitals and Mildmay Centre. Most of these are fee for service, though some free drugs are provided through research studies. By far the most important is Joint Clinical Research Centre (JCRC), the oldest and largest AIDS treatment center in sub-Saharan Africa. The center, which grew out of an initiative by the Ministry of Defense to deal with the enormous problem of AIDS in the army, developed a collaboration with the Ministry of Health and Makerere University. From its Kampala treatment facility in the beautiful grounds once belonging to the government of the kingdom of Buganda it has provided ARVs to over eight thousand people since 1991. Recently it opened clinical facilities in four other towns: Mbale, Mbarara, Masaka, and Kabale. JCRC does "intelligence work" to find the cheapest drugs. It purchases direct from the Indian firm Cipla, bypassing the distributor, but like the other treatment centers, it also provides brand name drugs for those who can afford them.

While the donor research and treatment programs and the gazetted treatment centers are not government financed, they are very much government approved. Although they are spotty—huge areas of the country are not covered at all—and reflect the different priorities of donors and researchers, they have a public character and presence. They are located in buildings with signboards. They have a staff and provide jobs; some even have vehicles with acronyms stenciled on the doors. They are advertised at local council meetings, in religious services, and on the radio. They produce brochures, posters, and reports. They have a professional character of the type that contributes to what an article in *Lancet* called "Preventing antiretroviral anarchy in sub-Saharan Africa." The authors write that "it is not just a matter of providing antiretroviral drugs, but also that they must be provided within a structured framework. There has to be a system to ensure regular procurement and distribution, good patient management, monitoring, and assessment" (Harries et al. 2001:410).

The third channel, private practitioners, is far more discrete and less open to surveillance. No one knows exactly how many private physicians are treating patients with ARVs, but David Bagonza, the sales representative for MSD, told us that his company was selling to forty private clinics as of mid-2003, almost all in the Kampala area. The Ministry of Health and the National Drug Authority are supposed to monitor the distributors to ensure that they sell to physicians in established clinics rather than to lay individuals, but someone who has a prescription can have it refilled without consulting the doctor each time. And this opens the door for more creative and less systematic uses of medicine.

The fourth channel is hardly a channel at all, but rather a web of capillaries through which ARVs seep out to those in need. People who are "in the system" help relatives and friends to obtain the drugs at the lowest possible cost. One pharmacist confided that he was helping fifteen patients in this way. Another revealed that the drugs were sometimes sold without a prescription and that pharmacists take on the task of counseling and advising even though they have not been trained to do so.

Whether anarchy, or at least disorder that is convenient for some, will set in remains to be seen. Other drugs in Uganda have active social lives (Whyte 2001). All kinds of prescription drugs are available over the counter or from someone's satchel in small shops and storefront clinics, at bus stops, and in the homes of health workers. Will ARVs be diverted from their enclaved positions under the monopoly of health professionals in quasi-public institutions?[3] Such valuable commodities, desperately needed in a poor country where people look for any way to make money, will provide a strong challenge to the kind of structured framework called for by the authors of the *Lancet* article.

## Inclusion Criteria: What about Me?

Drugs flow in channels that carry them mainly to the urban, the prosperous, and the better connected. The lives of most people in Uganda are rural and constrained by poverty. Only those who happen to reside in the catchment area of a project giving free treatment are likely to have a chance of getting ARVs. The channel that brings ARVs to donor-funded projects and on to beneficiaries is well demarcated. Research projects must have explicit inclusion and exclusion criteria; donor projects and programs have defined target groups and procedures for becoming a beneficiary. They are localized, linked to an institution with a catchment area, and usually meant for a certain category of people.

A prime example is the PMTCT program supported by UNICEF and other donors, so far in place at eighteen government hospitals. The plan is to scale up so as to eventually include maternity units at all government facilities; a major problem in access is that over two-thirds of births take place at home. Mothers coming to antenatal clinics are counseled about the possibility of receiving a free dose of the ARV nevirapine at the onset of labor and a dose for the newborn baby, which can reduce vertical transmission by about 50 percent.[4] Mothers wishing to participate must take an HIV test; the medicine is given only to those who test positive. It can save the baby but has no effect upon the mother, for whom no treatment is offered. This system requires women to confront distressing information, which will be made known to hospital staff, with differential consequences for themselves and the child. As one woman speculated: "I would like to know my status if this will prevent my baby from getting infected, but on the other hand I fear knowing that I am among the dead and I am to experience much suffering of AIDS, so I would not want to know my HIV status for fear of those deep thoughts" (Pool et al. 2001:608).

In fact, a majority of the women so far offered the opportunity have made the difficult decision to test: of fifty-four thousand attending antenatal clinics at the eighteen hospitals between April 2002 and January 2003, 77 percent were given information about the program, 65 percent agreed to test, and 12 percent tested positive. The coordinator of the research component of the program, Loyce Ariinatwe, told us that the possibility of getting a drug to save the baby is the decisive factor for women, who say: "It has been documented [that the drug can save the baby's life] . . . if I die and leave my child healthy, it's a blessing from God." But at the same time, they ask: "What about me?" Why does the child get the drug but not the mother? At Mulago Hospital in Kampala, women ask about ARVs, and the policy in this program is to tell them where the drugs are available and at what price. They are terribly disappointed to learn the cost: "It is too much. . . . . We have that hope but how many can afford?" Social pharmacy cuts across the most intimate of all relations—that between mother and child. The ARV is for the baby; as Loyce pointed out, the mother can only lick the free milk powder that was also intended for the child.

The solution to this dilemma is a new program, PMTCT+, in which the plus stands for free antiretroviral therapy for the mother, and also for the baby should it be found positive despite the preventive doses. But PMTCT+ is only beginning, supported by other donors in a few restricted locations. If you do not happen to live in that particular place and attend the antenatal clinic during the project period, you are left to fish in the other channel, the one where ARVs are sold to those who can afford them.

The unevenness of access to free therapy is illustrated in another way by recent developments within The AIDS Support Organization (TASO). In 2002, TASO decided to subsidize ARV treatment for its counselors. This famous organization has been a pioneer in promoting openness, positive living, and AIDS education by people living with AIDS. Its eight district centers are places where AIDS can be, and must be, talked about, where people can share experiences and get advice from other people living with AIDS. Facilitating ARV treatment for counselors introduced a deep rift into that commonality of experience because most clients of TASO had no chance of obtaining the same treatment. The steering committee of TASO Mbale felt this was wrong, and the manager of TASO Tororo commented that it was a challenge now to struggle to get ARVs for TASO members as well as employees. One person speculated that the staff members were not "shouting" demands on behalf of their clients because they feared losing their own privileges, perhaps in a scheme of cost sharing where both they and their clients would have to pay.

In the event, donor-funded research and treatment projects have linked up with TASO branches in Entebbe, Masaka, and Tororo to provide medicines and clinical care to clients who meet established criteria. In Tororo, the U.S. Centers for Disease Control (CDC) has recruited the first thirty-two of a planned one thousand adults for a three-year study (ARV treatment is promised for life for study subjects but is not yet funded beyond the study period). ARV drugs will be delivered weekly to people's homes by a fieldworker (with a U.S. embassy ID) on motorcycle. The researchers have thought carefully about inclusion criteria: membership in TASO, CD4 count under 250, sleeping seven days a week in the surveyed household. Priority for admission to the study will go to those who participated in a previous CDC study, then to members of the TASO Drama Club, and then chronologically in order of length of membership; those who joined TASO first get first chance. The effect this will have on all the people who are not part of the study is unclear. Awareness of ARVs will likely be raised by the weekly visits of the thirty fieldworkers to neighborhoods throughout the district. Yet most HIV-positive people in the district are not members of TASO; not even all of TASO's seven to eight thousand members will be given drugs; and not even all sexual partners of the study subjects can be included. The question "What about me?" is bound to arise as the project takes hold. Welcome as this project is, it shares with other donor-funded treatment initiatives a limited life span and access criteria that exclude many people. They are left to the "public-private mix-up" that constitutes healthcare obtained from government facilities, fee-for-service clinics, and retail drug outlets.

## Health Workers and Referral: The Blanket Sign

Most people, even if they have heard about ARVs, do not know where to get them. One source of information is the health worker. The women whose babies were to be saved by nevirapine at Mulago Hospital were told that they could buy treatment for themselves—which most could not afford. But this information is not always provided, either because health workers themselves do not know or out of sensitivity to the predicament of poor people.

Some of the most striking and poignant examples of this situation come from health workers in public facilities who must decide whether to tell their patients that life-saving medicine is available. At the pediatric immunity clinic of Mulago, many of the patients are orphans brought by family members who exhausted their resources caring for the now-dead parents of the children. The nurse at the clinic said that they do not normally mention ARV treatment to these families: "Just caring for an HIV-positive child is difficult — we can't mention ARVs which they cannot afford . . . and we can't tell the children about ARV medicine — that would be cruel."

The head of the Department of Medicine at the same hospital, Dr. Harriet Mayanja, explained that they do not have ARVs on the ward because most people cannot afford them and they do not want the spectacle of the lucky ones going to the dispensing window of long life while others look on hopelessly.[5]

> On our ward, we use the "blanket sign" in order to decide whom to inform about where they can go to buy ARVs. Our patients bring their own bed linen. You check the blanket, the bedsheets, how the patient and family are dressed, whether they are wearing shoes or rubber slippers. Do they bring a nice thermos flask, a basket of food with a crocheted cover, a radio? Do they ask for a private room? Or is the patient using old sheets, or maybe a woman's gown because they can't afford a blanket? On the bedside table, is there only a plastic mug with the cold porridge provided by the hospital? It's not fair to suggest treatment costing sixty thousand shillings a month to someone who has not been able to afford sheets at eight thousand shillings in the past five years.

The blanket sign as a test of financial means is evocative in Uganda, where a common way of describing poverty is to say that husband and wife have to sleep under the woman's only gown.

This situation is part of the general "bring your own" pattern that characterizes public healthcare in Uganda. Both in-patients and out-patients are routinely required to bring everything needed for their treatment: a school exercise book for recording diagnosis and treatment, a disposable hypodermic needle and syringe, rubber gloves and a plastic sheet for maternity, IV sets and fluids, and food. Hospitals and health centers regularly tell families that needed medicines are out of stock and ask them to purchase these from nearby drug shops. ARVs are thus a high-profile example of something with which most Ugandans are quite familiar.

Patients who are referred to AIDS treatment clinics are often disappointed that the expense is greater than expected. The AIDS Information Centre (AIC) in Kampala provides counseling, testing, and treatment of opportunistic infections. It has now started to give information about ARVs; patients are told that the price of ARV treatment at JCRC is $28 a month. Some who follow up on the referral return to the AIC doctor bewildered and discouraged because the cost was far higher. The $28 does not include necessary tests, other drugs for opportunistic infections, and ARVs other than Triomune, the cheapest generic. This uncertainty about what you will actually have to pay is again characteristic of healthcare in Uganda. The problem is not only cost, but the unexpected extra cost for which it is difficult to plan. Unless you can find a sponsor, as have a few of the volunteers at AIC, the financial headache is a family pain. AIDS care is not an individual matter between a patient and a healthcare provider; it is a concern of families.

### Painful Priorities in Families: Affording the Next Dose

With women bearing an average of seven children, Ugandan families of procreation are large; extended families are truly extensive.[6] And as every Ugandan knows, part of the practice of relatedness is giving and receiving assistance. About 80 to 90 percent of Ugandans live in rural areas, but agriculture seldom produces much cash surplus, so people face major problems in acquiring cash to pay school fees, build a house, and get medical care, not to mention buying commodities for daily needs. A crisis, such as someone needing an operation, may require a family member to sell a goat or cow or even a piece of land. Any member of a family in paid employment has to balance his or her own living expenses and hopes to accumulate a little savings with the needs of relatives. Ugandan colleagues of ours working at the university almost always pay school fees for children of less-well-off siblings. In the era of AIDS, people take orphaned nieces, nephews, and grandchildren into their homes and support them together with their own children. "High dependency ratios" is the social work jargon for what is idealized as the supportive African extended family and experienced by people with means as an often burdensome obligation.

People of all economic backgrounds depend on family help in dealing with illness. AIDS is different because of its long duration and the fact that it often strikes more than one person in a family. As the staff at the pediatric immunity clinic recognized, families with a member needing ARVs have already been burdened by caring for long and demanding illnesses, and possibly by the cost of funeral expenses and fostering orphans. Only families with relatively good resources consider undertaking the costly and lifelong treatment with ARVs. Even for them the burden is often too heavy. Almost everyone who has contact with middle-class Uganda has stories of family efforts and family dilemmas in paying for ARV treatment. Three themes are woven through these situations.

*Treating AIDS means withdrawing support to other relatives for other important life projects.* Even when the sick person has an income and can afford to buy medicine, he or she must prioritize other expenses. And that means considering and prioritizing social relations.

The compliance study carried out in connection with the UNAIDS Drug Access Initiative in 1998–1999 included twenty people who were financing their own ARV medicine. Even these people, who were well-off by Ugandan standards, reported that they considered obligations to family members when budgeting for their drugs. Some explained to relatives why they had to stop helping them with school fees and other expenses; others did not. "However," notes Kisuule (1999:59), "patients reported that it was not easy for them to decide stopping or reducing financial support because extended families, fictive kinship institutions, neighbours, and close friends were social assets, and were always mobilised or united when a disaster struck. So there was a fear that they would also lose such support in the future."

One patient at the AIDS Information Centre remarked to the doctor that she might be on ARVs if she were not paying school fees for her younger sister. People speculate about whether taking a child out of school would enable them to buy drugs and improve enough to keep a job so they could continue giving some support at least. They worry about using all their resources to buy drugs, not being able to continue after they run out of money, and then dying, leaving their children with nothing. The price of social relations and life chances is brought sharply to consciousness in such situations.

*Because frequently more than one family member is sick, treating AIDS means choosing whom to help.* Dr. Peter Solberg of the CDC project used the technical term *triage* for the terrible decisions that must be made: "I've heard many cases of difficult choices—how to triage if there's not enough money for treatment for a couple." The choice is not always made explicit. We know of one instance in which a very sick woman was refused help by her husband, only to learn later from a relative working in an AIDS treatment center that he was on ARVs himself.

Sometimes families do pull together and find enough resources for all, at least for a while. A friend told of how they raised money for her sister in-law, the husband, and their son to access ARVs. George and Lisa wed in 1990 and had been blessed with three children. When their last-born child fell ill, failed to respond to treatment, and died in 2000, they could hardly grasp the tragedy. But it got worse. When they tested for HIV, both George and Lisa and their second born were HIV-positive. George worked for one of the most powerful companies in Kampala and was doing well. Although he was from a prosperous family and had close relatives living outside Uganda, he was stressed, afraid of losing his job, and fearful that other people would learn about his HIV status. He and Lisa both started using ARVs, but he still kept his diagnosis a secret until his financial status was in jeopardy. He lost the good job and the family depended on Lisa's income. In 2002, George fell ill with symptoms of AIDS, and his condition was no longer a secret. It was rumored that both George and Lisa had stopped using ARVs because they could no longer afford them. At this point family meetings were organized every Sunday by George's family, later involving Lisa's relatives as well. Resolutions to fundraise and purchase ARVs for all three were passed, medical checkups were done at JCRC, and George improved enough to get another job.

The financial and emotional costs of treating AIDS force people to conceptualize and make explicit assumptions about relationships that usually remain implicit. George and Lisa's relatives formalized this process through weekly meetings. Our colleague Mary explained how her family network financed ARV treatment for one of her cousins during a period when the cousin was very sick. Now the cousin has recovered, is working as a tailor, and is paying for her own treatment. "It's a miracle," Mary said. "She was dying and now she is even paying school fees for her children." Another member of the family is also HIV-positive and in need of ARV treatment, but she has not managed to mobilize resources from the family network. Mary remarked: "That one—she is not responsible, she doesn't understand ARV medicine, she never finished school and doesn't have a job. How do you start to help a person like this? And where do you stop? . . . People have to prioritize their resources: Do you pay ARV medicine for a sister forever and give up paying school fees for your child?" Mary was weighing not just her relationships to her cousins, but also their characters and the likelihood that they will resume responsibilities within the family. Unusually, she put her deliberations into words. Many people prefer to keep silent about such painful decisions and just let things take their course, as if there was no decision to make (Mogensen 2003).

*People who are ill and unable to support themselves must consider the burden that antiretroviral therapy might impose upon their families.* From the point of view of the sick person, being so highly dependent is often a distressing situation. Some would rather die.

One of our young Ugandan colleagues fell sick with the sort of meningitis which is very common among AIDS patients. At the hospital where she was admitted she was started on ARV drugs by the doctor. The meningitis had made her disoriented and she had not understood the implications of the medicine. She was a very proud person, and when she realized that she would have to receive help from others for the rest of her life to stay alive, she made the decision to stop the medication and go back to her parental home in northern Uganda. That is where she died.

Another Ugandan colleague told of his cousin who was HIV-positive and was developing AIDS. The cousin's wife was sick as well, and the family decided to hold a meeting to plan how to raise money for ARV medicine. A few hours before the family was to assemble, the cousin hired a taxi to Bujagali Falls on the Nile. He threw himself into the wild water and drowned, leaving the family the easier task of supporting only one sick person and the children.

Papa M is a retired government official, a wealthy and well-educated man by local standards. He lives in a large home with his three wives and some of their twenty-two children and grandchildren. Three of his daughters knew that they had been infected with HIV. One died in 1998, before less expensive ARV medicine was available in Uganda. Another daughter, Prisca, started to lose weight after her husband died in 2000. When we discussed the cost of ARV treatment, Papa said: "Even if we can't afford this in the long run we have to try it — we have to try it. She might pick up and survive. If she dies we will know that we tried everything possible." She moved back to her parents' home, and her father and some of her brothers and sisters were buying the ARV drugs every month at a branch of JCRC in Mbale town, thirty kilometers from the home. But after some months, Papa began to worry about "the arrangement" of buying drugs in Mbale. How long would it be sustainable? He is retired and had imagined that at this stage in his life the adult children would be taking care of their old parents — financially and otherwise. Papa mobilized funds from daughters and sons for their sick sister, but most of them were unable to help in a significant way, having many children themselves to care for. When a third daughter, Lovisa, who had moved in to help care for Prisca, fell sick, she decided not to stay at home: "It is too hard for Mother to see our sister Prisca being sick. It reminds her of how our other sister died. . . . The medicine helps, but it puts pressure on Mother. She worries about how they will get the next dose, money, transport. . . . So I decided to move where she can't see me and worry about me." Meanwhile, Prisca had many side effects from the medication. Papa M said that he suspected she lost the morale to take the drugs. She died on Easter day 2003. The family was again in great pain, and Papa commented that it was depressing to have spent so much money and put great expectations in these new drugs, which proved to be worthless for his daughter. He did not talk about the third daughter, who is also HIV-positive, but from his facial expressions it was clear that his worries continued. Lovisa's sensitivity about being a burden to her family increased accordingly.

Ivan, a young man in rural Tororo, told how he was planning to get an HIV test because he had started falling sick and his former girlfriend had died recently. He said he would not be shocked if he tested positive, but still hesitated to do the test because it would bring a lot of conflict in the family. One of his brothers who works in Kampala had told him that he would help him with money for treatment if he tested positive, but Ivan was worried about getting the rest of the money for treatment: "I do not fear the first 150,000 shillings for making those first tests, but it is the monthly expenses of drugs I fear. . . . We are from a somehow rich family with many children, but we are just disorganized and there is too much disagreement. If my family would not help me when they knew my problem it would kill me very fast. So that is why I fear to make that test."

These family situations do not involve priority setting once and for all, but rather continuing decisions unfolding over time as circumstances change and one set of problems overshadows another. When a relative is desperately ill, it is usually possible to mobilize help. But if the patient improves after the first few months on ARVs, the family again feels the weight of other obligations and stops contributing to purchase of the drugs. The long-term commitment to buying ARVs is difficult for individuals and families to maintain in situations where needs are so abundant.

The medical consequences of these family dilemmas are nonadherence to treatment regimes and the possibility of "antiretroviral anarchy," with dangers of developing resistance, that experts fear. Although there is little systematic research from Uganda on adherence in the "natural" situation of people paying for therapy, it is thought that the main reason for not adhering to ARV treatment is inability to sustain the cost. Cissy Kityo, the research coordinator of JCRC and a doctor with great experience in fee-for-service clinical care, asserts that cost is the main constraint to using and adhering to ARV treatment. In a retrospective review of 577 patient charts from January 1998 to June 2001, JCRC personnel found that although most patients were from urban areas and high socioeconomic status, only a quarter were 80 percent or more adherent to treatment. About 60 percent were lost to follow-up. They did not return for continuing treatment, presumably because they could not afford the next dose of drugs (presentation by C. Kityo, 26 September 2002).

Health workers confront the realities of patients not being able to pay for treatment, and families with some means struggle to balance the cost of the next dose against all their other needs. At the same time, we found a recurring conviction that well-placed people could afford treatment or get it through connections.

## Connections, Secrecy, and Status: Those Big People

Most people in Uganda do not know ARVs by name, nor do they know exactly what they do or where they can be obtained. But we have many times heard people say in a general way that "those big people get medicines to prolong their lives." People who are better informed also relate the drugs to social position. When Betty Kyaddondo asked people attending a clinic at the AIDS Information Centre what they knew about ARVs, their responses revealed the social character of the drugs. One young woman said: "My boyfriend used to talk about people using expensive drugs to cure HIV while he worked as a driver at the president's office. He would say that people using these drugs get cured of HIV, but kept lamenting at the exorbitant costs."

Another woman, a teacher, told Betty: "In 2000, a friend at the school told me about drugs that cure HIV. She said these drugs are sold in pharmacies in Kampala and cost about 700,000 shillings a month. She said in order to buy the drugs you must produce a bank statement because it is an indicator that you will actually afford them. I have not interacted with anyone using them, but I heard about some ministers taking them and they are doing well."

These examples show that medicinal knowledge is social knowledge, or at least it is linked to people's image of the kind of society in which they live. But the political imagination about social status and access to medicine has one particular feature that is especially striking: the conviction that the elite take medicines secretly. This comes out most clearly in discussions with professional "insiders" following the epidemic or providing treatment.

From one point of view, secrecy is simply understandable discretion. David Bagonza, the sales rep for MSD, noted that only some of the big businesses subsidizing AIDS treatment for their employees have made public announcements about the programs.[7] "Many others have not announced because they are not offering treatment to all employees. If you want to provide for free, you want to treat your most valued employees, not casual laborers. One of the big hotels treats trained workers but not the unskilled ones. They do it silently because in the contracts, some have medical coverage and some don't."

From the point of view of patients, secrecy may be about the desire for confidentiality. Bagonza seemed to see this as a natural desire of elite people: "Many people want confidentiality — like government officials, army officers. This kind of patient wants privacy. They prefer private practitioners; they don't want to go to treatment centers." He gave an example of the means by which confidentiality could be ensured: "A big army officer used to get drugs every month and ask us to put them in different containers — unmarked tins — so his wife would not know."

Cissy Kityo of JCRC put a somewhat different slant on this desire for privacy. "Stigma increases with socioeconomic status. Wealthy and well-connected people do not want to associate their symptoms with HIV or to disclose their status. They fear to attend JCRC because it is known as an AIDS clinic. They want to spend the shortest possible time at the clinic because they don't want to be seen. They prefer to see physicians outside of working hours. They give wrong addresses and identities. Doctors are the worst offenders." For her, secrecy is associated with denial, an unrealistic and unhealthy attitude in patients. But she also sees how social differences mean that some people have more face to save than others.

That secrecy is a political and moral matter is the argument put forward by others. There are two issues here. One is the question of whether state money is being used clandestinely to favor the few. The other is the matter of the role of openness and solidarity in the fight against AIDS.

A few years ago, a Ugandan researcher presented a paper on the current state of HIV-AIDS in the country. During the discussion the researcher noted that some Ugandans in leading political and military circles have had discreet access to ARV treatment for many years, despite the high cost of medicine and testing. Other elites were also known to receive treatment. Pressed for details about this group, the researcher replied with one bitter word: "Relatives!"

The researcher was not against helping relatives — a practice considered moral and indeed necessary. The bitter tone was reserved for the way that public funds were being channelled *secretly*, by those in power, to their *own* relatives. There are clear overtones here of class and ethnic politics — "the rich people from the west" (the researcher was from central Uganda) — but perhaps also a reluctant recognition that in today's Uganda, the entitlements of citizens are few and far between. To paraphrase Patrick Chabal and Jean-Pascal Daloz (1999), Uganda "works" even though many of the initiatives of the Ugandan state do not. Apparent weaknesses of the state provide opportunities for covert practices that are to the advantage of the powerful.

Access to valued goods and services is often a matter of "know-who." Connections are crucial, be they to relatives and tribesmen, co-religionists, or simply "old boys." All connections, however, are not of equal significance. Most people agree that the demands of kinsmen are moral even when they are excessive. Likewise, one ought to help a fellow tribesman or co-religionist, and one ought to remember old connections such as those formed at school. As such, these sorts of connections resemble entitlements — not always honored but still honorable (though they are often cause for criticism or irony when people like the researcher quoted above comment about how the powerful help their kinsmen and tribesmen).

Another set of connections, having to do with politics, individual profits, and patronage, is far more ambiguous, covert, and suspect. Here we enter the world of patrimonial relationships and rewards for service described by Chabal and Daloz. There are no entitlements, merely utility and the pursuit of advantage. Suspicions of access to ARV treatment given as patronage to a political ally or military supporter embitter those outside the circle of connections, and — at least in the eyes of the outsider — bitterness clings to the treatment even when it is converted into the moral world of kinship obligation, into helping someone else's relative.

Whereas many Ugandans talk generally, and often cynically, about the politically well connected and wealthy, AIDS professionals and activists specifically criticize this group's fear of coming out of the closet. Not only do they get access to AIDS treatment that is beyond the reach of most citizens, but they have no solidarity with others; they save their own skins while keeping their HIV status secret. This is the theme of one of the most outspoken critics of the current pattern of access to drugs.

Major Rubaramira is the principal AIDS educator in the Ugandan army as well as the founder and leader of an NGO called NGEN+ (National Guidance and Empowerment Network of People Living with HIV/AIDS in Uganda). He is open about his HIV-positive status, which he discovered in 1989. He has been on ARV medications for several years, and he "finds" them himself; some he gets from contacts in Europe forged through his activism. A still-serving officer, Rubaramira was with Museveni in the original "war in the bush" which brought the NRM to power. He has become a political figure in Uganda thanks mostly to his publicly expressed disgust at President Museveni's attempts to smear his opponent as HIV-positive during the recent presidential campaign. In 2002, Rubaramira told us that there were perhaps a thousand Ugandans who receive medicine at any one time from different government sources. This includes army officers, politicians, and members of the Movement—the ruling "nonparty"—as well as their family members. Rubaramira insists that this has been the case for a number of years. "But no one talks about it. These are all big people and getting medicine makes them support the government." For Rubaramira, the worst part of the whole affair is: "They are silent; they will not admit that they are HIV-positive, and that is very wrong for them and for others."

Rubaramira is highly critical of the current Ugandan AIDS policy and in particular with the unwillingness of the country's leaders to press for the resources to make ARV medicines generally available. For him this is an issue of equity—without help the poor will never be able to afford such medicines. But he also stresses a pragmatic point: if everyone has access to treatment, people will be more open about their own HIV status—and openness is the key first step toward behavioral change. The misuse of public trust and public resources is not in itself so unexpected. Worse than the cheating are the hypocrisy and the hiding which are commonplace among HIV-positive elites. AIDS, for Rubaramira, is truly a crisis in Uganda, and secrecy encourages the continuation of the pandemic.

The moral ideal asserted by Rubaramira was evident in the account given by one of our colleagues of her friend, the widow Namwandu. After losing her husband, Namwandu tested positive in 1992 and went to TASO, where she was very active. At TASO she made contacts with development workers coming from abroad on study tours. These "good friends" helped her obtain ARVs. Like Rubaramira, she became part of an international network through which medicines flowed.[8] As our colleague said: "These 'Poles' [her pronunciation of PLWAS, people living with AIDS] have many advantages because of their outside contacts. These people, the Rubaramiras, they share experiences, have so many contacts who give them donations. They get free drugs. But the good thing, they carry the message to all parts of the country."

It is not so much that people resent wealth and advantage in themselves. New hotels and resorts, fine office blocks, and the like are generally applauded as signs of progress. Even the modern house in a rural neighborhood is progress (Whyte and Whyte 1998). What is objectionable is secret consumption and selfish unwillingness to affirm relations with others by sharing and helping. What is morally admirable, at least in the eyes of enlightened AIDS professionals, is the willingness to speak out and stand with others in the struggle against the disease. In this respect, the views of people like Major Rubaramira harmonize with a deeper theme in dealings with misfortune: the morality of open public affirmation of relationships and the ambiguity and potential evil of secret use of medicines for purely selfish ends (Whyte 1988, 1997). Just as medicines (both African and cosmopolitan) may be used secretly in the local rural communities where we have done our fieldwork, so do people imagine that ARVs can be taken without regard for sociality. As long as they are too expensive for ordinary people, the image of the powerful man getting them covertly through connections can only cause bitterness and raise questions about morality.

## Conclusion

Although this chapter focuses on access to ARVs, treating AIDS is so much more than antiretroviral medicines. It is ensuring proper care for tuberculosis, skin disorders, and all the other opportunistic infections that make people suffer. It is good food (what people call "soft food" like passion fruit juice, milk, and eggs), something that many families feel is difficult to provide for chronically ill members. It is emotional support and nursing care and all the rest. Even in terms of medicines, ARVs are not the most important. Many public health specialists, and many on the front lines of AIDS care in Uganda, think media attention to ARVs has distracted from all the other problems of delivering healthcare to people with AIDS. In any case, there are very few people in Uganda today for whom ARVs are a realistic option.

One of the reasons why we nevertheless chose to write about them is that, beyond their pharmacological properties, which have changed the epidemic in wealthier countries, they have such powerful symbolic potential. As concrete things, ARVs objectify relationships in both subtle and dramatic ways. Hope, concern, solidarity, power, money, selfishness are all enacted as those tablets and capsules move between people. Within families, the virtues of care are most clearly demonstrated by buying medicines for the sick person (Meinert 2001). On a global scale, claims of medical apartheid in refusing to make ARVs truly accessible in poor countries are accusations of injustice and immorality.

Access to ARVs in Uganda illustrates the social meanings of medicines with painful clarity. ARVs not only move people to conceptualize and weigh their relations to immediate relatives, but to envision social relations and distinctions on national and even international scales. Research and treatment projects with their inclusion and exclusion criteria, health workers who silently assess the financial capacity of their patients, families who have to choose which lives to support, and activists who call for social justice are all caught in dilemmas that can be expressed in terms of access to medicines.

As global pharmaceuticals, ARVs have captured the social and political imagination more powerfully than almost any other kind of medicine. At the same time, they are caught up in a process of fetishization that is the fate of any *thing* that so effectively objectifies a possibility. Providing things—the adequate supply of cheap or free medicines—is not sufficient. Ensuring their proper use through flexible and efficient systems of delivery and care is the real problem, and it is one that cannot be solved by pharmaceutical companies or international agreements on property rights and trade.

The advocacy and lobbying efforts that have brought down the price of ARVs and made it possible to produce and import generics are immensely important. So are the exemplary projects that demonstrate that ARVs can be delivered effectively to poor populations in developing countries, such as the high-profile efforts in Khayelitsha in the Western Cape (Médecins sans Frontières 2002) and the Clinique Bon Sauveur in Haiti (Farmer et al. 2001). Our review of access dilemmas in Uganda points to a further step: There is a need to examine the whole range of delivery channels and access possibilities on a national basis. There has been little research on the implementation of AIDS treatment and how it might be scaled up for a whole country (but see Teixeira et al. 2003; Biehl 2004). As the price of drugs falls, and if donors and politicians do make decisions to prioritize treatment as a concomitant of prevention, it will be essential to know how treatment and care can be delivered effectively not only in small projects with good resources, but to everyone (Barfod and Ullum 2003:68–69).

In the long run, we believe that medicines for AIDS should be free to those who need them. The fall in price makes it more feasible for governments and other agencies to purchase and supply them. In the short run, or rather in the process of moving toward the goal of equitable care, cheaper drugs make possible different kinds of access, different qualities of care, and a growing awareness of inequity. Uganda is an excellent example. The very qualities of openness to initiatives from different quarters that have made it a leader in prevention (Parkhurst 2002) have encouraged a variety of treatment projects and possibilities. However, there is not yet an adequate national policy on antiretroviral drugs (Okuonzi et al. 2003), and the public healthcare system remains woefully incapable of providing equitable and effective care for all citizens. The dilemmas we have described here show the painful realities of "social pharmacy" at one historical moment.

## Notes

1. The work described in this essay was carried out as part of the Tororo Community Health (TORCH) Project, a collaboration between the Child Health and Development Centre, Makerere University; the Institute of Anthropology, University of Copenhagen; and the Department of Anthropology and Ethnography and the Institute of Epidemiology and Social Medicine, both at Århus University. It was funded by DANIDA, under its Enhancement of Research Capacity Programme. We are grateful for many discussions with colleagues at Makerere and for the generosity of those who gave us their time and shared their concerns.
   This chapter was written for this volume, but in the interest of quickly reaching another readership it was first printed in the *Journal of Social Aspects of HIV/AIDS* 1(1). The journal kindly agreed to its appearance here with slight modifications.
2. New developments in AIDS treatment are happening rapidly and it is difficult to keep up. A useful report on access to ARVs in Uganda (Martinez-Jones and Anyama 2002) was

compiled for Oxfam, with lists of accredited treatment centers and prices of all the ARVS available on the market. But just one year later, prices had already fallen further and new initiatives had changed the picture. As this book goes to press, our account from mid-2003 is already "history" in some ways: new resources flowing into the country have allowed far more people to obtain treatment. But our basic argument about different channels of access, consciousness of inequity, and dilemmas faced by families and healthworkers still holds.

3. A hint of what could happen came with the fluconazole scandal in 2002. Pfizer had donated a large supply of this drug (not an ARV), which is even more expensive than ARVS and is used in the treatment of meningitis and fungal infections commonly affecting AIDS patients. The drug was distributed to government hospitals, but not long afterward it was found—marked as a gift from Pfizer—in private pharmacies in Kampala. The Ministry of Health came down strongly, but just a half year later, in May 2003, another sticky situation was reported in the newspapers. National Medical Stores had negotiated a favorable price reduction on Combivir and two other ARVS from GlaxoSmithKline and was preparing to reexport the drugs to Europe, despite an outcry about the damage this could do to Uganda's image vis-à-vis other drug companies and donors. The deal was stopped by the Ministry of Health.

4. The nevirapine is being donated to the Ministry of Health for a period of five years by Boehringer Ingelheim.

5. Her colleague was quoted elsewhere on the same point: "Why should we tell patients about ARVS when they will not be able to buy them? It will just make them more depressed" (Martinez-Jones and Anyama 2002:9).

6. Total fertility rate for the age group fifteen through forty-nine was calculated at 6.9 for the country as a whole (Macro 2001).

7. Among those who have announced that they will subsidize all or part of ARV treatment for employees with AIDS are *New Vision* newspaper, Bank of Uganda, Stanley Chartered Bank, the Civil Aviation Authority, National Water and Sewage, Shell, Total, Coca-Cola, and various embassies. The Uganda Business Coalition and the Uganda Business Council have been active in promoting AIDS prevention and care in the corporate world.

8. Nguyen et al. (2003) describe a similar phenomenon: the "recycling" of drugs from countries of the north to Burkina Faso either to patient groups or on an individual basis.

# REFERENCES

Abbott, Andrew. 1988. *The System of Professions: An Essay on the Division of Expert Labor.* Chicago: University of Chicago Press.

Abrams, Phillip. 1998. Notes on the difficulty of studying the state. *Journal of Historical Sociology* 1(1):58–90.

Abramson, John. 2005. *Overdosed America: The Broken Promise of American Medicine.* New York: Perennial.

Acordo TRIPS ou acordo ADPIC. *Diário Oficial*, 19 December 1994, 18889, n. 239. Brasília.

Acurcio, F., M. Guimarães, and C. Drew. 1996. Accessibilidade de indivíduos infectados pelo HIV aos serviços de saúde: uma revisão de literatura. *Cadernos de Saúde Pública* 12(2).

Agamben, Giorgio. 1998. *Homo Sacer: Sovereignty and Bare Life.* Stanford: Stanford University Press.

Agar, Michael H., and Richard C. Stephens. 1975. The methadone street scene: The addict's view. *Psychiatry* 38:381–387.

Agar, Michael, Philippe Bourgois, John French, and Owen Murdoch. 2001. Buprenorphine. "Field trials" of a new drug. *Qualitative Health Research* 11(1).

Alden, Edward. 2004. US interrogation debate: Dismay at attempt to find legal justification for torture. *Financial Times*, 10 June.

Alderman, J., R. Wolkow, M. Chung, and H. F. Johnston. 1998. Sertraline treatment of children and adolescents with OCD or depression: Pharmacokinetics, tolerability and efficacy. *Journal of the American Academy of Child and Adolescent Psychiatry* 37:386–394.

Alvarez, Sonia, Evelina Dagnino, and Arturo Escobar. 1998. *Cultures of Politics — Politics of Culture: Re-visioning Latin American Social Movements.* Boulder, CO: Westview.

Anderson, Warwick. 2003. *The Cultivation of Whiteness: Science, Health, and Racial Destiny in Australia.* New York: Basic Books.

Angell, Marcia. 1988. Ethical imperialism? Ethics in international collaborative clinical research. *New England Journal of Medicine* 319(16):1081–1083.

Angell, Marcia. 1997. The ethics of clinical research in the Third World. *New England Journal of Medicine* 337(12):847–849.

Angell, Marcia. 2000. Investigators' responsibilities for human subjects in developing countries. *New England Journal of Medicine* 342(13):967–968.

Angell, Marcia. 2004. *The Truth about the Drug Companies: How They Deceive Us and What to Do About It.* New York: Random House, 2004.

Appadurai, A. 1986. Introduction: Commodities and the politics of value. In A. Appadurai, ed., *The Social Life of Things: Commodities in Cultural Perspective.* Cambridge: Cambridge University Press.

Appadurai, A. 1996. *Modernity at Large: Cultural Dimensions of Globalization.* Minneapolis: University of Minnesota Press.

Appadurai, A. 2002. Deep democracy: Urban governmentality and the horizon of politics. *Public Culture* 14(1):21–47.

Applbaum, Kalman. 1998a. The sweetness of salvation: Consumer marketing and the liberal-bourgeois theory of needs. *Current Anthropology* 39(3):323–349.

Applbaum, Kalman. 1998b. Rationality, morality and free trade: U.S.-Japan trade relations in anthropological perspective. *Dialectical Anthropology* 23(1):1–30.

Applbaum, Kalman. 2000a. Crossing borders: Globalization as myth and charter in American transnational consumer marketing. *American Ethnologist* 27(2):257–282.

Applbaum, Kalman. 2000b. Marketing and commoditization. *Social Analysis* 44(2):106–128.

Applbaum, Kalman. 2004a. *The Marketing Era: From Professional Practice to Global Provisioning*. New York: Routledge.

Applbaum, Kalman. 2004b. How to organize a psychiatric congress. *Anthropological Quarterly* 77(2):303–310.

Arendt, Hannah. 1958. *The Human Condition*. Chicago: University of Chicago Press.

Arendt, Hannah. 1973. *The Origins of Totalitarianism*. New York: Harvest/HBK Book.

Arie, Sophie. 2001. Argentina hits rock bottom. *Observer*, 9 December 2001.

Arnold, David. 1993. *Colonizing the Body: State Medicine and Epidemic Disease in Nineteenth-Century India*. Berkeley: University of California Press.

Arrais, Paulo, D. Sérgio, H. Coelho, and L. Lutéscia. 1997. Perfil da automedicação no Brasil. *Revista de Saúde Pública* 31(1).

Avorn, Jerry. 2004. *Powerful Medicines: The Benefits, Risks, and Costs of Prescription Drugs*. New York: Knopf.

Bachmann, Christian, and Anne Coppel. 1989. *Le dragon domestique: deux siècles de relations entre l'Occident et la drogue*. Paris: Albin Michel.

Barbosa, Denis Borges. n.d. O acordo TRIPS e o prazo das patentes. MS.

Barfod, T., and H. Ullum. 2003. The option of antiretroviral treatment in Africa. In *One Step Further: Responses to HIV/AIDS*, 54–75. Stockholm: SIDA and UNRISD.

Barry, Andrew, Thomas Osborne, and Nikolas Rose, eds. 1996. *Foucault and Political Reason: Liberalism, Neo-liberalism and the Rationalities of Government*. Chicago: University of Chicago Press.

Bastos, Cristiana. 1999. *Global Responses to AIDS: Science in Emergency*. Bloomington: Indiana University Press.

Bastos, Francisco Inácio, and Christovam Barcellos. 1995. Geografia social da AIDS no Brasil. *Revista de Saúde Pública* 29(1):52–62.

Bastos, Francisco Inácio, and Christovam Barcellos. 1996. Redes sociais e difusão da AIDS no Brasil. *Boletim da Oficina Sanitária Panamericana* 121(1):11–24.

Baszanger, Isabelle. 1995. *Douleur et médecine: la fin d'un oubli*. Paris: Le Seuil.

Bayer, R. 1998. The debate over maternal-fetal HIV transmission prevention trials in Africa, Asia, and Caribbean: Racist exploitation or exploitation of racism? *American Journal of Public Health* 88(4):567–570.

BBC Online. 2002. Los Argentinos se sienten devaluados. 24 January.

Becker, Howard. 2001. Les drogues que sont-elles? In Howard Becker, ed., *Qu'est-ce qu'une drogue?* Anglet: Atlantica.

Bellow, Saul. 1996. *Mosby's Memoirs*. New York: Penguin.

Benatar, Solomon. 2001. Distributive justice and clinical trials in the Third World. *Theoretical Medicine and Bioethics* 22(3):169–176.

Benatar, Solomon, and Peter A. Singer. 2000. A new look at international research ethics. *British Medical Journal* 321(7264):824–826.

Bergeron, Henri. 1999. *L'Etat de la toxicomanie: histoire d'une singularité française*. Paris: Presses Universitaires de France.

Bergeron, Henri. 2001. Définition des drogues et gestion des toxicomanes. In Howard Becker, ed., *Qu'est-ce qu'une drogue?*, 162–180. Anglet: Atlantica.

Berman, Elaine S. 1999. Too little bone: The medicalization of osteoporosis. *Journal of Woman's Health and Law* 1:257–277.

Bermudez, Jorge. 1992. *Remédios: saúde ou indústria*. Rio de Janeiro: Relume Dumará.

Bermudez, Jorge. 1995. *Indústria farmacêutica, estado e sociedade: crítica da política de medicamentos no Brasil*. São Paulo: Editora Hucitec e Sociedade Brasileira de Vigilância de Medicamentos.

Bermudez, J. A. Z., M. A. Oliveria, R. Epsztejn, and L. Hasenclever. n.d. Implicações do acordo TRIPS e da recente lei de proteção patentária no Brasil na produção local e no acesso da população aos medicamentos. MS, 2000.

Biehl, João. 1999. *Other Life: AIDS, Biopolitics, and Subjectivity in Brazil's Zones of Social Abandonment*. Ann Arbor: UMI Services.

Biehl, João. 2000. Technology and affect: HIV/AIDS testing in Brazil. *Culture, Medicine and Psychiatry* 25(1):87–129.

Biehl, João. 2001a. Vita: Life in a zone of social abandonment. *Social Text* 19(3):131–149.

Biehl, João, with Denise Coutinho e Ana Luzia Outeiro. 2001b. Technology and affect: HIV/AIDS testing in Brazil. *Culture, Medicine, and Psychiatry* 25:87–129.

Biehl, João. 2002. Biotechnology and the new politics of life and death in Brazil: The AIDS model. *Princeton Journal of Bioethics* 5:59–74.

Biehl, João. 2004. The activist state: Global pharmaceuticals, AIDS, and citizenship in Brazil. *Social Text* 22(3):105–132.

Biehl, João. 2005. *Vita: Life in a Zone of Social Abandonment*. Berkeley: University of California Press.

Biehl, João, with Jessica Blatt. 1995. *Life on Paper: A Trip Through AIDS in Brazil*. Study document. Rio de Janeiro: ISER.

Biehl, João, Arthur Kleinman, and Byron Good, eds. Forthcoming. *Rethinking Subjectivity*. Berkeley: University of California Press.

Binder, Philippe. 1994. Le médecin généraliste peut-il prendre en charge des toxicomanes en ambulatoire sans recourir aux cures de substitution? Quels sont les produits qu'il utilise? *Annales de Médecine Interne* 145(3): 62–64.

Bloch, J., et al. 1996. Place des généralistes dans la prise en charge des toxicomanes: EVAL.

Bluebond-Langner, Myra. 1996 (1948). *In the Shadow of Illness: Parents and Siblings of the Chronically Ill Child*. Princeton, N.J.: Princeton University Press.

Boltanski, Luc. 1971. Les usages sociaux du corps. *Annales: Economies, Sociétés, Civilisations* 1:205–239.

Boltanski, Luc, and Laurent Thevenot. 1991. *De la justification: les economies de la grandeur*. Paris: Gallimard.

Bosk, Charles. 1999. Professional ethicist available: Logical, secular, friendly. *Daedalus* 128(fall):47–68.

Bosk, Charles. 2000. Irony, ethnography, and informed consent. In Barry Hoffmaster, ed., *Bioethics in Social Context*. Philadelphia: Temple University Press.

Bosk, Charles. 2002. Now that we have the data, what was the question? *American Journal of Bioethics* 2(4):21–23.

Bosk, Charles. 2005. *What Would You Do? The Collision of Ethnography and Ethics*. Chicago: University of Chicago Press.

Bosk, Charles, and Raymond de Vries. 2004. Bureaucracies of mass deception: Institutional review boards and the ethics of ethnographic research. *Annals of the American Academy of Political and Social Science* 595(1):249–63.

Botbol-Baum, Mylène. 2000. The shrinking of human rights: The controversial revision of the Helsinki Declaration. *HIV Medicine* 1(4):238–245.

Bourdieu, Pierre. 1999. Rethinking the state. In George Steinmetz, ed., *State/Culture: State-Formation after the Cultural Turn*. Ithaca: Cornell University Press.

Bourgois, Philippe. 1995. *In Search of Respect: Selling Crack in El Barrio*. Cambridge, New York: Cambridge University Press.

Bowker, Geoffrey C., and Susan Leigh Star. 2000. Invisible mediators of action: Classification and the ubiquity of standards. *Mind, Culture and Activity* 7(1–2):147–164.

Boyer, Robert and Daniel Drache. 1996. *States Against Markets: The Limits of Globalization*. New York: Routledge.

Braithwaite, John. 1986. *Corporate Crime in the Pharmaceutical Industry*. London: Routledge and Kegan Paul.

Brandt, Allan. 1985. *No Magic Bullet: A Social History of Venereal Disease in the United States since 1880*. New York: Oxford University Press.

Brass, P. 1972. The politics of ayurvedic education. In R. L. H. Rudolf and S. I. Rudolf, eds., *Education and Politics in India: Studies in Organization, Society, and Policy*. Cambridge; Harvard University Press.

Brescia, Bonnie. 2002. Better budgeting for patient recruitment. *Pharmaceutical Executive*. Electronic document, http://www.pharmexec.com. Accessed 10 September 2004.

Breslau, Joshua. 2000. Globalizing disaster trauma: Psychiatry, science, and culture after the Kobe earthquake. *Ethos* 28(2):174–197.

Briggs, Charles, and Clara Mantini-Briggs. 2003. *Stories in the Time of Cholera: Racial Profiling During a Medical Nightmare*. Berkeley: University of California Press.

Brodwin, Paul. *Medicine and Morality in Haiti: The contest for Healing Power*. Cambridge.: Cambridge University Press, 1996.

Bury, M. 1996. Caveat venditor: Social dimensions of a medical controversy. In D. Healy and D. Doogan, *Psychotropic Drug Development: Social Economic and Pharmacological Aspects*. London: Chapman and Hall.

Bury, M., and J. Gabe. 1990. Hooked? Media responses to tranquilliser dependence. In P. Abbott and G. Payne, eds., *New Direction in the Sociology of Health*, 87–103. Basingstoke: Falmer, Brass.

Business Communication Company. 2003. *The Clinical Trials Business*. Report B-171. Norwalk, Conn.: Business Communication Company.

Cadet-Taïrou, A., and D. Cholley. 2004. *Approche régionale de la substitution aux opiacés: 1999–2002, pratiques et disparités à travers 13 sites français*. Saint-Denis: OFDT.

Cadet-Taïrou, A., and D. Cholley. 2004. *La substitution à travers 13 sites français: 1999–2002, pratiques et disparaités régionales*. Paris: CNAMTS, OFDT.

Cadet-Taïrou, A., et al. 2004. Quel est le nombre d'usagers d'opiacés sous BHD? *Tendances* 37:1–2.

Cahuzac, Jérôme. 1999. Le poids des industries pharmaceutiques. *Pouvoirs: Revue Française d'Etudes Constitutionnelles et Politiques* 89(April):101–118.

Caldeira, Teresa. 2001. *City of Walls: Crime, Segregation, and Citizenship in São Paulo*. Berkeley: University of California Press.

Callaway, Enoch. 1996. Buprenorphine for depression: The un-adoptable orphan. *Biological Psychiatry* 39(12):989–990.

Cardoso, Fernando Henrique. 1998. Notas sobre a reforma do estado. *Novos Estudos do CEBRAP* 50:1–12.

Carpenter, Daniel P. 2004. "The Political Economy of FDA Drug Review: Processing, Politics, and Lessons for Policy." *Health Affairs* 23(1): 52–63.

Carpentier, Jean, ed. 2000. *Des toxicomanes et des soins*. Paris: Harmattan.

Carpentier, Jean, Jean-François Bloch-Lainé, and Serge Hefez. 1994. Intérêts et limitaitons des traitements de substitution dans la prise en charge des toxicomanes. *Annales de Médecine Interne* 145(suppl. 3):50–51.

Cassier, Maurice, and Marilena Correa. 2003. Patents, innovation and public health: Brazilian public-sector laboratories' experience in copying AIDS drugs. In *Economics of AIDS and Access to HIV/AIDS Care in Developing Countries: Issues and Challenges*, 89–107. Paris: ANRS.

Castilho, Euclides A. de, and Pedro Chequer. 1997. A epidemia de AIDS no Brasil. In Coordenação Nacional de DST e AIDS [CN]. *A Epidemia da AIDS no Brasil: Situação e Tendências*, 9–12. Brasília: Ministério da Saúde.

Cecchi, Horacio. 2001. Una noticia para comerse las uñas. *Pagina 12*, 16 August.

Center for Drug Evaluation and Research. 2002. *CDER Report to the Nation: 2002*. Washington: U.S. Food and Drug Administration.

CenterWatch. 2002. CenterWatch launches first-of-its-kind consumer guide to the risks and benefits of volunteering for clinical trials. Electronic document, http://www.centerwatch.com/newsreleases/4-1-2002. Accessed 1 September 2004.

Chabal, P., and J.-P. Daloz. 1999. *Africa Works: Disorder as Political Instrument*. London: James Currey; Bloomington: Indiana University Press.

Chambliss, Daniel F. 1996. *Beyond Caring: Hospitals, Nurses, and the Social Organization of Ethics*. Chicago: University of Chicago Press.

Charpak, Y., J. Barbot, and F. Nory. 1993. La prise en charge des toxicomanes par les médecins généralistes en 1992. EVAL.

Chen, Lincoln, Arthur Kleinman, and Norma Ware, eds. 1994. *Health and Social Change in International Perspective*. Cambridge: Harvard University Press.

Chernobyl's legacy to science. 1996. *Nature* 380(6576):653.

Cholley, D., et al. 2001. Tratiement de substitution par buprénorphine-haut-dosage: quel rôle pour l'assurance maladie? *Revue Médical de l'Assurance Maladie* 32(4):295–303.

Christakis, Nicholas. 1992. Ethics are local: Engaging cross-cultural variation in the ethics for clinical research. *Social Science and Medicine* 35(9):1079–1091.

Clary, François Prévoteau du. 1999. Drogues, médicaments, sustitution? Le médecin qui prescrit s'est-il fait une raison? In F. Diderot, ed., *Les médecins doivent-ils prescrire des drogues?*, 52–64. Paris: Presses Universitaires de France.

Cohen, Lawrence. 1999. Where it hurts: Indian material for an ethics of organ transplantation. *Daedalus* 128(fall):135–165.

Cohen, Lawrence. 2000. *No Aging in India: Alzheimer's, the Bad Family, and Other Modern Things*. Berkeley: University of California Press.

Comaroff, Jean, and John L. Comaroff. 2000. Millennial capitalism: First thoughts on a second coming. *Public Culture* 12:2.

Comaroff, John, and Jean Comaroff. 1992. Medicine, colonialism, and the black body. In John Comaroff and Jean Comaroff, *Ethnography and the Historical Imagination*, 215–235. Boulder, Colo.: Westview Press.

Conrad, Peter. 1985. The meaning of medication: Another look at compliance. *Social Science and Medicine* 20:29–37.

El consumo de tranquilizantes crecio entre un 8 y un 9 por ciento. *Clarín*, 3 October 2001.

Coombe, Rosemary. 2003. "Works in Progress: Traditional Knowledge, Biological Diversity and Intellectual Property in a Neoliberal Era." In B. Maurer and R.W. Perry, eds., *Globalization and Governmentalities*. Minneapolis: University of Minnesota Press.

Coordenação Nacional de DST e AIDS [CN]. 1997a. *Catálogo de organizações não-hovernamentais*. Brasília: Ministério da Saúde.

Coordenação Nacional de DST e AIDS. 1997b. *Coquetel contra AIDS faz cair numero de mortes e custos do tratamento*. Brasília: Ministério da Saúde (press release Oct. 31, 1997).

Coordenação Nacional de DST e AIDS. 1997c. *A epidemia da AIDS no Brasil: situação e tendências*. Brasília: Ministério da Saúde.

Coordenação Nacional de DST e AIDS. 2000a. *The Brazilian Response to HIV/AIDS: Best Practices*. Brasília: Ministério da Saúde.

Coordenação Nacional de DST e AIDS. 2000b. WTO panel calls Brazilian patent laws into question. Brasília: Ministério da Saúde (press release).

Coordenação Nacional de DST e AIDS. 2001a. *National AIDS Drug Policy*. Brasília: Ministério da Saúde.

Coordenação Nacional de DST e AIDS. 2001b. *Boletim epidemiológico, Janeiro a Março de 2001*. Brasília: Ministério da Saúde.

Coordenação Nacional de DST e AIDS. 2002. *A Experiência do Programa Brasileiro de AIDS*. Brasília: Ministério da Saúde.

Coppel, Anne. 1996. Les intervenants en toxicomanie, le sida et la réduction des risques. *Communications* 62:75–108.

Coppel, Anne. 2002. *Peut-on civiliser les drogues? De la guerre à la drogue à la réduction des risques*. Paris: La Découverte.

Cosendey, Marly Aparecida, J. A. Z. Bermudez, A. L. A. Reis, H. F. Silva, M. A. Oliveira, and V. L. Luiza. 2000. Assistência farmacêutica na atenção básica de saúde: a experiência de três estados brasileiros. *Cadernos de Saúde Pública* 16(1):171–182.

Costes, J.-M., and A. Cadet-Taïrou. 2004. Impact des traitements de substitution: Bilan sur les dix dernières années. *Tendances* 37:3–4.

Courtwright, David T. 2001 *Forces of Habit: Drugs and the Making of the Modern World*. Cambridge: Harvard University Press.

Crouch, Robert A., and John D. Arras. 1998. AZT trials and tribulations. *Hastings Center Report* 28(6):26–34.

Crozier, Michel. 1963. *Le phénomène bureaucratique*. Paris: Le Seuil.

*Current Index of Medical Specialities*. 2001. Volume 24, no. 3.

Dagognet, François. 1964. *La raison et les remèdes*. Paris: Presses Universitaires de France.

Dagognet, François. 2000. Complexité de la prescription médicamenteuse. In F. Diderot, ed., *Les médecins doivent-il prescrire des drogues?*, 14–22. Paris: Presses Universitaires de France.

Daniel, Herbert. 1991. We are all people living with AIDS: Myths and realities of AIDS in Brazil. *International Journal of Health Services* 21(3).

Das, Jishnu, and Jeffrey Hammer. 2004. Strained mercy: Quality of medical care in Delhi. *Economic and Political Weekly* Feb.: 951–961.

Das, Veena. 1995a. *Critical Events: An Anthropological Perspective on Contemporary India*. New York: Oxford University Press, 1995.

Das, Veena. 1995b. Suffering, legitimacy, and healing: The Bhopal case. In Veena Das, *Critical Events: An Anthropological Perspective on Contemporary India*, 137–174. Delhi: Oxford University Press.

Das, Veena. 1999. Public good, ethics, and everyday life: Beyond the boundaries of bioethics. *Daedalus* 128(4):99–133.

Das, Veena, and Arthur Kleinman, Mamphela Ramphele, Pamela Reynolds. 2000. *Violence and Subjectivity*. Berkeley: University of California Press.

Das, J., and C. Sanchez. 2002. Short but not sweet: New evidence on short duration morbidities from India. Paper presented to All Bank Conference on Development Economics. 11–17 March, Washington, D.C.

Davis, C. 2000. *Death in Abeyance*. Edinburgh: Edinburgh University Press.

De Grazia, David. 2000. Prozac, enhancement and self-creation. *Hastings Center Report* 30:34–40.

Deleuze, Gilles. 1995. *Negotiations*. New York: Columbia University Press.

Desjarlais, Robert. 1997. *Shelter Blues: Sanity and Selfhood among the Homeless*. Philadelphia: University of Pennsylvania.

Desjarlais, Robert, Leon Eisenberg, Byron Good, and Arthur Kleinman, eds. 1996. *World Mental Health: Problems and Priorities in Low-Income Countries*. Oxford: Oxford University Press.

Deux médecins dénoncent les dérives liées au Subutex. *Le Quotidien du Médecin*, 15 April 2002 (no. 7107).

de Vries, Raymond. 2004. How can we help? From "sociology in" to "sociology of" bioethics. *Journal of Law, Medicine, and Ethics* 32(2):279–293.

de Zulueta, P. 2001. Randomised placebo-controlled trials and HIV-infected pregnant women in developing countries: Ethical imperialism or unethical exploitation? *Bioethics* 15(4):289–311.

Dickersin, Kay, and Drummond Rennie. 2003. Registering clinical trials. *JAMA* 290(4):516.

DiMasi, Joseph A., Ronald W. Hansen, and Henry G. Grabowski. 2003. The price of innovation: New estimates of drug development costs. *Journal of Health Economics* 22(2):151–186.

Dixon, Peter. 1999. Towards a public health response for preventing the spread of HIV amongst injecting drug users within Nepal and the development of a treatment, rehabilitation and prevention program in Pokhara. *International Journal of Drug Policy* 10(5):375–383.

Doimo, Ana Maria. 1995. *A vez e a voz do popular: movimentos sociais e participação política no Brasil pós-70*. Rio de Janeiro: ANPOCS/Relume Dumará.

Dourado, M., M. Barreto, N. Almeida-Filho, J. Biehl, and S. Cunha. 1997a. Região nordeste. In Coordenação Nacional de DST e AIDS, *A epidemia da AIDS no Brasil: situação e tendências*, 123–143. Brasília: Ministério da Saúde.

Dourado, M. I. C., C. Noronha, A. Barbosa, and R. Lago. 1997b. Considerações sobre o quadro da AIDS na Bahia. *Boletim Epidemiológico do SUS*. Brasília: Ministério da Saúde.

Dumit, Joseph. 2000. When explanations rest: "Good enough" brain science and the new biomental disorders. In Margaret Lock, Alan Young, and Alberto Cambrosio, eds., *Living and Working with the New Medical Technologies: Intersections of Inquiry*, 209–232. Cambridge: Cambridge University Press.

Edwards, James C. 2000. Passion, activity and "the care of the self." *Hastings Center Report* 30:31–33.

Ehrenberg, Alain, ed. 1998. *Drogues et medicaments psychotropes: Le trouble des frontières*. Paris. Esprit.

Eisenberg, Rebecca. 2001. The Shifting Functional Balance of Patents and Drug Regulation. *Health Affairs* 20(5): 119–135.

Elkin, Nina, and Michael Tan, eds. 1994. *Medicines: Meanings and Contexts*. Quezan City, Philippines: Information Health Network.

Elliott, Carl. 2000. Pursued by happiness and beaten senseless. *Hastings Center Report* 30:7–12.

Elliott, Carl. 2003. *Better Than Well: American Medicine Meets the American Dream*. New York: W. W. Norton.

Encyclopedia of Global Industries. 2005. Pharmaceuticals. In *Business and Company Re-*

source Center. Farmington Hills, Mich.: Gale Group. See also online edition, http://galenet .galegroup.com.

Epstein, Steven. 1996. *Impure Science: AIDS, Activism, and the Politics of Knowledge*. Berkeley: University of California Press.

Escorel, Sarah. 1993. Elementos para a análise da configuração do padrão brasileiro de proteção social: o Brasil tem um *Welfare State*? *Estudos: Política, Planejamento e Gestão em Saúde*, no. 1. Rio de Janeiro: FIOCRUZ/ENSP/DAPS.

Estroff, Sue E. 1985. *Making It Crazy: An Ethnography of Psychiatric Clients in an American Community*. Berkeley: University of California Press.

Etkin, Nina L. 1992. "Side effects": Cultural constructions and reinterpretations of Western pharmaceuticals. *Medical Anthropological Quarterly* 6(2):99–113.

European Monitoring Center for Drugs and Drug Addiction. 2004. *The State of the Drugs Problem in the European Union and Norway*. Annual Report 2004. Luxemburg: Office for Official Publications of the European Communities.

Farmer, Paul. 1999. The consumption of the poor: Tuberculosis in the late twentieth century. In *Infections and Inequalities: The Modern Plagues*, 184–211. Berkeley: University of California Press.

Farmer, Paul. 2002a. Can transnational research be ethical in the developing world? *Lancet* 360(9342):1301–1302.

Farmer, Paul. 2004. *Pathologies of Power*. Berkeley: University of California Press.

Farmer, Paul, and Jim Yong Kim. 1998. Community based approaches to the control of multidrug resistant tuberculosis. *British Medical Journal* 317:7159–7163.

Farmer, P[aul], F. Léandre, J. S. Mukherjee, M. S. Claude, P. Nevil, M. C. Smith-Fawzi, et al. 2001. Community-based approaches to HIV treatment in resource-poor settings. *Lancet* 358:404–409.

Farmer, Paul, Fernet Léandre, Joia Mukherjee, Rajesh Gupta, Laura Tarter, and Jim Yong Kim. 2001. Community-based treatment of advanced HIV disease: Introducing DOT-HAART (directly observed therapy with highly active antiretroviral therapy). *Bulletin of the World Health Organization* 79(12):1145.

Fassin, Didier, ed. 1998. *Les figures urbaines de la santé publique*. Paris: La Découverte.

Ferguson, James, and Akhil Gupta. 2002. Spatializing states. *American Ethnologist* 29(4):981–1002.

Feroni, Isabelle, and Anne M. Lovell. 1996. Prévention du VIH et toxicomanie a Marseille: Esquisse pour une santé publique locale. *Annales de la Recherche Urbaine* 73:22–32.

Fischer, Michael M. J. 2001. Ethnographic critique and technoscientific narratives: The old mole, ethical plateaux, and the governance of emergent biosocial polities. *Culture, Medicine and Psychiatry* 25(4):355–393.

Fischer, Michael M. J. 2003. *Emergent Forms of Life and the Anthropological Voice*. Durham, N.C.: Duke University Press.

Fleising, Usher. 2002. ImClone's failed culture of expertise. *Trends in Biotechnology* 20(8):326.

Fonseca, M.G., C. Travassos, F. I. Bastos, N. do V. Silva, C. L. Szwarcwald. 2003. Distribuição social da AIDS no Brasil, segundo participação no mercado de trabalho, ocupação e *status* sócio-econômico dos casos de 1987 a 1998. *Cadernos de Saúde Pública* 19(5):1351–1363.

Foucault, Michel. 1980. *The History of Sexuality.* Vol. 1. New York: Vintage Books.

Foucault, Michel. 1991. Governmentality. In Graham Burchell, Colin Gordon, and Peter Miller, eds., *The Foucault Effect: Studies in Governmentality.* Chicago: University of Chicago Press.

Foucault, Michel. 1992. Del poder de la soberanía al poder sobre la vida. In *Genealogía del Racismo.* Buenos Aires: Editorial Altamira.

Foucault, Michel. 2000. "Omnes et singulatim": Toward a critique of political reason. In James Faubion, ed., *Power.* New York: New Press.

Franklin, Sarah. 1995. Science as culture, cultures of science. *Annual Review of Anthropology* 24:163–185.

Fraser, Nancy. n.d. Transnationalizing the public sphere. MS, 2002.

*Fundación ISALUD.* 1999. El mercado de medicamentos en la Argentina. *Estudios de la Economía Real,* no. 13. Buenos Aires: Fundación ISALUD.

Gabe, J., and M. Bury. 1991. Tranquillisers and health care in crisis. *Social Science and Medicine* 32:449–454.

Galbraith, John Kenneth. 1967. *The New Industrial State.* London: Hamish Hamilton.

Galvão, Jane. 2000. *A AIDS no Brasil: a agenda de construção de uma epidemia.* São Paulo: Editora 34.

Galvão, Jane. 2001. HIV/AIDS na América Latina: desigualdades, respostas e desafios. Seminário: Violência Estrutural e Vulnerabilidade frente ao HIV/AIDS na América Latina: Práticas de Resistência.

Galvão, Jane. 2002. A política brasileira de distribuição e produção de medicamentos antiretrovirais: privilégio ou um direito? *Cadernos de Saúde Pública* 18(1):213–219.

Garrison, John, and Anabela Abreu. 2000. Government and civil society in the fight against HIV and AIDS in Brazil. Study Document, World Bank. Europe and the Americas Forum on Health Sector Reform, 24–26 May.

Gasquet, I., C. Lançon, and P. Parquet. 1999. Facteurs prédictifs de réponse au traitement substitutif par buprénorphine haut dosage: étude naturaliste en médecine générale. *L'Encéphale* 25(6):645–651.

Gattari, Miriam, Susana Scarpatti, Inés Bignone, Ricardo Bolaños, and Ulises Romeo. n.d. Estudio de utilización de ansiolíticos y antidepresivos en cuatro entidades de la seguridad social de la Argentina, periodo 1997–2000. MS, 2001.

Geertz, Clifford. 2000 [1984]. Anti anti-relativism. In Geertz, *Available Light: Anthropological Reflections on Philosophical Topics,* 42–67. Princeton: Princeton University Press.

Geertz, Clifford. 2001. Life among the anthros. *New York Review of Books* 48(2):18–22.

Gibier, Lionel. 1999. *Prise en charge des usagers de drogues.* Reuil-Malmaison: Doin.

Giddens, Anthony. 1990. *The Consequences of Modernity.* Cambridge: Polity Press.

Giddens, Anthony. 1991. *Modernity and Self-Identity: Self and Society in the Late Modern Age.* Cambridge: Polity Press.

Glenmullen, Joseph. 2000. *Prozac Backlash*. New York: Touchstone.

Gomart, Emilie. 2002. Methadone: Six effects in search of a substance. *Social Studies of Science* 32(1):93–135.

Good, Byron J. 1994. *Medicine, Rationality and Experience: An Anthropological Perspective*. Cambridge: Cambridge University Press.

Good, Mary-Jo DelVecchio. 1995. *American Medicine: The Quest for Competence*. Berkeley: University of California Press.

Good, Mary-Jo DelVecchio. 2001. The biotechnical embrace. *Culture, Medicine and Psychiatry* 25(4):395–410.

Good, Mary-Jo DelVecchio, and Byron Good. 1993. Clinical narratives and the study of contemporary doctor-patient relationships. In Gary L. Albrecht, Ray Fitzpatrick, and Susan C. Scrimshaw, eds., *Handbook of Social Studies in Health and Medicine*. London: Sage.

Goozner, Merrill. 2004. *The $800 Million Pill: The Truth Behind the Cost of New Drugs*. Berkeley: University of California Press.

Gorman, James. 2004. The altered human is already here. *New York Times*, 6 April.

Government of India. 1948. *The Report of the Committee on Indigenous Systems of Medicine* [Chopra Report]. Delhi: GOI Publications.

Groupe de Travail de l'INSERM. 1998. Evaluer la mise à disposition du Subutex pour la prise en charge des usagers de drogue. Paris: INSERM.

Guess, Harry A., Arthur Kleinman, John W. Kusek, and Linda W. Engel, eds. 2002. *The Science of the Placebo: Toward an Interdisciplinary Research Agenda*. London: BMJ Books.

Guillemin, Jeanne. 1998. Bioethics and the coming of the corporation to medicine. In Raymond de Vries and Janardan Subedi, eds., *Bioethics and Society: Constructing the Ethical Enterprise*, 60–77. Upper Saddle River, N.J.: Prentice-Hall.

Hacking, Ian. 1990. *The Taming of Chance*. Cambridge: Cambridge University Press.

Hacking, Ian. 1995. *Rewriting the Soul: Multiple Personality and the Sciences of Memory*. Princeton: Princeton University Press.

Hacking, Ian. 1998. *Mad Travelers: Reflections on the Reality of Transient Mental Illnesses*. Charlottesville: University Press of Virginia.

Hacking, Ian. 1999. Making up people. In M. Biagioli, ed., *The Science Studies Reader*. New York: Routledge.

Hahn, Robert. 1999. *Anthropology in Public Health: Bridging Differences in Culture and Society*. New York: Oxford University Press.

Hahn, Robert, and Arthur Kleinman. 1983. Belief as pathogen, belief as medicine. *Medical Anthropology Quarterly* 14(4):16–19.

Harkness, Jon M. 1996. Research behind bars: A history of nontherapeutic research on American prisoners. PhD diss., University of Wisconsin, Madison.

Harries, A. D., D. S. Nyangulu, N. J. Hargreaves, O. Kaluwa, and F. M. Salaniponi. 2001. Preventing antiretroviral anarchy in sub-Saharan Africa. *Lancet* 358:410–414.

Harrington, Anne, ed. 1997. Introduction to *The Placebo Effect: An Interdisciplinary Exploration*. Cambridge: Harvard University Press.

Harvard AIDS Institute. 2000. *Consensus Statement on Antiretroviral Treatment for AIDS in Poor Countries*. Boston: Harvard School of Public Health.

Hassenteufel, Patrick. 1997. *Les médecins face à l'etat: une comparaison européenne*. Paris: Presses de la FNSP.

Hayden, Cori. 2003. *When Nature Goes Public: The Making and Unmaking of Bioprospecting in Mexico*. Princeton: Princeton University Press.

Healy, David. 1990. The psychopharmacological era: Notes toward a history. *Journal of Psychopharmacology* 4:152–167.

Healy, David. 1991. The marketing of 5HT: Anxiety or depression. *British Journal of Psychiatry* 158:737–742.

Healy, David. 1998. *The Antidepressant Era*. Cambridge: Harvard University Press.

Healy, David. 1999. Antidepressant psychopharmacotherapy: At the crossroads. *International Journal of Psychiatry in Clinical Practice* 3:S9–S15.

Healy, David. 2000. Good science or good business? *Hastings Center Report* 30:19–22.

Healy, David. 2001. The dilemmas posed by new and fashionable treatments. *Advances in Psychiatric Therapy* 7:322–327.

Healy, David. 2002a. *The Creation of Psychopharmacology*. Cambridge: Harvard University Press.

Healy, David. 2002b. Conflicting interests in Toronto: Anatomy of a controversy at the interface of academia and industry. *Perspectives in Biology and Medicine* 45:250–263.

Healy, David. 2003. Lines of evidence on the risks of suicide with selective serotonin reuptake inhibitors. *Psychotherapy and Psychosomatics* 72:71–79.

Healy, David. 2004. *Let Them Eat Prozac*. New York: New York University Press.

Healy, David, and Dinah Cattell. 2003. The interface between authorship, industry and science in the domain of therapeutics. *British Journal of Psychiatry* 182:22–27.

Healy, David, Marie Savage, Pamela Michael, Margaret Harris, David Hirst, Michael Carter, Dinah Cattell, Tom McMonagle, Nancy Sohler, and Ezra Susser. 2001. Psychiatric bed utilisation: 1896 and 1996 compared. *Psychological Medicine* 31:779–790.

Hilts, Philip. 2003. *Protecting America's Health: The FDA, Business, and One Hundred Years of Regulation*. New York: Knopf.

Hirschman, Albert O. 1995. *A Propensity to Self-subversion*. Cambridge, Mass.: Harvard University Press.

Homedes, N., and A. Ugalde. 2001. Improving the use of pharmaceuticals through patient and community level interventions. *Social Science and Medicine* 52(1):99–134.

Hopenhayn, Martin. 2001. *No Apocalypse, No Integration: Modernism and Postmodernism in Latin America*. Durham, N.C.: Duke University Press.

Ignatieff, Michael. 2001. *Human Rights as Politics and Idolatry*. Princeton: Princeton University Press.

Inhorn, Marcia. 1996. *Infertility and Patriarchy: The Cultural Politics of Gender and Family Life in Egypt*. Philadelphia: University of Pennsylvania Press.

James, Oliver. 1997. Oh no! We're not getting more depressed are we? *Guardian*, 15 September.

Jeffery, R. 1982. Policies towards indigenous healers in independent India. *Social Science and Medicine* 16:1835–1841.

Jeffrey, Roger. 1981. *The Politics of Health in India.* Berkeley: University of California Press.

Johansson, S. Ryan. 1991. Health transition: The cultural inflation of morbidity during the decline of mortality. *Health Transition Review* 1(1):39–68.

Jonas, Hans. 1969. Philosophical reflections on human experimentation. *Daedalus* 98(spring): 219–247.

Juma, Calestous. 1989. *The Gene Hunters: Biotechnology and the Scramble for Seeds.* Princeton: Princeton University Press.

Just how tainted has medicine become? 2002 Editorial. *Lancet* 359:1167. See also responses in *Lancet* 359:1775–1776.

Kamat, V., and M. Nichter. 1998. Pharmacies, self-medication and pharmaceutical marketing in Bombay, India. *Social Science and Medicine* 47(6):779–895.

Kapp, Clare. 2002. Counterfeit drug problem "underestimated," says conference. *Lancet* 360(9339):1080.

Karim, Q. A., and S. S. A. Karim. 1997. Informed consent for HIV testing in a South African hospital: Is it truly informed and truly voluntary? *American Journal of Public Health* 88(4):637–640.

Kassirer, Jerome. 2004. *On the Take: How Medicine's Complicity with Big Business Can Endanger Your Health.* Oxford: Oxford University Press.

Kaufman, Sharon R. 2005. *And a Time to Die: How American Hospitals Shape the End of Life.* New York: Scribner.

Kawabuchi, Koichi. 1998. *Introduction to Health Care Economics in Japan.* Tokyo: Yakuji Nippo.

Keller, Martin B., Neal D. Ryan, Mitch Strober, et al. 2001. Efficacy of paroxetine in the treatment of adolescent major depression: A randomized, controlled trial. *Journal of American Academy of Child and Adolescent Psychiatry* 40:762–772.

Kervasdoué, Jean. 2000. *Santé: Pour une révolution sans réform.* Paris: Gallimard.

Khan, A., S. R. Khan, R. M. Leventhal, and W. A. Brown. 2000. Symptom reduction and suicide risk in patients treated with placebo in antipsychotic clinical trials. *American Journal of Psychiatry* 158:1449–1454.

Kim, Jim Yong, Alec Irwin, Joyce Millen, and John Gershman. 2000. *Dying for Growth: Global Inequality and the Health of the Poor.* Monroe, Me.: Common Courage Press.

Kim, Jim Yong, Joia S. Mukherjee, Michael L. Rich, Kedar Mate, Jaime Bayona, and Mercedes C. Becerra. 2003. From multidrug-resistant tuberculosis to DOTS expansion and beyond: Making the most of a paradigm shift. *Tuberculosis* 83(1–3):59–65.

King, Nancy M., Gail E. Henderson, and Jane Stein. 1999. *Beyond Regulations: Ethics in Human Subjects Research.* Chapel Hill: University of North Carolina Press.

Kisuule, A., and J. David. 1999. *Compliance Study in Uganda: A Social, Economic, and Cultural Qualitative Study on Determinants of HIV/AIDS-Related Drugs Compliance in Uganda.* Geneva: UNAIDS.

Klein, D. 1996. Reaction patterns to psychotropic drugs and the discovery of panic disorder. In D. Healy, *The Psychopharmacologists*, 329–352. London: Arnold.

Kleinman, Arthur. 1980. *Patients and Healers in the Context of Culture: An Exploration of the Borderland between Anthropology, Medicine, and Psychiatry*. Berkeley: University of California Press.

Kleinman, Arthur. 1988. *Rethinking Psychiatry: From Cultural Category to Personal Experience*. New York: Free Press.

Kleinman, Arthur. 1989. *The Illness Narratives: Suffering, Healing, and the Human Condition*. New York: Basic Books.

Kleinman, Arthur. 1999. Moral experience and ethical reflection: Can ethnography reconcile them? A quandary for "the new bioethics." *Daedalus* 128(fall):69–99.

Kleinman, Arthur, Renee Fox, and Allan Brandt, eds. 1999. *Bioethics and beyond*. Special issue. *Daedalus* 128:4.

Kleinman, Arthur, and Joan Kleinman. 1996. The appeal of experience, the dismay of images: Cultural appropriations of suffering in our times. *Daedalus* 125(winter):1–24.

Klerman, G. L. 1988. Overview of the Cross-National Collaborative Panic Study. *Archives of General Psychiatry* 45:407–412.

Klerman, G. L. 1992. Drug treatment of panic disorder. Reply to comment by Marks and associates. *British Journal of Psychiatry* 161:465–471.

Klerman, G. L., et al. 1989. In reply to Marks et al. *Archives of General Psychiatry* 46:670–672.

Klerman, G. L., et al. 1992. Drug treatment of panic disorder: Comparative efficacy of alprazolam, imipramine and placebo. Cross-National Collaborative Panic Study Second Phase Investigators. *British Journal of Psychiatry* 160:191–202.

Knorr Cetina, Karin. 2001. Postsocial relations: Theorizing sociality in a postsocial environment. In George Ritzer and Barry Smart, eds., *Handbook of Social Theory*. London: Sage Publications.

Kopp, P., C. Rumeau-Pichon, and C. Le Pen. 2000. Les enjeux financiers des traitements de substitution dans l'héroïnomane: Le cas de Subutex®. *Revue d'Epidémiologie et de Santé Publique* 48:256–270.

Kopytoff, Igor. 1986. The cultural biography of things. In Arjun Appadurai, ed., *The Social Life of Things: Commodities in Cultural Perspective*, 64–91. Cambridge: Cambridge University Press.

Kotler, Philip. 2000. *Marketing Management*. Upper Saddle River, N.J.: Prentice-Hall.

Kramer, Peter. 2000. The valorisation of sadness. *Hastings Center Report* 30:13–18.

Kremer, Michael, and Rachel Glennerster. 2004. *Strong Medicine: Creating Incentives for Pharmaceutical Research on Neglected Diseases*. Princeton: Princeton University Press.

Kumar, M. Suresh, Shakuntala Mudaliar, and Desmond Daniels. 1998. Community-based outreach HIV intervention for street-recruited drug users in Madras, India. *Public Health Reports* 113(suppl. 1):58–66.

Lagnado, M. 2003. Increasing the trust in scientific authorship. *British Journal of Psychiatry* 183:3–4.

Lakoff, Andrew. 2000. Adaptive will: The evolution of attention deficit disorder. *Journal of the History of the Behavioral Sciences* 36 (2).

Lakoff, Andrew. 2005. *Pharmaceutical Reason: Medication and Psychiatric Knowledge in Argentina*. Cambridge: Cambridge University Press.

LaPiazza, Pier Vincenzo. 2002. A quoi servent les modèles animaux pour comprendre les maladies mentales? Séminaire sur Sciences Sociales, Psychiatrie, Biologie. Paris: EHESS.

Larvie, Patrick. 1997. Personal improvement, national development: Theories of AIDS prevention in Rio de Janeiro, Brazil. In A. Leibing, ed., *The Medical Anthropologies in Brazil*. Berlin: Verlag für Wisenschaft und Bildung.

Latour, Bruno. 1986. *Science in Action: How to Follow Scientists and Engineers Through Society*. Cambridge: Harvard University Press.

Leclerc, A., et al., eds. 2000. *Les inégalités sociales de la santé*. Paris: Ed. La Découverte/INSERM.

Lemmens, Trudo, and Benjamin Freedman. 2000. Ethics review for sale? Conflict of interest and commercial research ethics review. *Milbank Quarterly* 78(4):547–584.

Lemoine, Patrick. 2001. Médicaments psychotropes: le big deal? *Revue Toxibase* (2001):2–12.

Lert, France. 1998. Methadone, Subutex: substitution ou traitement de la dépendance à l'éhroïne? Questions en santé publique. In Alain Ehrenberg, ed., *Drogues et Médicaments Psychotropes. Le trouble des frontières*, 63–99. Paris: Ed. Esprit.

Leshner, A. 1999. Addiction is a brain disease, and it matters. *Nature* 398:45–47.

Leslie, C. 1973. The professionalizing ideology of medical revivalism. In Milton Singer, ed., *Entrepreneurship and Modernization of Occupational Cultures in South Asia*. Durham, N.C.: Duke University Press.

Leslie, C. 1974. The modernization of Asian medical systems. In John J. Poggie Jr. and Robert N. Lynch, eds., *Rethinking Modernization: Anthropological Perspectives*. Westport, Conn.: Greenwood Press.

Lévi-Strauss, Claude. 1967. The sorcerer and his magic. In *Structural Anthropology*, 167–185. New York: Anchor Books.

Lewin, Tamar. 2001. Families sue Pfizer on test of antibiotic. *New York Times*, 30 August.

Lexchin, Joel. 2001. Lifestyle drugs: Issues for debate. *Canadian Medical Association Journal* 164(10):1449, 3 pp.

Lexchin, Joel, Lisa A. Bero, Benjamin Djulbegovic, and Otavio Clark. 2003. Pharmaceutical industry sponsorship and research outcome and quality: Systematic review. *British Medical Journal* 326(7400):1167.

Lindenbaum, Shirley. 1978. *Kuru Sorcery: Disease and Danger in the New Guinea Highlands*. New York: McGraw-Hill.

Lock, Margaret.1993. *Encounters with Aging: Mythologies of Menopause in Japan and North America*. Berkeley: University of California Press.

Lock, Margaret. 2001. *Twice Dead: Organ Transplants and the Reinvention of Death*. Berkeley: University of California Press.

Lock, Margaret, Allan Young, and Alberto Cambrosio, eds. 2000. *Living and Working with the New Medical Technologies: Intersections of Inquiry.* Cambridge: Cambridge University Press.

Lovell, Anne M. 1980. Paroles de cure et énergies en société: les bioénergies en France. In J. Carpentier, R. Castel, J. Donzelot, J.-M. Lacrosse, A. Lovell, and G. Procacci, eds., *Résistances à la Médecine et Démultiplication du Concept de la Santé.* Paris: Collège de France and CORDES.

Lovell, Anne. 1993. Evaluation des interventions et estimation des besoins en santé mentale: tendances actuelles. *Revue d'Epidemiologie et de Santé Publique* 41:284–291.

Lovell, Anne. 2001. Ordonner les risques: l'individu et le pharmaco-sociatif face à la réduction des dommages dans l'injection de drogues. In J.-P. Dozon and D. Fassin, eds., *Critique de la Santé Publique: Une Approche Anthropologique,* 309–342. Paris: Balland.

Lovell, Anne. 2002. Risking risk: The influence of types of capital and social networks on the injection practices of drug users. *Social Science and Medicine* 55(5):803–821.

Lovell, Anne M., and Isabelle Feroni. 1998. Sida-toxicomanie: un objet hybride de la nouvelle santé publique. In Didier Fassin, ed., *Les figures urbaines de la santé publique,* 203–238. Paris: La Découverte.

Lowy, Ilana. 2000. Trustworthy knowledge and desperate patients: clinical tests for new drugs from cancer to AIDS. In Margaret Lock, Alan Young, Alberto Cambrosio, eds., *Living and Working with the New Medical Technologies: Intersections of Inquiry.* Cambridge, U.K.: Cambridge University Press.

Luhrmann, T. M. 2000. *Of Two Minds: The Growing Disorder in American Psychiatry.* New York: Knopf.

Luiza, Vera Lucia. 1999. Aquisição de medicamentos no setor público: o binômio qualidade-custo. *Cadernos de Saúde Pública* 15(4).

Lurie, Peter, Percy Hintzen, and Robert Lowe. 1995. Socioeconomic Obstacles to HIV Prevention and Treatment in Developing Countries: The Roles of the International Monetary Fund and the World Bank. *AIDS* 9:539–546.

Lurie, Peter, and Sidney M. Wolfe. 1998. Unethical trials of interventions to reduce perinatal transmission of the human immunodeficiency virus in developing countries. *New England Journal of Medicine* 337(12):853–855.

Lurie, Peter, and Sidney M. Wolfe. 2000. Letter to the National Bioethics Advisory Commission regarding their report on the challenges of conducting research in developing countries. HRG Publication no. 1545. Electronic document, http://www.citizen.org/publications. Accessed 12 December 2003.

Lurie, Peter, and Sidney M. Wolfe. 2001. Comments on the draft health and human services inspector general's report: The globalization of clinical trials (OEI-01-00-00190). HRG Publication no. 1591. Public Citizen's Health Research Group, 5 July 2001. Electronic document, http://www.citizen.org/publications. Accessed 12 December 2003.

Macklin, Ruth. 1999. *Against Relativism: Cultural Diversity and the Search for Ethical Universals in Medicine.* Oxford: Oxford University Press.

Macro, O. 2001. *Uganda Demographic and Health Survey.* Entebbe: Uganda Bureau of Statistics.

Maestracci, Nicole. 1999. Une nouvelle approche des conduites addictives. *Revue Française d'Epidémiologie et de Santé Publique* 47:393–396.

Malt, Ulrik F., O. H. Robak, H.-B. Madsbu, O. Bakke, and M. Loeb. 1999. The Norwegian Naturalistic Treatment Study of Depression in General Practice (NORDEP). I: Randomized double blind study. *British Medical Journal* 318:1180–1184.

Marks, Harry. 1997. *The Progress of Experiment: Science and Therapeutic Reform in the United States, 1900–1990.* Cambridge: Cambridge University Press.

Marks, Harry. 2000. Where do ethics come from? The role of disciplines and institutions. Paper prepared for Conference on Ethical Issues in Clinical Trials. University of Alabama, Birmingham, 25 February.

Marks, Harry. 2002. Commentary. Third Annual W. H. R. Rivers Workshop: Global Pharmaceuticals: Ethics, Markets, Practices. Harvard University, 19–21 May.

Marks, I. M., et al. 1989. The efficacy of alprazolam in panic-disorder and agoraphobia: A critique of recent reports. *Archives of General Psychiatry* 46:670–672.

Marks, I., et al. 1992. Comment on the second phase of the Cross National Collaborative Panic Study. *British Journal of Psychiatry* 160:202–205.

Marks, I. M., et al. 1993a. Alprazolam and exposure alone and combined in panic disorder with agoraphobia: A controlled study in London and Toronto. *British Journal of Psychiatry* 162:776–787.

Marks, I. M., et al. 1993b. Reply to comment on London/Toronto study. *British Journal of Psychiatry* 162:790–794.

Marks, I. M., et al. 1993c. Drug treatment of panic disorder: Further comment. *British Journal of Psychiatry* 162:795–796.

Marshall, Patricia, and Barbara Koenig. 2004. Accounting for culture in a globalized ethics. *Journal of Law, Medicine, and Ethics* 32(2):252–266.

Martinez-Jones, A., and N. Anyama. 2002. Access to antiretroviral therapy in Uganda (Kampala, June 2002). Electronic document, http://www.oxfam.org.uk accessed 17 July 2003.

Maurin, Eric. 2002. L'égalité des possibles. In *La nouvelle société française*, 1–78. Paris: Seuil.

Medawar, Charles. 1997. The antidepressant web. *International Journal of Risk and Safety in Medicine* 10:75–126.

Medawar, Charles, Andrew Herxheimer, Andrew Bell, and Shelley Jofre. 2003. Paroxetine, panorama, and user reporting of ADRs. Consumer intelligence matters in clinical practice and post-marketing drug surveillance. *International Journal of Risk and Safety in Medicine* 15:161–169.

Meinert, L. 2001. The quest for a good life: Health and education among children in eastern Uganda. PhD diss., University of Copenhagen, Copenhagen.

Ministério da Saúde [MS]. 1995. *Segundo relatório sobre o processo de organização da gestão da assistência à saúde.* Brasília: Ministério da Saúde (third version).

Ministério da Saúde [MS]. 1997. *Farmácia básica: programa 1997/98.* Brasília: Ministério da Saúde.

Ministério da Saúde [MS]. 1999. *Política nacional de medicamentos.* Brasília: Ministério da Saúde.

Misra, Kavita. 2000. Productivity of crises: Disease, scientific knowledge and state in India. *Economic and Political Weekly* 35(43–44):3885–3897.

Moatti, J.-P., M. Souville, N. Escaffre, and Y. Obadia. 1998. French general practitioners' attitudes toward maintenance drug abuse treatment with buprenorphine. *Addiction* 93(10):1567–1575.

Mogensen, H. 2003. Surviving AIDS? The uncertainty of antiretroviral treatment. Paper presented at the conference Uncertainty in Contemporary African Lives, Arusha, Tanzania, 9–11 April.

Moore, Sally Falk, ed. 1993. *Moralizing States and the Ethnography of the Present*. Arlington, Va.: American Anthropological Association.

Moreno, Jonathan D. 2004. Bioethics and the national security state. *Journal of Law, Medicine, and Ethics* 32(2):198–208.

Morris, David. B. 1998. *Illness and Culture*. Berkeley: University of California Press.

Moukheiber, Zina. 2001. Drug warrior. *Forbes*, 5 March.

Moynihan, Ray. 2002. Selling sickness: The pharmaceutical industry and disease mongering. *British Medical Journal* 324:886–891.

Moynihan, R., and I. Heath, D. Henry. 2002. Selling sickness: The pharmaceutical industry and disease mongering. *British Medical Journal* 324 (7342): 886–891.

Médecins sans Frontières. 2002. Mandela joins MSF to scale up AIDS treatment in South Africa. Electronic document, http://www.doctorswithoutborders.org. Accessed 29 September 2003.

Mundy, A. 2001. *Dispensing with the Truth*. New York: St. Martin's Press.

Murray, C. J. L., and A. D. Lopez. 1996. *Global Health Statistics: A Compendium of Mortality and Disability from Diseases, Injuries, and Risk Factors in 1990 and Projected to 2020*. Cambridge: Harvard University Press.

National Bioethics Advisory Commission. 2000. *Ethical and Policy Issues in International Research: Clinical Trials in Developing Countries*. Bethesda, Md.: National Bioethics Advisory Commission.

National Commission for the Protection of Human Subjects of Biomedical and Behavioral Research. 1974. *Protection of Human Subjects: Ethical Principles and Guidelines for the Protection of Human Subjects of Research* [Belmont Report]. Washington: Department of Health, Education, and Welfare.

Nguyen, V.-K., T. Grennan, K. Peschard, D. Tan, and I. Tiendrébéogo. 2003. Antiretroviral use in Ouagadougou, Burkina Faso. *AIDS* 17(suppl. 3):S109–S111.

Nichter, Mark, and Nancy Vuckovic. 1994. Agenda for anthropology of pharmaceutical practice. *Social Science and Medicine* 39(11):1509–1525.

O sexo inseguro. 1991. *Isto É/Senhor*, 20 November, 52.

Office of the Inspector General, Department of Health and Human Services. 2001. *The Globalization of Clinical Trials: A Growing Challenge in Protecting Human Subjects*. Boston: Office of Evaluation and Inspections.

Office of the Inspector General, Department of Health and Human Services. n.d. OIG Mission. Electronic document, http://oig.hhs.gov. Accessed 22 September 2004.

Okie, S. 2001. A stand for scientific independence. *Washington Post*, 5 August.

Okuonzi, S., H. Karamagi, and S. Kyomuhendo. 2003. *Evaluation of HIV/AIDS Policies in Uganda*. Technical report. Kampala.

Oliveira, M. A., A. F. Esher, E. M. Santos, M. A. E. Cosendey, V. L. Luiza, and J. A. Z. Bermudez. 2002. Avaliação da assistência farmacêutica às pessoas vivendo com HIV/AIDS no município do Rio de Janeiro. *Cadernos de Saúde Pública* 18(5):1429–1439.

O'Nell, Theresa Deleane. 1998. *Disciplined Hearts: Hearts, Identity and Depression in an American Indian Community*. Berkeley: University of California Press.

Paley, Julia. 2001. *Marketing Democracy: Power and Social Movements in Post-dictatorship Chile*. Berkeley: University of California Press.

Palier, Bruno. 2004. *La réforme des systèmes de santé*. Paris: Presses Universitaires de France.

Palomar, Jorge. 1996. El ranking de los remedios. *La NacionLine*. Electronic document, http://www.lanacion.com.ar.

Pan American Health Organization. 1998. *Health in the Americas*. Washington: Pan American Health Organization, Pan American Sanitary Bureau, Regional Office of the World Health Organization.

Paraguassú, L. 2001. Governo pode quebrar patente de remédio. *Folha de São Paulo*, 15 February.

Parker, Richard. 1990. *Bodies, Pleasures, and Passions*. Boston: Beacon Press.

Parker, Richard. 1994. *A construção da solidariedade: AIDS, sexualidade e política no Brasil*. Rio de Janeiro: Relume-Dumará, ABIA, IMS/UERJ.

Parker, Richard, ed. 1997. *Políticas, Instituições e AIDS: Enfrentando a Epidemia no Brasil*. Rio de Janeiro: Jorge Zahar/ABIA.

Parker, Richard. 2001. Estado e sociedade em redes: descentralização e sustentabilidade das ações de prevenção das DSTs/AIDS. Paper presented at the Fourth National Conference on DST/AIDS Prevention, Cuiabá, Brazil, 11 September.

Parker, Richard, Cristiana Bastos, Jane Galvão, and José Stálin Pedrosa, eds. 1994. *A AIDS no Brasil*. Rio de Janeiro: Relume Dumará, ABIA, IMS/UERJ.

Parker, Richard, and Kenneth R. Camargo Jr. 2000. Pobreza e HIV/AIDS: aspectos antropológicos e sociológicos. *Cadernos de Saúde Pública* 16(1):89–102.

Parker, Richard, and Herbert Daniel. 1991. *AIDS: a Terceira epidemia*. São Paulo: Editora Iglu.

Parkhurst, J. O. 2002. The Ugandan success story? Evidence and claims of HIV-1 prevention. *Lancet* 360(9326):78–80.

Peabody, J. W., M. O. Rahman, P. J. Gertler, J. Mann, D. O. Farley, and J. Luck, eds. 1999. *Policy and Health: Implications for Development in Asia*. London: Cambridge University Press.

Petersen, Alan R., and Deborah Lupton. 1996. *The New Public Health: Discourses, Knowledges, Strategies*. London: Sage.

Petryna, Adriana. 2002. *Life Exposed: Biological Citizens after Chernobyl*. Princeton: Princeton University Press.

Petryna, Adriana. Forthcoming. The human subjects research enterprise. Princeton: Princeton University Press.

Pfizer Expert Report. 1997. Sertraline hydrochloride for obsessive compulsive disorder in paediatric patients. Approved 20 October. Document available from David Healy upon request.

Pincus, R. L. 2002. From Lydia Pinkham to Bob Dole: What the changing face of direct-to-consumer drug advertising reveals about the professionalism of medicine. *Kennedy Institute of Ethics Journal* 2(2):141–158.

Pocock, Stuart. 2002. The pro's and con's of non-inferiority (equivalence) trials. In Harry A. Guess, Arthur Kleinman, John W. Kusek, and Linda W. Engel, eds., *The Science of the Placebo: Toward an Interdisciplinary Research Agenda*, 236–248. London: BMJ Books.

Pool, R., S. Nyanzi, and J. A. Whitworth. 2001. Attitudes to voluntary counselling and testing for HIV among pregnant women in rural south-west Uganda. *AIDS Care* 13(5):605–615.

Power, Michael. 1997. *The Audit Society: Rituals of Verification.* Oxford: Oxford University Press.

Prakash, Gyan. 1999. *Another Reason: Science and the Imagination of Modern India.* Princeton: Princeton University Press.

Rabinow, Paul. 1989. *French Modern: Norms and Forms of the Social Environment.* Cambridge: MIT Press, 1989.

Rabinow, Paul. 1992. Artificiality and enlightenment: From sociobiology to biosociality. In Jonathan Crary and Sanford Kwinter, eds., *Incorporations.* New York: Zone Books.

Rabinow, Paul. 1996a. *Essays on the Anthropology of Reason.* Princeton: Princeton University Press.

Rabinow, Paul. 1996b. *French Modern: Norms and Forms of the Social Environment.* Chicago: University of Chicago Press.

Rabinow, Paul. 1999. *French DNA: Trouble in Purgatory.* Chicago: University of Chicago Press.

Rabinow, Paul. 2003. *Anthropos Today: Reflections on Modern Equipment.* Princeton: Princeton University Press.

Ramesh, A., and B. Hyma. 1981. Traditional Indian medicine in practice in an Indian metropolitan city. *Social Science and Medicine* 15:69–81.

Rampton, Sheldon, and John Stauber. 2001. *Trust Us, We're Experts!* New York: Tarcher Putnam Books.

Ramsey, Matthew. 1994. Public health in France. In D. Porter, ed., *The History of Public Health and the Modern State*, 45–118. London: Wellcome Institute Series.

Rapp, Rayna. 1999. *Testing Women, Testing the Fetus: The Social Impact of Amniocentesis in America.* New York: Routledge.

Relman, Arnold, and Marcia Angell. 2002. America's other drug problem: How the industry distorts medicine and politics. *New Republic*, 16 December, 27–41.

Rettig, Richard. 2000. The industrialization of clinical research. *Health Affairs* (March–April):129–146.

Rhodes, Lorna A. 1995. *Emptying Beds: The Work of an Emergency Psychiatric Unit.* Berkeley: University of California Press.

Rieff, David. 2003. *A Bed for the Night: Humanitarianism in Crisis.* New York: Simon and Schuster.

Rodwin, Victor, and Claude LePen. 2004. Health care reform in France: The birth of state-led managed care. *New England Journal of Medicine* 351(22):2259–2262.

Rosário Costa, Nilson. 1996. O Banco Mundial e a política social nos anos 90: a agenda para a reforma do setor saúde no Brasil. In N. Rosário Costa and J. Mendes Ribeiro, eds., *Política de saúde e inovação institucional: uma agenda para os anos 90.* Rio de Janeiro: Secretaria de Desenvolvimento Educacional/ENSP.

Rose, Nikolas. 1996a. The death of the social? Refiguring the territory of government. *Economy and Society* 25:3.

Rose, Nikolas. 1996b. Governing "advanced" liberal democracies. In Andrew Barry, Thomas Osborne, and Nikolas Rose, eds., *Foucault and Political Reason: Liberalism, Neo-liberalism and Rationalities of Government.* Chicago: University of Chicago Press.

Rose, Nikolas. 1999. *Powers of Freedom.* Cambridge: Cambridge University Press.

Rose, Nikolas. 2003. Becoming neurochemical selves. In Nico Stehr, ed., *Biotechnology between Commerce and Civil Society.* New Brunswick, N.J.: Transaction Publishers.

Rosenberg, Tina. 2001. How to solve the world's AIDS crisis. *New York Times Magazine,* 28 January.

Rothman, David J. 1991. *Strangers at the Bedside: A History of How Law and Bioethics Transformed Medical Decision Making.* New York: Basic Books.

Rothman, David J. 2000. The shame of medical research. *New York Review of Books* 47(19):60–64.

Rothman, Kenneth, and Karin Michels. 2001. When is it appropriate to use a placebo arm in a trial? In Harry A. Guess, Arthur Kleinman, John W. Kusek, and Linda W. Engel, eds., *The Science of the Placebo: Toward an Interdisciplinary Research Agenda,* 227–235. London: BMJ Books.

Sabel, Charles. 1997. Constitutional orders: Trust building and response to change. In J. R. Hollingsworth and R. Boyer, eds., *Contemporary Capitalism: The Embeddedness of Institutions.* Cambridge: Cambridge University Press.

Sachs, Jeffrey D., Andrew D. Mellinger, and John L. Gallup. 2001. The geography of poverty and wealth. *Scientific American* 284(3):70–76.

Saradamma, R. D., N. Higginbotham, and M. Nichter. 2000. Social factors influencing the acquisition of antibiotics without prescription in Kerala State, south India. *Social Science and Medicine* (50):891–903.

Sassen, Saskia. 1996. *Losing Control? Sovereignty in an Age of Globalization.* New York: Columbia University Press.

Sassen, Saskia. 1998. *Globalization and Its Discontents.* New York: New Press.

Sassen, Saskia. 2000. Spatialities and temporalities of the global: Elements for a theorization. *Public Culture* 12(1):215–232.

Scheper-Hughes, Nancy. 1992. *Death Without Weeping: The Violence of Everyday Life in Brazil.* Berkeley: University of California Press.

Scheper-Hughes, Nancy. 1994. An essay: AIDS and the social body. *Social Science and Medicine* 39(7):991–1003.

Scheper-Hughes, Nancy. 2003. Rotten trade: Millennial capitalism, human values and global justice in organs trafficking. *Journal of Human Rights* 2(2):197–226.

Scheper-Hughes, Nancy. 2004. Parts unknown. *Ethnography* 5(1):29–74.

Scheper-Hughes, Nancy, and Margaret Lock. 1991. The message in a bottle: Illness and the micropolitics of resistance. *Journal of Psychohistory* 18(4):409–432.

Scheper-Hughes, Nancy, and Philippe Bourgois. 2003. *Violence in War and Peace: An Anthology* (Blackwell Readers in Anthropology). Malden, Mass.: Blackwell Publishers.

Schering-Plough. n.d. Subutex monograph. Levallois-Perret: Information Médicale Schering-Plough.

Schuklenk, U., and R. Ashcroft. 2000. International research ethics. *Bioethics* 14(2):158–172.

Scott, James. *Seeing Like a State: How Certain Schemes to Improve the Human Condition Have Failed.* New Haven: Yale University Press, 1998.

Sell, Susan. 2003. *Private Power, Public Law: The Globalization of Intellectual Property Rights.* Cambridge: Cambridge University Press.

Serra, José. 2000. *Ampliando o possível: A política de saúde do Brasil.* São Paulo: Hucitec.

Serra, José. 2002. *Ampliando o possível.* São Paulo: Campus.

Setbon, Michel. 1993. *Pouvoirs contre sida. De la transfusion sanguine au dépistage: décisions et pratiques en France, Grande Bretagne et Suède.* Paris: Le Seuil.

Shapin, Steven. 1994. *A Social History of Truth: Civility and Science in Seventeenth-Century England.* Chicago: University of Chicago Press.

Sheahan, David. 2000. Angles on panic. In David Healy, ed., *The Psychopharmacologists,* 3:479–504. London: Arnold.

Shorter, Edward. 2001. Historical review of diagnosis and treatment of depression. In Ann Dawson and Andre Tylee, eds., *Depression: Social and Economic Timebomb,* 25–30. London: BMJ Books.

Sikkink, Kathryn. 1991. *Ideas and Institutions: Developmentalism in Brazil and Argentina.* Ithaca: Cornell University Press.

Silva, R. C. S., and J. A. Z. Bermudez. n.d. Medicamentos excepcionais no âmbito da assistência farmacêutica no Brasil. MS, 2000.

Smith, Jane. 1990. *Patenting the Sun: Polio and the Salk Vaccine.* New York: William Morrow.

Someya, Toshiyuki, et al. 2001. Is DSM widely accepted by Japanese clinicians? *Psychiatry and Clinical Neurosciences* 55:437–450.

Spears, Timothy. 1995. *100 Years on the Road: Traveling Salesmen in American Culture.* New Haven: Yale University Press.

Spiegel, D. A., et al. 1993. Comment on the London/Toronto study of alprazolam in exposure in panic disorder with agoraphobia. *British Journal of Psychiatry* 162:788–789.

Starr, Paul. 1982. *The Social Transformation of American Medicine.* New York: Basic Books.

Stiglitz, Joseph. 2002. *Globalization and Its Discontents.* New York: W. W. Norton.

Strathern, Marilyn. 1992. *After Nature: English Kinship in the Late Twentieth Century.* Cambridge: Cambridge University Press.

Strathern, Marilyn, ed. 2000. *Audit Cultures: Anthropological Studies in Accountability, Ethics and the Academy.* London: Routledge.

Teen depression: 3 million kids suffer from it. What you can do. *Newsweek*, 7 October 2002, 52–61.

Teixeira, Paulo Roberto. 1997. Políticas Públicas em AIDS. In *Políticas, Instituições e AIDS: Enfrentando a Epidemia no Brasil*, 43-68, edited by Richard Parker. Rio de Janeiro: Jorge Zahar/ABIA.

Teixeira, P., M. A. Vitória, and J. Barcarolo. 2003. The Brazilian experience in providing universal access to antiretroviral therapy. In *Economics of AIDS and Access to HIV/AIDS Care in Developing Countries: Issues and Challenges* (forthcoming). Electronic document, http://www.developmentgateway.org. Accessed 15 September.

Temple, Robert. 2002. Placebo-controlled trials and active controlled trials: Ethics and inference. In Harry A. Guess, Arthur Kleinman, John W. Kusek, and Linda W. Engel, eds., *The Science of the Placebo: Toward an Interdisciplinary Research Agenda*, 209–226. London: BMJ Books.

Thase, Michael E., A. R. Entsuah, and R. L. Rudolph. 2001. Remission rates during treatment with venlafaxine or SSRI's. *British Journal of Psychiatry* 178:234–241.

Toulmin, Stephen. 1987. National Commission on Human Experimentation: Procedures and outcomes. In Tristram Engelhardt Jr. and Arthur L. Caplan, eds., *Scientific Controversies: Case Studies in the Resolution and Closure of Disputes in Science and Technology*, 599–613. Cambridge: Cambridge University Press.

Tribalat, Maryse. 1995. *Faire France: une grande enquête sur les immigrés et leurs enfants*. Paris: La Découverte.

Trostle, J. 1996. Inappropriate distribution of medicines by professionals in developing countries. *Social Science and Medicine* 42:1117–1120.

Trouillot, Michel-Rolph. 2001. The anthropology of the state in the age of globalization. *Current Anthropology* 42(1):125–139.

Tsutani, Kiichiro, ed. 1997. *Clinical Trials and GCP in East Asia*. Theme issue. *Drug Information Journal* 31(4).

Turkle, Sherry. 1978. *Psychoanalytic Politics: Freud's French Revolution*. New York: Basic Books.

Turner, Victor. *The Forest of Symbols: Aspects of Ndembu Ritual*. Ithaca: Cornell University Press, 1967.

Ueda, Keiji. 1997. Overview of the ICH GCP guideline. *Drug Information Journal* 31(4):1065–1070.

Uganda AIDS Commission. 2003. HIV/AIDS in Uganda. Electronic document, http://www.aidsuganda.org. Accessed 17 July.

UNAIDS. 2000. Brazil: Epidemiological fact sheets on HIV/AIDS and sexually transmitted infections. 2000 update (revised).

UNAIDS. 2004. *Report on the Global AIDS Epidemic*. Document. (http://www.unaids.org/bangkok2004/report)

Un généraliste sur cinq, deux pharmaciens sur trois. QDM, La Lettre Le Quotidien du Médecin 1999, 2002.

UNICEF/WHO. 1975. *Alternative Approaches to Meeting Basic Health Needs in Developing Countries*. Geneva: WHO.

United Nations. 2001. *HIV/AIDS: Global Crisis–Global Action*. New York: United Nations.

United Nations Development Programme [UNDP]. 2003. *Human Development Indicators, 2003*. UNDP Human Development Report. Electronic document, http://www.undp.org. Accessed 28 September.

U.S. Food and Drug Administration. 2001. International Conference on Harmonization: Choice of control group in clinical trials. *Federal Register* 66:24390–24391.

Van der Geest, Sjaak, and Susan R. Whyte, eds. 1988. *The Context of Medicines in Developing Countries*. Dordrecht: Kluwer.

Van der Geest, Sjaak, Susan Reynolds Whyte, and Anita Hardon. 1996. The anthropology of pharmaceuticals: A biographical approach. *Annual Review of Anthropology* 25(1):153–179.

Varmus, Harold, and David Satcher. 1996. Ethical complexities of conducting research in developing countries. *New England Journal of Medicine* 337(14):1003–1005.

Vastag, Brian. 2000. Helsinki discord? A controversial declaration. *JAMA* 284(23):2983–2985.

Vaughan, Megan. 1992. *Curing Their Ills: Colonial Power and African Illness*. Stanford: Stanford University Press.

Vuckovic, Nancy, and Mark Nichter. 1994. Agenda for an anthropology of pharmaceutical practice. *Social Science and Medicine* 39(11): 1509–25.

Vuckovic, Nancy, and Mark Nichter. 1997. Changing patterns of pharmaceutical practice in the United States. *Social Science and Medicine* 44(9):1285–1303.

Waisman, Carlos. 1987. *Reversal of Development in Argentina: Postwar Counterrevolutionary Policies and Their Structural Consequences*. Princeton: Princeton University Press.

Whyte, M. A., and S. R. Whyte. 1997. The values of development: Conceiving growth and progress in Bunyole. In H. B. Hansen and M. Twaddle, eds., *Developing Uganda*, 227–244. London: James Currey.

Whyte, S. R. 1988. The power of medicines in East Africa. In Van der Geest and S. R. Whyte, eds. *The Context of Medicines in Developing Countries: Studies in Pharmaceutical Anthropology*, 217–233. Dordrecht: Kluwer.

———. 1997. Questioning misfortune: The pragmatics of uncertainty in Eastern Uganda. *Cambridge Studies in Medical Anthropology* 4.

———. 2001. Creative commoditization: The social life of pharmaceuticals in Uganda. In J. Liep, ed., *Locating Cultural Creativity*, 119–132. London: Pluto Press.

Whyte, S. R., S. Van der Geest, and A. Hardon. 2002. *Social Lives of Medicines*. Cambridge: Cambridge University Press.

Wilken, P. R. C., and J. A. Z. Bermudez. n.d. Os descaminhos da assistência farmacêutica previdenciária no Brasil. MS, 1999.

Williamson, John. 1990. What Washington means by policy reform. In J. Williamson, ed., *Latin American Adjustment: How Much Has Happened?* Washington: Institute for International Economics.

World Bank. 1993. *The Organization, Delivery and Financing of Health Care in Brazil*. Study document.

World Bank. 1997. *Health, Nutrition and Population*. Washington: Human Development Network of the World Bank Group.

World Bank. 1988. *Brazil Public Spending on Social Programs: Issues and Options*. Vol. 1.

World Bank. 1999. Brazil: Partnerships in the fight against AIDS program considered model for others. Press release, 7 December. Electronic document, http://www.worldbank.org/aids/.

World Bank. 2002. Stemming the HIV/AIDS Epidemic in Brazil. Press release, July. Electronic document, http://www.worldbank.org/aids/.

World Health Organization. 2001a. *Atlas: Country Profiles on Mental Health Resources in the World*. Geneva: WHO.

World Health Organization. 2001b. *World Health Report 2001. Mental Health: New Understanding, New Hope*. Geneva: WHO.

World Medical Association. 2000. Ethical principles for medical research involving human subjects [Declaration of Helsinki]. *Journal of the American Medical Association* 284:3043–3045.

Young, Iris. 2004. Responsibility and historic injustice. Paper presented at the Institute for Advanced Study, School of Social Science, Princeton, N.J., 19 February.

Yunes, J. 1999. Promoting essential drugs, rational drug use and generics: Brazil's national drug policy leads the way. *Essential Drugs Monitor* 27:22, 23.

Yvorel, Jean-Jacques. 1992. *Les poisons de l'esprit: drogues et drogués au XIX° siècle*. Paris: Quai Voltaire.

# CONTRIBUTORS

Kalman Applbaum is an associate professor of anthropology at the University of Wisconsin-Milwaukee. He is author of *The Marketing Era: From Professional Practice to Global Provisioning* and a coeditor of *Consumption and Market Society in Israel.*

João Biehl is an assistant professor of anthropology at Princeton University. He is author of *Vita: Life in a Zone of Social Abandonment*, and co-editor with Arthur Kleinman and Byron Good of *Subjectivity: Ethnographic Investigations.*

Ranendra K. Das is an associate research scientist at Johns Hopkins University and retired as a professor of economics at the Delhi School of Economics. He is the author of *Optimal Economic Planning* and coauthor of *Basic Statistics.*

Veena Das is the Krieger-Eisenhower Professor of Anthropology at Johns Hopkins University. She is the author of *Critical Events: An Anthropological Perspective on Contemporary India* and coeditor of *Social Suffering, Violence and Subjectivity, Remaking a World*, and *Anthropology in the Margins of the State.* She edited *Mirrors of Violence* and *The Oxford India Companion to Sociology and Social Anthropology*, among her other authored and edited books on Indian sociology.

David Healy is a professor of psychiatry at Cardiff University in the United Kingdom. He is the author of *The Antidepressant Era, The Creation of Psychopharmacology*, and *Let Them Eat Prozac*, among many other books on the history of psychopharmacology.

Betty Kyaddondo, a physician, worked as a medical officer supervising counselors at the AIDS Information Centre in Kampala. She is now National Program Officer in the Family Health Department at the Uganda Population Secretariat, Ministry of Finance, Planning and Economic Development.

Andrew Lakoff is an assistant professor of sociology and science studies at the University of California, San Diego. He is the author of *Pharmaceutical Reason: Knowledge and Value in Global Psychiatry.*

Anne M. Lovell is Senior Research Scientist at INSERM, France. She is editor of *Santé mentale et société*, coeditor of *La santé mentale et mutation* and *Psychiatry Inside Out: Selected Writings of Franco Basaglia*, and a coauthor of *The Psychiatric Society.*

Arthur Kleinman is the Esther and Sidney Rabb Professor of Anthropology, and Chair, Department of Anthropology, Harvard University; and Professor of Psychiatry and Medical Anthropology at the Harvard Medical School where he chaired the Department of Social Medicine from 1991 to 2000. He edited or coedited more than seventeen volumes and is author of *Patients and Healers in the Context of Culture, The Illness Narratives, Rethinking Psy-*

*chiatry, Social Origins of Distress and Disease*, and *Writing at the Margin: Discourse Between Anthropology and Medicine*.

Lotte Meinert is an assistant professor in the Department of Social Anthropology, University of Aarhus. She has done fieldwork on schooling, health, and medicines in Uganda.

Adriana Petryna is an assistant professor of anthropology at the New School for Social Research. She is the author of *Life Exposed: Biological Citizens After Chernobyl*.

Michael A. Whyte is an associate professor at the Institute of Anthropology, University of Copenhagen. He has carried out ethnographic fieldwork in eastern Uganda and has a long-standing interest in AIDS policy and intervention projects.

Susan Reynolds Whyte is a professor at the Institute of Anthropology, University of Copenhagen. She is author of *Questioning Misfortune: The Pragmatics of Uncertainty in Eastern Uganda*, coauthor of *Social Lives of Medicines*, and coeditor of *The Context of Medicines in Developing Countries* and *Disability and Culture*.

# INDEX

Page reference followed by *t* indicates a table.

Academic medicine, pharmaceutical industry relations with, 32n.20

Accountability: biological citizenship in context of, 53–54, 238n.5; implications of Brazilian AIDS program for, 207–8; liability model of, 48

Active control trials, 45

Addiction: comparing French and other mainstream approaches to, 142–44; French toxicomania (*toxicomanie*) perception of, 140–42, 145; methadone substitution approach to, 138, 142, 143–44, 148, 165n.1. *See also* Heroin addiction

Addiction markets: globalization as creating demand for, 137–38; particularity of addiction pharmaceuticals and, 137–40; pharmaco-association and pharmaceutical leakage, and, 152–60; reflections on "French experience" with, 164–65. *See also* Buprenorphine market; Toxicomania addiction treatment

Advertising: celebrity endorsements as form of, 61; containment of negative publicity and, 67–68; FDA on direct-to-consumer, 9; geared to panic disorders treatments, 62–64; images of pharmaceutical, 2; Japanese restrictions on direct-to-consumer, 103–4; marketing of depression and, 64–66; profit motivation for, 3–4; of Zoloft and Paxil, 80–81. *See also* Pharmaceutical marketing

Africa: controversy over AZT placebo use (1994) in, 42–43, 44–45, 50; development of anti-HIV drug market in, 2–3; HIV-positive population in, 1–2; Nigerian Trovan research (1996) in, 48–51. *See also* Uganda

AIC (AIDS Information Centre) [Kampala], 249

AIDS activism: Brazilian organizations in, 210–11; international partnerships in, 207, 212–13, 216–17; role in Brazilian AIDS model, 217–18. *See also* NGOs (nongovernmental organizations)

AIDS crisis: affect on French drug users, 146–47; Brazilian model used for, 27–28; consequences of failure to address, 4; and emergent pharmaceutical markets, 220–22; failures of Uganda policies for, 28–29, 240–61; Global Fund to Fight AIDS, 3, 31n.11; images and impact of, 2–3, 207; and placebo use in African AZT trials, 42–43, 44–45, 50. *See also* Brazilian AIDS model; Disease

AIDS medicine: Brazilian AIDS model for, 27–28, 206–37; as socially and pharmacologically active, 241, 260–61. *See also* ARVs (antiretroviral therapies)

Alprazolam, 62, 63

*American Journal of Psychiatry*, 72

American Psychiatric Association (APA), 75, 115

AMM (*autorisation de mise le marché*) [France], 147, 148

Angell, M., 43

ANIT (Association Nationale d'Intervenants en Toxicomanie) [France], 142, 147

Anthropologists: and cultural and moral differences in healthcare, 35; on new biomedical technologies, 34; studies on policy impact on local epidemics, 36

Antibiotics: dispensed by Bhagwanpur Kheda practitioners, 190–92; penicillin, 2, 14; social transformations due to, 14

Antidepressants: advertising of, 65; demand and regulation in Argentina, 24–25; educating Japanese physicians on, 104–5; emerging Japanese market for, 24, 30n.5, 82–83n.4, 86–108; examining Argentine market in, 24–25, 112–34; FDA hearings

Antidepressants (*continued*)
on children and safety of, 76, 78; flawed
clinical investigations used for, 23–24;
growth of global sales of, 2; incidence of
suicides and suicide attempts in, 70*t*, 72.
*See also* SSRIs antidepressants

Antipsychotic drugs: growth of global sales
of, 2; and incidence of suicides and
suicide attempts, 76–77*t*

"Anxiety Disorders Week" (Argentina, 2001),
129

Anxiety marketplace, 62–64

Anxiety neurosis, 63

APA (American Psychiatric Association), 75,
115

Appadurai, A., 242

Applbaum, K., 19, 24

ARCA (Religious Support against AIDS)
[Brazil], 211

*Archives of General Psychiatry*, 71, 72

Arendt, H., 234–35

Argentina: antidepressant market trends in,
119–21; audit surveillance of prescription
practices, 121–23; demand for antidepressants in, 24–25; factors influencing
prescribing behavior of physicians, 128–
34; local knowledge marketing strategies
in, 126–28; history of pharmaceutical
industry in, 112–15; relationship between pharmaceutical firms and opinion
leaders in, 123–26; relationship between
pharmaceutical firms and physicians in,
115–16; U.S. case against, 134n.5. *See also*
Latin America

Ariinatwe, L., 246

ARVs (antiretroviral therapies): and "blanket
sign" in Uganda, 247–48; Brazilian laboratories production of, 226; Brazil's free
distribution of, 206; delivery of ARVs to
developing countries, 260–61; families
priority decisions on, 249–54; raising
awareness of, 247; Ugandan access to,
242–44, 247–61. *See also* AIDS medicine

Ativan, 64, 65, 81

AZT placebo controversy (Africa, 1994),
42–43, 44–45, 50

Bago, 129

Bagonza, D., 244, 255

Bahia death certificates [Brazil], 230–32

Bargaining theory, 60n.38

Basic Pharmacy Program (Brazil), 223

*BBC Online*, 129

Becker, H., 152

Bellow, S., 85

Benzodiazepines: dependence concerns regarding, 64; marketing impact of loss of,
66

Bernard, C., 150

Bhagwanpur Khedra. *See* India

Biehl, J., 27, 28, 241

Bioethics. *See* Ethics

Biological citizenship, 53–54, 238n.5

Birth control pill, 98

"Blanket sign" (Uganda), 247–48

Brazil: AIDS as hidden epidemic in, 230–32;
antiretroviral law of, 218; Basic Pharmacy
Program in, 223; government prevention
policies in, 210–12; history of AIDS crisis
in, 208–10; National AIDS Program of,
210, 215, 216–17, 224–25, 232, 233; patent
legislation of, 226; pharmaceutical market in, 219–20; progressive constitution
on right to health, 211; transnational
policy space affecting AIDS policies in,
212–17. *See also* Latin America

Brazilian AIDS model (state dispensation): implications of, 27–28; innovation
of, 206; outcomes of, 206–7, 236–37;
"pharmaceuticalization" of public health
and, 222–25; public sector science influencing, 225–30; role of AIDS activist
groups in, 217–18; social mobilization
affecting, 217–22. *See also* AIDS crisis

"Bridging studies" (Japan), 91

Bristol Meyers Squibb, 242

British College of Psychiatrists, 75

*British Medical Journal*, 72

Buprenorphine: AMM approval for commercializing, 147–48; as analgesic, 138–49; comparing heroin to, 153–54; harm reduction perspective of, 160–61; as orphan drug in France, 139, 166n.10; pharmaco-association incorporating, 152–55; shift from heroin to, 136–37; social uses of, 158–60; as substitution treatment in France, 144–51

Buprenorphine market: Americanization of French buprenorphine, 163–64; biopolitics of, 160–63; French experience with, 164–65; pharmaceutical leakage and, 138, 155–60; and state-run addiction management model, 25–26, 136. *See also* Addiction markets; France

Buspirone, 64

Caasah (grassroots care center) [Salvador], 232–36

CAEME (Council of multinational laboratories), 130

Canadian pharmaceutical spending, 2

Cardoso, F. H., 207, 215, 218, 224, 226–28, 229

Cassier, M., 227

Cattell, D., 71

CDC (Centers for Disease Control), 43, 243, 247

Center for Drug Evaluation (FDA), 44

Chabal, P., 257

Chequer, P., 215

Chernobyl nuclear disaster: consequences of government inaction, 59–60n.34; ethical variability of research following, 51–53; "experiment" perception of, 59n.33; hematopoetic growth factor molecule (rhGM-CSF) testing after, 51–52, 60n.36; medical research after, 40, 51; reframed as humanitarian crisis, 52

Children: FDA hearings on antidepressant safety and, 76, 78; medicalization of antidepressant treatment of, 74–78; and PMTCT (Prevention of Mother to Child Transmission) projects, 242, 245–46; suicidal tendencies among depressed, 72; Uganda AIDS policies and family priorities regarding, 249–54

China: nonstandardization of Chinese medicinal products, 16; regulatory practices of, 16–18

Chinese medicinal products, 16, 19

Chloramphenicol, 2

Cipla, 240

Clinical trials: aspects of sociology of, 78–80; bioethic issues of globalization and, 33–36; claims about Japanese lack of standards in, 94–101; controversy over placebo use in, 42–43, 44–45; CROs management of, 39–40; current number of, 57n.8; and DART (Development Antiretroviral Therapy), 243; developing countries as markets for, 56n.2; "equivalent medication" provided in, 46; establishment of randomized, 10; failure of active control, 45; as form of marketing, 23; and incorporation into medical protocols, 79–80; increasing number of participants in, 33; lack of U.S. regulatory policy in global, 47–48; and language of crisis in questionable trials, 51–53; medicalization and suppression of data from, 73–78; research ethics and, 23–24; suicides and suicide attempts in antidepressant, 70t. *See also* Drug development process; Human subjects; Standardization

Close Up (Argentina), 120, 121–22, 126, 128

CMD (Current Medical Directions) [New York], 69, 71–73

CNAM (national health fund) [France], 159

Cocaine, 153

Collor de Melo, F., 212

Correa, M., 227

CROs (Contract Research Organization) industry: described, 38–39; Eastern Europe recruitment by, 40–41; liability concerns of, 58n.24–59n.24; origins and develop-

CROs (*continued*)
ment of, 37–38; recruitment practices by, 39–40
Cross-border drug sales, 14–15
CSSTS (specialized drug treatment centers) [France], 142
Cultural relativism, 35
Customary laws, 49–50

Dagognet, F., 153
Daloz, J.-P., 257
Daniel, H., 210, 211
DART (Development Antiretroviral Therapy) trial, 243
Das, J., 193
Das, R., 26, 27
Das, V., 26, 27, 34
"Defeat depression" campaigns (1990), 75–76
Deleuze, G., 118–19
Depression: destigmatization campaign in Japan, 102–3, 104; emergence of literature and research on, 66–67; marketing of, 64–66; supposed universality of, 10
Developing countries: clinical trial markets of, 56n.2; controversy over placebo use in, 42–43; CROs alliances with site management organizations in, 39–40; delivery of ARVs to, 260–61; emergent HIV/AIDS pharmaceutical markets in, 220–22; lack of U.S. regulatory policy for trials in, 47–48; participation in American-sponsored research in, 47; treatment naiveté of human subjects from, 40–42
Disease: Ayurvedic principles on, 204n.12; demarcating disease as means of prevention, 41; historical transformation of, 14; self-medication study (India) of, 183–92; social construct of, 14. *See also* AIDS crisis
Doctors Without Borders, 49, 221
Doctors of the World, 147
DOT (Directly Observed Therapy) center (India), 189
Drug development process: four phases of,

57n.12; globalization of, 38; marketing role during, 73–78. *See also* Clinical trials; Standardization
Drug market. *See* Pharmaceutical marketing
"Drug pipeline explosion," 36
*DSM-III (Diagnostic and Statistical Manual)*: impact on psychiatry by, 61; Japanese adoption of, 89; pharmaceutical marketing strategies use of, 62–64
DTC (direct-to-consumer) advertising restrictions, 103–4
"Dynamic nominalism," 14

Eastern European human subjects, 40–41
Effexor (venlafaxine), 69, 80–81
Eli Lilly, 65, 67, 117, 125, 128
Equivalent medication, 46
Escorel, S., 235
Ethical dilemmas: challenges of pharmaceutical market, 7–8; globalization of clinical trials and, 33–35
Ethical variability: biological citizenship claims and, 53–54; of Chernobyl nuclear disaster research, 51–53; constructing global subjects through, 42–46; globalization of clinical trials and, 33–35; and language of crisis in questionable trials, 51–53; recruitment successes achieved through, 36. *See also* Human subjects
Ethics: anthropological focus on biotechnology, 34; cultural relativism versus imperialism of Western, 35; development of workable document of, 46–53; "moralizing strategies" and, 86; psychiatric medications as redefining research, 23–24
Evidence-based medicine. *See* Standardization

Farmer, P., 35, 171
FDA (Food and Drug Administration): globalization of clinical trials promoted by, 47; human subjects research guidelines of, 56n.5; new drug approval by, 17–18
FDA Center for Drug Evaluation, 44

Fluconazole scandal (2002), 262n.3
Foucault, M., 118
Foxetin, 117, 133
France: addiction pharmaceuticals discouraged in, 7, 25–26; AMM approval for commercializing buprenorphine, 147–48; antipsychiatry Lacanianism movement in, 141; buprenorphine as orphan drug in, 139, 166n.10; buprenorphine substitution in, 144–51; effect of AIDS crisis on drug users in, 146–47; national health system of, 149–51, 161; problematic drug use in, 140–42; rejection of methadone substitution model, 138, 142, 143–44, 148, 165n.1; state-run addiction management model, 25–26, 136. *See also* Buprenorphine market; Toxicomania addiction treatment

GAD (generalized anxiety disorder), 80
Gador, 117, 126, 127–28, 131, 133
Galvão, J., 214, 218
GAPA (Group of Support and Prevention Against AIDS) [Brazil], 210–11
GATT (General Agreement on Tariffs and Trade), 113
GCP (Good Clinical Practice), 91
Geertz, C., 40
GGB (Gay Group of Bahia) [Brazil], 210
Ghostwriting of medical articles, 68–69
Giddens, A., 10
Gift relations. *See* Pharmaceutical gift relations
Giscard d'Estaing, V., 144
GlaxoSmithKline: antidepression clinical trials by, 74–78; lawsuit for fraud (2004) against, 78; Paxil advertising by, 65; success in increasing SSRIs prescriptions, 133
Global drug marketing platform: elements of, 87–88; global guidelines adopted in Japan, 90–91; and Japanese depression market, 88–90; strategic measures to establish market, 91–94. *See also* Japanese

antidepressant market; Pharmaceutical marketing; SSRIs antidepressants
Global Fund to Fight AIDS, 3, 31n.11
Globalization: and demand for addiction pharmaceuticals, 137–38; of drug development process, 38; ethical variability of clinical trials impacted by, 33–35; of human subjects research, 22–29; pharmaceutical nexus and, 21–22
Gomes, C., 233
Good, B., 177
Good, M-J. D., 177
Government regulation: comparing practices of China and United States, 16–18; FDA on direct-to-consumer advertising, 9; of marketing, 16–20; medical standardization supported by, 9–10; and need for more human subjects, 36;

Hacking, I., 14, 230
*Hastings Center Report* (2000), 67
HDB (high-dose buprenorphine). *See* Buprenorphine
Healing as social process, 8–9
Health: Brazil's progressive constitution on right to, 211; changing focus of anthropological studies on, 34–36; culturally standardized breakpoint in continuum of, 194; global failure to address, 4–5; pharmaceutical advertising and images of, 2; relationship between income inequalities and, 4. *See also* Mental health
Health transition studies, 58n.18
Healy, D., 9, 23, 68, 115
Helsinki Declaration revision (2000), 43–44, 46
Hematopoetic growth factor molecule (rhGM-CSF) research [Chernobyl], 51–52, 60n.36
Heroin addiction: buprenorphine prescribed for, 25–26, 136, 149–50; comparing buprenorphine to, 153–54; French perception of, 139–65; language of, 153–55; methadone substitution model for, 138, 142,

Heroin addiction (*continued*)
143–44, 148, 165n.1. *See also* Addiction;
Illicit pharmaceuticals; Toxicomania
addiction treatment
HIV/AIDS crisis. *See* AIDS crisis
Homeopathy (India), 204n.19
"Houses of support" (*casas de apoio*), 232–35
Humanitarian crisis research, 51–53
Human subject protection: global regulations on, 43–44, 49, 56n.6, 59n.29; IRBs
(institutional review boards) monitoring,
38, 39, 48, 56n.6; and Nigerian Trovan
case (1996), 49–50
Human subject recruitment: competition of,
40–41; CRO practices of, 39–41; regulatory limitations on prison research and,
37–38
Human subjects: controversy over placebo
use for, 42–43, 44–45, 50; demand for
larger pools of, 36–40; from developing
countries, 40–41, 47; equivalent medication provided to, 46; prisoners as,
37–38, 54; research dynamics of using,
22–29; shrinking U.S. pool for, 37. *See
also* Clinical trials; Ethical variability

ICD-10 (International Classification of
Diseases), 89
ICH (International Conference on Harmoni-
sation), 44, 47, 88, 90–91; Good Clinical
Practice guidelines of, 4, 38, 93
Illicit pharmaceuticals: buprenorphine use
as, 158–60; informal economy of, 26;
methadone substitution approach to, 138,
142, 143–44, 148, 165n.1. *See also* Heroin
addiction; Prescription drugs
Illness. *See* Disease
IMF (International Monetary Fund), 4–5, 217
IMS Health (Great Britain), 120, 121, 126, 128
Income inequalities, relationship to health
of, 4
India: distribution of practitioners by
qualifications, 177–78t; homeopathy
in, 204n.19; patterns of illness in, 183–
92; self-medication study sites, 173–77;

use of medical categories by practitioners and patients in, 192–95. *See also*
Self-medication study
Interested knowledge: Argentine physicians
embedded in, 116; factors involved in
formulation of, 13
International Conference on Harmonisation
of Technical Requirements for Registration of Pharmaceuticals for Human Use
(ICH), 12, 44, 47, 88, 90–91
International Monetary Fund (IMF), 4–5,
217
IRBs (institutional review boards), 38, 39, 48,
56n.6

*JAMA* (*Journal of the American Medical
Association*), 71, 72
Japan: depression destigmatization campaign
in, 102–3, 104; *DSM-III* adopted by, 89;
launch of SSRIs in, 86–90; restrictions on
direct-to-consumer (DTC) advertising
in, 103–4; stigma of mental illness in,
102–3; U.S. market practices in, 24, 30n.5
Japanese antidepressant market: adoption
of ICH guidelines and, 91; impact of
clinical trials and pricing on, 94–101;
implications of, 106–8; mega-marketing
challenge of, 101–5; state of, 82–83n.4;
strategic measures for establishing, 91–
94. *See also* Global drug marketing
platform
Japanese "bridging studies," 91
Japanese Ministry of Health Labor and
Welfare (MHLW, *koseirodosho*), 90, 91
Japanese Pharmaceutical Association, 92
JCRC (Joint Clinical Research Centre)
[Uganda], 243, 254
JMA (Japan Medical Association), 92
Johansson, S. R., 194, 202
"Junk science" discourse, 96–101

Kim, J. Y., 6, 35
Kisuule, A., 250
Kityo, C., 254, 256
Klein, D., 62

Kleinman, A., 34
Knowledge: interested, 13, 116; relations between power and medical, 177, 178t
Koseirodosho (Japanese Ministry of Health Labor and Welfare), 90, 91
Kuhn, T., 73
Kyaddondo, B., 255

Lacan, J., 143
Lacanianism movement (France), 141
Lakoff, A., 13, 24, 25
La Nación, 130
Lancet editorial (2002), 68, 244
Latin America: human subjects recruited in, 41; "Washington Consensus" on, 212. See also Argentina; Brazil
Lévi-Strauss, C., 8
Liability issues, 58n.24–59n.24
"Liability model" of accountability, 48
Librium, 64, 81
Licensing agreements, 2
Los Vulnerables, 127
Lovell, A., 7, 25, 26
Lula da Silva, L. I., 229

Malaria treatments, 3
Marketing. See Pharmaceutical marketing
Marketing agreements, 2
Marks, H., 43, 46
Mayanja, H., 248
Medical Access Uganda Limited, 242, 243
Medical Inquiry Committee (Punjab), 179
"Medical nomadism" (doctor shopping), 156
Medical Registration Act of Bombay, 179
Medical writing agencies, 69–73
Menem, Carlos, 113, 114
Mental health: antidepressant treatment, 2, 23–25, 65, 70t, 72, 76, 78; antipsychotic drug treatment for, 2, 76, 77t; depression and, 10, 64–67; deteriorating treatment outcomes for, 79–80; DSM-III classifications for, 61–64; Japanese attitude toward stigma of, 102–3. See also Health; Psychiatry
Merck Sharp & Dohme (MSD), 242

Methadone substitution, 138, 142, 143–44, 148, 165n.1
MHLW (Japanese Ministry of Health Labor and Welfare), 90, 91
Mianserin, 72
MILDT (French drug agency), 162
"Mirroring" institutions, 88
Monoamine oxidase (MAO) inhibitor, 63–64
Moore, S. F., 86, 108
"Moralizing strategies," 86
Morbidity: availability of medical categories and, 194–95; cultural inflation of, 194
Mosby's Memoirs (Bellow), 85
Mulago Hospital (Kampala), 246
Multi-drug-resistant tuberculosis, images of, 2

National Bioethics Advisory Commission, 48
National Family and Heath Survey (1993), 174
National Institute on Drug Abuse, 163
National Institutes of Health, 43, 147
Nations for Mental Health (WHO), 103, 109–10n.22
Negative publicity containment, 67–68
New England Journal of Medicine, 71
Newsweek, 74
NGEN+ (National Guidance and Empowerment Network of People Living with HIV/AIDS in Uganda), 257–58
NGOs (nongovernmental organizations): ARCA (Religious Support against AIDS) [Brazil], 211; "dictatorship of projects" rule of, 214; Doctors Without Borders, 49, 221; Doctors of the World, 147; GAPA (Group of Support and Prevention Against AIDS) [Brazil], 210–11; Medical Access Uganda Limited, 242, 243; NGEN+ (Uganda) AIDS activism, 257–58; Pella Vida (Brazil), 211; PMTCT and PMTCT+ AIDS activism, 242, 245–46; TASO (AIDS Support Organization), 246, 247, 258. See also AIDS activism
Nigerian Trovan research (1996), 48–51
Nuremberg Code (1947), 49, 56n.6, 59n.29

*Observer*, 130

OIG (Office of the Inspector General) [U.S. Department of Health and Human Services], 48, 56n.2, 59n.26

Olanzapine, 76, 77t

Opinion leaders (Argentina), 123–26

Organon, 124

Orphan Drug Act (1983) [U.S.], 166n.10

Orphan drugs, 139, 166n.10

Outra Coisa (Brazil), 210

Paladin, 71

Panic disorder medications, 62–64

Parker, R., 213

Partners in Health, 221

Patent citizenship, 208, 238n.5

Patent laws (Brazil), 226

Patient compliance: literature on, 171–72; self-medication distinguished from, 203n.1. *See also* Self-medication

Paxil, 64, 65, 74, 76, 80–81, 133

PBM (Pharmacy Benefits Management), 132

Pella Vida (Brazil), 211

Penicillin: discovery of, 2; social transformations due to, 14

Perception management strategies: and buprenorphine marketing in France, 139–65; containment of negative publicity, 67–68; and ghostwriting of medical articles, 68–69; use of CMD (Current Medical Directions) [New York], 69, 71–73

Petryna, A., 7, 22

Pfizer Inc.: antidepression clinical trials by, 74–78; CMD coordination of article on Zoloft for, 71–72; fluconazole scandal and, 262n.3; Trovan research by, 48–51; Zoloft advertising by, 80–81

Pharmaceutical access: and ARV availability in Uganda, 242–44, 247–61; power and connections used to gain, 256–59, 260–61; well-being and health associated with, 2–3

Pharmaceutical gift relations, 73, 116–19

Pharmaceutical governance: new configurations in Brazil producing, 218–22; "pharmaceuticalization" of public health and, 222–25; public science sector and, 225–30

Pharmaceutical industry: history of Argentine, 112–15; history of modern, 2; level of secrecy within, 13–14; liability concerns of, 58–59n.24; local context of studies of, 14–15; medicalization and suppression of data by, 73–78; multinational and national enterprises of, 30n.6; perception management strategies used by, 66–73; relationship between academic medicine and, 32n.20; relationship between Argentine physicians and, 115–19. *See also* Standardization

Pharmaceutical leakage, 138, 155–60

Pharmaceutical marketing: in Brazil, 219–20; and celebrity endorsement, 62; clinical trials as form of, 23; of depression, 64–66; distinction between rational pharmacology and, 115; economic and moral paradoxes of, 2–4; and emergent HIV/AIDS, 220–22; ethical challenges of, 7–8; government regulations on, 16–20; lack of standardization in, 15–16; medicalization and suppression of data and, 73–78; "moralizing strategies" in, 86; of panic disorder medications, 62–64; rebranding SSRIs antidepressants as anxiolytics, 66–67; U.S. theories of practice to open new, 24. *See also* Advertising; Global drug marketing platform

Pharmaceutical nexus: described, 20–21; as empirical object, 21; as method of inquiry, 22; as problem of relating different interests, 21–22

Pharmaceutical spending: on development of each new drug, 11; U.S. and Canadian share of global, 2

Pharmaco-association: comparing biosociality notion to, 168–69n.37; incorporating buprenorphine through, 151–55;

pharmaceutical leakage and, 155–60; social uses of HBD impact on, 158–60

*Pharmakon*, 153

Phoenix House, 143

PhRMA (Pharmaceuticals Research and Manufacturers of America), 92–93, 94, 98, 99

Physicians: Argentine, relationship with pharmaceutical firms, 115–19; CMD information influencing, 69–73; factors in prescribing behavior of Argentine, 128–34; "freebies" influencing, 73, 116–19; French national health system and, 149–51, 161; ghostwriting articles for, 68–69; Indian, distribution and classification of, 177, 178*t*, 179–81; Indian, reports on illnesses and treatments, 181–83; Japanese, antidepressant education of, 104–5; "medical nomadism" (doctor shopping practice) for, 156; relationship between power and medical knowledge of, 177; toxicomania addiction treatment by French, 144–46; use of medical categories by Indian patients and physicians, 192–95

Pinheiro, E., 226–27

Placebo: AZT clinical trials (Africa, 1994) use of, 42–43, 44–45, 50; suicidal activity for antipsychotic drugs versus, 76, 77*t*, 78

PMDD (premenstrual dysphoric disorder), 90

PMTCT+ program, 246

PMTCT (Prevention of Mother to Child Transmission) projects, 242, 245–46

"Post-script on Control Societies" (Deleuze), 118

Power: access to ARVs in Uganda as measure of, 256–59; relations between medical knowledge and, 177, 178*t*

Practitioners. *See* Physicians

Pregnancy case study (Kamla), 197–98

Prescription drugs: cross-border sales of, 14–15; dispensed by Bhagwanpur Kheda practitioners, 190–92; FDA approval of, 17–18; increased patent applications for,

36; marketing of panic disorder, 62–64; particularity of addiction, 137–40; post-World War II boom in U.S. demand, 37–38; progressive price reductions of, 99–100; promotion practices for, 15. *See also* Advertising; Illicit pharmaceuticals

Prisoners as human subjects (early 1970s), 37–38, 54

Progressive price reductions, 99–100

Prozac, 65, 67, 153

Psychiatry: *DSM-III* classification system of, 61; ethics of research on medications, 23–24; French Lacanianism movement against, 141; U.S. shift to neuroscientific approach, 126. *See also* Mental health

"Psychotropic nihilism," 20

PTSD (posttraumatic stress disorder): influence of medical articles on, 71; SSRI treatment for, 90

"Public health machismo," 6

Rabinow, P., 208

Randomized clinical trials. *See* Clinical trials

Rational pharmacology, 115

rhGM-CSF research (Chernobyl), 51–52, 60n.36

Roche, 63–64

Rubaramira, Major, 257–58, 259

"Rups" (Rohypnol), 153, 154

Sanchez, C., 193

Saradamma, R. N., 173

Sassen, S., 20

Satcher, D., 43

Scandals: AZT placebo controversy (Africa, 1994), 42–43, 44–45, 50; Chernobyl nuclear disaster research, 40, 51–53, 238n.5; conflict of interest as cause of, 11–12; Nigerian Trovan research (1996), 48–51; Pfizer fluconazole (2002), 262n.3; prisoners as human subjects (early 1970s), 37–38, 54

Schering-Plough, 139, 150–51, 165n.2

Scott, J., 17

Seeing Like a State (Scott), 17
Self-medication: and genealogy of biopower, 172; depiction of social factors of, 172–73; described, 26, 171; distinguished from concept of compliance, 203n.1; and sense of self-sustenance, 26–27. See also Patient compliance
Self-medication study (India): biomedicine embodied in, 177, 178t; ethnographic sites for, 173–77; on failure of local practitioners, 195–96; on implications of illness and forms of sociality, 201–3; on Kamla's pregnancy, 197–98; on patterns of illness, 183–92; on patterns in practitioner distribution, 178–81; report on sickness and treatment, 181–83; on Sangeeta's tuberculosis, 199–201; on use of medical categories, 192–95. See also India
Serra, J., 217, 219, 225
Sertraline, 72
SmithKline, 64
SmithKline Beecham, Tobin v., 84n.13
Social good question, 7
"Social liveliness," 8
Social pharmacy: AIDS medicine as example of, 241, 260–61; realities of, 261; Ugandan access to ARVs as, 242–44, 247–61
Social phobia, 63–64
Solberg, P., 251
Solvay, 65
"Sorcerer and His Magic, The" (Lévi-Strauss), 8
SSRIs antidepressants: efforts to launch in Japan, 86–108; global adoption of, 85–86; global sales of, 87; marketing of depression and, 64–65; rebranding of anxiolytics as, 66–67, 81–82. See also Antidepressants; Global drug marketing platform
Standardization: claims about Japanese lack of, 94–101; difficulty of enforcing global, 12–13; drug marketing lack of, 15–16; evolution to global, 101–5; government regulations for, 9–10; ICH Good Clinical Practice guidelines, 4, 38, 93; impact of local contexts on, 14–15; importance of trustworthy, 12–14; as key to pharmaceutical globalization, 78–79. See also Clinical trials; Drug development process; Pharmaceutical industry
State: postnational era, 18–19; under rubric of global pharma, 19; types and powers assumed by, 19
Streptomycin, 2
"Stress, Anxiety, and Depression:" symposium (Argentina, 2000), 127–28
Subutex, 139, 149, 170n.53
Suicides and suicide attempts: antidepressants for children and, 72; and "defeat depression" campaigns claims, 75–76, 77t; risk for antipsychotic drugs versus placebo, 76, 77t, 78
SWOT (Strength Weakness Opportunity Threat) matrix, 88
Synanon, 143

Tamil rebellion (1996), 136
Taming of Chance, The (Hacking), 230
TASO (AIDS Support Organization), 246, 247, 258
"Teen Depression," 74
Teixeira, P., 210, 212, 213, 229
Temple, R., 44, 45
Theory of Social and Economic Organization, The (Weber), 152
Third World countries. See Developing countries
"3 by 5" Program (WHO), 236
Titan Pharmaceuticals, 163–64
Tobin v. SmithKlineBeecham, 84n.13
Toxicomania (toxicomanie), 140–41, 142, 145
Toxicomania addiction treatment: adoption of buprenorphine for, 144–51; historic development of, 141–42; strategies creating perception of, 140; two groups providing, 144–46. See also Addiction markets; France; Heroin addiction
Tranquilizers advertising, 65

Tranquinil, 129
"Transient" mental illness, 14
Triomune, 240
TRIPS (Trade-Related Aspects of Intellectual Property Rights): Argentine agreement to, 113; Brazilian agreement to, 218; new ecology role of, 6
Trovan research (Nigeria, 1996), 48–51
Tuberculosis case study (Sangeeta), 199–201
Turner, V., 8

Uganda: access to ARVs in, 242–44, 247–61; AIDS treatment priorities in families, 249–54; failure of AIDS treatment in, 28–29, 240–41; raising awareness of ARVs in, 247–49; social stigma of ARVs in, 255–59, 260–61. *See also* Africa
Uganda Cares Initiative (Masaka), 243
UNAIDS, 242
UNAIDS Drug Access Initiative (1998–99), 250
UNICEF, 245
UNICEF-WHO study (1975), 181
United Nations right to health resolution (2001), 218
United States: case against Argentina by, 134n.5; comparing regulatory practices of China and, 16–18; foreign markets practices of, 24, 30n.5; global pharmaceutical spending by, 2; Orphan Drug Act (1983) of, 166n.10; post–World War II pharmaceutical boom in, 37–38; shrinking pool of human subjects in, 37
University of Belgrano, 132
University of Buenos Aires, 124
Upjohn, 62
Uruguay Round (1986), 113
U.S. Department of Health and Human Services, 139
U.S.-Japan Enhanced Initiative for Deregulation and Competition, 91

U.S. Patent Office, 36
U.S. prison research, 37–38

Valium, 64, 65, 81, 131
"Values gap," 6
Varmus, H., 43
Venlafaxine (Effexor), 69, 80–81
Viagra, 98
*Vidal* (French physicians' desk reference), 154

"Washington Consensus," 212
Weber, M., 152
WHO (World Health Organization): on Brazilian pharmaceutical market, 220; on healthcare needs in developing countries, 181; HIV/AIDS Department of, 6; lobbying France on drug addiction, 147; Nations for Mental Health program of, 103, 109–10n.22; report on depression disability (1996), 65; "3 by 5" program of, 236
W. H. R. Rivers Workshop (Harvard University, 2002), 5
Whyte, S. R., 15, 28
World Bank: AIDS activism partnerships with, 207, 212–13, 216–17; failure to address health issues, 4–5; new ecology role, 6, 31n.13; SAPS (structural adjustment policies) of, 31n.13
World Psychiatric Association, 63
WTO (World Trade Organization): influence on Brazilian policies by, 219; new ecology role of, 6; U.S. threat to bring sanctions against Brazil at, 228
Wyeth, 68, 69

Xanax, 63

Young, I., 48

Zoloft, 65, 71–72, 74, 75, 80–81, 133

Adriana Petryna is an assistant professor of anthropology at the New School for Social Research. Andrew Lakoff is an assistant professor of sociology and science studies at the University of California, San Diego. Arthur Kleinman is the Esther and Sidney Rabb Professor of Anthropology and Chair, Department of Anthropology, Harvard University; and Professor of Psychiatry and Medical Anthropology, Harvard Medical School.

Library of Congress Cataloging-in-Publication Data
Global pharmaceuticals : ethics, markets, practices / edited by Adriana Petryna, Andrew Lakoff, and Arthur Kleinman.
p. cm.  Includes bibliographical references and index.
ISBN 0-8223-3729-0 (cloth : alk. paper)
ISBN 0-8223-3741-X (pbk. : alk. paper)
1. Pharmaceutical industry.  2. Pharmaceutical industry—Marketing.
3. Drugs—Marketing—Moral and ethical aspects.  4. Pharmaceutical ethics.
I. Petryna, Adriana, 1966- .  II. Lakoff, Andrew, 1970- .
III. Kleinman, Arthur.
[DNLM: 1. Drug Industry—ethics. 2. Drug Industry—economics.
3. Marketing—ethics. 4. Commerce. 5. Health Services Accessibility.
6. Internationality. 7. Socioeconomic Factors.   QV 736 G562 2006]
HD9665.5.G56 2006
338.4'76151—dc22      2005028222

23 95